STRANGE DAYS

Patricia Kennealy

Strange Days

MY LIFE WITH AND WITHOUT
JIM MORRISON

A DUTTON BOOK

DUTTON
Published by the Penguin Group
Penguin Books USA Inc., 375 Hudson Street, New York, New York 10014, U.S.A.
Penguin Books Ltd, 27 Wrights Lane, London W8 5TZ, England
Penguin Books Australia Ltd, Ringwood, Victoria, Australia
Penguin Books Canada Ltd, 10 Alcorn Avenue, Toronto, Ontario, Canada M4V 3B2
Penguin Books (N.Z.) Ltd, 182–190 Wairau Road, Auckland 10, New Zealand

Penguin Books Ltd, Registered Offices:
Harmondsworth, Middlesex, England

First published by Dutton, an imprint of New American Library,
a division of Penguin Books USA Inc.
Distributed in Canada by McClelland & Stewart Inc.

First Printing, May, 1992
1 3 5 7 9 10 8 6 4 2

REGISTERED TRADEMARK—MARCA REGISTRADA

LIBRARY OF CONGRESS CATALOGING-IN-PUBLICATION DATA:
Kennealy, Patricia.
Strange days : my life with and without Jim Morrison / Patricia
Kennealy.
p.   cm.
ISBN 0-525-93419-7
1. Morrison, Jim, 1943–1971   2. Rock musicians—United States—
Biography.   I. Title.
ML420.M62K46   1992
782.42166'092—dc20

[B]   91-41456
                                                        CIP
                                                        MN

Printed in the United States of America
Set in Goudy and Mona Lisa Recut

Designed by Steven N. Stathakis

For Jim,
in more than memory

Acknowledgments

With love, thanks and blessing to all who, over the past twenty years, helped, protected, encouraged, comforted, patiently listened or, rarest of all, truly heard; most especially to: Michael Rosenthal, Christopher Schelling, Lana Griffin, Kathleen Quinlan, Verity Lund, Jerry Hopkins, Pamela Hannay, Susan Donoghue, Janice Scott Gentile, Regina Kennely, David and Geli Walley, Stefan and Linda Bright, James and Susan Fox-Davis, Eileen Campbell Gordon, "Brân" and "Maura," Katherine Kurtz-MacMillan and Scott MacMillan, Kristine Zeronda, Rainer Moddemann, Ko and Joke Lankester, John Silbersack, Melissa Hayden, Michael Kaye, Dylan Jones, Bob Dolman, Pauline Rivelli, Janice Coughlan, Laura Scott Roberts, Terry Towne, Noreen Shanfelter, Bruce Harris, Bobbi Harris, Elin Guskind Defrin and Bob Defrin, Gina Mazzola (Gangi), Diane Gardiner, David Westgor, Sasha Harari and Oliver Stone.

Also to Trixie, my evil twin; my readers, those loyal subjects of Keltia; Nancy C. Hanger, DTJ, and Andrew V. Phillips, KTJ, for sanctuary, a place for me to hide; the Michaelines, the Templars and the Craft; Danny Baror and Henry Morrison, for daring to broach the forbidden topic; Malcolm Edwards likewise; Ron Jacobs, who brought a record to Walnut Street in the cold early days of that Annus Mirabilis, 1967, and "introduced" Jim and me; and, above all, the Goddess Whose faith in me, as mine in Her, has sustained me now as then.

NOTE ON NOMENCLATURE

In 1979 I legally altered the spelling of my surname from "Kennely" to "Kennealy." This was done for ease of pronunciation (Ken-NEEL-ee, not KENNEL-ee), orthographic esthetics and the greater glory of my Celtic heritage.

Additionally, I legally assumed at that time the name "Morrison" which I have used privately since 24 June 1970.

For purposes of clarity, however, my surname in this book will be "Kennealy" throughout. It's just easier.

NOTES ON SOURCES

This memoir is a true story. The material drawn upon is taken from journals, diaries, letters, notebooks and other memoranda kept privately by me during the period in question, and from my own recollection of events. Some names have been changed to protect the privacy of certain individuals; otherwise all names of people, places and events are genuine. Dialogue, dates and times are accurate to the best of my knowledge.

Some material has been reconverted to memoir form from my unpublished novel *The Voice that Launched a Million Trips*, a roman à clef about Jim and me that I wrote in 1971–72; other sources are the interviews, reviews, articles and columns written by me for the magazine of which I was editor from 1968–71, Jazz & Pop.

For the chapters dealing with Jim's death and the death of Pamela Courson, I have drawn upon material from published and private accounts by Jerry Hopkins, Rainer Moddemann, James Riordan, Bob Seymore, Albert Goldman and Alan Ronay.

In Chapter 25, I have been obliged to paraphrase from personal letters that Jim wrote me from Paris just prior to his death. Direct quotation was forbidden me, as according to law I own only the paper on which the letters are written—the physical letters themselves—not the contents thereof or the copyrights pertaining thereto (nor those of the several poems Jim wrote for me). Although these letters and poems were intended by Jim for me alone, the copyrights to all of them are the legal property of Mr. and Mrs. Columbus Courson and/or Admiral and Mrs. George S. Morrison, and I may not lawfully publish them. Presumably the loving sentiments, at least, expressed at length to me therein by the writer of both the poems and the letters *do* belong to me, as gift from him which no one else may claim . . .

"The opposite of a shallow truth is false. But the opposite of a deep truth is also true."

—NIELS BOHR

FOREWORD

This is not a biography. Nor is it an autobiography. It will tell you some things about Jim Morrison, and it will tell you some things about me, and it will tell you quite a lot about us.

What it will not tell you is what Jim's teachers or his childhood friends or even the other members of his band thought of him, or what happened when the Doors played Saratoga or Stony Brook or San Diego, or how much money they made on the third album, or how many groupies *really*, or what Jim was drinking on any night in question. There are other books for that.

What this book will tell you is as much of Jim Morrison as I know. There is *no* other book for *that*. Save for a few private moments and memories I have kept private, shared only and forever between him and me, I have been in all ways as open and as honest in this account as I know how to be, and as Jim has taught me to be, and as he would both wish and expect me to be. About him. About me. About us. Because I think that that is best for everyone, and for Jim most of all; and to me he is what matters most.

Although I was in the music business when I met Jim, a professional, the editor of a national magazine, I was by no means a Doors insider, a member of the Doors family or the Doors court: more like a sovereign Eastern empress, having certain treaty understandings extant with the Lizard Throne. (You are thinking Elvis and Priscilla, when you should be thinking Solomon and Sheba, or at least Spencer and Kate.) The only Door I knew was Jim; I didn't know about them, they didn't know about me, and that was how Jim and I both preferred it. Therefore do not wonder that this book is as it is.

In the years since Jim's death, I have kept well away from the necrocult that has sprung up around his name. I did so out of what seemed to me very good reasons indeed: unending grief, and abiding love, and the fierce wish to protect our privacy, to keep what we had for ourselves alone. I did so as long as I could; and when I saw what was passing for truth about Jim, and even about us, I knew my silent time was over. So I set my other books aside for a while and I wrote this one. It is no one else's truth but my own, and Jim's with me. My Jim; not anyone else's Jim (and there were many).

So this book will not tell you who was Jim Morrison really. But it will, I hope, tell you some of what he was: He was the Prince of Shadow and the beggar at the gate. He was the Emperor of Ice Cream and the Lord of Misrule. He dwelled in Morrisonia, in Jimworld, in the Lizard Kingdom; he dwelled there all alone, and he liked it best that way. He was beyond question the most incredible person I have ever met.

PROLOGUE

July 1971

STANT WITH THE END, AND SEE WHERE YOU CAN GO from there . . .

The truth of the graves.

What a time trying to get to him out front, ripped on jet lag, grief and too many downers: four years out of college and trying to wrap my tongue around eight years of French again, after an engine fire on the plane over, a bad cab ride from Orly and now a hotel clerk who loftily informs me there is no reservation in either of my names. It is my first time overseas, and I have been in Paris for less than one hour.

But will, or fate, or brute force, prevails; and all at once there is a charming chamber way up under the roof of this great old hotel, across the way from the Tuileries. I wash my face, brush my hair and change from my travel clothes—black tunic over black pants—into a long black dress. Outside the hotel, I hail a cab and give the driver Jim's new address.

There are high walls of buff-colored stone around the ancient grave-yard of Père-Lachaise; to keep people out or keep people in? I pass through the southwest gate that opens on the Boulevard Ménilmontant; just inside is a little guardhouse, and I go in and explain to the person on duty who it is that I am seeking.

"Je cherche le tombeau de Morrison—James Douglas Morrison?"

It takes a while to sort out; apparently he has been listed in the records as Douglas James, not James Douglas. Still, how many Morrisons can there *be*?

"Américain? Poète? Décédé le trois juillet?"

He still cannot find him. "Mor-ri-son . . . ah. Mais ce n'est pas un 'tombeau,' mademoiselle, ce n'est qu'un terre-plein."

Whatever! Who cares! Just tell me where it is! Before I rip your throat out! He gets the message—something in my eyes, perhaps, that does not require translation, or maybe it is just the way the air has begun to glow and vibrate in my immediate vicinity—and pulls out a map he had apparently not the smallest intention of showing me until now. With penciled X's and circles and lines he indicates where the grave is located and how to get to it.

Outside again in the shining summer morning, I look around and I see nothing of what is before me; in all my life I have never felt, never imagined I could feel, so utterly alone. I know no one here, have never been out of the United States in my life, must cope with French and the French—and the man I love is lying in his grave a few hundred yards away.

I have begun to shiver uncontrollably, not with the chill even July air can strike in Europe, and I reach down to take off my shoes. Barefoot bereaved all in widow black; well, maybe, though I did not plan it. (I am even wearing a long black veil; not so much that I do not wish the casual or curious to see me—though I don't—as I do not wish to have to see them.) But all at once it seems a thing I must do, walk barefoot to his grave; and I would do it were it deep midwinter and the cobblestones under snow. Something necessary, something instinctive: Instinct has brought me here in the first place, veiled me in black and set me shoeless on the stones, and instinct will take me where I want to be in the end.

I consult the map I have wrested from the guard and begin to walk, not really sure of my way. An old Frenchman in what looks like a morning coat, with a rose in his lapel, crotchets past me, muttering something that sounds obscene even in French. Because I have no shoes on? Doesn't he recognize a pilgrim when he sees one?

My sense of direction, usually infallible, is all but gone, and I lose myself at once in the twists and turns of Père-Lachaise, adrift amongst the tombs. It is so quiet and so lonely; I feel as if I am walking through neck-deep water, the air, or me, slowed and resistant. Or maybe this is just what a hundred-plus milligrams of Valium since takeoff from New York can make you feel like: It seems as if there is a hand planted firmly against my center of gravity, pushing me back even as I strive with all my strength to move forward . . .

A little old lady steps right out of the air in front of me as I wander vaguely, and with one imperial gesture directs my attention to the large, ornately canopied tomb before me.

"C'est le tombeau d'Héloïse et son Abélard."

"Vraiment, madame," I agree politely—well, it says so right on the thing. We talk for a few minutes of the famous medieval lovers, and the conversation has all the flavor of a bad acid trip. I remain staring at the two carved effigies, stretched out for eternity side by side, long after she has vanished as abruptly as she appeared.

There are armies of cats in Père-Lachaise, darting through the trees, flashing like minnows in and out among the tombs, all of them either black or black and white. They are bold, and lie on the tombstones in the sun as if they too are effigies.

I walk all round that southwest part of the cemetery. Grief and the sense of urgency that drove me all the way from New York recede somewhat under the rustling trees. I remember from somewhere—oh, right, my half-comprehending perusal of the map—that there are a great number of the renowned buried here: Chopin, Balzac, Edith Piaf, the French Communards, dear Oscar Wilde. Suddenly I am blinded by tears and frustration. Ah God, where *is* he? Why can't I find him? All you people, tell me where your new friend is; you tell me, who can tell me.

And they must hear and take pity on me, for they send me by a little lane I have not noticed before though I must have passed it half a dozen times, a little lane that runs up a slope and then dips down again to meet another path under tall trees. And then it is as if a psychic homing device, jammed until now by some strange interference, suddenly clears and switches on; and I walk forward straight to him without a falter or misstep, in through the trees, in amongst the houses of the lost, a narrow path between a marble mansion and a pile of newly turned dirt.

At the surprise of the dirt I check for an instant, thinking for one shattering moment that this must be where he is; but I realize my error at once. And with that comes the equally shattering, the inescapable inferral: This is the dirt that has been dug out of a nearby new-made grave. I force myself on a few steps more and no mistake about it this time, he is there.

Is it possible, then, is it real after all? I have come thousands of miles of Atlantic air because I never would have accepted it otherwise; and maybe I still do not accept it, but I knew from the first—before that, even—that it was true. But now it is here before me, the end of the trip: I approach with hushed carefulness, these last few feet of all our distances. Glassy uncertainty, so fragile now; catsoft, as if too harsh a step would set off unendurable atrocity; silent and held in hard, like a skittish racehorse, like a surgeon drawing near some unimaginable wound.

For it is real, real. There is a barrier between us now, something I cannot get past. I unpin the black veil so that it hurries down over my face, and I go to my knees upon that barrier: sand and grit and gray grainy dry earth unlike any soil I have ever seen. Bonedirt. No, I have never seen this earth with any sight; I have never dreamed it, and I have always known it.

What lies before me is a small raised uneven mound of rocks and dirt and broken stone, outlined by an oval of white scallop shells, with withered flowers strewn anyhow on top and fresh red roses head and foot. A homemade wooden cross laid on top of the dirt, about where his heart would be, says in neat block printing:

Douglas   MORRISON   James

artiste   chanteur

I stare at it through the veil. I do not weep. But my arms are aching with reaching to close around remembered chest and back and ribs and shoulders, closing now only on air: a formless phantom pain, the way amputees feel pain in a long-since-severed hand or foot. And how not: So much more than that was severed from me here. Amputation in one's karma hurts just as much, removes just as surely; astral amputation, throb of dull karmic loss.

While I still retain some command over myself, I take a roll of pictures; I know very well that in only seconds now I will be in no condition to do anything of the sort, and I know too that I will be glad of these pictures later, and that they must be taken now, at the first, for history—his and mine. As I pace around the grave, taking the dozen or so shots, I find my thoughts going not to him but to those at home who tried so long and hard to dissuade me from coming here.

He's dead, they said, not ungently. I know, I said. It's just a grave, they said. You can't see him. Why torture yourself? But it never for one instant entered my mind that I should *not* go. Doing all the things necessary to get me here—acquiring a passport in one day ("compassionate reasons," not a clerk in the Rockefeller Center office, seeing my face and hearing my story, expressed doubts as to the need or to the truth); booking a plane ticket; buying some francs for immediate need and travelers' checks for the rest; packing every piece of black clothing I own—I know I must have done all these things, for I allowed no one to do them for me; but I have no recollection of most of them.

Only little flashes of recall, moments illuminated as if by brief flares of soundless lightning in one great overspreading darkness... I remember sitting at the desk in the airline office; I remember coming out of my Valium daze on the plane, to hear in the midst of baffling uproar an announcement that we are returning to JFK as one of the engines appears to be on fire; I remember thinking 'Fine with me!', I would have been at that moment perfectly content if all four engines went out and we fell straight into the sea right there; I remember the douanier at Orly next morning looking sharply at me and asking with real sympathy if there was anything he could do for me, mademoiselle did not look at all well. And I remember too, clearest of all, with a dreadful clarity I wish I *could* forget, when the voice on the phone, so unearthly gentle, told me he was dead... But no more than this; and perhaps that is best for me.

It never once enters my mind through all this that those who care about me are genuinely upset about this totally unswervable departure. To me it makes perfect sense: He *DIED!* The only thing for it is to go; and as soon as I am sure that those who left him here are safely back in L.A., I do. I am where I am supposed to be, where I want to be and have to be, with the only one I want to be with. He called me, and I have come; I am not alone, so why should anyone be worrying?

I put the camera back into my shoulder-satchel and kneel again by the foot of the grave. What a remove is here, what finality: the knowledge that from now on I will always know exactly where to find him... And that thought is the last strand snapping of this cord of incredible control I have bound about me since New York: I stare blindly at his name on the little wooden cross and I begin all at once to weep. I am here, I have done what he needed; now I am free to do this thing *I* need, that I have needed for days now. And I kneel, back straight as a spear, hands clasped to my mouth under the veil, face set as iron, and shiver head to foot with silent grief.

How can he *be* there, under all that weight of rocks and roses, all that cover of earth and stone? How can I go away and *leave* him there, how get up and walk away from him, just leave him alone in the dark and the cold and the rain and the night, with cats running over his grave, all alone under the wet plastered leaves? No one has ever died on me before. This is my first true encounter with the last discontinuity, the final problem. It is the biggest thing that has ever happened to me, or that ever *can* happen, to me or to anyone: the death of the beloved. It doesn't get any worse than this, whether you face it when you are eighty and have had a lifetime together, or when you are a few months past your twenty-fifth birthday and have had a rather unorthodox two years.

Still, it is only a matter of time and space, and hardly permanent; no matter what else I may have changed my mind about over the years, I sure as hell still believe that. There is no way not to, not now; and even when I cannot believe—in my despair, in the dark mists of grief and pain and anger—even then I still know that it is true, and still I try to believe.

I take out some of the things I mean to leave here: little things, loving things—a lock of my hair, a picture of us together, some lines of his poetry that I have copied out, a letter to him, a piece of driftwood he picked up for me on the beach at Venice, a shell I found on the beach at Miami, a few other objects. I take them out, stare at them and hastily, gently, put them away again. It is not yet time to leave them; I will stay in Paris for as long as it takes.

I kneel all day in the dusty French sun. Weeping comes and goes: I am kneeling in silence when someone comes up to stand beside me. We do not acknowledge one another's presence; he leaves, and then a little later he, or someone else, returns. But now I am shaking violently with suppressed silent weeping, tears streaming down my face beneath the veil; and all at once I feel a gentle touch upon my arm.

A young Frenchman is kneeling beside me, peering anxiously at what he can see of my face. He is slight, not so tall as I, with long blond hair—hippie-looking. He asks if I am all right, if there is anything he can do to help me.

I stare back at him through the black veil and wonder if my French and my strength are both going to be up to this. Then somehow, miraculously, they are: Memory, or something higher, kicks in; endurance, or something greater, armors my pain. When I begin to speak, it seems more telepathy than speech: I say things in French I can barely say in English, express concepts I never learned in French 101.

"Êtes-vous sa femme?" he asks diffidently.

I answer in a steady voice that I am the mother of his dead child, the only woman with whom he ever exchanged wedding vows of any sort ("malgré la loi"), indeed I am his wife; besides, in French, 'sa femme' can mean not only 'his wife' but 'his woman'—and certainly I was that.

He seems to understand my carefully phrased distinctions, and to be moved; he tells me, moving me in turn, that he and his friends saw how the grave was left bleak and markerless, in less honor than the grave of a dead pet. This they could not bear, and so they lined out the ring of shells, left the fresh flowers, made the cross for him, even though they did not know the dates of his birth and death or whether he would wish a cross at all—and, following the cemetery listing, accidentally perpetuated the reversal of his given names.

He actually seems to be apologizing to me for their presumptuousness in doing all this. I hastily assure him it is nothing of the sort; he is embarrassed but shyly happy at my praise, and gives me a small snapshot of the grave as it had looked a few days ago, before they undertook their loving tending, then asks me, with even greater shyness, if I would possibly deign to write in the proper dates on the cross. I do so at once, carefully, through tears; it seems right that I am doing this.

Are you a friend of his, I ask presently—"Êtes-vous un ami?"

"Non, pas un ami; mais un admirateur."

But this unknown admirer did something for him not even his own longtime friends, who buried him, had seen the need of doing . . .

We kneel together in silence for a while, praying, thinking, imagining, remembering; then he kisses the hand I hold out to him in farewell, and bids me a blessing. I bid him the same and more, and he is gone. I never learn his name.

I kneel there as I am, unmoving, until the gritstone cuts through the thin black fabric of my dress and my knees bleed into the dirt; the long veil whips behind me in a wind that is so cold for July. No one else comes near.

I read him rituals, the only way I know to balance things. Over the past two years and a half, I have learned from him something about balance.

PART
ONE

I know you
I know you
You are Valor & Desire.

CHAPTER

1

January 1969

IT IS A COLD, CLEAR, BRIGHT, WINDSWEPT DAY NEAR the month's end. Dressed in what seem to be the right clothes for the job—gold velour tunic, brown leather pants, suede boots and black fur coat—I enter the Plaza Hotel on Central Park South and head for the house phone. As I do so, I note rather than like the fact that several groupies—clad *way* more exotically than I—have checked out my tape recorder and notebook, and, nodding to one another, are casually closing in from three different directions.

I ask the operator for the room number I have been given and she puts me through at once. One ring only; then a sleepy soft California voice comes through the receiver and almost buckles my knees. I know immediately who it is.

"Hi! Want to talk to me?"

"Ah, hi, I'm from Jazz & Pop, may I speak to Diane?"

"What kind of an *accent* have you got?"

"Me? Accent? No accent."

"Ah, sure y'do. I'm very hung up on accents, I've made an exhaustive special study. What kind is it?"

"None, really. Can I talk to Diane?"

"Yeah, sure, in a minute. First you have to tell me what kind of accent it is."

"New York."

Soft scornful laughter. "*That* is no New York accent, miss!"

"Sure it is. New York Irish."

"Well, *now* it is. My name's Jim."

"I know. Mine's Patricia. Please, is Diane there?"

"Yeah, she's here. But, *Pa-tr-r-r-r-i-s-s-s-e-e-e-a-a-a*"—the voice draws my name out to about seventeen caressing syllables—"you did come to talk to me, you know. Why don't you just come on up and we'll, you know, talk. I'll be waiting."

Despite the teasingly ominous invitation, I hold out for Diane, and she tells me to come upstairs right away. I dodge round the groupies, making sure they don't trail me, and in the elevator on the way to a high floor of the hotel, I think back on the previous night, sitting in the dark a mile downtown at Madison Square Garden . . .

"Ladies and gentlemen, *THE DOORS!*"

Over the past two years, I have heard those words a dozen times or more, in varied venues; the scene that follows hard upon them this night is something I have never witnessed before. The capacity Garden crowd, some twenty-two thousand souls, had shivered once collectively as the lights went down and stayed down. Now, as handlers and rent-a-cops hustle the Doors onstage in darkness out of the tunnel entrance, the noise that greets them is deafening and immediate and barely recognizable as human. I flinch at the sheer mass of it: a tidal wave, a physical, palpable thing—a half-agonized, half-triumphant, vocalized animal cry. The yearning in it is implicit. I have never heard a sound like it in my life, and never will again.

Flashbulbs go off in tides as Jim Morrison reaches the edge of the stage, steps into the light and grabs for the microphone—staggered flares so fast and so bright and so many that you can actually for one instant read by the light of them, one gigantic stop-action strobe, sweeping in waves from one end of the huge arena to the other and back again to overlap itself. The people I am with, mostly other press colleagues and personnel of Elektra Records, the Doors' label—I am seated directly behind Jac Holzman, Elektra's fortyish president, and his young son

Adam—turn to one another with expressions ranging from delight to disbelief.

Through all this the Doors cut like a terrible swift sword, with the lead-in to "Break On Through"; from there the concert rolls at breakneck pace. Morrison is in great voice and towering spirits and perfect command of both himself and his audience: The more he pulls me in, the further and deeper into my seat I sink, and after the band does "The Unknown Soldier" I find to my amazement I am trembling like a puppy. In front of me, someone leans over to whisper to Jac, "He's absolutely magnificent with a crowd," and Jac nods complacently. It has begun to dawn on me that in less than eighteen hours from now, I will be having a private audience with the man in the center of the cross of red light, who is just this minute pointing to my side of the arena and shouting, "You are life!" Then, turning and pointing to the other side: "You are death!" Another tiny pause, and I can hear the grin in his voice: "I straddle the fence—and my balls hurt!"

Could be an interesting conversation, I think. Why do I also have the strangest feeling that it is going to change my life forever?

So, as I walk down the Plaza hallway, what seems like my last mile, the walk to the scaffold, to the door of Jim's suite, I remind myself of all the warnings I have received about this person I have come to interview. Like Byron, they all dourly cautioned me, when I announced, thrilled and terrified, that I was going to be talking to him; and like a good Lit. major I cap the quotation now in my mind: "Mad, bad, and dangerous to know." I wonder what Lady Caroline Lamb, lover of Byron, would have thought of James Douglas Morrison.

The door is immediately opened to my knock, by someone who can only be Diane Gardiner, publicist for the Doors, with whom I have had a most pleasant phone relationship for some months: a short, cheerful blonde who tends to talk in italics. We greet one another with affection.

"Oh *Patricia*, I'm so glad you *got* here all right, Jim's really psyched to *meet* you, he's read some of your stuff and he really *likes* it so much, I just know everything is going to be *fantastic!*"

I do not have the nerve to ask her on what she bases this assertion—after all, she has been kind enough to set up a private interview for me with Jim, no other press have been invited this afternoon—and I follow her inside, through the bedroom, all rumpled sheets and tossed clothes and bottles of Poland water, into the suite's living room.

It is not what I have been expecting. I have trouble even remembering to put one foot in front of the other. I *know* you, I want to cry out. Across the room, out of a chair by the window where the suite overlooks Central Park far below, a tall figure rises at my entrance.

He holds out his hand to me, and I reach out to take it; as our fingers close upon one another's there is a visible shower of bright blue sparks flying in all directions. Carpet friction, combination of suede boots and fur coat and dry room air and cold weather; but it makes for great copy and greater memories. Actual apocalyptic storybook sparks, when the prince and the princess touch hands for the first time not the last. When I manage to look up into his face he is smiling; he holds my hand in his, very deliberately, and we *look* at each other, mutually aware, a little amused, and not at all surprised.

"Portent," he says in that impossibly soft voice, his eyebrows up and his gaze speculative out of clear blue eyes.

"A sign," I humbly agree, and retire, deeply shaken and hoping to hell I am hiding it from him, to the wing chair he politely holds for me. He had leaped to his feet as soon as I entered the room, and this combined with the chair politesse only serves to fill my mind with one thought: My God, not only did his mother teach him good manners, but I can't believe he actually *remembers* them!

Not the usual sort of thing you encounter in the rock mulch. But why am I so shivery? I am, at twenty-two, the editor of a national and highly respected music magazine; I am a professional person here to do my job; this guy, however chivalrous, is just a musician like all the other ones I've interviewed over the past year and, if reports are to be believed, even more obnoxious than most. But I look at him and I do *not* believe: I know already that this is so different, that he is different, that I am different with him. This is not editor and interview subject; nor is it star and starstruck groupie, as it would have been with those little girls downstairs. This is something else, something more, something realer; the amazing thing is that both of us seem to have recognized that instantly, and though we also seem to know that it might not be for a while yet, it is plain to us both that it will be. Just *what* it will be has yet, I think, to be determined; but it will be nothing like anything else there has ever been before.

None of this, you understand, is a comforting thought; I am thrilled to my soul, but also scared to my marrow. He has gone to fetch me a drink from the bottles lined up on a sideboard, exchanging some words in an undertone with Diane en route. I take the opportunity, while his back is half-turned, to scrutinize him, shyly, critically and absolutely shamelessly.

He is bigger than I had thought, taller too, dressed in last night's concert clothes of unbleached white linen peasant shirt, black jeans and black leather boots. His brown hair is a little lighter than it looks onstage or in photographs, a deep rich brown with no red in it, shoulder-length and shaggy. The eyes are blue, and there is depth in them, none of that shallow empty washed look blue eyes can so often have. The voice is soft, the smile frequent and charming, the grin devastating.

The Myth of Morrison—slender young flowerfaced tousle-tressed androgyne lion—is utterly demolished. He is the most masculine thing I have ever seen in my life and he looks as strong as a horse. But I had not guessed the bigness. The way he fills a door.

Given a choice between bourbon and cognac, I choose cognac; he holds out to me a filled snifter. Diane is talking animatedly, and I silently bless her for it: I am a rather shy person, and suffer untold agonies on interview assignments. Unlike most of my journalistic colleagues, who are only too pleased to hang out with artists, I have a definite distaste for this fakery of levels and roles, the rock gamesmanship which many consider to be the whole game, and if only I could, I would much prefer to stay home and listen to records, write my piece from there. Also I have a fear of ultimate silence in the room, my questions exhausted and the subject unhelpful and the tape flapping in the breeze. Which is worse, I wonder now, to be so well-informed about your subject that there is nothing left to ask, or to know little, rudely, and have to ask even the simplest, stupidest questions like How did you get the band started?

But Jim is looking at me, and Diane is discreetly edging out of the room, and with a start I realize it is showtime, and I'm the one who's on. I take a deep breath, straighten my shoulders under the velour tunic and lean forward in my chair.

Before I can open my mouth, he sees my difficulty. "Well, don't let me just sit here," he says with a smile. "Come on, ask me some questions, Patricia. Easy ones," he adds. "I'm not sure I'm going to be up to you New Yorkers today."

I begin warily working my way through my question list. Diane pops in and out through all the next hour and a half, as if she's checking on a particularly fidgety soufflé, beaming on the proceedings. Jim answers easily, with a string of socko quotes.

"You can say I'm an actor-musician-dancer-politician— There were five of them, what's the other one? Oh yeah, writer, that's it."

" 'Erotic' politician?" I ask, recalling a familiar quote from earlier days.

He grins, a little embarrassed. "No, just a politician."

"It's a very low occupation," I remark, and he throws me a sharp glance, unsure if I am taking him at all seriously.

"Well, politician only in the broadest sense—"

Shyness has made me bold. "Ah, then perhaps you mean in the Shelleyan sense, where he says—was it in 'Alastor'? No, 'A Defence of Poetry'—that 'Poets are the unacknowledged legislators of the world'?"

The blue eyes spark and widen, and he sits up a little in the white-and-gold French Provincial chair that's too small for him. He doesn't seem to have heard *that* sort of thing too often from interviewers, and I am vain enough of my literary scholarship to be pleased. After a few more exchanges, the talk shifts to less airy planes; Diane comes in again, and she and I get into a teasing riff about the alleged alligators in the New York City sewer system.

Here Jim seems on firmer ground. "Bullshit."

"Oh, I don't know, Jim, I had this friend used to be lead harpoon in the alligator patrol boat, his name was Queequeg—"

He gets it but won't let me have it. "Bullshit," he repeats, but he is smiling. "Alligators like to lie and bask in the sun, where're they gonna find sun in the sewers? I am a native of the great state of Florida and I know these things. Now *I* will tell *you* a story: There is in Manhattan a rat population twice that of the entire city, and they all live underground, and they are held in check by an irregular army of two hundred thousand *cats.*"

I mutter something to the effect that I liked the alligators better and I hope that they are all mutating into monsters down there. The Lizard King (Jim has over the past year or so become known by the title he will die by) likes this, and we discourse for a few minutes on reptilian themes, a show he'd seen on television about Komodo dragons, serpents in myth and history.

I look down at my hands, then up at him. "Did you know—well, I'm sure you know—the badge of your clan is a serpent? The

Morrisons—who are a *minor* Scottish clan, founded by a bastard son of a king of Norway—have a snake as their totem animal. And according to some authorities, the snake is one of the sacred beasts of the Mother Goddess."

He takes the teasing in good part, but the rest of it has most powerfully caught his attention. "Well, that sounds right to me. And just what might yours be, miss? Or don't the Irish go in for that sort of thing?"

"How do you know I'm Irish?"

A chortle of laughter. "With that hair and that attitude? Are you kidding? Anyway, you told me so on the phone, when you called before."

I have the grace to blush. "Yeah, right—well, as it happens, my family name—of royal Milesian descent, *much* grander than the Morrisons—means 'wolf's head.' That was the mark of the ancient Irish tribal shamans: As a sign of their office, they would wear a whole wolf's pelt, the head on their heads and the rest hanging down their backs. Presumably that's where the family's name comes from; so I'm one of a line of hereditary shamans."

For some reason, this seems to affect him more than anything I have so far said. I have not yet heard the famous story he often tells, of how, when he was a small child in New Mexico, he witnessed a road accident in which several American Indians were killed, and how he has believed ever since that the soul of one or more of them leaped at that moment into his own body, making him a shaman, or at the least awakening his own shamanic potential.

But he is looking at me in a rather different way, and to cover my confusion I turn the conversation to the previous evening's show.

"It was a good night," he says, sounding pleased, if surprised at the sudden change of topic. "I had a good time, and I think the other guys did too. The new material—we did that 'cause when you play New York, the Garden, you want to do something special, not just the same old stuff. That's why we had the strings and horns. It probably won't be a permanent part of our sound; well, not live, anyway, the logistics of traveling with all those extra people would be a little too much, and we wouldn't want that sort of sound for everything we did anyway. The new album, that we're working on now, will have a lot of those songs we did last night, and that sound, on it; but not the one after that. We just wanted something different, just expanding a little, that's all."

The new sound and new songs he refers to will come to comprise the fourth Doors album, *The Soft Parade*, and will also come to be almost universally excoriated by critics and fans alike. But that is several months down the road: Now, here, he picks up a copy of the January issue of Jazz & Pop—I have brought a few with me—and studies the cover. It is a photograph of the members of Jefferson Airplane dressed up like a tacky lounge act of the 50's: Grace Slick in a tarty red satin dress and gold spike heels (which I still have), the guys in pink tuxes and greased-back hair.

"Ho, is that—sure it is. Well, well—how come they're on the cover and we're not?"

I instantly promise a later cover, but he is more eager to make his real point.

"You know, this cover symbolizes to me the death, the decadence of rock. Decadence is when you become self-conscious and languorous, when you're not doing anything new"—he says this with a total lack of irony, apparently unaware, or uncaring, that those precise charges have been thrown against the Doors for many months now—"and to me that says that the form of the music we now call 'rock' has progressed to the point of no return, where everybody is good, every group that comes out is a great group, and nobody stands above the crowd."

"But that's a good thing, surely? It shows development—isn't greatness always better than mediocrity, no matter how much of it there is?"

Again the searching blue laser-look. I am confused again; am I not supposed to be asking questions that show I have brains and opinions?

But he says only, "No, I think it's decadence. The Jefferson Airplane dressed up like 1950's cats, man, you know what that says? That says the 1960's didn't happen."

I disagree. "Well, I think it just means we've gotten to a place where we can kid about it a little."

"Look at it like this, then," he says kindly; his tone is patient, a teacher explaining things to a nice but slow child, but I can also tell he is amused and intrigued. "Each generation has to have its wild rebellion and its effulgence of energy and we're here. Write it just like that—we're here. In the past this was called jazz, and blues, and in the immediate past it was called rock and roll, and now it's called rock. I personally think that it's being proven and shown everywhere today that rock is now in its declining phase. It's the tail end of things," he says mournfully.

I murmur something meant to be consoling.

"It's the tail end," he repeats. "Nothing is really happening, no mass hysteria"—this in the face of the memory of last night's incredible force and fury!—"no vital movement. I feel sad to have come in on the end, you know, people like to feel they're in on the beginning of things. But it's still fun. And in five or ten years it's going to be a whole new thing. The new generation will need their own means of expression. I can't say what it will sound like, but they'll make up some sound that's as much above rock as rock is above rock and roll, and they'll have some nonsense word name to call it, and that will be the music."

He pauses to thoughtfully refill my empty snifter—I have been sitting silent and open-mouthed and pop-eyed all through this remarkable recitation—and puts it into my hand, favoring me with a quick grin. I blush and take a hefty pull on the cognac.

"By then," he continues, not missing a beat, "everybody will be into new things, though. I hope myself to expand into writing, into films and stage work in particular. I am primarily a word man; music is great, I love it, and I love performing. But there are some things I have to say that can't be put to music, and could be best communicated in a book —I'll be publishing a book of my poetry pretty soon—or even on the stage, a play or spoken-word performance of some sort. We have made this film, forty minutes long, sixteen-millimeter, color, that in a way is a first step to all this. It has stuff from our concerts and backstage, but we're only an excuse. The film isn't really us." He looks up at me with a wicked glint. "Got all that?"

I match the glint with scorn. "Sure." I have been casually memorizing everything for the past hour or so, of *course* I have it . . . "You're pretty good at this," I say, determined to win one skirmish in what already I have seen to be a lost battle. "Do you practice, or what?"

He grins, clearly trying to decide again if I am being hostile or just teasing. "They usually don't go half as well," he offers generously. "You really did your homework."

"My pleasure," I say with some demureness. "Oh, and 'Oi washed me 'ands an' fyce afore Oi come, Oi did', too."

His eyes sparkle, probably more at the attempted Eliza Doolittle cockney accent than the quote itself. "Boy, real cut-and-thrust stuff today! You should have warned me about this one, Diane. Maybe I should have gone on that photo shoot with the other guys, not stayed here to let some smartass New Yorker walk all over me."

"How could they do a photo session without you?" I ask unwisely.

"They can't," he drawls. "I'll do mine later—after all, I have *you* to keep me company... Well, come on, Pa-triss-eee-a, ask me some more zingers. I just hope I have something left to tell you."

But he has no problem finding things to tell me for the next half hour and more. I have run out of questions long ago, and by now am just listening to him riff, watching him as he talks. When he is animated, as he is now, his whole face comes alive, in a manner so different from his ordinary pleasant expression as to seem a thing of awe. It doesn't stop there, though: There can never have been more incredible bone structure handed out in the history of genetics—cheekbones, the outlines of strong shoulders and an epic rib-cage, thighs that seem to go on forever. He sits quite still when he speaks.

In mid-flight of fancy he sees my glass is empty again, and he pours me another drink. As he reaches across the coffee table to give it to me, he puts his hand over mine on the glass, then reaches up to stroke my hair, which is dark auburn and at this time in my life just about long enough to sit on.

"Beautiful. Don't *ever* cut it."

To my eternal disgust and his obvious delight, I shiver a little at his touch. But we both pretend to ignore it, and tacitly agree that the interview per se is over. Yet neither of us seems willing to end the conversation: We talk of books and music and college and New York vs. L.A. Diane has been in and out rather less frequently as the afternoon wears on, intercepting phone calls in the other room so as not to interrupt us, either under orders from Jim or as if she perceives the thing that has been moving between him and me for the past two hours, the thing I refuse to put a name to just yet though I know exactly what it is, the thing both of us seem to know beyond words is happening.

He leans forward again, closer this time, as close to me as the table's width will allow. His eyes are wide open and fixed on mine.

"What *are* you?" he asks, suddenly, softly, guilelessly.

And I find myself looking straight back at him, dark brown eyes into lucid blue, and answering just as softly, "I'm a witch."

The expression that crosses his face then is extraordinary, as if he is thinking, 'Oh, right, that explains *everything*!' It is a smile of the most singular sweetness, a look of surprise and delight and speculation and intrigued curiosity: of wanting to know a *lot* more and of being just a little afraid to ask; of pleasure at being confounded, apparently not a thing that often happens to him; of possibility and inevitability—

as if he has been waiting a long time for this, for someone to say this very thing to him. It is something new, something unexpected; and I will come to learn that Jim Morrison loves the unexpected.

He sits back in his chair. "Well!" he says. "I guess you'd better tell me some more."

CHAPTER

2

WITCHCRAFT—MORE COMMONLY JUST THE CRAFT—IS the modern-day worship of the Mother Goddess who predates the patriarchal religions of Judaism and Christianity and Islam; who at one time was worshipped by humans in just about every corner of the planet, everywhere there were people who needed Her power and sought Her help. It is the honoring and the drawing upon of the female principle of the Universe, as logical and natural as the honoring of a male God, and perhaps even more deeply seated in human nature.

And in physical, earthly nature as well: The holy days celebrated by witches are the great wheel of the seasons, the solstices and the equinoxes, the Quarter-days that announce the beginning of spring and autumn, summer and winter—Imbolc and Lughnasa, Beltane and Samhain. And with the Goddess, the God is worshipped, Her consort, male principle of the Universe, the Horned Lord of death and hunting and winter and darkness.

(None of this is Satanism, by the way, not the least littlest bit. As witches do not worship or accept the Christian god—though many, myself among them, revere Jesus Christ as a holy and enlightened teacher and avatar—they can hardly worship or otherwise honor that god's adversary. Nor would they even particularly wish to: Paganism is deeply informed by a loving reverence for all living creation—scarcely a tenet of the Satanist creed—and no true witch holds any truck with the negativity and nastiness Satanism seems to thrive on. Neither Jim nor I nor anyone I know ever engaged in, or even spoke of, any Satanic practice. It's a common error of the ignorant and misinformed, to confuse witchcraft and Satanism, but I advise you to put it well and firmly aside, *now, FOREVER.*)

The tradition I came to, at about seventeen, is Celtic witchcraft—though I use the term 'witchcraft' advisedly, and not just because of the Satanic taint the word still has among the masses. There is no generally accepted name for my particular faith: 'Draíochtas,' meaning something like 'wise-lore,' 'arcane knowledge,' probably comes the closest, and its many adherents like to think that this is the way the ancient native faith of Celtdom would have grown over the centuries, had not Christianity and secularism and cultural imperialism so brutally and finally intervened. Many of the rituals are modern reconstructions, working off ancient texts and sourcebooks and even literature, and as the Celts had an oral culture in any case much is lost forever. Yet such as can be retrieved, we gather together, and we hold it in honor as the faith of our fathers and mothers before us, and we practice it; I live it in my life, and I write about it in my novels.

Our deities are the gods and goddesses of the traditional Celtic pantheons: the Irish and Welsh deities of wisdom, magic, love, art, war, music, literature; of the sea, the sky, the earth, the stars, the beasts, of death and birth, of all the many facets of life itself. And above all these there is the Goddess, the feminine face of the Supreme, with Her consort, the Sacred King.

So I explain all this now to Jim, and he listens with rapt attention, as if I am imparting to him the secret of the world.

"So, you were initiated into a coven, and that makes you—what, a priestess?"

"Yes; and if you were initiated you would be a priest. We believe that each woman, each man, should deal directly with the High Ones, the Powers. In ceremonies, in fact, women *become* the Goddess, men *become* the God. Other religions ask you to have faith in God; we ask our gods to have faith in us as well."

He smiles, but ponders this, asks questions, comments; I can tell he is taking this very seriously indeed, and we discuss it for another twenty or thirty minutes. If I have surprised and impressed him by this unexpected quirk, he impresses me in his turn with his erudition in such matters. I already know that he is one of the best-read people I have ever met, better-read maybe even than myself; but now he quotes great slabs of Frazer's *Golden Bough* at me, I counter with Robert Graves and we bat Yeats back and forth. I recommend some Celtic sources (some of which he is already familiar with: His stock skyrockets still further when we discuss his derivation of the "Crystal Ship" motif from an ancient Irish legend), and I think both of us could have gone on quite happily for hours.

But reality intrudes: The other Doors have been coming and going, whispering briefly in his ear; Babe Hill, a sort of roadie, puts in an appearance. After a while Jim and I are joined by some people who stay: David Anderle, a producer from Elektra's Los Angeles office; Fred Myrow, a classical composer working with the New York Philharmonic; my press colleague Ellen Sander.

Diane is a bit put out by Ellen's arrival—"I'll make her leave if you want, Patricia, I *told* her she couldn't come talk to Jim today 'cause he was only going to be talking to *you*"—but I say No, it's fine, it's okay, let her stay, let them *all* stay. In all honesty, I am beginning to react to the strain of the past few hours alone with Jim—it seems years, or else mere minutes—and I am suddenly glad of other people there, to somehow dilute the power of his unadulterated presence and attention. He is getting to me, big-time, and all at once I am a little scared of—not him, but the moment.

We all sit around the room in a loosely arranged circle, unplanned, as if assisting at an impromptu seance. Jim calls room service for more drinks, beer, coffee, fruit, munchies. Outside the windows it is beginning to get dark.

The Doors were born in the doldrum summer of 1965, when Ray Manzarek and Jim Morrison, fellow graduates of UCLA's famed film school, met by chance on the beach at Venice, California. Morrison, who had been living rough, sleeping on the sands as well as on people's rooftops, his only caloric intake apparently in the form of LSD, shyly showed the older Manzarek some scribbled poems and incipient song lyrics. They decided then and there to get a rock group together (Manzarek already had some blues-band experience with his brothers) and make a million dollars.

When Manzarek brought in Robby Krieger, guitarist, and John Densmore, drummer—fellow meditators from the Maharishi Mahesh Yogi's L.A. center—the Doors were complete. And named, too; from you have a choice of stories—Aldous Huxley's (ultimately William Blake's) *The Doors of Perception* ("When the doors of perception are cleansed/ Things will appear as they are, Infinite"), or Jim Morrison's "There are things known and things unknown; in between are doors."

The fledgling band began its career with bare-survival gigs at small and long-since-defunct Sunset Strip clubs. A stint as the prestigious Whiskey à Go-Go's more or less house band was abruptly terminated one night when they performed the Oedipus section of "The End" for the first time. It is part of Doors legend that Morrison was on about ten thousand mikes of acid at the time, which might or might not explain it. The owner of the Whiskey, however, was not sharing the trip: He was outraged, the audience was scared out of its tiny mind, and the Doors were history in more ways than one.

But, fortunately for them and for the subsequent history of rock and roll, they had been signed by then to an Elektra recording contract; and soon there was a song that Robby Krieger wrote, a song called "Light My Fire" . . .

"A crucifix is the cheapest thing to do," mutters Jim to himself. "All you need, man, all you need is two sticks."

So much for my observation that, the night before at the Garden, from where I was sitting the four red spotlights on Jim came together to form a cross of light.

"Well, from where *I* was," offers Diane, "you couldn't see the spot beams at all, Jim, just the red light falling all over you. All the little teenies thought it was a miracle. 'Oooohh, he's smoldering! All red— he's burning up!' "

Comfortable chuckles run round our circle. Not even Ellen is pretending that this is any sort of interview at all by now, and for my part I am quite happy to sit back and drink my cognac. Someone kicks a discussion of music into a lumbering trot; Jim, eyes closed, begins to talk about his cherished Dionysian-Apollonian approach to music and communication. Nietzsche would have been so proud to hear him; but, at least by my accounting, Nietzsche's got a lot to answer for. (Years later, a Door will put it more bluntly: "Nietzsche killed Jim Morrison." And, well, yeah, I can see what he means, but it was just a *bit* more complicated than that . . .)

The phone in the bedroom has been ringing like the bells of hell, and Diane has been running in and out to answer it; the rest of us pretty much manage to tune it out. Then suddenly the phone next to Jim's elbow shrills, startling us all; we all come down about ten degrees at once. But Jim picks up the receiver, still earnestly expostulating, and holds it at arm's length, intent on finishing his point. The operator's shriek can be heard clear across the room.

"Jim," someone reminds him politely. "Jim. The phone?"

"Oh, yeah . . . Hello—yeah, well, this is Mr. Morrison? The, uh, the *doctors* are here now, they're in the middle of this operation. Yeah —on my *throat*. Right—very difficult and dangerous, it's a very delicate situation as I'm sure you can appreciate, so I'd be grateful if you didn't call back until it's over. We'll let you know how it goes." He goes back to his Nietzschean rap without missing a beat. Ellen breaks out the cannabis chocolate-chip cookies; they taste like the floor of a barn, but they do the job just fine, and not very long after we are all sitting paralyzed in our chairs.

Fred gazes meaningfully around the circle, then down into his glass. "I suppose you're all wondering why you've all been gathered here this afternoon."

Everybody chuckles; nobody moves. But what if he's *right?* I think.

"Knowledge is creation," says Ellen. Actually, knowledge is power, but I do not feel impelled to correct her. In fact, I can barely see her on the couch a few feet away: The room is dark now and no one will turn on a lamp; the only illumination comes from the bedroom and the little connecting hallway. "Like this apple," she continues. With one swipe of a knife she slices it in half. "You see the word 'apple,' and right away you make it into an apple in your mind." She bites into her illustration.

" 'Ringo' means 'fish' in Japanese," says Fred. I have no idea if this is true.

Jim leans forward, eyes closed. "Ohhh—where did the *ringing* start?" he whispers. "Rrrrinngg—what Ellen said, then it went right into 'Ringo.' "

Fred nods wisely. Ellen denies she ever said anything that went rrrrinngg, and tries to bust the tiny brass Indian bells on the ends of her pigtails as plausible ringers.

"No, no, it was something you said," insists Jim, "and Fred just made it right into rrrRingo."

David is flashing on a stoned Japanese person going to a Beatles concert and seeing a fish playing drums. Outside, far below in Central Park, they are ice-skating; if one person falls, six others trip over his prostrate form before he can get up again.

I sit watching little red lights fly in tight circles over the park, hoping against hope that they are really UFOs or something. My journalistic objectivity has been shot all to hell: It seems that I have been sitting in this chair since time began, that I was born here, that I will live out my life here, and that I will die here as well, and I *don't even care*.

Diane comes in, whispers to Jim and they disappear for a few minutes; conversation languishes in their absence, as if we need all our component parts to continue speaking. I am shaking a little by now, but it is with sheer relief: at not having made a fool of myself in front of Jim, at having asked everything I was supposed to ask, at having myself been asked some things I never in a million years expected to be asked. I feel like a show jumper who has completed the course without knocking down a single fence, and there is a feeling a little like Forever in the room.

Jim comes back, takes his place in the circle again and closes his eyes; against the last twilight gleam through the uncurtained windows behind him, he looks as if he is floating. I wonder why he likes to keep his eyes closed; does he see better that way? But I am not brave enough or stoned enough to inquire, and I am glad that it is so, for suddenly the blue eyes blaze wide open, and with an indescribable feeling that jolts my entire body I realize that Jim is staring straight at me.

He looks at me for what seems like eternity, and I stare back at him. I would guess the room has gone silent, but I can't hear anything so I really couldn't say: All my being is in my eyes, and those eyes are still fused with Jim's.

Finally he speaks, in a voice that sounds as if he is assuring me of something.

"Wait till I finish my drink."

Well, is that a threat, or a promise? I am not sure just now which

I would indeed prefer . . .   Luckily, I am not called upon to decide, because just then Jim throws himself down violently upon his knees, pauses an interminable instant, then walks, still on his knees, slowly and deliberately, across the room and past the coffee table to where Ellen is sitting on the couch. At his approach, she draws her feet up underneath her, nervously, and moves back as far as she can get.

Jim is masking his intent but making the most of his audience: He crashes to a halt before Ellen, weaving back and forth a little on his knees, then sneers at her, eyes still closed.

"C'mon, we're all gonna *sing* now, ever'body, we're gonna sing 'Oh Say Can You See'! Okay, Ellen, you first."

I can hear her voice quaver in the darkened room, but she throws it right back at him.

"No, Jim, you're the singer here. I'm a critic, just a professional audience, I can't sing. Why don't you sing for us?"

Nice try! I am impressed, quite certain that I will not be able to think of anything half so good when he turns next on me, as doubtless he will, and I try frantically to come up with a suitable defense.

But he's not finished baiting Ellen; and it is only afterwards that I learn why: She wrote something about him that he didn't like, and he's pissed. He remembers *everything* that *anybody* ever writes about him, good or bad, and Ellen had called him a "Mickey Mouse de Sade." Well! I guess that did it, because here he is, weaving back and forth like a cobra in front of a terrified cat. But Ellen is more of a scrappy mongoose; she doesn't give, not even when he moves as close to her as he can get and starts bellowing.

"I SAID *SINNNGGG!*"

I don't know what to do: I know I don't like what he's doing to someone I work with, but I know even better that I don't want to get between them. And looking around at the carefully neutral faces I can see that I am by no means alone in this discreditable feeling.

Finally Ellen, probably figuring she might as well just sing and get it the hell over with, comes across with the first verse of "Hey Jude," in a clear tiny voice that is on key and doesn't shake very much at all.

Jim smiles, eyes still closed, and heads back to his chair, using feet this time; the room breathes again. But he mutters under his breath as he goes, " 'Mickey Mouse de Sade,' am I?"

It has been a fairly unpleasant five minutes: But I get the feeling that Jim didn't really mean it, that he was just doing it because he wanted to see what would happen, it didn't matter to him one way or another. I don't like it; it is the first time I've met him, and this is what he chooses to show me . . .   Perhaps it is a warning; if so, I do not pay heed; and, out of deference to Ellen's feelings, I do not write about it.

Somebody needs to know the time/Glad that I'm here . . .   I say, very carefully, that in New York you call N-E-R-V-O-U-S to get the time, but that in San Francisco the number is P-O-P-C-O-R-N.

Jim is amused. "That says a lot, y'know, about the respective character of these two great cities. I mean, what else *would* you call in New York but 'Nervous'?" He grabs the phone and thrusts it at me. "Here, honey. Call them. I want to hear it."

I can barely read the pushbuttons in the dim light, so use phone Braille; to my surprise, it works. I listen attentively, then hang up.

"Well?"

"They said five-forty-eight-and-twenty-seconds." Pleased surprise all round: It's not as late as everyone had thought. "No, wait, *six*-forty-eight? *Seven*-forty-eight? I am so *stoned* . . ."

General laughter. Jim is looking at me with a half-smile.

"But you *are* sure about the forty-eight and the twenty part of it?"

"Oh yes."

"Good."

Years later. Ellen and I are making the vague movements that one makes preparatory to splitting. Jim is watching me put my coat on, his eyes not only wide open now but alarmingly aware, and he is laughing softly to himself.

"Jim?" I ask, wonderingly.

"Did you bring your gun?" he inquires. "I left mine in L.A."

"Do you have a gun, Jim?"

He closes his eyes again and smiles. "No."

Ellen has vanished, and I don't blame her one bit. Jim accompanies me to the door of the bedroom, out of sight of the rest of the party, then takes my arm and escorts me to the outer suite door.

"I really enjoyed this afternoon," he says then, and I can tell by his tone that he means it. There is now no faintest trace of alcohol daze in his eyes or his voice or his manner; it is as if his body has converted all that bourbon to spring water in his veins, just negated the intoxication he was showing only minutes ago. It must be a new frontier in metabolism; or maybe it's meditation?

"I'll call you the next time I'm here, give me your number," he adds. "We have to talk some more. Is that okay, will that be all right, if I call?"

I can't believe I'm giving him my number—what does this one make, about the thousandth?—but I do. I look up at him—I am a tall woman, he's maybe four inches taller—nod, thank him for his time and courtesy.

He smiles. "Be careful going home, will you? New York's a dangerous place." And then he leans down and kisses me lightly on the mouth.

"I know," I say, with the last shred of wit he has left to me. "That's why I live here."

He smiles again, and closes the door behind me.

CHAPTER

3

BORN THE HEIR OF INTERGALACTIC ROYALTY, I WAS abandoned by gypsies and raised by wolves.

Well, no, I wasn't; I only act that way. For the record, I was born in New York City on 4 March 1946 at seven in the evening (which makes me twenty-seven—there's that number again—months younger than Jim). For the zodiacally inclined, that also makes me Pisces, Virgo rising, Moon in Aries, Venus in Pisces.

I grew up on Long Island in a strict, traditional, Irish Catholic family, the eldest of four children, two girls and two boys. My father, now retired, was a POW in Germany during World War II, and came home to become an executive at one of the many local defense plants; my mother is a watercolorist and a stained-glass artist.

Growing up, I was considerably more successful academically than socially: reading before I started school, A's and A-pluses in most everything but the hated math. I won scholarships, edited the literary magazine, played field hockey, tennis and basketball, was literary editor of my yearbook, a columnist for the school paper, a member of student government, the choir and the National Honor Society, won trophies for French and creative writing. And I had *maybe* three dates in all four years of high school. No one asked me to the senior prom, and I spent the day in New York instead. I was, in fact, a nerdette; and proud of it.

Things changed when, at seventeen, I went away to college in western New York State: lovely country, deep snow-belt, rural mountain areas on the northern fringes of Appalachia. I spent two years at Saint Bonaventure University, where I majored in journalism and got engaged to Jim's forerunner, another dark, poetic, smoldering Heathcliff type; and finished up at Harpur College (now SUNY-Binghamton), the Berkeley of the New York State educational system, where I suffered through my broken engagement and graduated in June 1967, with a bachelor's degree in English literature.

It was at Bonaventure, under the purview of the Franciscan order, that I first began the involvement with Celtic paganism that has played so vast a part in my creative and spiritual life. I had been interested since early childhood in anything to do with Irish mythology or King Arthur, and at about age fifteen had suddenly realized that there was a great deal more to all that than just folktales and legends. Bonaventure—operating perhaps on the principle of "Know thy enemy"—had a superb library of books on this newly compelling field of interest, and Harpur was not far behind; and many enlightening hours were spent in the stacks.

After graduation, I headed straight to Manhattan, moving in with two sorority sisters of mine from Bonaventure (in case anyone is keeping score on my political correctness, let me add that I had also been the captain of the women's rifle team—which I fought patriarchs both priestly and military to establish, and on which I was a crack shot—a fencer, and a member of S.D.S.). I have never lived anywhere else: New Yorkers, especially born ones, know in their DNA that, as John Updike put it, people who live anywhere else have to be, in some sense, kidding.

In the time-honored tradition of English majors looking for work, I found a job with a publishing company; then one day in August 1967 I saw a magazine on the newsstand. It was called Jazz & Pop, and as soon as I flipped through its pages I knew this was the job I wanted: I loved the progressive rock that had been for the past year or so making its presence so thunderously known, and I wanted more than anything to write about it.

So in the fall I sent a letter to the magazine's editor/publisher,

Pauline Rivelli, asking if there was by any chance something going that a journalism/lit major might put her hand to. As it turned out, there certainly was.

On the top floor (cheapest rents) of a rundown building at 1841 Broadway (also home at that time to Atlantic Records, and across the street from Elektra—this was all before the Warner-Elektra-Atlantic merger of the mid-Seventies), Jazz & Pop magazine had its unprepossessing offices.

Three cluttered, interconnecting, ramshackle rooms on one side of a dingy hallway housed Pauline Rivelli, founder, editor and publisher, who did everything from layouts and mechanicals to selling ad space; Laura Roberts, the only eighteen-year-old in the country who was both circulation manager of a national magazine *and* its receptionist; and me, editorial assistant—which meant columnist, critic, feature writer, interviewer, record reviewer, proofreader, type spec'er, pasteup person and just about everything else.

That was it; though later on the staff would be augmented by Janice Coughlan, assistant to the publisher and staff photographer, and by assorted part-timers such as jazz editor Robert Levin and art director Louis Queralt. The rather impressive masthead listing—associate and contributing editors like Ralph Gleason, Nat Hentoff, and Ornette Coleman, among others—and the equally impressive critic roster—J&P gave an early start to the likes of Dave Marsh, Lenny Kaye, Vince Aletti, Robert Palmer, Stephen Holden, J Marks (Jamake Highwater), Ellen Sander and Pete Fornatale—were composed entirely of volunteer labor.

The magazine was so minimally funded, in fact, that Pauline, Laura, Janice and I even did all our own subscription fulfillment—mailing labels, postage, stuffing envelopes, sorting renewals, bagging thousands of issues each month and lugging them to the post office down the block—right there on the premises. With a few exceptions such as Hentoff and Gleason, and token case-by-case payment for major pieces, no one was paid for writing, ever. Reviewers were remunerated with bylines, free records, press tickets and glory, and that was about it.

And it worked: The quality and integrity of the magazine were unimpeachable. From the first, when Pauline had launched it single-handedly in 1962 as Jazz, it had been a progressive, highly politicized liberal rag; and with the title change in 1967 to Jazz & Pop, the politics, reflecting the music, went radical.

Interestingly enough, the magazine's circulation was overwhelmingly male, something like 80 percent—this for a publication created, produced and physically assembled (not to mention artistically envisioned) 100 percent by women. (Which on occasion could make for some interesting fan mail . . .) But we had the blessing of such martyrs to the radical cause as political prisoner John Sinclair (head of the White Panther Party, long-terming it in a Michigan slammer for possession of *two* joints), and were also deeply involved in the New York wing (entertainment media division) of Robert Kennedy's 1968 Presidential campaign. Though we never made Nixon's enemies list, even simple association could seem guilt enough to some: My sister, applying for a college summer job at a defense-plant supplier, found her security clearance delayed forever by a passel of gimlet-eyed suits, who kept asking her ever so casually-but-insistently just what her sister was up to lately. (She was thrilled, and gave away absolutely nothing, and never got that clearance after all.)

By the summer of 1968, I was writing a monthly column, "Pop Talk," in addition to record and concert reviews and general editing; by the end of my first year Pauline had made me the magazine's editor, herself retaining the title of publisher. She also raised my salary to the princely level of $175 per week—more than twice what I had been earning at the publishing company.

And more than enough to let me move out on my roommates and get my own apartment, a few blocks from the Fillmore East, and to keep me in clothes from Biba and Paraphernalia and Trina Robbins (herself a onetime Morrison paramour, though I do not learn this until many years later; but I'd still have bought her clothes, she made the most beautiful patchwork velvet bellbottoms), and drugs from my favorite dealers, and books, books and more books.

By the time I was looking at that fateful issue of Jazz & Pop, in August of 1967, rock was in what would later be held up as its Golden Age moment, its highest and finest exponent: artistically, culturally, musically, socially, politically, intellectually, spiritually. Never again were there to be so many bands massed above so high a minimum level of excellence. Even the bad bands were not bad at all, the middling bands were memorable, and as for the good-to-greats, well, there has never been anything to touch them since. To me, and to the many others lucky enough to have enjoyed such dazzling plenty (and to be un-brain-damaged enough to actually remember it), every musical movement since then has been, in some sense, kidding.

It sounds naive enough now—even a bit goofy—to those who were not there for it (and even some of those who were there for it were not *there* for it), but in those days music really *could* tear down walls, really *could* create a shared sense of community and context. The bands knew this too, and fed it back to us in a symbiotic and mutually beneficial manner.

At least, most of them did. The Doors were different.

The Doors *wanted* to be different, and the Doors did their flat-out best to ensure that they *were* different. You either loved the Doors or you loathed them, a pattern that seems to have persisted to this very day. They never allowed you any middle ground, and they did not suffer the half-hearted. As they themselves proudly put it, "We're not one of your peace-and-love bands," and in the flower garden that was 1967, the Doors were the black rose.

They got everybody, though, sooner or later; the sheer excellence of the music made sure of that. They began by aiming for the hip fringe, the intellectuals, the literate, the artistic avant-garde; but soon they were pulling in the teenyboppers and the beerdrinkers and the acid casualties as well, and they apparently had something to say to them all.

The Doors antagonized as many as adored them, of course—another pattern that has lasted—maybe even more. They were called pretentious, perverse, boring, obsessive, repetitive, and—worst of all—silly. They revelled in it all, and they deliberately provoked criticism as much as they consciously courted like-mindedness. The Doors, and most especially their lead singer, strove to be as intense and as contradictory and as maddening and as inflammatory as the times, and they almost always were.

I loved them. Their only serious rival for my musical affections was Jefferson Airplane. So when, in February 1968, I joined Jazz & Pop with the exalted title of Editorial Assistant (instead of lighting out for San Francisco with some friends from college), I knew beyond any doubt whatever that I had the best job in this world or indeed any other.

The first time I saw the Doors perform live was at Ondine, in the snowy early winter days of 1967, driving all night down from Harpur specifically to see them play.

A few of us who were really into music did this whenever we could:

We saw the Airplane before *Surrealistic Pillow* hit, at the tiny Cafe au Go-Go on Bleecker Street, sitting right in front of the speakers with our backs to a brick wall and Grace Slick, pale and beautiful, in full cry not six feet away (we were deaf for two days); the Mothers of Invention, the Fugs, you name them. It being 1967, we were of course stoned as usual; grass almost exclusively, occasionally acid or hash, never anything harder.

It has become fashionable of late to revisionistically bash one's own drug use in the 60's and 70's, to recant all those bright swirling times. I think those who do so are cowards. One may not be proud, exactly, of some of those excesses, and certainly it is nothing one would do now, but those days can only be judged in their own context. I loved drugs, and I'm not going to cop out now and go all handwringingly contrite about it. I loved the way they made me feel, and I'm not sorry for one *minute*. I loved all the mad clandestine rituals of buying pot—we used to pack it, *clean*, in those big green Excedrin bottles, enormous quantities of de-twigged and de-seeded grass for five or ten dollars. (Dealers who left in seeds and twigs were scorned, and lost face as well as custom.) Sometimes somebody would score a key, and we'd all buy into it, however much as we could afford or could use—a couple of ounces, maybe. Then we'd all assemble at the dealer's apartment—watching over our shoulders all the time for the dreaded (and mostly imaginary) narcs—and split it up like a pizza, everybody getting the slice he or she paid for.

Acid began to move into Harpur in 1966, brought back by exotic voyagers to the West, latter-day Marco Polos coming in from the Haight. And, too, though this was still rare and considered a bit risky, more potent hallucinogens, such as mescaline and peyote and psilocybin. But only the most dedicated heads tried those: The rest of us were still happy with our little stashes of pot and hash, and the odd hit of acid every now and then; speed freaks were looked down upon, and heroin and cocaine were nowhere to be seen.

But in those days we marked our time by music, dating events by the soundtrack of what we heard: the Airplane's first album, the newest Stones, the first Dead LP, *Sgt. Pepper* in June 1967 (*major* landmark, half the freaks at Harpur ran to the only music store in Binghamton the day it came out; I'd even ordered my copy in advance); and, in January of that year, an unheralded album with a darkly enigmatic jacket, called, simply, *The Doors*.

*   *   *

James Douglas Morrison was a war baby, born at five minutes to noon on 8 December 1943 in Melbourne, Florida; first child of Steve and Clara Morrison, a career Navy couple. He was born a Sagittarius, Aquarius rising, Moon in Taurus, Venus in Scorpio (well, where the hell else would it be?). A sister and brother would follow within a few years.

He had the usual Navy-brat childhood, a vagabond existence that took the family from one coast to another and back again: largely absentee father (who will command a warship during the Gulf of Tonkin incident that was prelude to the U.S. Vietnam involvement, eventually becoming an admiral; and who at the time of his retirement in 1975 was naval commander on Guam), mother who seems of necessity to have reared her children pretty much on her own.

From what Jim will later tell me, it seems to have been an unhappy and difficult childhood as well, and not in the sense in which my own childhood was difficult. Both of us experienced the sort of thing that gifted children invariably encounter; but if I also at times suffered from what I thought was an excess of unreasonable parental strictness and was in fact loving overprotectiveness, Jim seems to have suffered from a lack thereof; or so at least he will later say. Of the two of us, I have no doubt that he fared worse.

Needs, if recognized at all, were ignored (weakness, not to be tolerated) or simply not met (self-indulgence)—he will tell me this on more than one occasion, never with anything but pain. Frequently the least things were given the most weight: forced togetherness, conformity, length of hair, a veneer of family unity to the onlooking world, exacerbated because of the Navy factor—and all the while the underlying tensions went untreated and uneased, creaking and straining like wires in a high wind, like the rocks of the San Andreas Fault building to a break.

Was it any real surprise that the break came, inevitably, so huge, with aftershocks? Any wonder that as soon as he commanded any sort of control over his own backstory he swore to all that his parents were dead and he had no other kin? Or that, in his mind if nowhere else, they in truth *were* dead? What pain could spawn such negation, what roots of rootlessness could compel him to declare himself a sib-less orphan? Was it denial on a grand scale, or merely a means of sparing himself more pain? Or was it, at heart, revenge?

He went to high school in Alameda, California and Alexandria, Virginia; his parents sent him to college in Florida, under the stern God-fearing eye of his paternal grandparents, until he cut loose from all of it, and against his parents' wishes, transferred to UCLA, indulging himself in film school, the new hip medium for self-reinvention.

His college career was less than spectacular: He spent much of his time stoned out of his mind on hallucinogens, reading his brains out with books having little to do with academics, or both together. Sometime around then, he met Ray Manczarek (as Ray was then spelling it), and the ground was prepared for that other, later and more fateful meeting on the beach. His student film (the film-school equivalent of a senior thesis) was less than triumphant: montages of TV sets, Nazis, voluptuous blondes; professors were bewildered, fellow students scornful. He graduated more by courtesy, apparently, than out of any real academic commitment.

He had few romantic involvements during his college years—ironic in light of what was to follow—and some mean-spirited detractors have recently put it down to pudge. He wasn't—one has only to look at contemporary photographs—but plainly he had not yet grown into his bones and his beauty, was still an Ugly Duckling fledging into a rare black swan.

But the estrangement from his parents—he saw them for the last time in 1964—endured until the day he died. He never told me—or anyone, really—what it had been to cause him to hate his parents so immitigably (he even issued orders barring his mother from the venue, when she appeared once or twice at a theatre where the Doors were playing). Shadowy references have been made over the years to an episode in his childhood of alleged abuse by an adult whom he trusted (nature of abuse and identity of adult unspecified by sources), and his subsequent rejection and angry dismissal by the parent to whom, in his shame and pain and bewilderment, he had turned for help. I can't say; but it would explain much.

But all that was past now: Jim was living in Venice, writing, thinking, planning, vaguely intending to go to New York and pursue an artistic life there. In the event, he didn't; at least not just then, and that road not taken changed more lives than Jim's alone.

I am sitting in Ondine, a hole of a place practically under the Fifty-ninth Street Bridge; I am feeling groovy. We—four of us, down from school—are still buzzing pleasantly from all the grass we smoked in the car, and we are clad in sympathy and style: I am wearing my favorite brown paisley pantsuit, with about four pounds of silver and beads on ears and neck and fingers. None of us has ever seen this group perform live; although their first album has been living on my turntable for a while now, nothing has prepared me for what is about to happen this night.

The general anticipation runs up a couple of notches as the musicians come out and start tuning up—they look like heads, this is promising —but it is not until the guy in the leather pants hits the tiny stage that I sit up and pay startled attention. I know karma when I see it.

It's not just that it is of course love at first sight, that goes without saying; but more is going on here than simply that. Things to do with what this guy is singing about, as well as how he is choosing to sing it. The subtext here is for me strangely and subtly compelling: not just sensuality, though that is certainly part of it. But attractive as the package undeniably is, for me it's the brain on display here, not the lizard, that makes me sit up and take such notice.

But it's more even than notice: Something way far within points its finger at him and says, "You." Says, "That's for me." I know I'm right—what I don't realize is that about a million other women are looking and saying much the same thing. And quite a few of them, as it turns out, will also be right. But I will be right in a somewhat different way . . .

Still, the thought just now in my reeling brain is: My GOD, this guy is SMART! Gorgeous is good, fated is good, but smart is soooo much better. He's too pretty just now anyway, androgyny does nothing for me; let him put on a few years and a few pounds. The fact is, here is somebody singing about all those things I have spent so much time with over the past five or so years, that will (though I do not yet know this) play so great a part in my own future creative life: mythology, symbology, arcana, animism, archetypes, MYSTERY . . .   Not dryly pedantic, but made rich and meaningful and transmuted into art by the most compelling music imaginable.

It is difficult now, at two decades' remove, to convey just how staggering all this was, on how many levels, to college kids who were themselves just beginning to experiment with limits, to rush variously into drugs and mysticism and radical politics. We were all explorers; now here was somebody who seemed able to see around a few more corners a little farther in advance of the rest of us. The attraction or connection was by no means universal—I knew plenty of heads who couldn't stand the Doors at any price—but if once you made that first crucial suspension of disbelief, took that first willing step into their Roman wilderness, the Doors would richly repay you for your faith.

So I watch and listen and marvel. I don't know how this is going to happen, or when; all I know is that it will be, though after that evening at Ondine, Jim Morrison is no part of my life for many months to come, save as a voice reaching out for me from the speakers, or a dark blazing presence on a darkened stage. Tucked away for safekeeping is the absolute certain knowledge that he and I will meet and will matter to one another. Though it is to be two years more before this happens, in that span I see him in concert some score of times, and one of the very next occasions is at Forest Hills, in August of 1967.

The Doors are playing second on the bill to Simon and Garfunkel (whom I last saw at Winter Weekend, playing in the Harpur gym)—one of the zanier bits of creative programming you could ever hope to see. I have dragged my two best friends from college, roommates Sue Donoghue and Noreen Shanfelter (both of whom will become involved themselves in the music business over the next few years). They have made it quite clear to me that they are only coming along to see the headline act, and have absolutely no interest whatever in that pretentious Oedipal crooner from L.A. and the drony band that backs him.

Fine with me! I am here for a different purpose altogether, and the Doors have barely taken the stage in front of the diametrically split audience—half theirs, half Paul's and Artie's—before my purpose is met. I see that I had been right, back at Ondine, back at the Scene: This lunatic in the black leather pants, who is even now falling into the drum kit, is going to be of the most tremendous importance in my life; and I am either second-sighted or utterly insane. Or both.

Whatever, I am gripped by the utter conviction that our paths will cross; that out there along the cosmic sidewalk, he and I are waiting to stick out a casual foot and trip the other up.

We arrive at the Fillmore East in good time; after the free-for-all of the Janis Joplin concert two weeks ago, on opening night, 8 March 1968, we are pleasantly surprised to find that not only do the tickets now have actual seat numbers on them—the seats too! every luxury!—but that crowd control has been vastly improved. A cadre of T-shirted, no-nonsense longhairs moves everybody along with minimal fuss, if little affection on either side.

We don't care. Our seats are in the third row center; though by now I have seen the Doors so many times, this is special: This is my first professional gig with Jazz & Pop, my first night as a ROCK CRITIC and it's with the Doors. Also it is Ron's first sight of them in concert, and he is really up for it. Since he is the one who turned me on to the group in the first place, bringing their album over to my off-campus pad in Binghamton, along with what must have been a pound of grass, it seems only fair and right that I have asked him to accompany me.

I am pretty up myself: The joints we smoked on the way here probably help, and may possibly explain why I am dressed in two lace tablecloths. Oh, I've sewn them into a pantsuit—cut so that design medallions cover strategic areas, it's not as if I've just draped them round me—and the monk's cloak that Susie brought me from Bonaventure, gift of a friendly friar, goes over it all. I am by far not the most creatively dressed person here.

The crowd settles down as the blue lights dim, and we endure the supporting acts: Crome Syrcus, a forgettable bunch of lightweight pop-pers, and Ars Nova, a knockout Renaissance-brass rock ensemble. But everyone is waiting for the Doors; patiently and politely waiting, too, maybe incapable of anything else. There is a thrillingly ominous under-current building up through both these sets, and a jolt of anticipation when the stage crew finally pulls out the equipment platform for the evening's third act.

The lights go down again at last, the Joshua Light Show explodes; a modal moan seeps like smoke out of the huge speaker banks, and Morrison stalks down center stage, like the rough beast whose hour has come round at last.

He doesn't do very much at first; just stands there, hanging on the mike stand, eyes closed, head lifted, swaying slightly, light spilling over the planes of his face. That face is pale against the dark burgundy of his velvet shirt; his brown hair falls below his shoulders; his eyes, when he opens them at last, to actually *look* at us, are like desolation craters of the moon. He stares, smiles, sneers, "Five to one, one in five, *nobody* here gets out alive," and I believe him as he laughs.

Familiars "When the Music's Over," "Break On Through," "Back Door Man"; then "Money," and something whose name escapes me. He sings one line over and over again; the music falls away from under him, and we begin to clap softly to the unheard beat. He glides into "Moonlight Drive" segued with "Horse Latitudes," then:

"Is everybody in?" Conversational; shouts of Yeah, sure, we're in!
"Is everybody IN?" Challenging; louder Yeah's challenge back.
"IS EVERYBODY IN?" Silence. "The ceremony is about to begin."

And begin it does: This is "The Celebration of the Lizard," and New York has hardly heard it before. He has us totally by now—where did he learn to grasp like this?—me and Ron and everyone else, spiraling inward, always at his side, never slowing; we had come so far already, and we would have followed him right over the edge of the world. I am not exaggerating.

When the song ends some twenty minutes later, there is a blackout, silence, no one stirs; I think we are afraid to move, to breathe. I know I am . . . Then music leaps out of John and Ray and Robby like tongues of flame, and the lights blaze crimson, roaring into the great conflagration of "Light My Fire."

Crude, but smashingly effective: As they leave the stage—nobody believes for a minute that this is all there is—a film begins to roll on the lightshow screen. The Doors with instruments and bunches of flowers, Jim in a brown jacket, no shirt or shoes, walking to a beach in the early morning. It is "The Unknown Soldier," one of the first times, if not indeed the first, that a film has been made for the specific purpose of accompanying or illustrating a rock song—music video is born! what a horrible thought!—and though it is shamelessly manipulative it is also eerie and effective. Morrison is tied to a pile of timbers; machineguns blast; he falls forward against the ropes, blood pouring from his mouth to sprinkle the banked flowers at his feet. Film of Vietnam, dead children, dead cities, VJ Day in Times Square, signs reading "The War Is Over!"; his voice on the audio track exults "War is over!", and we scream *YES!*, shout, raise our clenched fists, leap out of our seats in catharsis and agony and joy.

When the Doors return to the stage for the encore, I truly do not expect to see Jim with them; but he comes out last of all, almost humbly. You're *dead!*, I think, stoned and stunned and three years too soon, You *can't* come back! And from the audience reaction I can tell that I am not the only one to think so . . .

But the first notes of "The End" arc out, shining and trembling,

golden in the silence, and we all shiver and settle down again. He's got
everybody by now, even the cynics; well, especially the cynics, they always
fall the hardest at the last, but they do fall. He sings, dances a war dance,
a love dance, the music takes wing and he kneels at the edge of the
stage apron. Then, finally, "the end of nights we tried to die—"; and
he looks up, waves once and leaves the stage.

It is a suitable introduction to my new profession, even though this night
I am here with bought tickets (the press passes are for tomorrow night's
shows, also incredible; I wear a brown velvet Cossack shirt, in tribute
to Jim's own, and a matching microskirt atop leather thigh-boots). Not
counting a rather unsatisfactory appearance at the Westbury Music Fair
in April, the next time I see the Doors is at the Singer Bowl, one hot
and hellish August night.

For this occasion I go in style: A publicist friend who works for the
Doors' p.r. firm commandeers a limo, and we drive to the gig feeling
like supergroupies or jetsetters; it is the first time either of us has ever
been in a limousine, and I like it, it appeals to my elitist tendencies,
but it also makes me very uncomfortable indeed.

We do some drugs on the way out—it is a beastly summer evening
in New York, hazy and sultry, with poisonous air, and we figure whatever
works . . .   In fact, we *are* mistaken for supergroupies—my companion
is wearing black harem pants and a big fringed scarf tied around her as
a top, I am in backless braless see-through silk. We probably deserve it.

We are glad of the limousine, though, when the concert tends toward
riot before it is more than a few minutes old. The Who, playing second
on the bill after an unwanted opener called Kangaroo and before the
headlining Doors, do their usual destructo-derby, but it looks bogus, and
they play a lackluster set anyway.

So by the time the Doors make it to the stage, the crowd is hot
and pissed and bored and cranky, and Morrison doesn't help. He takes
his own sweet time getting on stage, letting the band play without him,
then strolling out behind a phalanx of rent-a-cops, a film crew following
close behind.

Once onstage, he doesn't sing, but slurs and mutters and makes up
his own lyrics—not exactly what this crowd has been wanting to hear.
Worse, he breaks off singing to launch into poetic raps, lewd asides, even
flirts with stageside chicks, throwing himself down on the stage and

writhing around like a, well, snake. All of which makes for great footage for the film crew, but not much of a concert for the sellout crowd.

Just past midnight all hell breaks loose, as Morrison finishes "The End" (most appropriate), flops down with a theatrical shriek, and several *hundred* people rush the stage. Cops clog the stage front as broken folding chairs start to fly, in pieces and entire, at anything that moves. Jim fields a few and lobs them right back into the seething mass. More missiles are incoming now, and there are so many cops onstage that the Doors are invisible behind their human shield.

We have not strayed far from the limo—it is parked on the edge of the seat area, easily accessible, we had a feeling a quick escape might be called for—and as the first chair becomes airborne, we turn in unison and head for the car. But in those few moments, even our own immediate area, far from the center of Morrison's storm, has become agitated, and we have to push our way through waves of frenzied fans. It is really unpleasant, and quite genuinely scary: Is this the sort of thing that rock stars have to go through all the time? Man, I would *hate* that . . . I start out politely excusing myself to everyone as I inch along, then just unapologetically straightarm anybody who dares to stand between me and the limo.

Safe at last in the car, we look back as the driver, clearly edgy, pulls away in no uncertain terms: Behind us now is total chaos; we will hear tomorrow that the riot went on for almost an hour, many people were hurt, some hospitalized, and several were arrested. Jim Morrison was not among either the bashed or the busted: The Doors play Cleveland, Ohio the next night, and there is a riot there too.

The Doors do not return to New York in 1968, ending the year with a big European tour and some dates in California and the Midwest. That fall I get to meet my other favorite band, Jefferson Airplane, when they pose in lounge-act clobber for the magazine's cover (the one Jim will take such exception to); after the shoot, Grace gives me her gold lamé stiletto heels.

I also go to my first Fillmore East Thanksgiving dinner: For the benefit of musicians and anyone else who might otherwise miss out on turkey day, or who is feeling a little lonely over the holiday weekend, no grandma's house to go to, Bill Graham sets up communal tables in the lobby of the Fillmore East, laying on a spread of turkey and trimmings for all. I palm off my slice of pumpkin pie on Janis Joplin, who is sitting across from me; she likes it, I don't, so it's hers—and she offers me a swig of her Southern Comfort in return. Seems fair.

The year ends quietly, sliding into 1969; and soon Diane Gardiner, who does press for the Doors now as well as for the Airplane, calls to tell me that the Doors will be playing the Garden in January, and Jim would like to talk to me, do I think I might like to talk to him too . . .

CHAPTER

4

March–May 1969

AFTER THE PLAZA EVENT, I DO NOT HEAR FROM JIM FOR a while, unless you count the flowers he sent to Ellen and to me: apology, presumably, in her case; in mine—promise? Or threat, after all? I write up the afternoon, including a brief section on the rather less entertaining time I had talking to two of the other Doors, and it runs in the March issue of Jazz & Pop. Pauline loves the piece, praises it as warm and funny and honest. She doesn't know the half of it.

Jim seems to like it, too: After it appears at the end of February he sends me a letter of appreciation and thanks, the first letter I ever get from him. It is written on steno-pad lined paper, the kind with the raggy top edge where you rip it out of that spiral wire thing; his handwriting is an oversized and sprawling scrawl, often taking two lines of paper to write one line of script. I am thrilled.

Then, the first week of March, word comes out of Miami that Jim has behaved with more erratic abandon even than usual, at a concert there on the first day of that month of storms (ironically, or perhaps just hubristically, the very same date that director Oliver Stone will choose, twenty-two years later, for the premiere of his movie called *The Doors*).

Although no one knows it just yet, this concert at the Dinner Key Auditorium will be for the Doors the equivalent of Pearl Harbor or the battle of Châlons or the Archduke Ferdinand getting it at Sarajevo: the fatal moment, the hinge where history turned; in this case, turned *on* them. They would never be the same again; and to my mind, what happened as a result of Miami is one of the chief contributory factors to Jim's death.

But we are not thinking anywhere near so cosmically at the time; by now everyone is so accustomed to the various and usually entertaining excesses Jim brings to a concert—diving off the stage, hanging on rising curtains, swinging in on ropes, feigning electrocution, miming assassination, the usual fun stuff—that few in the music press or indeed in the larger hip community pay much attention at first. There are a few half-laughing, half-despairing groans about how Morrison *will* diddle while Amerika burns, but that's about it.

But then the true message of Miami begins to sink in, and suddenly no one in the music press is paying anything *but* attention. But it's still the wrong kind of attention, for the most part: People persist in viewing this as another stupid Morrison stunt, equating it with the New Haven bust of December 1967 (in which Jim was maced backstage while making out with an admirer, discussed it onstage later and was dragged off by cops, the first onstage rock star bust in history), writing dismissively about it if they write about it at all—praising with faint damns. Even so, there are some already who see it for what it is. And here we all thought it was just another dumb Doors concert . . .

It appears to have been a doomed and fated night from the start: Jim arrived late and drunk and surly (exceptionally late and drunk and surly even for him, it seems); the audience, who had been kept waiting hours, was hot, unruly, angry, too many of them crowded into a too-small venue by too-greedy promoters. Something plainly had to give, and it was, of course, Morrison. For over an hour he berated, abused, harangued and insulted, single-handedly managing to piss off the audience, the cops, the State of Florida, most of the social order of the Western Hemisphere, and even his own band.

Not a bad night's work for the Lord of Misrule; but Jim didn't stop there. Under the influence of the Living Theatre, whom he had just seen perform in California and with whom he had been powerfully impressed, he proceeded to involve the entire audience in a piece of living theatre of his own. Very little music was going on through all this, though the other Doors kept trying valiantly to get Jim to remember that this was, after all, a concert; but even when music did happen Jim refused to interrupt his tirade long enough to sing at all seriously. He had bigger things in mind.

At last the crowd became tense and expectant and eerily quiet, the kind of quiet that settles over a trailer park just before the tornado touches down. Into that silence, Jim snarled into the microphone, "You didn't come just for MUUUUSIC, didya? No! You came for something *else!*" And then those incredible lips framed the fateful words, the terrible words, the words everyone would later unanimously agree that they had heard: "Ya wanna see my cock?"

Wham! But that is the last thing on which eyewitness accounts agree: Some said he pulled it out. Some said he didn't. Some said he tried but couldn't get his zipper down. Some said the zipper came down but he had boxer shorts on and a roadie was pulling on his pants waistband from behind. Most said they just weren't sure. Many said they saw it. Many more probably wanted to think they saw something. Jim himself was to tell several different stories—he did, he didn't, he couldn't remember—and in any case was not supposed to be talking about it at all.

But most of this happens later. At the moment, all we know is that once again Jim Morrison has behaved like a jerk in public, only worse (we do not trouble ourselves with his reasons for doing so, not right off). Yet, somehow, incredibly, it begins to look as if the Feds are taking more than a passing interest, possibly thinking they can put Jim away, even, at least for a while. As the days pass, it begins to look, horribly, as if they might very well succeed, and it starts to dawn on at least some of us that something more is going on here than we had thought at first.

Then, four days later, the charges roll out of Miami like the opening salvos of a whole new war, the guns of March: felony lewd and lascivious behavior, misdemeanor indecent exposure (two counts), misdemeanor public profanity (two counts), misdemeanor public drunkenness. (And here we all thought it was just another dumb Doors concert...)

But it doesn't stop there, no! So great an outcry rises up out of the dark howling heart of the Moral Majority that Doors concerts are canceled all across this great land of ours, causing the group to lose hundreds of thousands of dollars in bookings; airplay vanishes virtually overnight (lost record sales); a "fuck clause" is inspired, written into rock concert contracts to guarantee payment of bond should naughty words or, indeed, naughty bits intrude themselves into the course of a performance. By now the FBI has stepped self-importantly in, no doubt seeing in this a chance of glory for themselves, and Jim is charged as a *fugitive from justice*; this despite the fact that he was surrounded by cops onstage and nobody seems to have had the idea of busting him right there. Indeed, he and the other Doors left Miami unhindered and unpursued, *days* before any charges were even thought of by self-seeking politicians or opportunistic Federal serfs.

Most stupefying of all, though, a Rally for Decency springs up, spearheaded by such publicity-grubbing pillars of moral rectitude as Jackie Gleason (who, you will recall, made a long and lucrative career out of playing alcoholism and wife-beating for laughs), gay-basher Anita Bryant, and, not one to miss a chance he doubtless thought his own small god had sent him, that whitest of whited sepulchres, Richard Milhous Nixon.

They have all joined hands and hearts under God (whose God?) to roll over Jim Morrison and all his works and pomps and minions. If it were not so utterly terrifying it would be hysterically funny, and indeed there are, even in the hip community, many who still cannot bring themselves to take it seriously. But the message is clear for those of us to read who can, and we are not laughing: Get Morrison, get the Movement.

The two are by no means identical, of course—and neither would thank you for equating them—but those out to do the getting seem neither to know nor care. All they can see is some damn hippie longhair dope-fiend degenerate up on a stage in Florida, in front of a hall full of impressionable high-school kids (they should only know about those kids . . .), screaming about fucking and disorder and cocks and changing the world and "No limits, no laws!" No wonder they're scared: This guy really means it, and even they can see it.

The strangely dissociated attitude in the hip/music press is paralleled by the attitude of the fans, and it is this which Jim and the other Doors are to feel most keenly. Ever eager to push Jim to new benchmarks of outrage, for some reason the fans take Miami as a personal slap in the face. Somehow, Jim has made *them* look bad, too, and that is going too far even for the man they themselves had made a god.

"It's like they thought I'd betrayed them," he will tell me much later, genuinely hurt and puzzled. "But they were the ones who seemed to want it. No matter what I did, it was never enough; they always wanted something weirder or grosser or wilder. And then when I did it they just turned around and called me a buffoon. They didn't get it, and blamed me that they didn't. I think what they really wanted was to see me die onstage. Literally." The Sacred King is always torn to pieces by his people in the end . . .

In any event, the legal maneuvering and moralistic posturing go on well into April and May—Jim is even threatened with extradition (you can tell they'd really like it to be execution; who do they think he *is*, John Wilkes Booth?)—but though in Doorsland the reverberations are profound and long-lasting and ultimately tragic, in the outside world the flap soon begins to fade. Jim, bewildered in the eye of his own storm, takes advantage of the enforced furlough from touring to work on pet projects of his own—film and poetry—and the whole band buckles down to the business of finishing up their still-in-progress fourth album.

But there is a deep hurt here, a graver wound than Dade County jurisprudence's self-serving slings and arrows could ever inflict: The hip press and the fans together have dealt it, and Jim (and to a lesser extent, the other Doors) will never recover from it.

In April, I get a phone call from Ricki Franklin, a producer at New York's public television station, WNDT/Channel 13. She loses no time telling me all about a series she is involved with called "Critique," an hour-long arts program devoted to showcasing one artist at a time, in-depth: in this case, the Doors. Yes, those same bad old Doors who can't find work on any stage in America just now, for them public television will buck the Philistine tide and give them a gig. I am delighted to hear this; then Franklin lowers the boom: She's read the piece I did on Jim in J&P, and thinks I'd have a lot to offer in a critics' panel discussion of the group on the program.

"I've never been on television," I say immediately, the subtext being clear: And I never intend to be on television in a million years if I can possibly avoid it. "I really don't think I'd be very good, I'm very shy and it's much better for me when I can write things out."

Franklin dismisses all this: Nonsense, you love the group, we need a critic on the panel who's an unabashed Doors fan, we need a woman, you'd be perfect. She continues in this vein for some time.

"Well, what exactly would I have to do?" I ask at last. I don't think I'm going to win this one.

Franklin explains that the show will be of course mostly the Doors themselves: playing live in the studio (though they will not be actually playing live on the air, it'll be taped for broadcast); being interviewed by the episode's host, pop critic Richard Goldstein; being discussed by the panel of critics; and playing again to close out the show. The panel is where I come in: It will consist of four critics, with Goldstein (another Doors loyalist) as moderator and participant both.

I have the greatest misgivings as to the wisdom of all this. But Pauline says go, talk, hear. So a few days later, I walk over to the station's West 58th Street office, just down Broadway, to discuss it with Franklin and the series' producer, Steve Rabin.

They both seem to think that I would do just fine on the show, repeatedly referring to the piece in J&P, the obvious love I have for the Doors' music (I don't think they know how I feel about the Doors' singer) and for the music in general, my youth and hip appearance and editorial credentials (though they also admit they've talked to a few other women as well). Oh, you mean I might not get the job after all? But very likely they are concerned chiefly with the politically correct mix of the panel: The final lineup is a gay white man, a straight white man, a straight white woman, and a straight black man—about as politically correct as you can get.

When they call a day or two later and offer me the gig for real, in a fit of something or other—probably hubris—I agree to do the show.

The status of women in rock at that time was, to say the least, iffy. But then, that was pretty much the case with women in society as a rule. It was the cusp of change, when women were beginning to make their move, as a force, into places and spaces that had never before been thought of as available to them. And I'm sorry to have to say that for all rock's self-aggrandizing postures as the one true free and equal art form, the cold clean wind of change that would clear out the fust of generations, rock was every bit as sexist, homophobic, gynophobic, obdurate and reactionary as the institutions it claimed to challenge. (And it still is.)

It put on a good show to the contrary, though, at least back then, and that's why we all *thought* it was so different; maybe even why, on some subliminal, peripheral level that we didn't find out about until years later, it *was* a little different. But then, out front, it was just as hard for a woman to cut it in rock as it was for her to make a place for herself in any other male-dominated business, profession or craft.

It was a new experience for me: Through a combination of luck and other fortuitous circumstances, I had never yet been told that I couldn't do whatever I wanted to do simply because I was a woman. Not because I had only ever encountered enlightened and liberated souls, but because at the simplest level, and in all modesty, I had always been smart enough for people to feel extremely stupid telling me anything of the sort.

But just because people feel they can't *tell* you something sexist doesn't mean they still can't or don't or won't *behave* to you in sexist fashion; and, as Jim too was to learn to his cost, a 140-plus IQ can't do it all.

Still, I was lucky enough, or had earned sufficiently good karmic credit, to encounter Pauline Rivelli as my first real boss and mentor and role model. She was one of that generation of independent women, ten years or so older than the boomer vanguard, who *really* broke through, who without polemics or posturing or tiresome feminist rhetoric did more for the cause of women in the workplace than any number of strident ranters. She just *did* it, and so made it easier for us to do it too.

Pauline saw to it that I was involved in every aspect of the magazine she had founded, and a year later had the confidence and the generosity to make me editor. No doubt there were political and business reasons as well involved in that decision, but she made it, and did not seem to regret it, and I never really saw until much, much later what a tremendous thing she had done. I was grateful and thrilled and proud at the time, of course—twenty-two and the editor of a national magazine, who wouldn't be?—but the size, the magnitude, the nature of the gift and the trust, the strength of the helping hand, all did not become apparent until years later.

But most women in the rock field (or indeed any other field) were not so fortunate. There were not all that many women who were given, or who seized for themselves, the freedom to write like men, like *writers*: Annie (Diane) Fisher of the Village Voice, Anne Marie Micklo of Rock, Ellen Willis, Ellen Sander, Karin Berg, Deday La Rene, Alice Polsky, a few others. Most of the women in rock journalism were little more than glorified gossipers, whether through circumstance or inclination; and some, of course—lacking greater talent, deeper sensibilities, or even the brains God gave a goat—were not even that (and still aren't).

Women could always find a home as flacks, needless to say, the thinking being that women could brag about "their" groups the way they'd brag about their children. Men were no slouches in the puffery

department, either, hype aptitude being by no means a sex-linked characteristic; but p.r. was by and large a female preserve, and nobody thought
twice about the implicit, or indeed explicit, sexism that this entailed.

But for a field that male critics often railed was devoted to, supported
by, and furthered for specifically female interests (all those leather pants
and lacy shirts, I guess), the business end of rock was ever notably sparse
in female prime movers.

No women promoters (the odd festival consultant here and there,
a sop to the women's movement or to superior skill too blatant even
for men to ignore). Few if any women managers, or booking agents,
or personal agents, or recording engineers, or promotion "men,"
or producers, or A&R "guys," or disc jockeys, or record company
executives, or talent agency honchos, or program directors, or even, yes,
rock editors, critics and journalists.

There were of course exceptions: d.j.'s Alison Steele of WNEW-
FM in New York and Dusty of KSAN in San Francisco; Nonesuch
Records' Tracy Sterne. Ten Wheel Drive had a female equipment manager who schlepped amps with the best of them, but then Ten Wheel
Drive also had a formidable female frontperson, Genya Ravan, who just
might have had something to say about equal hiring practices. As a rule,
though, women were thought unsuited to such low (read well-paid and
powerful) occupations as sweating over a Scully 12-track or beating up
some hapless promoter for a bigger share of the gate or dragging the lead
singer out of a bar at three in the morning.

There were, of course, groupies, the only role that most male artists
of that time (and probably even this present time) seemed willing to
allow a woman to fill: a fetching device of roughly the same convenience
quotient as a knothole, only a bit more decorative and hopefully more
fun; who should, nonetheless, be just as undemanding afterwards as said
knothole, go away without a fuss and have kept her mouth shut all night
(except of course when otherwise required).

It was this egregious attitude that made it so difficult for those of
us who indeed had our minds on the music as music and not on the
musicians as groins to get this across to the primal slime we so often had
to deal with. Okay, yeah, maybe I *shouldn't* have worn my lace-tablecloth
pantsuit backstage to talk to Led Zeppelin at the Fillmore East, thereby
allowing Robert Plant to dare address me with, "Hey, you in the lace
nightie, get over here and sit on my face!"

But why the hell could I not wear just what I pleased (the guys certainly did, including Plant) and still have been spared such affronts to my professionalism and personhood? Plant, needless to say, was immediately set straight, and in no uncertain terms, and of course he was a Brit anyway; but the larger point remains: No male critic, regardless of what he wore (or indeed his sexual preference) would ever have been spoken to so, and such incidents were by no means isolated ones—no matter *what* a woman wore.

Some of course deserved this sort of thing: There *was* the time a low-caste rock writer (well, "writer" by courtesy, anyway), now a middle-aged film critic, reportedly kept guests, and her then husband, locked out while she went at it with a second-rate rocker . . . But by and large this was rare.

All the same, whatever one's credentials, women rock writers were very often condescended to by the people they wrote about as, indeed, little more than well-connected groupies. One could always, in such cases, exact a bit of instant revenge, and cause the interviewee male to drop his drink by tossing off a casual remark as to, oh, the comparative influences of Cotswold morris music (as opposed to other morris strains) and Irish-Scottish broadside ballads on his own work—or Karlheinz Stockhausen, or Django Reinhardt, or almost anything at all with more intellectual heft than "What's your favorite color?" It could at times even be fun; and sometimes you did encounter artists who were sympathetic and smart—people like Alvin Lee or Paul Kantner or Elton John. But that too was rare.

Male reporters never had to put up with insulting suspicion ("Well, who coached *you*, sweetheart?") or equally insulting amazement ("My God! It can think!"). But what the offending male rockers so often found out, later, to their terror and dismay, was not only could "it" think, "it" could write well enough to blister their balls (such as they were) off. And, very often, "it" did.

But women artists themselves fared little better. With my own disbelieving ears I heard a member of an all-male band (British, not surprisingly; the Brits always were the worst offenders in this regard) tell me that women in rock bands were bad news because they were "too emotional." Whatever that means. Oh, and guys aren't, I guess. Too manly or something, probably.

But what *does* that mean? Does it mean female musicians miss gigs because they're washing their hair, or they're too smashed to go on, or they're too busy with a groupie, or they screwed up a concert because they had a fight with their old man, or that they behave unprofessionally on tour or in the studio? Or does it just mean they've got PMS and can't be trusted? Well, I and other women writers could give chapter and verse (and names) about *male* musicians who could be charged with the same crimes (yeah, even the PMS), and worse besides.

On the other hand, even those few women who had fought past all this and won a place in a group were held to one of two (male-specified) roles: Earth Mother or Ice Princess (one fucks, the other doesn't). Same with rock lyrics, women in, position of (usually supine, unless kneeling). In all the vast creative panorama of 60's rock there was no female counterpart to a Jim Morrison or a Mick Jagger (we would have to wait until the 80's, and the total construct that was Madonna, before we would see anything even remotely analogous; and you will note how carefully I do not say "equivalent").

Even now, in this last decade of the millennium, there has yet to be a dangerously intelligent, supernally beautiful, musically brilliant young woman who would do onstage for guys what Jim did for girls. Grace Slick, in the 60's, probably came the closest—she was arguably the loveliest, certainly the smartest and the funniest—but for all her excellence, she never possessed the kind of fatal magnetism Jim threw off without even trying. (And any woman who could say, apparently without irony, speaking of women in rock bands, "If you had a group of five cows and a pig you'd look at the pig because it was different" is not precisely the sort of standard-bearer women of the 60's were looking to for a musical idol.) Latterly, perhaps Chrissie Hynde, once; but no one since.

If Emma Peel, say, had been a real-life rock star instead of a TV-fictional Avenger, we might have seen it. We haven't yet. And given the state of rock today—all product, no creation—I do not think we will. Not any time soon.

CHAPTER

5

May 1969

THIS THEN IS THE STATE OF THINGS WHEN ON A BLIS-
teringly hot afternoon I go over to the Channel 13 studios on Ninth
Avenue to tape "Critique." On the advice of my personal media con-
sultants (Pauline, Laura), I have brought a choice of outfits: a cream-
colored Mexican wedding dress from Fred Leighton, and a cocoa-brown
slubbed cotton tunic with an elaborately beaded front from Knobkerry.

The TV people, uniformly helpful and cheery, tell me the brown
top will look better on camera; so I change, then go into makeup, where
I am pancaked and shadowed and have my hair tampered with, pulled
back straight and smooth and held with a comb.

What happens next is sort of like being a human sacrifice: confusing,
demeaning, and over before you can really think about it. As the youngest
and most televisually inexperienced person on the panel (and maybe too
the only female person on the panel?), I am given little chance to speak;
and as the only polite person on the panel, I find myself unable to just
wade in all over what someone else is saying. All three of the others are
all talking at the same time, Goldstein seems out of his depth as a

moderator, and as a result I get to say very little, giving me a distaste for public debate situations that has lasted ever since.

The only good thing that comes of this is that I get to have dinner one night with Jim. The Doors have already taped their portions of the program—the performance segments (including a staggeringly good version of "The Soft Parade," one of my absolute favorite Doors songs —no horns, no strings, just Doors) and the interview with Goldstein— and have a brief layover before they head back to L.A.

Judging from their performance for the show, it would seem that those old first-album Doors are back: It was real Doors music, which sounds like nothing else on earth, and it *worked*, people were bouncing up and down in the control room, technicians were boogying around the cameras. No strain, no stridency, no posturing or pressure. No clap-trap about rock as ritual, or Morrison as Lord of the Newts, or whatever. Just incredible rock by incredible musicians, played simply and superbly.

We meet this time not at his hotel but at a restaurant on West 57th Street (Piraeus My Love—Greek, which I do not particularly care for). On entering the place, I see Jim before he sees me, and I am startled. Not just by the Che Guevara drag—beard and shades and cigar—but by his air of exhaustion, of psychic fragility, visible clear across the room. He looks more beat, in fact, than I have ever seen him look, wiped out on more levels than the merely physical, and I am a little alarmed.

Although I am here by invitation, I can tell he is not expecting me just yet by the further differences in how he looks: People, when they are unaware of being watched by someone who knows them, always seem to lose all resemblance to their own selves. Their expressions change and shift, there is an alteration in their posture, a different way of holding their facial muscles, a defense in their eyes—all adding up to a palpable difference, a distance. And when one is a star besides, and has a certain interest in maintaining that difference, that defense . . .

Even so, I truly think for one instant that I have made a mistake, that it's not Jim after all over there at that table in the corner but a stranger, just somebody else tall, blue-eyed, dark-haired. And full-bearded.

"It's new," I say, smiling down at him. "I like it—"

He looks up, recognizes me and comes back into his face with astonishing speed, leaps to his feet even more swiftly.

"Patricia! Oh man, it's so nice to see you again—"

I can tell that it is, too: His mouth and eyes now have that look you can't counterfeit, of real pleasure in someone's presence.

He pulls out the chair for me; I seat myself, smile shyly at my plate as I settle myself and my belongings, then indicate the beard, with a little nod that is more in my eyebrows than anywhere else.

"Any particular reason?"

He smiles. "No, not really. It just sort of happened. No conscious decision. You'll get used to it."

"It suits you, somehow. Are you planning on keeping it?"

"For a while, anyway. I'll get bored with it and then it'll go, and then I'll probably grow it back again."

All that can be said about the beard has now been said, so as we order before-dinner drinks (Scotch for him, sherry for me) I cautiously bring up the subject of Miami. He is courteous but firm in his refusal to discuss it.

"The lawyers, you know. They never let you say anything. When I *can* talk about it, though, I promise you'll hear the whole thing."

He looks so woebegone that I decide to tease him just a little. "Oh, well, let's just have a regular old interview then— Tell me, Mr. Morrison," I say in my tape-recorder voice, tipping the flower vase under his chin in lieu of microphone, "how did you get the band together?"

"Oh, you know, it was just one of those things." He smiles, and falls into the spirit of the game. "It was really Ray's band first; I think he only asked me to join because nobody liked his singing."

"Cruel, but unsurprising. And you had sung before?"

"Not a note. But I had written some poems and tales and fables that we put to music, and we needed more lyrics, and I had these notebooks . . .   I'd say it worked out okay."

It is almost a question. "For you, sure," I say, abandoning my role as interviewer. "But what do the other guys think about it? *Really* think about it. I don't notice too many people asking young Robby or young John for *their* comments on Music, Art or the American Dream. Nobody takes pictures of Ray half-naked for Vogue, or busts *him* onstage for being incredible. What do you think they think about it all?"

"*I* think they *don't* think," he says straightfaced.

"Oh, come on, you don't mean that! I've talked to them, they think just fine."

But he will not be budged, and I am beginning to learn that mules are the soul of obliging cooperation compared to Jim Morrison when he sets his mind to mulishness. Our dinner has arrived by now, Hellenistic conglomerations of lamb and foliage and Zeus-knows-what, and we talk of other things.

"Artists aren't nice people," he offers, after dinner has been cleared away, returning somehow to an earlier theme. "If I ever had to choose between, say, my poetry—you know I'm into writing poetry, I think I told you I'll be coming out with a couple of books soon—and the band, I'd sell them all into slavery if that's what it took to keep on writing poetry. It's like that for any artist—you told me you want to write novels; well, I bet you'll feel the same way when it comes to your books, what will be your books. You can't think about anyone except yourself; and when you really get into your own work, your novels, you'll see that. And even with me telling you this now, it'll be as big a surprise to you as it was for me. The guys feel the same way, I'm sure, about their music. It's not nice, but it's true."

I cast around for another topic. "Tell me more about the poetry."

His face lights up, shyly. "Oh, it's stuff I've been working on for a long time, since college, actually. It'll be two books; I'm publishing them myself, private editions."

"I don't think you'd have a very hard time finding a real publisher for them," I say incredulously. "If they're anywhere near as good as the songs are, they'll be terrific."

"Thank you, that means a lot to hear you say that." He seems to mean it, adding, "I know how much it takes to impress *you . . .*   But I thought it would be best to try it this way first, see what happens."

"What are the poems like? I mean, are they lyrical, abstract free verse, *sonnets*, what?"

"They're kind of personal and descriptive—they've been I guess you could call it patched together, over a few years. They weren't originally intended to, but they seem to hang together and tell a kind of tenuous story. One book is more obviously 'traditional' poetry, the other is more, ah, media-oriented, film-oriented. That's the one called *The Lords: Notes on Vision*. It's almost a collection of aphorisms, little comments and perceptions, mostly on film and the way people see things."

"And the other?"

"That's going to be called *The New Creatures*. That's the more deliberately—consciously—poetical one." He shrugs, looking a little embarrassed. "I don't even like to describe it as poetry, y'know, call myself a poet. 'Poet' seems to me to be one of those gift words, a mantle that other people confer upon you. You'd be arrogant and boastful if you claimed it for yourself. If I call myself a poet, it's only because there aren't really any other words to convey just what it is I'm trying to do. I don't mean to be pretentious about it."

"I know that—but that *is* how you'd like people to think of you, poet rather than rock star?"

He shifts in the chair; he hasn't taken his eyes off mine for the past five minutes—I've finally found somebody who can hold my stare.

"Well, sure, wouldn't you? Anybody can be a rock star if they put their minds to it, find a decent band. Do we really remember the pop artists of two, three, four hundred years ago? No; but we remember the poets."

"Well, if you think about it, the pop artists of four hundred years ago really *were* the poets. There wasn't the kind of separation we have now between popular culture and higher culture. Even Mozart and Shakespeare weren't afraid to use pop themes in their work, because they had to appeal to that segment of society, as well as the royalty and nobility. I think art was more—of a piece back then."

He nods vigorously. "Yes, and probably because, also, so few people could read; it was a much more oral culture than today, and the pop element made songs and ballads and poetry and plays more accessible. Though sometimes I think we're going back to that sort of society today, kids don't like to read the way we did when we were their age. Did you graduate, when you went to college?"

"Sure. I never thought I wouldn't." I start to say that it was because I had had such a good time in college, just reading my little heart out for four years and not having to worry about grades or anything else, but he is nodding fiercely again, off on a tack of his own.

"Right, right! We were so *programmed*, weren't we, we were still so hung up on finishing. Though we were probably the last group to be like that: Kids in college now—if *I* was still in college today I'd never bother with graduating, I'd just drop out and do what I wanted to do. Maybe I'd never even have gone in the first place."

I feel compelled to put in an oar for higher education, try to turn it around.

"Oh, I don't know, I found it very useful for my writing. Not *writing* courses, I don't believe anyone can actually teach anyone to write, and I think workshops and things like that are a waste of time—I mean, if you want to write, just go and *write*. But things like Latin, which I *loved*, it did more for me as a writer than anything else—and other languages, French and German, and editing, and journalism courses, and literature . . . You should just read as much as you can, and your own voice will come out of that. But courses like those teach you to think about where the words come from and how they work together and how you can put them together, how to organize your thoughts and express yourself almost by instinct. I think *that's* how you learn to be a writer." I cast back to an earlier answer of his. "So, is that what you're really after, Jim, to be remembered as a poet four hundred years from now?"

His real smile, as distinguished from the half-strength public version, splits his face; it really does light up the room, and only someone with a heart of steel and a countenance of basalt could keep from smiling along.

"Oh, Patricia, I'd be happy if they remember me five years after I'm gone! Memory is such a strange thing—like, what's the very earliest event *you* remember?"

"Oh, that's easy. We had a house on the Jersey shore one summer, on the beach, I wasn't even two yet. And my father and I were walking along the boardwalk when I dropped my little rubber ball onto the sand, and a man below caught it and tossed it back up to me. I can still see it, how far away he seemed, how close I seemed to the slats of the boardwalk—I guess because I was so little myself—even how hot the boards were, the way they smelled, like hot tar. Then my dad took me on the carousel with two of my cousins, the first time I was ever on a carousel, and I rode on a lion." I glance curiously at him. "You?"

He unfocuses a little, his eyes reflective. "I don't remember how old I must have been—a bit older than you, I guess. Anyway, I was staying with my grandparents in Clearwater, that's over by Tampa, and there was a hurricane coming. They brought me and I guess my sister —or maybe she wasn't born yet, but I seem to remember her being there—out on the porch in our jammies to watch. I can remember the way the trees were moving back and forth in the wind, and the clouds blowing before the storm really started breaking loose. It's strange what stays in your mind from your childhood, especially when you think of all the other stuff you've forgotten. Maybe someday I'll get hypnotized, just remember it all." He gives me a look from narrowed eyes, and already I am beginning to recognize his put-on look. "My mother's family was so poor they had to live in trees."

At least, I *think* this is a put-on, it's hard to tell with him. But for some reason it strikes me as extraordinarily funny, and I giggle helplessly about it for many moments. It can't be true, surely: I know nothing of his family except what he told me in January—his father's an admiral, he has a brother and a sister, and he's effectively estranged from all of them (at least he had the grace to look embarrassed when he confessed his folks weren't dead). But I don't think a future admiral would marry a tree-dweller, even a former one. He must be putting me on.

"Now tell me something about *you*," he commands. "Tell me more about being a witch. We talked about that the last time."

"I know, and, actually, I'm kind of surprised you remember."

His face brightens. "Oh, like I'd really forget somebody telling me something like *that*! If I recall correctly, and I'm sure I do, you told me you belonged to a Celtic coven, that it was a religion—pre-Christian, polytheistic—and that magic per se is neither black nor white but neutral. You said the blackness or whiteness of it comes according to the use you put it to."

I stare at him. He is obviously pleased with himself, and I am very impressed. Flattered, too, though I don't say so.

"There are lots of witch traditions," I remark after a while. "Mine is just one. Everybody does something a little differently, and people are drawn to what works best for them. Covens don't go out like missionaries, recruiting; somehow you just seem to find each other, when you're both ready. For instance, I found my group through some research I was doing into Irish mythology and genealogy; I was working in a private library, and I met some people, who knew some people, who knew some other people . . . Well, anyway, they thought I was promising material, and they *really* liked the idea of my family's alleged shamanic origins"—he grins at that—"and it sort of went on from there. The magic's not the important part; the worship is."

"But there *is* magic—how would you define magic?"

"I would personally define 'magic' as a particularly effective form of prayer. Maybe even an extra-insistent form of prayer. What's prayer, really, but asking a higher Power to do something for you that you can't do for yourself? Or thanking that Power, or just communicating with that Power. Magic is just a form of concentrating your attention so that what you have to say is maybe heard a little bit more clearly. That's all."

"And now you're a priestess."

"Every woman who's a witch is a priestess, and every man is a priest.

What I am now is the Maiden of the coven, the High Priestess's assistant. I probably shouldn't be telling you this"—he leans closer to me, with exaggerated eagerness to hear—"but there's been some discussion as to making *me* the High Priestess later this year. Maura—Lady Maura, she's the one who's run the coven with her husband for the past ten years— feels it's getting a bit much for her, so we're thinking maybe I'll try running things for a while." Now it's my turn to tease. "You know, Lord Brân, the High Priest, is an ordained minister in *your* religion—well, the one you were born into, anyway."

He breaks up. "A *Presbyterian* witch?"

I nod. "He's got no problem with it—though I bet his elders or moderators or whatever you call them would have some *big* ones."

He is still smiling. "I bet they would... I find this fascinating," he says then, frankly staring at me, as if he's busy with a mental reap-praisal. "I know from my reading that all the ancient peoples of the earth worshipped goddesses. It makes more sense, y'know, to believe in a Mother Goddess than a Father God—it's a lot more natural, more fun, too, that's for sure. But I like that polarity you were talking about last time—the Goddess and the God, the High Priestess and the High Priest, the woman and the man. It's real, it's of the earth, you can see it and touch it and feel it."

"I like it because it's of our own heritage, Celtic, before other influences got their hands on it—Irish, Scottish, Welsh. To me it feels stamped into our cells, a kind of race-memory, if that's possible. I've never felt drawn to any other religious tradition, not even the great Eastern ones. It just didn't feel right for me."

His face sparks at that, the look I am starting to know as the one he gets when you have said something to him that particularly engages his mind or his imagination.

"Yeah—maybe that's why I never got into the Maharishi the way Ray and John and Robby did. It never seemed to have anything to say to me, I don't know why. I was more into—other things."

Yeah, I'm hip... "Well, in the Craft, it's often suggested that one—the entity that is oneself, the entity that is now going by the name Jim Morrison or Patricia Kennealy—is drawn most strongly to things it's already familiar with. If you've been initiated before, you'll be an initiate again; in fact, you'll never *stop* being an initiate. And you'll usually be drawn again to a Path you followed in a previous life, or to a Path that has something to offer which you need to learn." I look at him for a moment in silence. "I get the feeling I'm preaching to the converted ... From what you've written in your songs, certainly, and the way you've said you see yourself onstage, I think you know all about this. I don't think you'd be doing what you're doing otherwise. It's not the kind of thing you just fall into."

He's got his show-me look on again. "Oh? And just what *is* it, then, miss?" He takes a single drag off his cigar, then puts it out at once; he knows how I detest it.

I look right back at him, with my best looking-through-you-into-the-middle-of-next-week gaze. He doesn't flinch, and he doesn't look away, either, after a couple of seconds, as so many people do.

"Functioning in a priestly capacity," I say at last, still watching him closely. "Serving as a shaman, as you seem to feel most comfortable calling it. It's real, you know, what you're doing. It's a concert, a great rock show, for those who can see only that, and that's legitimate and good and fine. But that's not all it is."

He looks a little frightened, and very surprised, as if I have caught him out in a truth he didn't think anyone else knew he was telling, or would have believed if they had.

"Intermediating between the people and God," I continue. "It's what priests do, and what artists do—becoming the link between God, the Goddess, the God, the gods, the Highest Power, the Supreme Being, the primal creative force, whatever you want to call it. Deity, anyway, in all His/Her/Its manifestations."

Jim sits up excitedly. "*That's* it, *that's* what it is! It seems more logical to believe in all the aspects of God—Deity—than in just one aspect. It seems logical to me that an all-powerful, all-knowing, all-loving Supreme Being would not put any limits on how creation perceived Him, or Her, or Them. It's like that old riddle about the three blind men and the elephant—every religion sees their own little bit of God, and they're all absolutely right."

He is silent for a while. "I fell asleep on the beach once at Venice," he says then. "In the light of the full moon; and when I woke up the moon was looking down on me, only me, not on anybody else, and it was the face of my mother."

"It was the face of your Mother, all right."

He sighs and stretches and favors me with a spacious smile.

"Well. Well ... That was an extremely interesting conversation; now I know who to look up in New York for theological discussions.

And it was also a very pleasant evening," he adds, as we stand up to depart the restaurant. Most of the other diners are long gone, and the bored staff is hanging around over by the kitchen door waiting for us to split.

On our way downstairs to the street, I comment on something, I can't remember what, and when we get to the bottom of the stairs Jim turns to look at me.

"You sound a little cynical," he says doubtfully, as we emerge onto deserted 57th Street.

"Cynical! I'm the world's biggest romantic—haven't you noticed?"

He smiles. "We make a good pair then."

But whether he means a cynic plus a romantic, or two romantics together, I am not sure.

When he kisses me goodnight—a real kiss, our first—hands me gallantly into a cab and overpays the driver to take me home, giving him explicit instructions as to how to best convey me to my comfort and safety, I am a bit more certain; but I am *absolutely* certain I am crazy about him.

CHAPTER

6

May–August 1969

BUT NOT CRAZY ENOUGH TO *DO* ANYTHING ABOUT IT just yet, even if he had suggested we do anything, which so far he has not. One or two kisses notwithstanding, I do not even know if he sees me in that sort of context. Which does not entirely displease me: I'd far rather he got to know me first as somebody he can talk to on his own level, not somebody he can go to bed with (though naturally I'd like to work up to that eventually, of course . . .).

Still, over the next few months, while the Doors are playing out the meager handful of concerts that survived the Miami fallout (one upcoming date, in Mexico, gives me such a second-sighted turn when I hear about it a few weeks beforehand that I get a message to the Doors via somebody at Elektra to be *really, really careful*—it's one of the scariest vibes I've ever had, and it's all to do with Jim, something terrible happening to him—but the Elektra guy, who also believes in precognition, passes on the warning, and in the end all is well), Jim does not forget me.

There are calls every three or four weeks, then letters start arriving at odd intervals—not many, and short ones at first, becoming gradually chattier and lengthier—sometimes two in one week, then none for two months. He even sends me a poem or two, not to publish or even to criticize, but just for me to have (one, a kind of Yeatsian diatribe, is called, what else, "Crucifiction").

It is very nice and rather sweet, sort of like being back in college and you're at one school and your boyfriend is at another halfway across the state, but he isn't really your boyfriend just yet, neither of you is really ready for that, but you both know you're on the way to it, and so you send these odd little letters, have these excruciating phone calls, full of shyness and fear and naive romance, and you both know what the subtext is, and even the fear and uncertainty are fun. That's what this feels like.

Well, at least it does until I hear about Pam. Pamela Susan Courson, longtime on-again-off-again girlfriend of Jim. When I do hear about her for the first time, that summer, I am surprised by just *how* surprised I am to hear about her. Logically, I am quite sure I never expected him to be, ah, unencumbered by someone of the sort—but I find myself, of all things, inappropriately and ridiculously hurt to learn of her existence. What the hell is the matter with me? Needless to say, I immediately inquire.

"She's our age," says my Elektra spy. "Short, no tits, and she had great hair until she started fooling around with it. Oh, it's really pretty now, too—fire-engine red, about half as long as yours—but it was prettier before. *Not* intellectual, and I don't think she actually *does* anything but be the girlfriend—when she *is* the girlfriend. No, wait, my mistake, he did set her up in a boutique, we'll see how long before it folds . . . But still. Why *do* they insist on clinging to their high-school sweethearts? Scared, probably."

Probably. I do not mention my new knowledge to Jim when next we speak, do not ask about Pam or even hint to him that I am now aware of her. Or, indeed, of any of his other rumored involvements: Popular opinion has made him out a slut, groupies by the shoal and girlfriends all over the place; but from what I have observed he seems not so much actively promiscuous as amenable to what's near and going. I might do well to remember this.

Still, having heard about Pam, I now feel a certain constraint even just talking to Jim on the phone. But, between the paltry few dates in places like Eugene, Oregon, and a couple of gigs in San Francisco and at L.A.'s Aquarius Theater, Jim seems as wishful as I of keeping up our acquaintance, and I find myself unable to distance myself quite so far as I might wish, or as might be best.

Little more information can be gleaned about Pamela anyway— yeah, yeah, I ask around, okay?—nobody seems to know very much about her, or even much care, and at this stage I am of course still parsecs away from even the beginnings of a glimmer of a thought of a possible future rivalry: I haven't even slept with Jim yet, and she has been with him, however stormily, for a consistent few years. One thing my sources do tell me: They're not committed to living together. Sometimes they do, just as often they don't, and both have no shortage of outside relationships. Not promising; but hey, I'm not interested, am I. We're just friends.

In any case, I have a relationship of my own going just now: Sometimes it is good, sometimes it is terrible, and pretty soon, it is over. He moves out; but we find we make better friends than lovers, and we are to remain close friends for more than twenty years.

In late June, the "Critique" segment on the Doors finally airs, and I watch it with friends. I am appalled to see myself on television, an attitude which is not to vary by one micron even two decades later, when circumstances will require me once again to subject myself, several times too, to ordeal by cathode. But the Doors look great and sound incredible, and that's what matters.

On Thursday, the third of July (ironic; but that day's fatefulness is still two years in my future), a contingent from Jazz & Pop heads up to Newport, Rhode Island, for the Newport Jazz Festival, to be held over the Independence Day weekend. En route, we hear that Brian Jones of the Rolling Stones has been found dead in the swimming pool at his country home in England. A downer, to be sure, yet I wonder why no one but me seems greatly surprised.

This festival is not expected to be quite so cosmic as last year, when Janis Joplin and Big Brother blew everyone out past Jupiter at the Newport *Folk* Festival. But it is far from shabby even so: not with such as Sun Ra, Jethro Tull, Ten Years After, Blood Sweat & Tears, Jeff Beck, Roland (not yet Rahsaan Roland) Kirk, Miles Davis, John Mayall, the Mothers of Invention, Sly & The Family Stone . . .

But none of my real favorites (and oh, wouldn't the Doors and Jefferson Airplane have been *perfect* here?). Still, the weekend is for me noteworthy in that it is here on the rocks at a Newport beach that I take my very first mescaline trip.

Gleeful as two mad chemists, we—the by-now-ex-boyfriend-but-still-friend, David Walley, and I—have dissolved the mescaline powder in water (it makes a lovely purple drink, like liquefied amethysts), and swilled it down. Then we go off to the beach.

Nothing happens, and nothing continues to happen for a *very* long time; then wham! The earth turns over all at once, time is slowed and s-t-r-e-t-c-h-e-d, and I climb up on a huge rock halfway into the ocean, and just sit there, looking out to sea like the Little Mermaid, watching the rushing seawater separating into its constituent ions of hydrogen and oxygen and recombining into water. I find this endlessly fascinating, and I sit there for *hours*. I get a sunburn all down one side where the light has reflected off the water and onto me; I look very strange, pink on one side and dead white on the other. I think David has turned into a hermit crab.

Years later. Pauline and her squeeze, record producer Bob Thiele, come looking for us and take us away and feed us and laugh at us. We are very happy. That night, before, during and after the festival program, there are parties at the venerable Viking Hotel, impromptu jams all over the place, hordes of hip longhairs who would not usually have been caught dead at a *jazz* festival drifting smiling through the narrow Newport streets. Pot-smoke is in the air like the scent of burning autumn leaves.

We hang out with everybody from Alvin Lee (nice) to Frank Zappa (not). Pauline and Bob introduce us to jazz legends I should by rights be curtsying to; but I can only think how much more fun I would be having if Jim were here, or the Airplane, or Janis, or the Dead. Mostly I can't wait to do some more mescaline, and when somebody from a British blues band tells me I can actually *snort* the stuff, I don't have to drop it at all, my joy knows no bounds.

On Monday we all drive home, and a week or so later I find myself at Madison Square Garden for the American debut of the Supergroup of the Month, the aptly, and cynically, named Blind Faith. Blind Faith (or Dumb Luck, as David insists on calling them), has for its constituent parts Eric Clapton, Ginger Baker, Stevie Winwood—and that other one, the one nobody ever heard of before, oh yeah, Ric Grech.

This maiden performance was originally supposed to have taken place at Newport; not at the festival, but at a separate concert a few days after. But jittery officials, apparently fearing a resurgence of the benevolent but raggedy hippie tide that had lapped through the town over the festival weekend, canceled the gig only three days before. So now the previously scheduled Garden date becomes Blind Faith's U.S. debut. Reportedly, the band is ill-pleased, having wanted to open out of town, not before the hanging judges that are the New York rock audience and critics. But hey, that's rock 'n' roll . . .

I don't know about Blind Faith. I am not numbered among the ranks of those who scribble on walls (and *believe*) "Clapton Is God." I loathe drum solos (oh, *please*, Baker, not "Toad" *again*!); and although I think Stevie Winwood (a very sweet man, we had him on the cover of Jazz & Pop back last November—along with Bill Graham and Ornette Coleman) was certainly the weight in Traffic, I don't really care.

In fact, I hate the whole idea of supergroups: Four, or three, or five, virtuosi playing simultaneously is not my idea of a rock band. And when I see, that evening at the Garden, the kind of audience reaction that Blind Faith pulls (huge roars at Clapton's most insignificant slur, Baker's slightest rim shot, Winwood's tiniest organ riff), I am even more alarmed.

It's cultism, plain and simple: It is the *idea* of Blind Faith that the crowd has come for, not the music. I don't think they even *hear* the music—the audience response is so ludicrously disproportionate to the merits of what is actually being played that I cannot believe they and I are even at the same concert.

It's not just Blind Faith, though, even if it is at their concert that this trend is made plainest. It's Janis and the Who and the Mothers and just about every British blues band I can think of, and, yes, every now and again, even my own best beloved Doors and Airplane. The audiences seem more taken with the idea of the musicians as Brand Names, as Personages, with what and who they are, than with what they might be playing, or how well or badly they might be playing it.

It was not ever thus. In the beginning, anyway, people who went to rock concerts were better critics than the actual critics (and that is saying a lot—critics were artists back then, people like Paul Williams and R. Meltzer and Sandy Pearlman and the early Richard Goldstein). Rock moved in a way that no other art form even came close to, reflecting conditions and shifts with an immediacy that only political cartooning could match. Moreover, not only was rock inextricably bound up with the shaping forces of the time—politics, race, sex, sociology—but it was itself one of those shaping forces, and when you went to a rock concert, you were participating in something that went way beyond the licks and riffs and jams being presented onstage.

Not everyone was aware of this, of course, or believed it even if they were; just because you happened to listen to music didn't necessarily mean you heard what it was really saying. And when it was Doors music, that went double with brass knobs on . . .

A heap of hooey has been talked by people over the past two decades about what Doors concerts were really like. They were mystical occasions. They were triumphs of flummery. The Lizard King's Leather Pants vs. The Emperor's New Clothes. The most overhyped band in the Western World. The greatest rock group in captivity. It's all true.

What I remember best about Doors concerts, at least in New York, was that you never *moved*. At an Airplane concert, a Grateful Dead concert, a Janis Joplin concert, you were up on the seats and swinging from the chandeliers. But at a Doors concert, especially in the early days, you were almost always nailed to your seat.

Partly this was a function of fear: You didn't want to make any sudden moves and maybe draw Morrison's attention—so you skulked in your chair, like some wary Greek shepherd hoping to avoid the Medusa's gaze. But mostly it was because you were incapable of movement: The music and the vocal combined to turn you to stone, they did all the moving for you. Only your mind was moving; all you had to do was sit there and supply the psychic energy the band fed on. A Doors concert took a lot out of you.

Now, on occasion—maybe too many occasions—this dynamic broke down: Jim was too drunk, the audience couldn't get into it, the band didn't care and just served up rote—a standardized bag of predictable tricks that they would zip through like a well-rehearsed troupe of trained seals. But there is no getting round the fact that when the band was up for it and Jim was up for it and the audience was up for it and the stars were right in their courses, the Doors could produce a force of psychic violence that would freeze you to the heart.

It sounds utterly ridiculous now, of course, from the vantage point of twenty years' distance and sophistication and cynicism; and maybe it was, a little. You had to be there. But the things that most modern and/or revisionist commentators find so pretentious about the Doors are precisely the things that were so great and true and real about them in their time and context. Given the parlous state of modern rock (let's talk about the classical scholarship of Paula Abdul, shall we, or the spiritual sensibilities of Vanilla Ice?), perhaps critics should not be quite so swift to retrospectively bash a band that was trying to accomplish something a little more rarefied. There was always a lot more going on at a Doors concert than people invariably knew, and it did not always have to do with the lead singer's blood alcohol level at any given moment.

Jim, of course, had a far more acute and self-deprecating sense of humor about it than most of his critics would ever give him credit for. "It's not easy playing sacred king," he will complain to me in a teasing drawl, after the Felt Forum dates.

"Better playing one than being one, don't you think?"

"Oh, I don't know—not a bad way to go, all in all. Drink and debauchery until you're just too whipped to care and you never even see the knife coming—"

"I'd *want* to see it," I maintain. "I'd be too scared otherwise."

But, much as I love them, the Doors are not my only cherished group. Sharing most-favored-nation status is Jefferson Airplane, that gang of rugged San Francisco individualists, another one-of-a-kind assemblage. In fact, Jazz & Pop probably devotes more space to the Airplane than to just about any other group (other pets are the Mothers of Invention, whom David and Pauline adore but whom I personally find technically brilliant but cold-hearted, and of more than usually repellent aspect, and Janis Joplin, whom *everybody* adores).

Since being turned on to the Airplane in the fall of '66, with their stunningly erratic first album *Jefferson Airplane Takes Off* (not yet with Grace Wing Slick on board, but fronted by strong-voiced Signe Toly Anderson), I have seen the Airplane perhaps even more often than I have seen the Doors (well, they neither of them come to New York and environs all that often, do they). I meet the group for the first time early in my rock career: Although we do not become friends, we do evolve into cordial acquaintanceship, and so when Diane Gardiner calls to tell me that the Airplane will be in New York early in August, I am delighted to pop by and say hello.

I am down the block at the Fillmore East, to catch Jefferson Airplane in rehearsal for their weekend gigs. Or, rather, the formless jam the Airplane *calls* a rehearsal, which even so is about fourteen times better than the regular performances of any other band around (except the Doors, of course).

The Airplane doesn't like New York all that much (though New York loves them—proving it conclusively at a free Central Park concert on the Sunday after the Fillmore dates, fifty thousand people in the Sheep Meadow, a record for the time). This is the first time they've been here for many months, and they're refusing to leave their hotel rooms during the daylight hours (well, in August, perhaps wisely); instead, they creep out around seven or eight every night, like some bizarre form of collective nocturnal psychedelic snail.

The Fillmore is strangely unfamiliar in its rehearsal clothes: empty of the usual throngs, it reminds me of my college auditorium when there was a play in rehearsal—expectant, hollow, half-asleep. Not for long, though, not with this group.

I sit in the front row with Spencer Dryden, Airplane drummer, and tease him with a quote from the last time we talked: " 'Our band doesn't look good onstage at all.' "

He looks surprised. "Did I say that? Well, it's true! We look like living shit. No stage presence whatsoever, just six freaks standing there giggling and can't even count to one . . ."

He goes on happily and very tongue-in-cheek in the same vein; I am privately marveling at how healthy they all look, like they've even been having a *meal* once in a while, lead guitarist Jorma Kaukonen actually has a *tan*. Incredible.

Jack Casady, blond bassist from Mars, drops like Errol Flynn from the stage lip just in front of us, grins hello and tells Spencer they're ready to start. From the other side of the auditorium, Grace leaves a cluster of people and heads for the pass door to the stage. I settle back, get wine from one direction and a hash pipe from another. Diane comes over to join me.

The rehearsal gets serious right away, with a strange and oddly melodic song Grace has written and Paul Kantner, for reasons of his own, has named "Eskimo Blue Day" ("*I* don't know what he means by it, either," Grace confesses later). "Day" caused serious gnashing of teeth over at RCA, the Airplane's label (as did another song on the album— *Volunteers*, their sixth—a Marty Balin protest rant called "We Can Be Together"): There were two words, one in each song, that were giving the suits coronaries every time they thought about it, and the more they thought about it the more they wanted the words to go.

The Airplane, quite rightly, refused. It wasn't the first time by any means that rock bands had had trouble with censorship—not only had there been Miami, but the Doors had been censored (unsuccessfully, as it turned out) on Ed Sullivan's show as far back as 1967. But that's concerts and TV: Recorded lyrics have as a rule been pretty sacrosanct, if only because it takes a mere mixdown to make the problem largely academic. Just fudge the mix, and don't print any liner notes, and any problems an overly sensitive ear might have had are solved.

But that's not good enough for the Airplane, and "Eskimo Blue Day" is only the latest series of tussles with the label (in the end, RCA will be reduced to taking out ads that announce with somewhat pitiful bravado, "If you think Jefferson Airplane has problems with each other, you should see the problems they have with us"; it fools no one).

All this is far from what's going on just now, however. They do the song three or four times, and nobody cares about the word, but they are unable to move on to anything else because Marty Balin has not yet shown up, and he is after all their other lead singer. Jack and Jorma begin a jam to pass the time; Spencer and Paul join in, and Jorma's guitar takes off like a runaway horse. After, Jack steps to one of the open mikes and inquires of the auditorium itself, it seems, "Was that inhumanly loud?", clearly delighted that it was.

After a while Marty slouches in, his hair now almost as long as Jack's below-the-shoulder locks. The energy level zooms into the red; good, *now* they can get going. And for the next two hours, they do: balls-against-the-walls rock and roll, and I have to tear myself away.

"Come on over, we're having an acetate party!"

No, it's not some exotic new drug—acetate being merely the informal name for the first test pressing of a new record. And the record in this case being the Airplane's new one, *Volunteers*, wild weasels wouldn't keep me away.

It's the afternoon following the rehearsal: I'm up at the Jazz & Pop offices, and Diane Gardiner is urging me to come over to the Holiday Inn, of all places, way west on 57th Street.

After a bit of Twilight Zone stuff (she said Room 200; I get off the elevator and there *is* no Room 200; it turns out to be merely the wrong wing of the hotel), I am met by Diane and escorted firmly to the proper floor.

Grace is sitting in the middle of the unmade bed, playing an acoustic guitar. She is dressed in violet panne velvet pants and tank top, wears no makeup and has her dark hair in a frizzed cloud. She looks about sixteen years old. Paul Kantner—Airplane rhythm guitarist, tall, blond, prognathous, for the past few months Grace's new consort—offers greetings and various mind-altering substances, liquid and otherwise.

But the record?

"It's been and gone," Paul admits. "The record player they sent us was a piece of crap, so we didn't want to risk playing the thing and maybe ruining it. But there's a cassette, you could do a review right now—"

He wrestles a cassette into a small portable player; it won't go in. "Spencer's goddamn machine . . ." He succeeds in getting the cassette into position; it stays there exactly five seconds and then pops out like a piece of toast, flying through the air and under the bed.

"Wasn't that the best record you ever heard?" asks Grace earnestly. "It's really even better than that. I can't believe it's our sixth."

"There's this thing Kienholz did," says Paul, fiddling with a little blue-and-white tin box. " 'Confessional'—you walk in off the street, go into it, and do whatever you feel like, be father-confessor or penitent. And another piece—he had a vacant lot, and he filled it up with trash, you know, papers, old tires, and he fenced it off, and that was the work of art. Then one afternoon, a drunk wandered in and fell asleep, and he was part of it too! That's a nice approach to things; to our music, if you like."

He takes leave of us, so he can go down to RCA's offices and hear the record properly. We start talking about him as soon as the door closes behind him.

"He's the disciplinarian of the group," confides Grace, eyes wicked. "Actually, he's the Nazi of the group. Very logical. Blond, Teutonic, obstinate—you know you've had it with Paul when he gets this little smile on his face, and then he stands up and puts his hands in his pockets and starts talking through his teeth. Sitting down, he can still be reasoned with. But once he stands up, you haven't got a prayer."

We talk a bit about the "Eskimo Blue Day" furor.

"The guys at the label are still having conniptions every time they hear the songs," giggles Diane.

Grace grins. "Yeah—I like it . . . Actually, they did ask us, very nicely, if maybe we wouldn't consider changing the words; they said some record-store chains might even refuse to carry the album."

"What did you say?"

"We said fuckem, the words were staying, and that was that. It's fairly strange, isn't it? I mean, everybody talks like that—I think someone once figured out that the word 'fuck' or 'shit' is used once every twenty seconds in ordinary conversation—so it's not as if people are gonna be turned to stone by any of this. It's natural to use those words in songs, because they *are* familiar, and they convey a certain mood and feeling. But then along comes somebody and says, 'Look! What's *that*?!' And then immediately you start to wonder, 'Yeah, what *is* that? What's it doing there, who put it there and what does it mean?' The emphasis becomes fixed on the wrong thing, and if that's what you start to focus on, that's what people who hear the song will start to focus on."

Diane mentions an upcoming outdoor concert in upstate New York, at which the Airplane will be playing with about twenty other major bands, and to which everyone in the music business is planning to go. It sounds pretty hyped, but who knows, it might even be fun: I'm going myself.

Just then the phone rings beside Diane; for an instant it seems like a replay of that afternoon with Jim at the Plaza . . .

"Hello—no, she isn't—no, I'm not her sister—no, really, I don't sound like her at all"—(Grace: "Say I'm dead!")—"no, she really isn't here just now."

Diane breaks off, looking a little dazed, and silently hands the phone to Grace, who listens with an expression of entirely suspended judgment. Diane turns to me with wonder on her face.

"He just said, '*I* sing, too,' and then he started to sing 'White Rabbit'."

"Sure it wasn't Jim?"

She giggles. Grace, still glued to the receiver, makes a gesture and face to the effect that whoever he is, he is still singing it. When she finally hangs up, she shakes her head and says, "Yeah, all of it, and the first verse of 'Somebody to Love,' too."

The conversation shifts to media, and journalism, and books; I lament the fact that nobody seems to read anymore. Grace sits up.

"Yeah, right! Remember when you used to really *read*? Just sit by yourself and turn the pages of a book, and read the words, and maybe take a week to think about it all. That was nice, I liked it; I miss it, I don't get much chance to do that sort of thing anymore. But everything's pre-digested these days anyway—pre-explained, mainlined. Books, TV, knowledge, experience. Mainlined life. Just shoot it all up."

The phone rings again; Grace picks it up. "No, there iss no vun here, no vun atall . . . Yess, I vill leaf a mess-ahge."

Diane laughs. "That was Margaretta, if I ever heard her."

"Yeah, Margaretta, Jorma's wife," says Grace, grinning. "Margaretta got into this really bizarre thing one night, where everything Jorma said she would say to him, 'Yorma, a vooman vould not say that,' 'Yorma, a vooman vould not haff a cat like that,' just went on and on. He was flipping out after about five minutes of it."

The whole thing is beginning to degenerate into three chicks sitting around being wiped out and gossipy; it would be fun, but the afternoon is wearing on, and Grace needs to take a nap, so after a while I stand up to leave. There's another rehearsal tonight that I'm going to, as well as all the concerts; more time to talk.

"Are you coming to the rehearsal?" asks Grace. "Good—I think the more you hear the songs the better you'll like them."

"I like them just fine already," I say with some surprise.

She looks pleased. "Really? Thanks—but we're only just learning them, you know."

"But you've already recorded them."

"Oh, yeah, sure, but we're still learning how to play them. We'll probably never learn how to do them really right."

CHAPTER

7

August 1969

" 'THREE DAYS OF PEACE AND MUSIC,' " SAYS PAULINE, reading from the press release. "A rock festival in the Catskills—sound like fun?"

"Sounds like pure hell."

"Well, you're going."

I grumble a little, but after I talk to a few people—Grace and Paul among them—it all begins to sound as if there might be a few cheap laughs in it, and certainly some of my most favorite people are booked to play: Janis, the Who, the Dead, my darling Airplane. But I'm not going alone, and I prevail on Sue Donoghue to come with; besides, she's got this really cool green Mustang, and I don't drive.

As it turns out, we remember we have friends from Bonaventure who live in a tiny mountain town called Long Eddy, on the banks of the Delaware not far from the festival location. This thing is called Woodstock, after an earlier site incarnation that had to be abandoned due to protests from townsfolk over that way, who displayed an astonishing degree of prescience in wanting nothing whatever to do with this. (Actually, it was going to be held in a place called Wallkill, but "Woodstock" sounded so much better . . .) But Bethel/White Lake, in the resort-area Catskills of Sullivan County, steps in, and the festival moves west.

Susie calls the Long Eddy people, who are delighted to put us up, and on a sunny Friday morning, 15 August 1969, we hit familiar old Route 17, heading northwest. This is the way I went back and forth to college for four years, and it seems somehow strange to be going this way as a member of the music biz; indeed, we even have an official Woodstock press sticker on the windshield. We take back roads, and stop for lunch in Monticello—the best kosher roast beef sandwiches in the universe—then drive unsuspectingly on, straight into vehicular history.

It is the biggest traffic jam I have ever seen, and I can only see a tiny part of it: We turn on the radio to hear about it, see it as we crest a hill. With the decisiveness of a rally driver, Susie slews off Route 17 just in time; if we'd been caught in that thing—later we are told it went on for *ten miles*—we'd have been there for days. Instead, we return to the back roads and twisty green country lanes, a Grand Circle Route, congratulating ourselves on our prior knowledge of the terrain, cutting over to Liberty, roundabout to Hancock, listening with awe and horror to the radio bulletins telling us to forget it, that the campgrounds at the festival site are already full, that the site itself is full, that the roads leading to Bethel and White Lake from Route 17 are impassable, with as many as a *million and a half* still on the way.

The festival began happening earlier this week, officially known as The Woodstock Music and Art Fair at Bethel, New York—An Aquarian Exposition. Bethel (which means "house of God" in Hebrew, a fact not unnoted by the seeking hordes) is a quiet green backwater in lovely rolling hills, with a permanent population of around 3,000 and a summer influx of holidaymakers to the nearby resorts.

It seems an unlikely place for a rock festival; but when the original deal fell through, it was Max Yasgur who said that the organizers could rent his dairy farm's 600-acre back pasturage; and it is to this huge natural grassy amphitheatre that Susie and I, having dropped in on Long Eddy twenty minutes away, are now heading.

It is early Friday afternoon. The press sticker on the car gets us clearance to drive into the festival grounds, along Hurd Road, a winding one-and-a-half-lane dirt track now nearly solid with shuffling freaks. As we inch forward, they briefly shuffle a little faster out of our way, then drop back to their former pace. None of them looks at either the car or us; so stoned I guess they don't have to actually *look*, they just see out of their skin . . .   I am flashing on oil-rich Bedouin bimbos in a black Cadillac plowing through crowds of barefoot dust-covered peasants on the road to Mecca. It is not an association I feel I can particularly deal with just now, so I light a joint and pretty soon I don't have to.

We reach the press parking mudhole, position the Mustang for a quick getaway should one be needed (though I can't imagine how we'd ever actually make one), and get out to join the multitudes streaming by. As we come over the top of the hill, I see it for the first time: The city is there. It looks like the biggest gypsy camp in the world, the bazaar at Samarkand, both Fillmores, a Third World disaster area, the New Jerusalem and London during the blitz, all in one. It is absolutely staggering. It is also rather scary.

It is, in fact, a city of almost half a million souls—bigger than every upstate burg but Buffalo!—almost all of whom are well under the age of thirty and deeply under the influence of substances: a city with no buildings and no conveniences to speak of, a city that will live for four days on this Catskill hillside with no violence whatsoever. Half a million, to offer a downstate comparison, is about half as many as just now live on Manhattan Island; there has yet to be a four-day period in which half of Manhattan Island is totally non-violent. Think about it. (Then again, there has yet to be a four-day period in which half of Manhattan Island is so stoned it can't move, let alone shoot . . .)

Richie Havens is on, and he sounds just fine as we walk along, skirting the last rows of people on the hill sloping down to the giant stage almost half a mile away. I am clutching a package wrapped in brown mailing paper, which arrived in the J&P offices only yesterday: Jim has sent me copies of his private edition books, *The Lords* and *The New Creatures*, and I am so thrilled I cannot bear to part with them even for a weekend—even though the latter volume *is* dedicated to Pam. For three days I lug them proudly around in the rain and the mud and the drugs, fending off the curious with modest little cries of "Oh, they're just nothing, just some books Jim sent me," taking care to ensure that the Doors' office address is clearly visible to inquirers at all times.

I am not sure just *why* I want people to know that Jim sent me his books—it's most likely just vanity, he only had a hundred copies printed up of each, probably not all that many others here present were so honored—but there it is, and I'm not examining my motives very closely just now. Maybe it's simply that it makes him feel closer, to have his books with me. Besides, it's so cool to be able to read them *here* . . .

Our press passes, Susie and I quickly discover, pull weight only to get you telephone access at a bank of rather unreliable pay phones down by the parking puddle; the actual official press section was overrun days ago by kids who arrived early and staked their claim, and who are by now solidly dug in. No one with a mere press pass is allowed onstage, backstage or in the performers' pavilion—in short, nowhere near the real action.

The remnant of Friday afternoon is therefore spent wandering from trailer to trailer in the summer twilight, trying to obtain what publicist Pat Costello, a dear and droll woman, sardonically refers to as "upward pass mobility." There are two levels of nirvana to which I might aspire: guest pass and performer pass; and in a fit of hubris and crankiness, I decide to go for the gold. By the time I have gone through my routine for at least half a dozen people, zonked, straight, and in-between (making damn sure they all see Jim's book package, just for additional leverage), and score performers' passes, unqualified, for Susie and me, I feel that I have earned them.

The crowds are by now of Biblical proportions (and aspect: This is a real Old Testament scene in more ways than one—you've got your beards, your sandals, your long hair on all sexes, your bare feet and lots more, your incense and tents and livestock and copulations and even, on Saturday and Sunday, your thunderbolts from above). Susie and I (and my tiny black Persian kitten, Nefer, whom for some insane reason I have brought with me, tucked safely into a big soft suede shoulderbag) bolt for the relative serenity of the performers' tabernacle—oops, pavilion. The Pav, as it is sarcastically dubbed, is an open-sided psychedelic mead hall, a surrealistic-pillared galleon with redwood beams and canvas roof like a great sail and floor of redwood chips. It is quite handsome, and there is food, and chairs, and once you are inside you do not want to move ever again, just sit facing the stage (or not) and write your piece from there.

But, hey, that wouldn't be responsible rock journalism; so after some sandwiches and a few glasses of champagne, I leave the kitten with Susie and Diane Gardiner, and get up to move around a bit, flinching at the helicopters taking off and landing a few hundred yards up the hill, airlifting press and musicians and emergency cases in and out. What the hell *is* this, Nam? Incoming!

There is a bridge leading from the Pav over the high cyclone fence that protects its territorial integrity against the unprivileged: over the field, across the road, over a fenced work area, right into the stage. It looks like a down-at-heel Bridge of Sighs and it is outlined in festive red Christmas lights. I gingerly cross over, like one of the Billy Goats Gruff wary of trolls, and step onto the vast wooden stage, where Tim Hardin is just going on.

It is dark by now, and the longhaired m.c. asks the audience to light matches, "Let's see how bright we can make this place!" Oh please. This is a familiar riff to anyone who attends Doors concerts—and it's pretty corny *there*, too—but the fire that is instantly lighted on that hillside puts Madison Square Garden to shame. It blazes in the soft summer night, and is really almost bright enough to read by. Looking out at the murmuring faceless human ocean, I am, in spite of myself, a little awed.

There are tons (literally) of people on the stage with me that night; in fact, I learn some years later that one of my future close friends was standing not ten feet away from me at that very moment. More to the immediate point, I overhear a security guy, seriously concerned, mutter something about not letting anyone else onstage because it might not be able to support the weight upon the muddy wet ground. Not wishing to be a party to the Bethel Mining Disaster of 1969, I head back to the pavilion, where we feed the kitten and ourselves shrimp and cheese and water, and talk to friends, and leave the grounds long after midnight.

It has grown chill and wet and windy; back at the house, amazingly, our hosts are still waiting up for us, like good children wanting to hear the tale of the grownups' glamorous night out. We do our best, but we are smashed and not feeling grown-up at all, and we stagger to our rooms to fall out. I can't *believe* we have to go back the next day and do this all over again.

Saturday begins with pours of rain: thunder, lightning, bigger than ever crowds. I am cranky and freezing, and *I* had a nice warm house and a roof over my head and a bathroom and breakfast and even a bed to sleep in, not like these waifs and strays. The people who have slept out are sodden and tending toward pneumonia, but they are all *smiling*, and *really meaning it*, that damn Woodstock Smile, as they slog through the ankle-deep red mud on the way to laughably nonexistent sanitation.

We have found where Hurd Road comes out on the opposite side of Max's farm—a brilliant bit of scouting by Patricia, worthy of her new deerskin Iroquois moccasins (which are immediately replaced with sneaks to spare them from the mud)—so Susie aims the car that way instead. Unfortunately, about a million other people—well, maybe a couple of hundred—have had the same idea before us (better scouting), and it takes us two hours to go two miles. As we inch closer to the heart of the site again, the rain stops and the sun breaks waterishly out; there are people skinnydipping in the Yasgur stockpond, much to the dismay of the neighbors and the cows.

As we wait, we are regaled with incredible travelers' tales, told to us by harmless souls who wander over to chat: twelve-hour waits to get from Monticello to Bethel, ten-mile hikes to parked cars, battalions of resident and vacationing Samaritans distributing water and free sandwiches to the parched hungry masses in the vast parking lot that was once Route 17B. It's too weird for words, it must all be true.

Our patience is rewarded with a parking space right in the middle of the festival, at the crossroads facing out. I am feeling like a rather uncomfortable elitist—must be the drugs—so instead of making a beeline for the security of the pavilion, Susie and I set out to explore.

On the way, we check out the music—nothing is happening at the moment; between rain delays and drug delays and the groups beginning to pull power plays ("If we don't get paid in cash we don't go on," that kind of thing, it wasn't *all* peace and love and vibes—not that they should have gone unpaid, but still), there are big holes in the fabric of seamless music everybody seems to hear in memory's headphones.

Half an hour later we are back in the Pav. I feel as if I have been briefly shanghaied to some Third World country—one with no food, pidgin speech patterns, indifferent latrine habits, little clothing, even native handicrafts to buy and take home—and I'd sooner be trapped naked in a stalled elevator with Idi Amin than accept any of the profusely offered drugs of dubious provenance.

I am not usually put off by crowd situations, but this is different. *This* is what it was like to be straight at Woodstock: The onslaught of varied vibes is psychically deafening and is affecting me physically, and the plain fact of half a million wiped-out freaks sitting perched on a hill, like some acid avalanche looming above a hapless village, is just too much. I am at the point where if one more person, just *ONE*, says to me "Good vibes, huh?", I am going to punch him/her in the mouth.

I am so pissed off, in fact, at all the mindless drug-induced we-are-all-one-let-it-all-hang-outness that I take out the antler-hafted dagger I bought in Hancock along with my warrior mocs—it's not sharp enough to cut cheese, don't worry—and defiantly strap it to my waist in plain sight ("You want vibes?? *I'LL* give you vibes, you zonked-out little twerps! Dig *this!*"), just to freak people out. Not surprisingly, it keeps my personal space very clear; which is just fine with me.

So now we are back in Valhalla, the pavilion, with just about everyone you have ever heard of in rock and roll: every performer (except of course my beloved Doors, who either were not invited or who chose not to come, depending on whose story you buy), every writer and critic and parasite gossiper, every record exec and publicist and manager and hanger-on and titan. It is in fact my idea of HELL, and I am trapped here. Armed, but trapped.

I am sitting at a table with Diane, some members of the Airplane —Grace drifts by, immaculate and radiant in fringed white leather, she gives us a greeting and a big smile—Jerry Garcia and a few other suspects, when Ellen Sander sits down beside me. I am very happy indeed to see her—hey, Ellen's New York, even if she will move to Marin County not long hereafter—and in the course of our rap I allow as to how the scene is splitting my head.

"Have you been Out There?" she asks earnestly. "Well, *get* Out There, then! Those kids are beautiful, they're beautiful and together and you'll see it. It just amazes me, how people can pull it together in a crisis situation. *Go!*"

I look at her. Crisis?? This is supposed to be Three Days of Peace and Music, what the hell happened to *that*? I know that people are performing great works of charity and mercy—the Hog Farm feeding multitudes with muesli and bulghur wheat, not loaves and fishes but a miracle all the same; the medical personnel over yonder in the hospital tents—and others are doing miracles of another sort, simply keeping the music going at all. Yes, the kids are beautiful, especially when you think of the sort of unenlightened trash-heads who stayed home. Yes, I was Out There with them in their squelchy multitudes, for as long as I could damn well stand it. And yes, I did see a great deal of beauty.

But also I saw thousands upon thousands of the walking wounded of this Revolution we all talk so fine and large and smug about: kids who haven't got faces yet, kids filled up with drugs they don't know how to make proper use of, and only take because they think it's required of them, because they want to be hip and cool and accepted, because the Scene makes it easy and essential.

Kids like this hurt me. I didn't start taking drugs until I was twenty years old; I had some semblance of my finished personality, my real self, fairly well in place by then, so that the drugs did what they were supposed to do: expand my mind and enhance my consciousness. At least there were both mind and consciousness there for them to work on . . . These kids are babies, unsure, eager, unfocused, with all a baby's insistent wants and demands, and none of a formed soul's strengths and resistance—no defenses.

I feel compassion for their confusion, pity for their bewildered pain; I want to weep when they look at me as if I've got some answers for them, and I wonder if this is how Jim must feel. And guilt too is there, big-time media guilt: that we who are older and supposed to have it together, we who have power to set fashions and examples and opinions and styles, have used that power to push them into this before they were ready for it. Kids who try to hitch a ride in your car with a V-sign, then snarl obscene viciousness at you when you tiredly explain that you already have a full load and the axles really can't take another passenger. Kids who have all the right hip clothes and know all the right hip words and drop all the right hip stuff, but whose essential heads—the true inner hipness—haven't been affected in the slightest, it's all surfaces. Kids who have come to this festival and who are going to consume vibes and dope and music, but what are they going to take home with them? (Is it all really just consumerism, in the end?) And even more importantly, what have they brought here?

So I sit looking at Ellen as she tells me of the beauty of the children; and part of me is yelling "Right on, sister!", but most of me is feeling like Scrooge listening to Bob Cratchit. Unrepentant to the last, I scope out the rest of the Pav's inhabitants. A majority of those present is probably of Ellen's politically correct persuasion, but I don't notice too many of them flinging their passes to the muddy ground and running out to actually *join* those beautiful children . . . No, they are all sitting in here, swilling champagne and scarfing strawberries and cream, with all the best-quality dope on either coast to choose from should the need arise. French aristocrats, huddled heedlessly in Versailles, while outside the sandwichless and toiletless masses press against the cyclone fence and suck up Hog Farm granola. (Comes the Revolution . . .) And I am no better; worse, maybe, because I see it, sense it, know it, and still I stay here.

But what is going on outside is not something I would care to be a part of; it's massive, it's historic, it may well be fun, even, once you're in it—but, bottom line, it's mindless, and for me, Apollo must be served as well as Dionysus. (You *can* do both, Jim . . .)

There has been music going on all day and all evening—Creedence, Janis, Sly, the Who, Canned Heat, Melanie; I can't even remember who was on when, though I did get to see Pete Townshend belt Abbie Hoffman upside the head with a guitar, a fine sight—but it seems to be of only peripheral importance. Janis is not at the top of her form, seems anguished and angry; even the Grateful Dead, who have been such fun to be around in the afternoon, can't turn it on when they finally get onstage about ten Saturday night, and return to the pavilion looking disgruntled. But *nobody* played well at Woodstock. It must have been so frustrating: all that energy and you can't get your music off. To me, it's just another indicator: These are *not* the sort of people I want to be tripping amongst.

But the strain isn't just onstage: There has been a rather ugly incident, to my probably politically incorrect way of thinking anyway, earlier that evening, when somebody casually tossed acid into the bowl of fruit punch on the caterer's table, an unsuspecting girl drank some of the now-electric beverage, and freaked.

"Really, acid in the punch?" I ask, thanking all my gods I stuck to champagne.

"Yeah," some blond cowboy giggles, "isn't that wild?"

I fail to see the humor in the situation, however, and the memory of that girl, who couldn't have been more than eighteen, stays with me all that evening. I even go to the medical tent to see if she's okay, but can't find her in the melee. Just one more soul to worry about.

Under protest, I have disarmed myself at my friends' behest—well, I have put the knife away, is all—which is probably a wise move, for it keeps me from pulling it on Joan Baez when she and I have a polite disagreement later on over the last dish of ice cream left in the caterer's freezer. I suppose I really should give it to her—she's so saintly and queenly and pregnant, and she's worked a lot harder than I have this weekend, and I really do admire her, and I loved the way she did "Henry Martin" on that early album—but drugs and vibes and sugar deficiency have made me dangerous, she'll have to rip it out of my hands if she really wants it. (Crazed Critic Slays Peckish Folksinger . . . film at eleven.)

Non-violence prevails, though, and she graciously cedes me the snack (making me feel terrible, of course). I take my melting prize back to the table, where half the New York press corps and lots of our West

Coast pals and large chunks of Ten Years After and the Grateful Dead and Jefferson Airplane and Crosby Stills & Nash are all sucking down more Moët than you'll see any New Year's Eve. I open yet another bottle—huddled over, totally paranoid, I trust no one in *this* crowd to pop the cork or even undo the damn foil and wire (I knew that knife would come in handy!), who knows what they'll sneak into it when I'm not watching?—and drink more of it than I can quite remember. For purely medicinal purposes, you understand.

By now I am running on survival vibes, scraping by on nerve sheaths; it is about three in the morning, the pavilion is taking on the aura of being the rock world's ultimate press party, the groups are taking longer and longer to get onstage—and there is a cat sitting next to Albert Grossman, Dylan's manager, in a black porkpie hat, yellow shades and a trenchcoat, with *short* hair, who I am *convinced* is an F.B.I. agent or a narc or a Fed of some stripe.

When I realize it is actually Johnny Winter, delusionally incognito, that blazing white hair stuffed up under the stupid hat, I think it might be time to go home quietly. Even with performer's passes, we couldn't get near the stage that night; the music has continued to be less than ecstatic; the minimal stash I have brought with me is exhausted (oh, like that's really a problem *here*! But it is: I'm probably the singularly most unstoned person here at this hour, and given what's available— coke-laced orange sunshine, or maybe it's the other way round; killer grass; bad acid—I'd really rather stay that way). And I may have an iron bladder, but it has been, after all, quite some hours since I have last peed.

But then I look around, and I think, Well, we've been here so long already, it's only rock and roll— So it is that I am there to hear the Airplane greet the dawn. They should have been on at ten Saturday night, but kept getting bumped by other acts—Janis, Sly, the Who— and so it is not until Sunday morning sunrise that they finally take the stage.

I am so tired by now that I'm not even sure it's happening; or maybe somebody finally got me with something after all and I just didn't notice. But the sky is pale pearl and there is mist in the little valleys, and just at this minute, as that music rings out for ten miles around, it is my favorite music in the world. It almost makes it all worth being here.

We go back to Long Eddy and crash, not getting back to the festival until early afternoon. Being straight has not been quite so much fun, so maybe today I will just do something major—Owsley is reportedly around, that might be interesting—but in the end I only do a joint or two and a small hit of certified adulterant-pure coke to keep from falling asleep from sheer fatigue. I don't know how the bands can actually get up there after all this and *play*; of course, they don't play very *well*, but still.

Sunday is sort of an anticlimax—I can't remember anybody who actually played except maybe was it Crosby Stills & Nash?—so Susie and I look at each other, nod, and agree without a word exchanged that we've been too long at the fair. For us, Woodstock's over.

As we are just about to make good our escape, we are suddenly held up in traffic for the longest wait we have so far endured, turning out of Hurd Road onto the county blacktop that will get us back to Long Eddy. On the trunk of the car in front of us, a little girl is perched between her parents, little kid with long blond braids, fringed buckskin jacket— can't be more than six or seven years old.

After exchanging smiles and peace signs with us (well, it's a *kid*, what was I gonna do, give her the finger?), she speaks to her mother and hops off the trunk, coming round to my window and proceeding to discuss, with incomparable aplomb, the faults of the festival's programming and sound system and facilities, how much she had wanted to hear Ravi Shankar on Friday night but he was on too late and they had to get back to their motel. My jaw drops lower with every sentence. Seven-year-old kid.

Then traffic starts up somewhere far ahead, the line of cars begins to move, the girl's father calls her back. She smiles at us and says, "It's really a good festival, but not for music. I feel safe here." She skips away, vanishing into her parents' car, which turns left while we head right.

I sit and wonder, and my thoughts are dark and hard. In ten years or so, maybe less, is that little girl going to be one of the casualties I have just spent three days among, her personality stolen by drugs before she can even get it in place to enjoy? (And you must remember we are talking here about "good" drugs, not stuff like heroin and crack . . .) Are those hip-looking, concerned parents of hers going to tell her that even good things can hurt when used wrongly or prematurely or inappropriately? And what about the rest of those beautiful children: Are they rare souls, or lobotomized robots?

Tough questions, and a cold message to take home from Three Days of Peace and Music; especially in the face of the media euphoria, the self-induced autohype, which is the Woodstock aftermath and legacy for years to come. Susie is cynical; Jim, when I tell him about it next time we speak, philosophic.

"You should be pleased and proud you weren't there," I say to him severely. "It was *not* a Doors kind of gig."

"The guys sort of wanted to go," he admits. "I think John, or maybe it was Ray, was even there for a day or so, hanging out—but it just didn't happen. Must've been our *karma*," he adds teasingly, "don't you think?"

"They wouldn't have liked you there." I am reaching for something, but can't seem to put my verbal finger on it. "Wouldn't have heard you—I don't know, *something*—"

Jim understands what I am driving at. "They wouldn't have wanted to hear what we would have wanted to say to them." Which is, of course, exactly right.

I read him, with great glee, the memorably demented New York Times editorial of August 18, titled "Nightmare in the Catskills," in which the sanity of festival participants is unfavorably compared to that of lemmings hurling themselves into the sea. (The Times is remarkably schizoid on Woodstock: The editorials say one thing, but on-scene reporters are filing stories that say very different; and in subsequent editions the editorial is altered, withdrawn, and, the next day, contradicted by a fulsomely favorable one. So much for the collective head of the journal of record.)

Jim is highly amused. "So, it worked out okay, didn't it? We shouldn't have been there, and we weren't; and you're sorry you were there but glad you can bitch about it now."

"Well . . . sorry I had to *be* there. Not sorry I *was* there."

And I'm not. Rock and roll, and some other things beside, came and were seen and did conquer in an upstate pasture on a stormy August weekend. For whatever reasons, I'll always be grateful I didn't miss that "crisis situation" after all.

PART
TWO

your Surrender
is not defeat
& my love is
your Portion.

CHAPTER

September 1969

THINGS SETTLE DOWN AFTER WOODSTOCK. THERE IS a Stooges concert at the New York State Pavilion, out at the old World's Fair site in Flushing, a suitably bizarro venue for Iggy's antics. I enjoy the Stooges' music—it's sort of like Doors music only without the laughs—and Iggy himself, whom I have met earlier this year up at Elektra, is charming and polite, only a year younger than I. But I just can't stand watching him idly carve up his bare chest with a broken drum-stick, or swandive into the crowd, confident that angels or strangers will surely catch him and bear him up. (Thankfully, I was never witness to Jim's dive phase—more a California thing for him, anyway, perhaps it was geographically linked—and I'm glad of it, I don't think I'd have liked to see Jim hurling himself carelessly into space.)

But outside of Jimi Hendrix at Salvation and Sha Na Na at El Morocco (now there's an inspired booking), things are quiet in New York. Until Jim hits town.

The first I hear of it is a call one afternoon.

"Hi!"

Man, I *hate* it when people do that... But I know very well who it is, because before my synapses can even supply me with the name every bone in my body has melted. My voice drops two octaves.

"Hi yourself—where are you?"

"Here!" He sounds very pleased with himself, as if it's a major achievement. "We're in town for a few days between gigs—to rehearse, and so I can show *Feast* to the public TV people, they think they may want to run it."

"Ah." This would be *Feast of Friends*, the Doors self-documentary, which he told me about back in January at the Plaza; oddly enough, someone at Channel 13 has already set up a screening for me. I pass it along.

"Great—why don't I meet you after you see it, and then we can go out for dinner and talk about it. Or you could come over to the hotel, or something."

Or something. *That's* the part that's giving me butterflies; as soon as I heard his voice in my ear I knew where this was headed, and though I am of course thrilled and joyful I am also scared to death. It's hard to get what you've been wanting. But I can't tell him that.

"Oh Jim," I say. "I'd love to."

We talk for a few minutes, then he tells me where he is staying (the Hotel Lexington, an industrial-grade hostelry on Lex and 48th Street, hardly the Plaza), and where the Doors will be rehearsing (Upsurge, a rental studio on a rather grimy block of West 19th).

I go to the screening the next day, down the block at the Channel 13 offices. Well, it's not *The Seventh Seal*, or even *The Magnificent Seven*, but *Feast of Friends* has some very exciting Doors concert moments very nicely photographed. There's a great sequence of Jim doing one of those long taunting silences during some epic or other—"The End" or "When the Music's Over"—just hanging on the mike for maybe two or three minutes, letting the audience get it all out, a grin flashes across his face just for an instant, self-aware, self-mocking. I grin in spite of myself to see it. What a fraud.

The fraud and I run into each other, almost literally, outside on the wide pavement in front of the Coliseum; he smiles warmly on seeing me, and I blush.

"You cut your hair!" is all I can think to say.

"Yeah—I was getting bored with it. But you didn't cut yours." He reaches out for a handful, and I am soooo glad I washed it last night (I'm glad it's all my own, too, all three red feet of it).

As it turns out, he is up to the screening room himself to see *Feast* again—I had a private showing, just Janice and me from the magazine and someone from Elektra, and I am torn between relief and regret that Jim wasn't an hour earlier. We make plans for dinner at a nearby pubbish sort of place, later on that evening—which means I can go home and change.

The first thing he asks about as we sit down in the booth is the Irish lessons I told him—in an April letter—that I was beginning. I am floored that he actually remembers this; he just smiles, pleased with himself for recalling it, and pleased too that I am so impressed by his remembering.

"Well," he explains, "I guess it must have made kind of an impact on me—"

Yeah, probably . . . We talk about the Irish language—at his insistence, I try out a few phrases on him—and the difference between Irish and other Celtic languages, and from there we get into Yeats and his occultism and his furry little friends of the Celtic Revival. From there—I don't know how—to film.

He tells me about putting *Feast* together, and the people he worked with on it, and then confides his larger plans, film-wise: a feature-length production he is already working on, writing the screenplay with his friend Michael McClure, author of *The Beard*.

"It'll be compared to *Easy Rider*, I know, but it was a written story when *Easy Rider* wasn't even a twinkle in somebody's lens. Michael and I are writing the screenplay conjointly, just improvising on the typewriter from his story. We even have an office."

"What else do you have to do with it?"

He looks down at his plate, a little embarrassed, then up at me. "Well—kind of a lot, actually." He's almost apologetic. "The movie will be—obviously—mostly me: I'll be co-authoring it, co-directing it, co-starring in it. So if you don't like me, you won't like this film."

"It sounds as if you're making a pretty easy target of yourself."

"Maybe—but I couldn't imagine being involved in a film and not having some say-so, some degree of control over the finished product."

"James Morrison, auteur? 'Un film de James Morrison'?"

He laughs. "No—I don't believe in auteur theory. I don't think any one individual has that much of a stamp on what a film ultimately becomes. There are simply too many other people involved. You—you the director, you the screenwriter, you the producer, whatever—

obviously will have a bigger stamp than, say, the cat who does the lighting, or the caterer, or the chick who does the costumes, but they're important too to the overall work, and you still don't have that iron-clad total control. It's really more of a team effort."

(Ah, Oliver, would you had been there . . .)

"What about the band? Where does all this leave the four of you?"

"I have no plans for this other work interfering with my music," he says sternly. "I have a feeling that the Doors aren't doing as much as we could, as an entity. We haven't pushed as much as we could—or should."

"What would you want to do—you yourself?"

"Oh man"—the face lights up—"I would *love* to do an album of all old blues standards, 'St. James Infirmary,' stuff like that. But the other guys don't seem to care so much for the idea, so—   Also, I'd like to get into production, do a Caedmon-type recording of my own poetry—new poems, not the material from *The New Creatures*—with a kind of esoteric musical score in the background. But really make the poetry and the music hang together, not just be some poems over some music."

He sounds a little tired and a little wistful, and I say so, adding, "You sound as if you don't really want to be doing rock much longer."

The eyes go very wide. "I *can't* see myself doing it very much longer—for one thing, I couldn't stand it—maybe two or three years more of it at most. Five years from now I want to be into writing and films. You know I majored in film at UCLA—though I *know* what you think of the poetry!"

I blush and mutter something noncommittal; he just laughs.

"You told me to reread Aristotle's *Poetics* last time we talked," he reminds me. Again, I can't believe he remembers these things . . . "I haven't gotten around to it again yet, but thanks for that 'reread,' at least you don't think I'm a total poetic illiterate."

"Well—not *total*."

We go back to my apartment as if by some unspoken agreement; no one suggests, no one accepts, it's just understood that it's time.

"Nice place," he says. "You live alone?"

"Go check the closets if you're so uptight," I reply with some asperity. "Of *course* I live here alone! I certainly wouldn't have brought you home with me if I didn't."

"Somebody said you might have an old man," he says vaguely.

"Well, I don't. It's just me here, and I'm not with anybody."

He picks up one of the fencing foils I have left lying on the couch after yesterday's session, holds it inexpertly at arm's length.

"I just don't want to find myself challenged to a *duel* or anything."

"Relax. I do all the dueling around here."

I get out the silver wineglasses, bend over to pick out a bottle—a nice vintage Bordeaux—from the wooden rack. When I straighten up again, I see, in the big carved mirror, Jim watching my velvet-covered rear; he quickly looks away.

"Pretty lethal, aren't you," he says then. "Maybe I should get out now, while I still can."

"Suit yourself."

Amazingly, he seems every bit as nervous as I am, both of us a little skittish with each other, shy with our eyes. He wanders around the three small rooms—which suddenly seem a whole lot smaller with him in them—as if he is at a particularly fascinating and informative yard sale. Everything seems to interest him: He leafs through books, checks out the records, examines pictures and artifacts and knickknacks, respectfully studies—from a carefully non-touching distance—my magical implements; sipping wine, full of questions.

"Is this your axe? You play?" He draws his fingers over the steel strings of my Martin dreadnought, where it hangs on the wall.

"Sort of. I had a serious folkie phase in college—you know, singing songs about house carpenters and unquiet graves, dyeing my hair black."

"Well, don't do *that* again!" he says severely. "You have the prettiest red hair."

I look up, but he is paging through my prized first edition of T.E. Lawrence and does not see the glance I give him. Red hair indeed! It is more deep auburn than real red: Irish-setter color, and certainly not as red as I've heard Pam's is, though about two feet longer than hers. But I guess red enough to qualify for his penchant: Bruce Harris, a friend who works for Cash Box magazine and will soon be publicity director at Elektra, has teased me more than once with the speculation that Jim really only goes for redheads . . .

He looks up from the book to meet my stare. "Why do people call you 'Kennealy'?"

"Oh, they called me that at college, and some of my close friends still do. I kind of like it."

"Can I call you that?"

"If you want. Though I prefer 'Patricia.' "

"What do your folks call you, your family?"

" 'Your Imperial Highness.' "

" 'Trish'! I bet it's 'Trish.' "

"Well, it isn't. It's 'Patty,' if you must know."

He cracks up. " 'Patty'! It's perfect—oh man, you are so not a Patty . . . well, not on the outside, anyway."

"And on the inside?"

But he just looks at me, still smiling, and then visibly decides to come clean about something.

"I wanted to make it with you, that first afternoon, you know, at the Plaza? Then everybody else came in, and we sort of, uh, lost the moment."

I am astounded. "You were really thinking about—" I cannot even say it, and to my chagrin and his amusement I am blushing furiously. I never do that with anyone but him; strange, that.

"You *bet* I was thinking about it. I was hoping you'd say yes—if I'd asked you."

I am so cool again. "Why *didn't* you ask?"

"You might have said yes . . . Oh, because you were too *smart*, okay? I needed somebody stupid that night."

Maybe every night, from what I've heard; so why's he here with me now?

"Too bad," I say airily. "I might have said yes." But this is a boastful lie, me trying to sound like Mae West. Sure, I *wanted* to. But I wouldn't have. Not then. Not yet.

He is sitting on the couch now, pouring out more wine for us both. I am curled up facing him at the couch's other end. For all Jim's notoriety as a drinker, in all the time I am to know him I will see him abusively drunk only one time, maybe one-and-a-half times. With me, he drinks very little: Tonight, for example, he had two Chivas-and-Cokes (which he is trying to get me into; I'd rather drink furniture polish) over dinner, and I had a vodka and tonic, and now we are into this bottle of wine, which we will barely finish between us.

We talk quietly for a while—somehow his head has found its way into my lap, the ends of my hair trailing across his face and onto his chest as he looks up at me. And then he turns over the hand he has been holding, and kisses the middle of my palm. I close my eyes and stop breathing.

"Want me to stay tonight and keep you company?" he says softly.
"Only if you understand it's not obligatory."
That eyes-wide flash of comprehension and amusement that I love.
"I know what you mean. It's not."
We turn to each other like plants to light.

I wake suddenly and completely, nothing moving but my eyelids; well, they're about all that *can* move, after last night . . . I throw the cat on the floor, shut off the alarm clock before it rings, and turn to the man asleep beside me in my bed.

Talk about your faits accomplis: I draw back the sheet a little and prop myself on one elbow, just wanting to look at him. Body more Roman than Greek, like that statue of Augustus in armor, and a hell of a lot more impressive than people have been snickeringly implying. I think he is the most beautiful person of either sex that I have ever seen, and I go right on thinking so until—well, I still think so. He was far too pretty for my tastes when he was the Young Lion of the famous bare-chested photographs, all pouts and scowls and curls; I like men to look like men, not underage Hellenic wineboys. But this is no pouty pretty boy, this is one extraordinarily handsome man. Except that his hair really is too short—he assures me several times, when I lament the shear job, that it *will* grow back—I like it best when it is down to his shoulders, very Cavalier. The beard is good too, the beard is *great*; I think any guy looks so much sexier with a beard, especially when he's so sexy to begin with. But it too is vanished; though again he promises a return engagement, a little amused that I am so vehement about it. But I just think everybody should have as much hair as possible. It must be a Celtic thing.

He is asleep on his left side, his back to me, though we did not sleep like that, and now I fit myself against him spoon-fashion, my breasts against his back, my crotch against his rear. What I really like is the discovery, made last night, that when I put my arm around him, as I do now, my hand barely reaches to the other side of his chest; like playing a dreadnought guitar as opposed to a concert-size, there is that same extra reach, arch and stretch of my arm from the shoulder.

I run my hand down his chest onto his hip and around to the front. He is starting to wake up, moving and purring, rolling onto his back; I hit him lightly on the shoulder as he reaches out for me and pulls me on top of him.

"Morning, stranger!" I kiss him on the ear.

He gives me a smile that lights the room. "Hi—I feel *great!*"

"Well of *course* you do. You spent the night with *me*—"

We make love a couple of times, and it is even better than last night, if that is possible—though the first time with someone you love is always magic. Then I reluctantly pull myself away from him, and go out to the kitchen to make us breakfast, we are both ravenous. While Jim plays with Nefer the cat, none the worse for her great Woodstock adventure, I fix tea and toast and eggs and bacon, put it all on a tray and carry it back to bed. We stuff our faces, feed bits to the cadging cat, speculating on how she truly perceives us, what is her feline reality.

"Neffie probably sees us as gods," he muses. "We appear, and there is food and warmth and affection. We go away, and hunger and loneliness come. Does she think she's a worshipper? In ancient Egypt cats were the gods—what does she think we do?"

After a lazy interlude, and making love several times more, we get up and dress; he has to go to Elektra and then to another rehearsal, and I have to put in at least a token appearance at work, though Pauline is privy to all this and thrilled to bits. But we arrange to meet for a late lunch at Max's—Max's Kansas City, center of the known hip world—and then walk over to the rehearsal studio, a few blocks away.

"Leon'll be with us at lunch, it'll look more like business, and he and I have to do some things anyway."

We share a cab uptown, kissing away madly in the back seat; I drop him off, and go on to the office. At Max's that afternoon they put us *upstairs*—which I actually much prefer to the trendoid back room, but which is considered to be outmost Siberia by the hipper-than-thou. I wonder with some amusement if this is a judgment of some sort, and if so, who is being judged. Not that I care one jot: Jim is there, across from me, our legs intertwined under the table (and I was never before so glad that Max's tables are so narrow), our faces bright enough to be seen in Hoboken. But we are cool, and Leon—Leon Barnard, new Doors publicist—seems to be unaware that there is anything more going on here than just a star-editor lunch.

Which is fine with me. I'd really rather nobody knew about this at all, but failing that then at least as few people as possible. To me it is as if we are together inside a bright isolation bubble, no one can see us or hear us but we can see everyone else; we are alone in our crystal sphere, just us—which is why I will be continually surprised whenever

I find out that other people *do* know about us, because to me it is only, always, him. It is all sacred and special and beautiful: I am insanely in love, as I have never loved before or since; but even so, already I seem aware in some tiny far part of my being that the operative word here is, of course, 'insane'. . .

After lunch we walk out into the sunshine on lower Park Avenue, and stroll over to Upsurge. I am wearing a blue-gray maxicoat over a Biba knit minidress and knee-high suede boots, and the weather, though lovely, is about ten degrees too warm for this sort of thing; by the time we reach the studio, I am a little puffed.

The other Doors are already there, doing things with amps and leads and monitors; I say hello, then quickly get out of their way, taking a seat in an inconspicuous corner, on an empty drum case. Jim gives me a quick kiss and cuddle when nobody's watching, then picks up a mike and starts to vamp on "Heartbreak Hotel."

He does a dead-on Elvis; I am always amazed by this sort of thing, but maybe musicians do not find it quite so astonishing. When I recount this to Bruce Harris, with awe and incredulity ("And *then* he did Ricky Nelson, 'Be-Bop-A-Lula'—!"), Bruce tells me a story of hearing David Crosby (!) do the best Jim Morrison anybody, including Jim, ever heard.

I sit watching Jim as he sings, his back to me, perched on an overturned amp trunk, moving around, lighting on a metal folding chair, moving again. I cannot believe any of this. It has finally come to pass: Jim and I have become lovers; and as to what is going to happen in the long run—well, I really don't want to think about it just now. Nor short run neither, for that matter. All I know, all I care to know, is that I was right again, as usual. . . I knew it would happen, and now it has. I have wanted, and I have gotten, and this is not the end of it. The gods are just after all. (They will show me the other side of the labrys, to be sure, but not just yet; and that too is part of the deal. . .) Or is it just one of life's major paybacks, something I—and he—richly deserve? Or is that the same thing? Or is it magic, have we just reeled one another in on the old karmic fishline? Or is *that* the same thing?

Whatever it may be, at least I manage to have the class to keep any destiny raps strictly to myself. I just sit there and watch him, listen to him sing, and there is such a shaking within me that I am amazed no one else notices.

The band is in great form. This is the way to hear the Doors, this is what it must have been like to hear them at the Fog and the Whiskey, back when they were working things out onstage. They do a few things I have not heard before: "Ship of Fools," "Land Ho," "The Spy," all from what will be the new album, called *Morrison Hotel* ("Because I wrote ninety percent of the stuff on it, that's why; all the words and all the music except for two lyrics which Robby wrote"). The sound is new, too, a bluesy amalgam that also has its roots in their scuffling days; the Doors always were a rock and roll band underneath it all, and it's so exciting to hear that coming back out again. They are working hard, too: at least four hours of rehearsal every day they're here.

At last they knock off for a break; Jim turns and looks at me, a smile on his face that is too intimate by half.

"What're you looking at, girl?"

"Your eyes," is all I can say, but that is not entirely it. Yet it is true: They are full of light, blue and luminous as an owl's clear across the room. I hope no one notices this exchange, but I am past caring.

"Twenty-twenty."

"Oh Jim. Oh God. I hope so."

After the rehearsal, we all go out for a bite to eat, six or seven of us, to a greasy spoon down the block. No one lingers especially over the meal; we hang out a while, talking, then everyone begins to drift out. The musicians want to get in some more practice time, Jim and Leon have to head back uptown to another commitment, I want to get home and wrap myself in my grandma's afghans and think about all this, before I disintegrate into a billion tiny glowing pieces. Jim walks me to the corner of Fifth Avenue to put me in a cab.

I have been searching my heart for something to say—something cool, something memorable (oh please Goddess don't let him forget about me!), something that will not make me look like a complete fool.

But nothing comes to me. It seems that Jim too has the same difficulty: In the end we just look at one another, as if words have indeed been exchanged between us—and maybe on some level they have. So we smile, hug, kiss goodbye, let our eyes possess the other's—then, as I am getting into the cab, he suddenly pulls something out of a pocket and loops it all in a hurry round my neck.

It is the gold-mounted tiger claw on a black cord I have seen him occasionally wearing—or one of them, actually; I have noticed two or three different ones—one of the very few pieces of adornment he goes in for: these, a cross or two, an elephant-hair or Navajo bracelet, things like that.

"Here, take this. I want you to wear it."

He kisses me again and walks away down the block. It is the first real gift he has ever given me—me, Patricia, the woman, the lover; not Patricia Kennealy the editor and critic—and I do not take it off for days thereafter (going so far as to wrap it in plastic when I shower or wash my hair). And though we are soon back to our routine of phone calls and letters—now perceptibly more intimate—I do not see him again for several months.

CHAPTER

9

September 1969–January 1970

NOW THAT JIM IS GONE AGAIN (HAVING JUST PLAYED Toronto, the Doors are on their way to gigs in Philadelphia and Pittsburgh; more than twenty concerts were canceled in the wake of Miami—these are among the few that remain), I sit for a while, just thinking about all this, then I get out my notebook and write everything down. I have been doing this from the first—from Ondine right through to the afternoon at the Plaza, and after that of course in greater detail.

I have always written things down: when things were too joyful to believe, too painful to bear. It is a defense as much as a recounting; somehow it does not seem real to me until I have set it down on paper, as if the physical act of writing, as much as the mental exercise of remembering and the spiritual discipline of changing emotions into words, somehow validates the event. I am a writer; this is what I do, how I deal with things. But even more than that, this is the only way I can handle something so huge and significant and all-important that I still can hardly believe it.

*   *   *

Well, *I* think so, anyway. The flip side of this is, of course, that that's it right there, one night. He was curious, he fucked me out of curiosity, and that's the end of it. I torture myself with this for a while (conveniently forgetting all those letters and calls, which have not diminished), then take it to Maura, the retiring High Priestess of my coven. I am scheduled to take over the office from her at Samhain (it's pronounced Sah-win and it's the Celtic New Year; known as Halloween by the non-pagan), with one of the senior male witches to act as my pro tem High Priest. (Although it often happens that the High Priestess and High Priest are mated partners as well as magical partners, it is by no means necessary: Aengus, who will be the most compatible of my working High Priests, is himself happily married to another witch of the group, and assures me Jim will be taking initiation and becoming my High Priest within the year; and, if Jim had lived, he probably would have.)

I tell Maura all my doubts and hopes and fears; she never makes light of the problems people bring to her, but her gift is that she lightens the weight of them. She is also one of the best psychics in the group, so when she tells me not to worry about retaining Jim's interest, I accept what she says, and she even goes so far as to predict a handfasting— which I don't dare even imagine.

But she would not be the High Priestess she is if she did not also tell me what else she sees, and, after the usual cautioning, she does.

She speaks first to my uncertainty, my fear that this with Jim has complicated or compromised my ability to assume the High Priestessly duties; she tells me it is not so, that if anything Jim will enhance it, will bring me strength, echoes Aengus's thought for the future.

And she tells me to love, and not to fear; that that's the job for me here, this time, this trip, and that the rest is not for me to worry about.

The day before Thanksgiving I go to the Rainbow Grill, on the sixty-fifth floor of the RCA Building, for a press conference the Rolling Stones are holding prior to their big concert at the Garden that weekend.

It is more of an Event itself than a mere gathering of ink-stained wretches: open bar, a string quartet from Juilliard playing Haydn and Mozart while we wait like courtiers for the Stones. But long before the group appears, the conference turns into a pitched battle between the straight press and the hip ("Move *over*, hippie, I'm here to get a story!" "Well, so'm I." "Oh yeah? Then why aren't ya taking any *notes*?"), punctuated by periodic omnidirectional bellows of "*COMMUNISTS!*" from one particularly puzzling TV gentleman. When the Stones finally show up, they are greeted with a round of applause, which seems to sum up the whole thing.

The Stones aren't giving this conference just to boost the Garden gig: On December 6, they announce, they will give a free concert in California, by way of thank-you to the fans—although the idea had been kicking around for a few years, and was in fact originated by members of Jefferson Airplane and the Grateful Dead, and reanimated by the vibes of Woodstock.

Unlike its East Coast paradigm, however, Altamont will be forever known as the great anti-festival, a citadel of negativity and evil fu. It's not entirely the Stones' fault: The organizing has been less than ideal, the location is uncertain right up to the actual concert morning, police and civil authorities work out long-standing antipathies through vengeful hassling.

Woodstock may have been disorganized, but this is *un*organized: It is chaos, it is ego trips, it is somebody thinking what a bright idea it would be to recruit the Hell's Angels to serve as security forces. Their fee is five hundred dollars' worth of beer, and they work hard for their pay.

On the day of the concert, the Hell's Angels enforce the security of the Rolling Stones by beating some of the 300,000 audience members senseless with wooden sticks, pool cues, studded belts and bare fists. They even take exception to some of the talent protesting this activity: During the Airplane's set, Marty Balin leaps off the stage to the defense of a black kid the Angels were stomping, and is himself punched unconscious for his trouble. The kid, 18-year-old Meredith Hunter, is later stabbed to death by "assailants unknown"—you can see it in the movie (*Gimme Shelter*, released in 1970).

The joylessness that prevails at Altamont comes as a harsh awakening for heads conditioned by the gentle give-and-take of festivals such as Woodstock, Hyde Park, the Isle of Wight and the earlier Monterey Pop. It isn't made any better by the fact that when the Stones, their audience bloodied and themselves unbowed as ever, get home to England, they immediately give a series of interviews to the British press in which they state that Altamont and the tour that had preceded it (which had been widely reviewed as static and formulaic) were the best things ever to hit the States.

Writing in the San Francisco Chronicle, Ralph J. Gleason, one of J&P's editorial board, has somewhat of a different take on it, pointing out that although the concert was ostensibly a free one, "there *was* a tab, in money and ego. The Stones did it for money . . . the name of the game is money, power and ego, and money comes first and means power. Whoever goes to see that movie [*Gimme Shelter*] paid for the Altamont religious assembly."

Grace Slick (whose band the Stones had been reluctant to have play on the same bill, pouting that the Airplane had actually outdrawn the Stones in Florida), remarks afterward, "How was Mick Jagger supposed to know how it was at Woodstock?" But that begs the question; and besides, he could have asked . . .

"This is the backstage pass?"

I turn it over in my hand, a little exasperated. It is January 1970, and the Doors are back in New York, to play a four-show gig at the Felt Forum, downstairs from Madison Square Garden. The pass for the concerts is a playing card of a pneumatic brunette, holding up the scanty pink nylon nightie she has apparently just removed. Terrific.

"Boys will be boys—"

Leon looks a little embarrassed. "It wasn't *my* idea!"

No, probably not. I look at Jim, who goes into one of those helium giggles of his. We are at another one of our interview lunches—a midtown Japanese restaurant this time—before the Doors launch into the first of their four shows, two nights from now. This is the first time I have seen him since September, and although we have of course been exchanging our usual calls and letters all these weeks, so far this trip he and I have not had a chance for a private meeting.

"You have to show it if you want to get into the rehearsal tomorrow afternoon," Jim helpfully points out.

"Yeah, I kind of figured that out for myself . . . Any other surprises you'd like to tell me about?"

He pretends to consider. "Don't you like surprises?"

"No. I hate them."

"Well, come to the rehearsal anyway." He stands up politely as I get up to leave, kisses me chastely on the cheek. "See you later."

The Felt Forum is an acoustically cheerful, crescent-shaped auditorium seating about five thousand, below the Garden's huge main arena; it is divided by a walkway into an orchestra section and a sort of mezzanine. I think the Doors are very wise to choose to play here rather than upstairs, and I am looking forward very much to the shows—all of which I am going to.

Arriving as invited for the rehearsal, I go in at the side Forum entrance, creeping down through the Garden's cement innards, flashing the porno playing-card at regular checkpoints, resigned to the snickers of the security guards. After what seems like a half-mile hike, I come to the dressing rooms, still smelling faintly of feet and circus, an olfactory legacy from the last acts that probably played here.

Leon comes to meet me, and we are standing in the corridor talking when a short, slight girl with bright red hair just past her shoulders emerges from the depths of the dressing room. She sees us and comes forward with a friendly smile, wide eyes under deep Julie Christie bangs.

"Hi, I'm Pam, Jim's wife?" She says it with a questioning air, as if I might challenge the statement.

Well, not quite *yet*, maybe . . . and didn't I tell Jim only yesterday I *hate* surprises? I say nothing, but just hold out my hand; and after a moment she takes it limply, seemingly bemused by the courtesy, as if a handshake is some arcane ritual she seldom has occasion to practice.

Leon introduces us. "Oh, Pam, this is Patricia Kennealy, she's the editor of Jazz & Pop magazine . . ." As he goes on about what a great magazine and what a terrific writer and all that, I check her out.

Pamela Susan Courson, nine months younger than I, three years younger than Jim, is a staggeringly pretty woman. Skin as white as my own (only freckled); slightly prognathous though delicate jaw; small thin nose with a teensy pinch across the tip, a tiny little ridge like a thousand bad nose jobs I've seen since (though I suspect hers is come by naturally, rather than store-bought). She's wearing L.A. fatigues, jeans and panne velvet tie-dye; I'm in a Betsey Johnson whose hem ends well short of my fingertips.

We chat for a few minutes; and as we talk I begin to see that though the lights may be on, nobody's home—and it looks as if the fuse needs to be replaced. All in all, she is about what I expected, and I am perversely pissed off. How can he want this and want me at the same time? I am vain enough to be smugly gratified that of course I am a whole lot smarter and have a college degree and run a magazine and can write and all the rest of it, but somehow I cannot help feeling that a worthier adversary would have done us all more credit.

I smile apologetically and indicate the stage area. "Well, I guess I'd better go in there . . . I did promise to say hi to Jim."

She understands completely, or says she does, and heads back into the dressing room to watch TV some more. Leon points me toward the stage.

As I thread my way through the tunnely maze, I hear him long before I see him; just turn a corner and his voice comes at me like a fist. He is in the middle of a song, and his voice fills the concrete passage from wall to wall, throbbing off the stone, the Minotaur bellowing in the Labyrinth.

My head comes up like a fire-horse's, and I shiver. Even after all this time, he still blows me away out front. I hear him on two levels, inevitably, double-tracked in my own head: the amplified baritone now riding so easily above the storm of the music, and the remembered whisper in the dark, against my ear, my neck, in my bed.

I walk with long strides around the ring of orchestra seats, super-conscious of him away off on my left, on the projecting stage. I wait until he finishes the song; then his head turns to where I am standing, his eyes meet mine, with the same click as always, as the first time, the last time. I smile and come forward; he reaches out a hand and I vault up onto the stage.

Another kiss on the cheek; we exchange greetings, small talk, then the band starts making some pointedly purposeful vamping noises, like, Jim, let's go, okay? I head back down into the orchestra, take a seat halfway back, drape my legs over the chair arm and just listen; later, I get up to move around, sampling the sound from various vantage points. They do four or five numbers, concert pace and strength; then Jim calls a break and joins me where I am sitting.

We look at each other for a long silent moment. Then:

" 'Wife'?" I ask. " 'WIFE'???!!!"

Jim half-closes his eyes and gives me a lazy smile. "She's not my wife. We're not married."

"Then why does she say she is?"

The eyes open wide again and he sits up in the seat. "I guess she thinks she's put up with a lot from me—on and off—over the past couple of years. Maybe she feels she's entitled. I'm not crazy about it, but I couldn't care less what she calls herself; it's not true and it's no skin off my nose anyway."

"Apparently."

He squirms a bit, stung. "Oh, hey, listen, it has nothing to do with you and me! She does her own thing, and I do mine. You—well, you're you. What we have is different, you and I. She's *nothing* like you."

"Got *that* right . . ."

"We don't even live together, not really," he continues, intent on making this as clear as he can. "She has her apartment, and I stay at the motel most of the time, or crash on the couch at the office."

"Listen, you don't have to explain to *me*! It's no business of mine."

He reaches out and takes my chin between his fingers, turning my resistant head around to him, so that I must meet his eyes.

"Isn't it?" When I remain stubbornly silent, he changes the topic. "How'd we sound?"

I know what's called for here ("Oh-darling-you-were-wonderful!"), and I let my face blaze with animation, glad to be able to tell him so with a clear conscience.

"Like Joshua fitting the battle of Jericho! You're a lot tighter than last time."

"Yeah, I really whipped them into shape for this tour." He pauses, whispers, "I want to fuck you so much, right here on the floor, make love to you right here in front of everybody."

I close my eyes. "Don't tempt me . . .   I haven't stopped thinking about you since yesterday. Well, since the last time, really, if you must know."

He looks pleased and surprised. "Really?"

I laugh in spite of myself. "Yes, really! Don't look so modest, I'm sure it's not all *that* unheard-of, for women to tell you they want you."

I am obviously angling; but he won't bite. "Oh, you might be surprised—"

Now it is my turn to change the subject. "Are you going to be at Jac's, for Ellen's party?" Jac Holzman, president of Elektra, and critic Ellen Sander are now an item, and he is giving a birthday party for her next week, at his apartment in the posh Butterfield House on West 12th Street.

"Oh yeah, sure—especially if you're going to be there. Tell me," he says abruptly, "was that going on—the two of them being together, I mean—when you were up to see me that day at the Plaza and she showed up, or did they only get started later?"

"Oh, later; I think a few months later."

"Interesting." He stands up, obedient to increasingly agitated signals from the stage. "Well, back to the salt mines. Stop backstage in between shows, if you feel like it. Bring a friend."

I just might do that.

Opening night at the Felt Forum. Once again through those pungent tunnels, now choked with groupies beating like butterflies on the successive sets of glass doors, Takeuswithyou!, pleading, hoping, fluttering. We—Bruce Harris and his wife, Bobbi, and David Walley—push past them without acknowledging them, not so much out of hauteur or rudeness or terminal coolness as because we have done a good bit of assorted drugs on the way here, and we are just a lit-tle blasted.

In between sets is good for visits backstage: The rule is, between and after, not before. Prior to a show musicians want to concentrate on the upcoming performance, not entertain visitors like the Sun King at some levée. But now we are all clumped together in the dressing rooms and spilling over into the corridors; the first show went extremely well, and the Doors are in a good collective mood.

I have dressed very carefully indeed for this evening, and am wearing a black jersey minidress over thigh-high black leather boots. The dress has a bare laceup back, about a foot wide and down to my waist; I am wearing it back to front. When I took off my fur coat, outside before the show, silence fell in a twenty-foot radius of my seat; I glance down now, as I did then, to make sure I am still inside the dress. It was a rather gratifying moment—though next to Pam just now I feel like a cow—and Jim, when he comes over to greet me, has a hard time keeping his eyes above my collarbone. Even more gratifying. As I head back to my seat for the second show, I surreptitiously push myself a little deeper into each side of the dress, pull the lacing a little tighter. Excess is a fine thing, but a little caution is good too.

The second show is even better than the first, though I am starting to come down a little off the mescaline I snorted earlier. I am barely back in my seat before the lights go down and a very familiar voice leers encouragingly from the stage. My heart nearly stops.

"YEEEAAAHHH—we're really gonna get it ONNNNN t'night, right?"

The audience giggles and emits a few polite catcalls, plainly unimpressed, but long before the show is over, most of it is clogging the aisles and thronging at the foot of the stage, arms upstretched and waving like Christmas ferns, Touchmetouchme, as if the white-shirted Morrison, glowing like faint radium in the semidarkness, were a piece of the True Cross.

I sink down into the depths of my seat. God, I love to hear him sing, his voice is so perfectly suited to my taste and his songs. But I know I am lost. Sunk. Doomed. He's got me. All the dozens of times I have sat like this in the dark to hear him, watch him performing his appointed task, and it's always like that first time at Ondine all over again. There he is, singing his heart out, being pelted with flowers, joints, bras, panties, lighted cigarettes and other tokens of affection: the man who says he wants to fuck me right there on the Forum floor.

The music is superb, they are so on tonight: things like "Money" and "Who Do You Love," even that scaly leviathan of a theatre piece, "The Celebration of the Lizard," stuff that New York Doors freaks seldom get to hear; songs I first heard them rehearsing back last fall: "Roadhouse Blues," "The Spy," "Maggie M'Gill."

"Now we're gonna give you a famous radio song," Jim announces, and Robby Krieger smirks his way into "Light My Fire" . . .   The tone is pretty much set for the other shows—at one, John Sebastian comes up to blow harp on the encores—and the proceedings are being recorded for future album use (*Absolutely Live*).

For all the musical excellence, though, I notice that Jim cannot control his crowd the way he used to: Several times he is even outshouted, and he taunts back ("Well, that's New York for ya, the only people who rush the stage are guys"; later, protesting, "You can pick your teeth with a New York joint . . ."). Finally it comes to an end, though the Forum is shaking to the foot-stamping of the insistent audience, wanting Moremoremore even after endless encores, shaking as the Alps must have shaken to the tread of Hannibal's elephants. I choose not to revisit Jim backstage—I really don't much feel like having to watch Pam hang all over him, and I might say something I'd regret and that might not even be mine to say. Instead, I head home alone in the bitter cold night.

Monday night sees me back uptown again, at the New York Hilton on West 54th Street, where Elektra is throwing a party for the Doors in the West Penthouse ("Better view," says Jac Holzman, "you can't see the park from the East one"), which nobody in New York would miss for all the farms in Cuba.

The venue, reached by private elevator, is a spacious expanse of

floor-to-ceiling windows overlooking Central Park (Jac is right), furnished in glass and modern—sleek puffy low sofas, leather and chrome
and mirrors. The most decorative things there are the guests: the rock
press corps in its droves, of course, but also such as newscaster Pia
Lindstrom and assorted Warhol superstars and other musicians who happen to be in town, and naturally the Doors themselves, looking tired
and a little daunted but very game, relieved to be done with the Forum
grind and pleased they have done so well.

I have snorted a little cocaine before leaving home, and again in
the car on the way here; it is beginning to wear off, so I go to the powder
room, pun intended, and do some more from the surprisingly capacious
depths of my jade and silver poison ring. When I return to the party,
I ensconce myself on a velvet divan strategically placed to catch most
of the downstairs action (place is a duplex, after all); the upper regions
will just have to take care of themselves.

My back knows when Jim comes in; I swing my hair across my face
and turn for a quick look. He is of course with Pam—who has made a
real fashion effort for the event, and is clad in a tie-dyed T-shirt, jeans,
clogs and a mirror-and-embroidery Indian vest. She is hanging on his
arm, and I have to turn away.

I console myself with another hit—brazenly in the open this time,
nobody seems to care—and wander around talking to friends and enemies
impartially; my escort of record—just a friend from the magazine—has
vanished and I don't see him anywhere. Probably trying to score.

Plowing through a clutch of Warhol oddities, in the open space
beyond I suddenly come face-to-face with Jim. He is alone, and he smiles
down at me.

"Nice outfit," he says, the smile widening and warming; as at the
rehearsal studio back last fall, a smile that is far too intimate and easily
read by others to risk giving me in public.

"Thank you," I say coolly, but I am nervous for other reasons too:
I am upholding New York's dress honor tonight (well, only *just* holding
it up . . .) in a cream leather sleeveless tight-bodiced tunic cut down to
my nipples (matching skin-tight pants stuffed into suede boots), and I
am afraid to breathe. There seems to be a bosom theme this week, a tits
subtext . . .   Only a braided knot holds the bodice closed, there is bare
skin down to my navel and a gold snake twines itself around my right
bicep. It is unbelievably excessive even for *this* room, and I am very

proud, for I have made the leather outfit myself. (The real triumph comes later, when Pamela actually compliments me on it, wants to know where she can get one like it—all this in front of Jim.)

He offers me a drink. "Why are you dressed like Genghis Khan's favorite wife?" he teases. "I like it, I like it! But I don't usually see you wearing clothes like that, do I."

"Well, no, I don't guess you do."

"Now, why is that, I wonder?" He pretends to ponder deeply this little foible of mine, not wearing sexy leather outfits where he can see them.

"Oh, I don't know," I say vaguely. "What's this movie later on?"

"Jac's showing *The Thirty-nine Steps* at midnight. Hitchcock," he adds helpfully.

"Very appropriate."

"Why don't we just go over here and talk—"

He takes my arm and draws me aside, out of the ebb and flow of the party. Out of earshot, maybe, but not out of sightline; I am all too uncomfortably aware of the covert and not-so-covert eyetracks all *over* us.

Jim leans down to whisper into my hair. "I want to fuck you."

"A man of fixed ideas," I whisper back, and he laughs.

"You know I'm going to be in town for a while? I really want to spend some time with you."

"Well—call."

When the phone rings the next afternoon I am not at all surprised.

"That was an—interesting evening."

"Wasn't it."

"Can I come over?"

He's in bed with me an hour later. We make love passionately for a couple of hours, almost without a word exchanged, he was tearing at my clothes before the apartment door was even closed behind him. Then we just cuddle for a while.

"Jim?" I ask presently. He is lying so still beside me, staring up at the hammered-tin ceiling, watching the reflections of the candle flames in the silver panels; my head is on his chest.

"Tell me about your family," he says out of nowhere, rather abruptly. "Do you have any sisters, brothers?"

"One sister, two brothers, all younger; we're all four years apart . . . You?" (Though I already know.)

"A sister and a brother. I'm the oldest too."

I snuggle closer, wondering at his willingness to speak of this. He has mentioned his family to me several times before, but only in the briefest of fashions, all but parenthetically, and I have never dared to press him.

"Did you have to go through all that stuff I did, that groundbreaker trip? The oldest child always has to go through torture, doing everything before everybody else, and then all the others have it easier when it's their turn to do it." I sit up, stare down at him, suddenly struck by what seems a totally stoned insight, though we have had neither drugs nor drink. "That's really what you're doing now, isn't it? Only you're just doing it on a much, *much* bigger scale—"

He looks at me, amused, a little frightened, a little embarrassed. "Hey, you know, it wasn't *my* idea—"

"Oh, was it not! Then whose *was* it? You just *happened* to find yourself in the right place at the right time looking the right way and thinking the right thoughts, with the right talent to bring it all off—"

"Must've been my karma," he drawls, in that pinched, dumb-Southerner voice he likes to affect.

"Yeah, probably." He looks annoyed at my easy agreement; he was being sarcastic, not expecting me to take him literally. Little does he know . . . "But don't you think there might be just a little more to it than that?"

"Well, you seem to know all about it, you tell me."

"No, Jim, *you* tell *me*." It is a chance he has never given me before, a chance to ask below the surface and not seem to push or pry. But he remains resolutely silent, and after a while I ask very gently, "What about your parents?"

The eyes flicker. "They were bullies," he whispers.

"What, you mean they *hit* you?" I am immediately outraged, angry and fiercely protective of him.

"No. Worse."

"They didn't know what you needed?"

He smiles, and it is that smile you smile in the face of howling pain, bleak and gallant and a terrible thing to see. He is not faking *this*, not lying about *this* as he once lied about his folks being dead. This is most real.

"They didn't know I was there needing."

I tighten my arms around him and kiss him above his heart. "I'm so sorry—"

"No, it's okay, it all happened a long time ago. I don't think about them anymore, don't want to talk about them."

"No, right, you just tell people they're dead—"

"Not for a long time," he murmurs. "C'mon, honey—"

"It's lying."

"Sort of."

"Would you ever lie to *me*? I think I could take almost anything from you but a lie. Promise me you won't ever lie to me."

"I could—but I might be lying when I promised it."

"I'd know."

At that he smiles with real delight. "Yeah—I think you might at that— But what does it matter? And I don't want to talk about my parents anymore either, okay?" He is a little cross, with me or with them I can't tell.

"Okay! Sure! Fine! *You're* the one who brought it up—"

But for whatever reasons, he can't leave it alone. After a moment or two of tense silence, he asks, "Do you, you know, *talk* to your parents?"

I shift back onto my side to look at him. "Well, yeah. Sure. There's lots of stuff I don't tell them—I wouldn't tell them about this, for instance"—I gesture to our two naked and intertwined bodies in the candlelight—"but I talk to my mom at least twice a week; my sister and my grandma too."

I look to see if this is boring him, but strangely enough he seems deeply interested, so I go on for a while, about my love and friendship for my sister, and how as children she and I, as the eldest, would gang up on our brothers, and the fifteen first cousins we have on my mother's side and the six more on my father's, and my grandparents all of whom are still living but my mother's father who died when I was a child. Every few moments he interrupts to ask me questions, shyly curious, eager to know; as if he had had no idea that people of our generation, living very different trips, could actually be on affectionate terms with parents and siblings and yet keep the trip's integrity intact. I wonder just how much of an act it all is, and then am ashamed of myself for wondering, as he says very quietly, "You're really lucky, you know."

"I know," I say, as softly. "*You're* here; how much luckier could I get?"

CHAPTER
10

I ARRIVE AT JAC'S PROMPTLY AT SEVEN. AFTER SOME thought I have decided it would be best to have a beard along for the evening, so I have asked David to accompany me. This, I realize, could be a mistake—he's got this weird jones about Jim, thinks if he's Socratic enough with him Jim will straighten up his poet act—but I'd rather have an escort than go alone, and I know I can trust him. So I ask; he's delighted to oblige, and I'm grateful.

Jac—tall, professorial-looking—meets us at the door, kisses us both. "Come on in, you're both beautiful!" Yeah, Jac, we're hip . . .

It is a cheerful company assembled to celebrate Ellen's birthday, and many of the faces from the concerts and the Hilton party are among it. They sure looked a lot better behind coke, or that mescaline even—but I begin the round of hugs-and-kisses. Jim is already here, off in a corner with a small admiring multitude, telling the mild little impudicities he fondly calls dirty jokes. Bruce Harris, seeing us, detaches himself from Jim's audience and comes over at once.

"Welcome to the Breakfast Club!"

I give him a withering look. "I've been up and working since ten this morning, not lying slugabed and debauched until half an hour ago, like most of this lot." No—nor like Jim and me, either, but he's not supposed to know *that*.

"Jim worked," Bruce protests. "He had two interviews this afternoon alone."

I chortle about that all the way in to dinner, a very fine repast that ends with plum pudding and hard sauce and a playing of Phil Spector's original mix of *Let It Be* on Jac's astrotechnical system—it looks as if it could launch moon rockets at the very least. After some mild conversation with acquaintances who happen by, I decide I am too much in the traffic pattern, and head for a big squashy armchair over by the window to remove myself from the loop. I am not there two minutes when somebody takes the chair next to mine, leans over without a word and puts a glass of sherry into my hand. I don't even look at him.

"Thanks, Morrison."

"Good party," he says after a pause, with the conviction that comes of drink taken.

"Yis, 'tis," I agree in my best Dublinese.

He squirms a bit in the chair, leans closer. "Who's that guy you came in with, is he your husband?"

"That's David Walley, you've met him three times in the past week, and no, he is *not* my husband."

"Well, why didn't you bring your husband, then?"

I stare at him. "Hey. This is *me*. Patricia. Remember? I'm not married. Not to him, not to anybody. He's not even my boyfriend. I don't even *have* a boyfriend. I only have you; you *do* remember *that*? I just brought him along so people wouldn't get the wrong idea about you and me."

"What idea would that be?"

"Oh, you know, the same old one, the one where I rip your clothes off and then I—" I detail what I'd like to do to him, in a voice that sounds about as excited as if I'm describing a crochet pattern, determined to make him blush. He does—the color is marvelous—but he also looks intrigued.

"Well! Listen, why don't you come back to the hotel with me?"

"Oh, right, and Pam can sleep on the couch? I *don't* think so! Besides, I'm still not sure I believe you."

"About what?"

"About not being married."

"Well, I'm not. I'll show you my passport— Patricia! I *swear* it! I'm not!" He's laughing, but he also sounds a little alarmed.

"Okay—but there's one thing *I'm* not."

"What's that?"

I give him a very straight look. "A starfucker."

Jim stares at me for a long, long moment, then closes his eyes and smiles beatifically, nodding to himself. Still nodding and smiling, he gets up and walks away. See you later . . .

Ellen, Bobbi Harris, David and I are having a thoroughly exhilarating discussion of rock roots in classical music when Pam comes up and takes the empty chair beside me, on the other side from where Jim had been sitting. She is wearing some Moroccan rag (I have still not managed to break free of the need to flaunt my tits—wonder why—and have on yet another scooped-down-to-there piece of excess, this one in beaded suede); she looks hopeful and eager, like a little girl wanting to join a game being played by the big kids.

"Can I get in on this? It sounds really good."

"By all means," I say graciously. I am dying to find out if the little pieface can talk.

Ten minutes later, the vote is split: There is indeed a Basic Californian vocabulary, of about the usual eight hundred words, operating somewhere behind those red bangs; but I don't know if I could describe, under oath, what she does with it as 'talking.'

Semantics aside, Pam is talking about Jim, and it took her all of about one and a half minutes to get onto him.

"Jim's SOOOUUULLL is gone from his BOOOODDDYYY," she trills, fluttering her short little fingers and rolling her big bluish eyes up to the ceiling, where presumably Jim's soul is now hanging out.

Ellen gives a disbelieving delicate snort. "Pam, dear, you're very young and very *here*. If that was true, he wouldn't be able to write songs anymore, would he—"

"Oh, he can still write *songs*," she says scornfully, doubtfully. "But they're just not the same as they used to be, they used to all be about *me*, and now on the new album there's maybe only one or two . . . It's really an accident that we're still together at all, that's what it is, a cosmic accident."

David mutters something by way of excuse and exits in one damned hurry; I glare suspiciously after him, certain I can see his shoulders quivering with suppressed mirth. Pam is not checked in her rap for even a tiny instant.

"We met—it was like fate!—I was walking down the street thinking about dropping out of art school and there he was. It was, it was truly fate, we were both very young and impressionable, it was a very crucial and important time for each of us. Then he got really famous, with the band and all—but we kept seeing each other, and breaking up, and getting back together and breaking up again. I keep telling him, *Jiiimmm,* you've *outgrooowwwnnn* me"—this in a girlishly charming little whine —"You're so much more *advaaanced* in your development than I am, Jiiimmm; but he just laughs. Still, I think his soul really *has* left him. He's a shell, now."

" 'Scuse," I say politely, and follow David to some other room. I wish it were some other time zone.

On my way there I run into the shell. I look up at him, and— slowly, utterly helplessly—the same grin transfigures us both.

"Don't say it, Patricia," he begs. "Don't even *think* it—"

"I don't *have* to say it, do I . . ."

"No. No—but just don't, okay?" He pauses, half-expecting me to blast him with it anyway. I just look guilelessly up at him. "I'm staying on in New York for a while, can I see you again later in the week?"

My smile turns wicked. "As a matter of fact, you can. Tomorrow night. I've been invited to dinner with you and Pam and Leon and Raeanne." Raeanne Rubenstein is a photographer who lives a few blocks from me in the East Village; she has taken some photos of Pamela's new boutique, Themis—or rather pictures of Pam and Jim and assorted hangers-on in the boutique Jim is paying for, to be more accurate about it. I couldn't resist the invitation, and I say so now.

Jim shakes his head, but I can see he finds it as funny as I do. "Man, the Irish really like to live dangerously, I had no idea—"

"What dangerously?" I say with some scorn. "Pam doesn't know you and I are—involved, right? Right, and neither does Leon or Raeanne, unless *you've* opened your mouth about it. I'm bringing David with me, and he does know, but he's a good friend and he won't say anything. It'll be fine. You'll see."

"Yeah, I guess I will."

"Jim really likes you," says someone to me in the bathroom, where we have gone to brush our hair and fix our makeup; no drugs, not tonight.

I drop my hairbrush at this unsolicited and not entirely welcome observation; she watches with interest.

"You were the only person he went up to tonight, did you know
that," she continues. "Everybody else had to go up to him themselves.
Are you avoiding him or something? Or don't you like him? I know you
like the music."

"Let us say I could like him much too much," I say lightly and
truthfully, "and we'll leave it at that."

"You're probably right. No good getting unethical."

I think about that all the way home, and for much of the night.
Then I laugh. If I'd been *less* ethical I'd be spending the night with Jim
right now at the hotel, or here; he'd be with me, I wouldn't be lying
here alone trying not to think of him uptown with Pam. But perhaps
there's a bigger point here . . .

Perhaps, just maybe, I haven't been as—unbiased about him, critically, artistically, as I should be, or could be, or, indeed, used to be.
I don't *think* I've been any easier on him in reviews and such since we've
been lovers—if anything, I think I've been harder on him, and that
might be just as unethical as the other—but really, am I the one to
judge? If you fuck a star, does that always make you a starfucker? Doesn't
it count if you're in love with the star, and he seems to care about you?
If he'd been a lawyer your best friend had fixed you up with, would that
make you a lawyerfucker? I'm in the music business, I meet music business
people—who the hell *else* am I supposed to fall in love with?

I go round with this one well into the postmidnight hours, and
finally decide that it's okay that I, a rock critic, am in love with Jim,
a rock star, only because I am going to be twice as hard on him in print
as I am on everybody else. This seems to me fair and right, and at last
I fall asleep.

David and I walk over to Third Avenue, to Raeanne's apartment-studio
in a tenement building over shops. Jim, Pam and Leon are all in the
kitchen with Raeanne, looking at the Themis photographs, which are
intended for some fashion spread in a glossy pop magazine. We all know
one another by now; everybody says hi, how are you, nice to see you
again. Jim and I very carefully do not look at one another straight on,
but I can see his smile out of the corner of my eye.

We talk for a while, and I mention that the snowstorm going down
for the past couple of hours has worsened, we'd better go now if we're

going to get anything to eat. We decide to walk to dinner anyway, to Café Il Faro, a local favorite on East 14th Street. Bundling up to venture forth into the storm, Pam admires my shaggy, embroidered sheepskin Afghan coat.

"It's really groovy—and it looks so *warm*."

"Yes, well, sometimes you need that in New York. I don't suppose it gets cold enough in L.A. for one of these."

"Ohhhh—I don't know, Jim, how cold does it get in L.A.?"

I run down the stairs and miss the end of the climatology lesson. Hell, she's got on a maxicoat with a raccoon collar, I don't *think* she's going to freeze . . . worse luck. If I look at Jim just now, both of us will lose it completely, so on our walk I try to keep my eyes off him.

Hard to do: He looks so happy in the swirling snow, walking along with his face turned up to the falling flakes as the storm deepens, his features screwed up like a little boy's under the streetlamp glow as the snow falls on him, trying to catch the melting flakes on his tongue, slipping once or twice and landing on his rear in the ankle-deep drifts.

Dinner is—strange. David, as I knew he would be, is a great help, steering the conversation into cultural-intellectual waters where Pam can only dog-paddle, while the rest of us play like dolphins. Mean, but there it is.

I am sitting facing Jim across the table, with Raeanne on my right across from Pam; David is on my left at the table's head, Leon facing him on Raeanne's right at the table's foot. About halfway through the meal—I am so nervous I can't eat, and they have *good* food here; I choke down a few shrimp and that's it—the vibes between Jim and me have grown almost visible, and quite definitely palpable. Raeanne looks quizzically at Jim, then turns to me with a look of wondering, half-laughing curiosity.

"*What* is going ON here?" she exclaims. I blush and shrug my shoulders.

Jim saves the moment with a little anecdote about how the police came to bust Pam for traffic tickets one morning, just came right into the unlocked apartment, the two of them lying there naked and asleep. Not exactly what I feel like hearing, but it serves to break the twangling tension of the moment—in another thirty seconds I'd have 'fessed up to everything—and Raeanne seems distracted. Jim and I and David just look at one another, then at our plates.

At last it is over, and we all trail back outside. It is still snowing, that unearthly quiet and light that come over New York in a snowstorm thick and bright around us. It is only eleven; still time for Jim, Pam and Leon to catch the midnight showing of Alfred Hitchcock's *Topaz* uptown, if they hurry.

We bid them goodnight under the restaurant canopy—hugs and kisses from all for all, the only time Pamela Courson and Patricia Kennealy are ever to embrace in amity; then they head for First Avenue and a cab uptown, while the three of us walk back to our East Village homes. Nobody looks back.

Two nights later Jim bursts through the door I have opened to him, his coat barely off before he takes out a little box from a pocket and puts it into my hands.

"Go on, open it, it won't bite." He drags me through into the living room, eager to see whatever it is in decent lamplight.

It is a lovely antique ring, obviously costly, which he slips on my hand, trying several fingers until he finds the one it best fits. I stare down at it; nobody has ever given me anything half so beautiful before.

"Oh, Jim, it's gorgeous, but it's *way* too valuable, I can't possibly accept it."

"You have to."

"I don't *have* to do anything."

"Well, I want you to. Please, Patricia. I saw it and I wanted to give it to you. Wanted *me* to be the one to give it to you."

I am silent for a moment. This is getting serious, and after a bit more of a pause I say so.

He is unconcerned. "Sure. Because I'm a serious kind of guy." The tone is light, the expression anything but. I thank him prettily and profusely, and don't take the ring off for *weeks*.

It is snowing again tonight; we do not make love at once, but lounge on fur throws and big squashy pillows in front of the fireplace and talk for a long time. Then:

"Sing me something," he demands.

Pardon me? *I'm* supposed to carol away a cappella to one of the greatest rock vocalists on the face of the planet?

"Are you *crazy?*" I riposte. "What if I don't? Are you gonna pull one of those numbers on me like you pulled on Ellen Sander last year?"

He unleashes one of those insane giggles. "That was really cruel, I'm sorry I did that to her—and she even invited me to her birthday party the other night in spite of that. Now, if that had been *you*, I bet you'd have lit the candles on the cake with me... But you're just gonna have to sing, Kennealy, and that's all there is to it."

"Oh yes? Or what?"

"Or—or I'll tie you to the bed, just fuck your brains out." His eyes are closed, a faint smile on his face, his voice low and teasing.

"Go ahead. I'd kind of like you to tie me up. Well—once in a while, anyway."

He looks at me, clearly surprised, and more than a little nonplussed. This is either major challenge or big-time trust, and he is not yet sure which it is, or what to do about it.

"It's not just to fuck," he says after a while. "It's to fuck *you*, make love to *you*—"

"I know that. And it's because it's *you*— But first I'll sing to you."

He settles down expectantly into the furs, his head on my thigh. I ponder a little—I don't think some Child ballad lament would be really the thing here—and then it comes to me.

" 'Western Wind, when wilt thou blow,
     The small rain down can rain?
     Christ, that my love were in my arms,
     And I in my bed again,
     And I in my bed again.' "

It is a medieval love lyric, something he remembers at once from his college reading. My voice is a typical amateur folk alto—I can carry a tune and that's about it—but after a quavery start I gain confidence as I sing.

Still with his head in my lap, he starts to hum the simple melody, and then joins in on the vocal. The baritone and alto sound surprisingly sweet together—I still can't believe I have the nerve to sing a duet with Jim Morrison—but then we really get into it. We sing in unison, we sing in canon, we sing in varying harmonies. We sing our hearts out: bits of liturgical music, a beautiful Tudor "Alleluia" that I teach him, even a chant to the Goddess.

We finish off with sighs of satisfaction. "Nobody ever sang to *me* before," he remarks. "It's nice, I like it... If I'd known you could sing like that, I'd have made *you* sing last year instead of Ellen..." He seems all but asleep; the house is very quiet. "Now that the buffalo's gone, the tribes will all go hungry this winter."

"What?!" I start to laugh. "What the hell does *that* mean?"

"Got me, honey," he says with a grin. "Let's go to bed."

The next morning is clear and bright; the snow has stopped, though it is still very cold. I wake up with him warm beside me; I look at him, then stare for a long time at the ring on my hand, resolutely barring from my mind and my mood all thought of Pamela, presumably uptown alone at the Navarro, though I wouldn't put money on it. But later, after we make love a few times, *very* intense even for us—Jim invariably likes to fuck by the dawn's early light, much more so than I do, though he is quite happy to continue amorous activities until any hour of the night as well—he mentions her himself.

"You know, it's really all right—you and me. I mean, as far as Pam is concerned. I can tell it's been bothering you."

I look up sharply. "You mean she knows about this? About us?"

"Well, not specifically you, I don't think. But she knows I've been spending time with someone—well, she'd have to, wouldn't she, since I haven't been at the hotel the nights I've been with you—and I think she knows it's not just some groupie but somebody real."

"And that's okay with her?"

"Sure. But I don't really care if it isn't. She's not my wife, I don't have to answer to her. Besides, she's got, uh, *friends* of her own, this French count or something, some movie cat, bunch of other guys as well. I told you before, we don't live together or have an exclusive arrangement; we're not married and what I do is really my own business." He pauses, clearly debating whether he wants to say this, then says it. "And considering the fact that she's into heroin, nothing I do should be *any* business of hers."

I gasp. "Heroin! But that's—are you sure, Jim?"

He really doesn't want to elaborate on it, a little sorry he brought it up, but obviously thinking it's something I should know.

"Yeah—she tries to keep it this big deep dark secret, but I've known about it for a long time. It wasn't so much at first, but lately—well, I guess I just thought you should hear it from me before you heard it from somebody else. It sort of explains why. Why I'm here, I mean. With you."

He glances over at me, as if willing me to ask—something. But I am still far too shy and insecure in our relationship to question him on anything of the sort: why me, why Pam, whyever, certainly not about Pam's smack habit (though I do know junkies aren't big on sex . . .); and the moment passes.

Instead, we change the subject with a vengeance: We talk about the concerts, Ellen's birthday party, the band, the new album, the Hilton party ("I had the feeling," he says wickedly, "that Jac wanted us all to clear out early, so the two of them could run around that living room naked, jumping from one couch to another"), the dinner at Il Faro.

But it is time to get up for real: I start by brushing out my tangled hair—he's really rough on it, can't keep his hands out of it and it always ends up in knots—on my knees in front of the big mirror, bent sideways so that the ends of the strands almost touch the floor. Jim watches for a while in silence.

"It's like watching the sun come up," he says at last. "Power, inevitability, ancient mystery—no, don't stop, it's beautiful. It's like drowning. Let me do it."

He takes the brush from me and pulls it through my hair; I close my eyes against the feel of his hands and the tug of the brush. Now I know how my cat feels when I brush her; I'd be purring if only I could.

Jim is in town for the whole next week as well, though the rest of the Doors entourage has gone back to L.A. Pam's still here, too, but that doesn't stop him coming down to see me every other night or so, even some afternoons: We go out to dinner in Chinatown and at Luchow's on 14th Street; sometimes I make him dinner and we just stay in. Of course I would like to see even more of him than I do, but I have calls upon my time too: I'm still an editor, I still have a column to write, there's John Sebastian at the Bitter End, Jack Bruce at the Fillmore East, an upcoming party at Ahmet Ertegun's East Side townhouse for Delaney & Bonnie (Bramlett, who will later, like me, have a cameo in the Doors movie—she plays a barmaid, I play Maura).

On the last night we spend together this trip, Jim is more distracted than I have yet seen him. I have made a private resolution not to inquire into things he does not choose to tell me—as much for fear of the answers I might get as out of respect for his privacy—but after a couple of hours I decide I just can't stand watching him try to fight it.

"What's the matter?" I ask, as gently and nonthreateningly as possible. "Jim? Do you want to talk to me about it?"

I have used the voice I have heard Maura use so many times, and to my amazement and delight, it works. He turns to me at once, a look of openness and relief on his face.

"You know, I think I do, actually. If anybody could help— It's the trial, the Miami one. It's coming up later this year, and I'm getting a little nervous. Somebody was talking about it today, and I guess it just —got to me." He laughs. "Why don't you come down there and be with me, I'm going to need all the friendly faces I can get—maybe I'll just fly in a bunch of people for courtroom support, a cheering section."

I hesitate. "Was the concert as—weird as we all heard it was?"

He really laughs this time. "You mean did I really do it? No, Patricia. No, I didn't. I think I thought I *wanted* to do it, maybe I even started to do it. But I didn't."

"Hey, I'm not on the jury, you don't have to convince *me*! I'm on your side already. I'd be happy to be a character witness for you, but I'm afraid I'm much too prejudiced in your favor."

"Well, let's *hope* so."

I roll over onto him, resting my chin on his chest, looking up with wonder into his face.

"You're really worried about this, aren't you, really scared. Do you think they have any kind of case? Surely not!"

He meets my eyes consideringly. "Who knows? It's all so fucking political. I'm just afraid of being the sacrificial lamb for everybody else; the scapegoat, the ritual victim. It's what happens to shamans sometimes, when they take on the 'sins' of the people. You know, all that The King Must Die stuff."

"Don't say that," I protest, instinctively, immediately; because I *do* know, because he has named, however jestingly (and I think not jestingly at all), something I have been feeling for a long time now, and already I would do anything to ward off harm from him.

He's flip again. "Maybe you could put a curse on the judge."

I smile, which was his intention. "No, I couldn't do that—but I could put some protection on *you*. . ." Well, *extra* protection; I've had a few protective numbers on him for quite some time now—though I know already nothing will ever be enough to keep him safe.

He thinks about it for a while. "No," he says at last, definitely but reluctantly. "I think I'd better do this one straight, leave the fates untampered with and all that. Tell me some more about witchcraft," he commands abruptly. "Are there witch—for lack of a better word, sacraments?"

I respond to his obvious wish to change the subject. "Oh, sure. Only we don't call them that, of course. But we've talked about this a couple of times before, you know. Do I really have to go through it all again?"

"No. Just tell me about witch marriage."

"We've talked about that before, too; even more than a couple of times."

"Well, tell me again."

My defenses begin to go up, as if by instinct, and I rattle off the salient points in a kind of hasty rote gabble.

"It's called handfasting, it's not legal unless you also get a license and get done by a civil authority, within the Craft it's religiously valid and binding."

"How binding?"

"As binding as the two people want to make it. They can take a vow for a year and a day, or a lifetime, or forever. It's their choice."

"Suppose one of them dies?"

"They're still married. As the ceremony says, death does not part, only lack of love. As long as there is love, there is a bond between them."

He is silent a very long time. "Would you ever want to get married like that—you yourself?"

It is more than a question, less than a proposal: a suggestion, perhaps, along the lines of 'If I were to ask you, what do you think you might say?', and it creates immediate tension in the air as it hangs between us.

I look at him and speak my heart. "It's the only way I ever *would* get married, quite honestly; the only marriage ceremony that would ever mean anything to me. For me, that would be the only bond that'd be real to me, no matter what it might look like in other people's eyes, or before the law. It's the promise I would make before the Goddess to the man I love, and he to me. I don't care about the rest of it." I give him a teasing grin to lighten the astounding solemnity that has settled upon us both as I was speaking. "And, of course, if worse ever came to worst, it'd never see the inside of divorce court. There's a lot to be said for handfasting, actually."

"So it seems, so it would—seem." Again a silence, and I do not dare look at him, afraid to let him see what he could not fail to see in my face.

"Patricia—" he says at last, and I inhale raggedly against the unknown. "Patricia. I can't talk about it now, not yet. I just want you to know, though, that I— If I ever—"

That word is in the air, but neither of us will say it just yet, out of fear, out of pride, out of terror that the other won't say it back. Yet for some time now our letters have been signed so, more intimate salutations than 'Dear' have long graced them . . .

"Let's go to bed," I say softly. But once there he makes no immediate move toward me—unprecedented—and I look over at him curiously.

"Is anything wrong? We don't have to, you know."

"I know," he says, marveling. "That's why I want to, and why we will, in a few minutes. There's something I have to say to you first—"

Again it is as if I have been flash-frozen by his words; I go still and small with fear of what he might say: He's really married to Pam after all, he's got a hundred other girlfriends and he likes all of them better than he likes me (well, I know he sees a *few* others, plus the groupies; but I don't think about it), I'm no good in bed—a million fears flip past like cards.

But he does not see my terror, is too absorbed in what he is feeling, and goes on talking with a kind of shy amazement, as if this is something he hadn't ever expected to be saying, and is filled with wonder at the fact that he *is* saying it.

"I know this may be a little difficult for you to believe, especially right now, but this is the first time I've ever felt like this. When I came back here with you that first night, I was a little apprehensive as to what, uh, physical intimacy was going to do to our friendship. But it only made it better, and then, the other night, when you told me you weren't a starfucker—like I really didn't *know* that, right? And just, you know, keeping in touch, calls and letters—it's so relaxed, because we've been friends all that time, and it's so exciting too, because we've been so much more than that all along, and now it's here. I'm really—surprised."

"How—surprising." Actually, I am beyond thrilled to hear Jim say all this, especially with his earlier half-spoken implication of spiritual commitment as well. I am at a strange place within, certain I have heard at least the promise of a promise, and just as certain I have not heard the word I myself cannot yet manage to speak.

"Ah, c'mon, Kennealy, you know what I'm trying to say! You and I— It's like—like I was just any guy you—cared about."

I roll my eyes. "Well, what else do you think you are *but* somebody I care about? Listen, rock stars really don't interest me, they're vain and stupid and shallow, and the only good thing about them is their music. And musicians are fucking *crazy*: It's usually a big mistake to even meet the people you admire, let alone go to bed with them. But with you—well, with you it was never like that. You, the music, everything together—*you, your* music—right from the first minute I ever saw you—"

I am growing increasingly flustered, trembling a little, plagued by blushes, full of things I want so much to say to him and am so shy and scared of saying, of *thinking*. He is just grinning hugely now, waiting, not helping me at all. I pull myself together and try again.

"You just love seeing me like this, don't you— Okay, right! There's only been one rock star I ever thought was good enough to come home with me—who *deserved* to come home with me—and he's the one in bed with me right this minute. You really are—and it was in spite of the fact of the stardom, not because of it, but it was because of the music, can you understand that? All *I* have to say is, it sure took *you* long enough to decide you wanted to come home with me. Didn't you think I might be somebody you'd—you know, want?"

" 'Want'!" He stares at me, then kisses me, very gently, between my breasts. "I told you the last time I was here, how much I wanted you. It took as long as it did because I think I knew from that first afternoon that there'd be more to it than just that."

"And? So?"

"You know how shy I am, Patricia."

That's it: I melt. "I do know. It's what endeared you to me in the first place. Didn't *you* know?"

We make love then, more fiercely than ever, and again several times more that night. Then, as we are lying half asleep, tangled together, exhausted and happy, he asks suddenly, "Do you trust me?"

I startle back to wary wakefulness, torn between the desire for utter honesty ("*YES!!*") and the instinct for cautious self-protection (he might not love me after all).

"I *want* to trust you, more than anything," I begin. Then something in his eyes, something he has not said, makes me throw self-protection to the winds, gives me courage and words, and I say them.

"I love you. I love you, Jim. More than I've ever loved anybody. More than I ever *will* love anybody." Before the moment can become unbearable, I add, "Of course, that still doesn't mean I'd trust you with, say, my library card . . ."

He does not seem insulted by the qualification. "You just said you love me."

"Yes."

"That's the first time you've ever said that to me."

"Yes."

"Do you mean it?"

No, of *course* not, I always go around telling jerks I love them, just for practice—

"Yes. I mean it. Does it bother you?"

"No! Oh, no. I don't *think* so. —Well?"

"Well what?"

"Well, aren't you going to ask me if *I* love *you?*"

I look at him, but he will not meet my eyes, and all at once I am consumed by a white flaming anger at what has been done to him: by Pamela, by his parents, by his friends, by others over the years who have said to him what I have just said to him—the ones who hurt him and lied to him and took from him, who held out trust and then ripped it away, who taught him to be suspicious of even a gift of love, who have stolen from him that simple fearless acceptance, that ability to believe without question when someone says I love you. Rage too that they have tainted by their seller's equations this most uncontingent of givings, that their barterous souls have made his own believe that love always carries a price tag, not just a price. Rage, love, protectiveness, tears—

"No," I say then, very gently, letting him see the love, the protectiveness, even the tears; but not the anger. "No, Jim, I'm not going to ask you that. That's not the way I do things. That would be— No, I'm not going to ask you." A tiny pause. "But why did you ask that?"

He smiles and looks at me then, and his eyes are suspiciously bright.

"Now, miss, that would be telling—" He takes my hand and kisses it, draws my hair across his face, like a veil, like a shroud. "I love you, Patricia."

I close my eyes, letting his words go through me, back to the Plaza, back to Ondine, back to a record player in Binghamton; and ahead, to something already dimly revealed; and I accept it all.

And then I look at him. "I know," I say. "I know, Jim. That's why I didn't ask you."

CHAPTER

11

May 1970

THE DOORS ARE PLAYING IN PHILADELPHIA: ALTHOUGH I know Jim will be in New York the week after, and presumably I shall be seeing him then, I suddenly need to see the band in concert, just see *him*, even if I don't get a chance to be with him or even talk to him. So at the last minute I call Leon to tell him I'll be there and I jump on a train.

It being Beltane, May Eve—one of the holiest days in the pagan calendar, the beginning of summer—I have made arrangements to visit some witches in the area, as long as I am down there. But the real reason, of course, is Jim, and I'm not fooling anybody.

It has been a quiet few months, for the Doors as well as for me. They have never really gotten back up to full concert-schedule strength in the wake of the Miami cancellations—since the Felt Forum dates in January they have played only eight gigs, not counting this one—and no doubt the renewed publicity over Jim's upcoming date with Dade County justice is further reducing their workload.

But he keeps the letters coming, even sends me a birthday gift (!) in March (belated, due to the fact that he's on trial in Phoenix, for a bit of hijinks aboard an aircraft last fall—it proves to be a case of mistaken identity, Jim being blamed for the drunken antics of a friend, and the case against him is dismissed), calls me from Boston when the Doors play there in April. I try to get up there, but it doesn't work out, and they're off to Denver and Honolulu before returning to L.A. and back East.

My college friend Noreen is living in Philadelphia now, working as a journalist, and I stay with her in her flat in a lovely old house. Later that Friday evening, we set off for the concert at the Spectrum, a huge sports hall facility clear across town.

I am more than a little nervous, since the morning before I left, I got a telegram from Jim in L.A., reading in its entirety, "Thanks for the pat on the back." This, of course, is his response to my review, in J&P, of his books *The Lords* and *The New Creatures*, now out in a one-volume, purple-jacketed hardcover public edition from Simon & Schuster. I have rapped his knuckles good for self-indulgence, praised his songwriting and command of structures and mood, and advised him to go check out the Preface to the *Lyrical Ballads* one more time before committing any more poems. I have also allowed myself a personal reference that will have—consequences. In return, the telegram: time-dated three in the morning, which doesn't help my nerves.

Leon has left tickets and backstage passes for us—plain manila, no naked females this time—and I know the passes are meant for after the show. Noreen and I take our seats shortly before the lights go down; I do not know it then, but it is to be the last time I will ever see the Doors in concert.

And it's a great way to end my Doors-watching career: a high-energy show ("Hey, PHILADELPHIA!") and a very good one too. Noreen, who has not seen the band since Forest Hills three years back, is impressed. Afterwards, backstage, we are standing in one of the dreary locker rooms talking to Leon and a few others, when Bruce Harris, also down from New York for the gig, comes up to me and grabs my arm. He is looking very grave.

"Boy, Patricia, you better make yourself scarce! I just talked to Jim, he saw your review of his poetry and he's going around saying 'Where the hell is Kennealy, gonna punch that bitch in the mouth when I see her'—"

He is kidding, I think. At least I pray he is, when a voice suddenly comes up behind me and lassoes me into immobility.

"Patricia?"

I close my eyes briefly against the soul panic, then open them and turn resolutely around.

"Jim."

"I thought it was you," he says with satisfaction. "I saw the hair, you know—"

A horseshoe of awed listeners immediately starts to form behind each of us, like the Montagues and the Capulets when Mercutio and Tybalt are getting ready to square off.

I figure I'd better just get into it. "I hear you've been going around saying where the hell is Kennealy, gonna bust her in the chops for that review—"

His face lights up with amusement and a certain considering awareness. "Oh no, no. Did you get my telegram?"

"Indeed I did. Why do you think I'm here?"

"You, uh, have a very excellent prose style."

"Why, thank you, Jim; you have a very promising poetic style."

"I wish you'd said that in the review," he remarks a little wryly.

"Read it again, sweetheart. I did." He looks a little skeptical; I elaborate a bit, to the mingled horror (lèse-majesté!) and delight (*you* tell him, Patricia!) of our audience, then offer some consolation. "Look at it this way: W.S. Gilbert, you know, Gilbert and Sullivan, he only read his bad reviews, and the worse they were the better he liked it. When somebody asked him why, he said that he knew very well how good he was, but what he didn't know was how bad he was."

Jim grins. "I take the point."

I turn suddenly shy, rummage through the depths of the big fringed suede bag slung over my shoulder.

"I have something for you, actually." I hold it out to him: It is a book by A.A. Milne, the one with the "James James Morrison Morrison" poem in it. I found it at the Strand, a famous, huge Village second-hand bookstore where I have taken Jim a few times; it seemed like a message or something, so I have brought it with me to give him.

He knows the poem, of course, and reads some of it aloud; we talk about Milne and Victorian children's literature, and the odd sort of chaps who tended to write it, and I marvel once again at the extent of his erudition. Perhaps bored by the unremittingly intellectual tone of the conversation, the spectator circle begins to break up and drift away.

Which seems to have been Jim's intention: He draws me aside a little.

"I'll be in New York on Monday—I want to fuck you so much, I haven't seen you for so long this time—"

"Last of the big-time romantics, aren't you, Morrison?" But I want him just as much. "Well, call when you get in; or I'll call you, where are you staying?"

"The Chelsea, I think; if not there, then the Navarro." He does not kiss me in front of the watching crowd, but squeezes my hand. "Well, Patricia," he says in a louder voice designed for public consumption, "it's been really nice talking to you again, we should talk more often—but now I have to go and drain my lizard."

He exits with a last grin thrown over his shoulder at me, and I sag all over in relief. Bruce comes over again a few minutes later, shaking his head.

"I can't get over it," he says. "Jim can't stop talking about that review you did—he says it's the first time anyone's ever criticized his *work* and not *him*."

"Well, yeah; but, Bruce, I think most of the poems suck *eggs*. I *said* so. As a poet, he's a great songwriter."

"I know; and Jim knows, but it was just what you had to say about them, constructive criticism, what he could do to improve the style, literary allusions, that kind of thing. He's really impressed."

Bedfellows make strange politics—but I can't say that in front of everybody, though Bruce knows all about it. Later on, I talk to one of the other Doors, though I never take my eyes off Jim across the room.

"Jim seems in good shape," I suggest tentatively.

"He's weird," says the Door with a shrug. "We don't see him too much anymore. We get to the place where we're playing, and he rents a car at the airport and drives himself into town, then buys a case of beer and just drives around all day. When he gets tired he pulls off the road and crashes for a while; when he gets dirty he goes back to the hotel and takes a shower. By then it's usually time to head for the gig. But his stuff always sounds great, so I guess he's basically all right."

"Well, there was that time in San Francisco when he was playing matador with the cable cars," somebody else offers; a Doors associate.

"Good God!" I am really angry. "And you assholes let him do it? Don't you take care of him when he's drunk?"

The associate looks at me with a very level gaze. "You must know by now that nobody at all can do anything at all with Jim when he's drunk."

I wonder if this is a message, or a warning, or what . . . As the party begins to break up, I see Jim looking for me, and I let him do the searching. He comes over hurriedly, tells me yet again to call him, bids me a quick farewell and departs. They're on the road to Pittsburgh the next day.

The rest of my visit goes well—my conference with the witches and old-home week with Noreen—and I return to New York on Sunday primed for anything at all. Out of some stupid idea of pride, or maybe just sheer bloody-mindedness, I do not call Jim until Tuesday morning; but the calls are not returned.

At last I cannot bear it another minute, and after lunch I go over to the Navarro—it's only three blocks from the office—to leave a personal message at the front desk. As I am leaving the hotel, a cab pulls up at curbside; I don't really register the tall figure getting out of it (or maybe I do on some subliminal level and choose to let him pursue *me*), and I turn left to head back to the office along Central Park South. In seconds I am up to New York cruising speed and steaming past the Essex House, when someone looms up beside me on my left and grabs my arm.

I look up, startled, about to deliver a karate chop to a presumed mugger, when I see just in time that it is Jim. He is smiling down at me and a little out of breath, and I am very glad I didn't hit him.

"Why do you New Yorkers have to walk so damn fast?" he complains. "I ran half a block after you to catch you."

And I am caught forever.

We go back to the hotel for him to change his clothes; he puts on a maroon shirt of wool so fine-spun it feels like cotton, a pair of pale gold corduroy pants over brown Frye boots. His hair is down to his shoulders again, the length I like it best, and he looks relaxed and happy. While he changes in the bedroom, I sit on the living room couch listening to records on the small stereo set he has brought with him, or sent out for: the soundtrack to the Costa-Gavras film Z, very stirring and dramatic. We talk about the film as he dresses.

Finally he comes out into the living room, pulls me up off the couch and into his arms for a real kiss. I am a little overwhelmed, and to cover my confusion and sudden shyness I suggest we go for a walk, or for lunch, or for both.

It is a gorgeous spring afternoon; he is hungry, so we stop off briefly at the Jazz & Pop office, then go on a few blocks uptown to the Ginger Man, where he orders steak tartare and I a cheese omelet. But we are both so caught up in one another that neither of us touches more than a bite or two; we are simply talking too hard to eat. The waiter notices, and comes over to inquire.

"Sir? Madam? Is there something wrong with your lunch?"

Jim grins up at him, then across at me. "It's spring, we're in love, we can't eat—"

I blush; the waiter smiles knowingly and departs, reassured. After a glass of wine—no more than that—we leave, walking lazily hand in hand over to Central Park a half-block away. We end up under some white-flowering tree, me sitting, Jim stretched out on the grass with his head in my lap, as usual. We are silent for a long while, just being in the moment; then Jim begins to talk.

"The last time I saw you, my, uh, *friend* and I were having major problems. I just want you to know that it's finished now, it was a poisoned relationship, half pity and half habit. It's been finished for a long time, but now it's over; it's you now, I guess it has been for a while, and when I saw you in Philly the other day I was sure of it."

As he speaks, I have started to tremble, thrilled beyond all measure and also more than a little frightened at what I am hearing; it is too perfect, it can't be happening, it's so much what I *want* to hear that it can't be true . . .

"You don't have to say this, Jim, you know."

"I know I don't. I want to. You never asked me about her, because you're a lady and you knew you had no business asking, so you didn't, not really. I liked that. Well, now it *is* your business, and I wanted you to hear it from me. But that's not all I want you to hear from me—"

He tugs on my hair until my face is bent to his. "The last time I was here we talked about this, and I've been thinking about it a lot lately. You told me about occult marriage, how witches marry—"

"Handfasting. It's how we marry in the Craft. It's only a religious ceremony, strictly private, between the two people and the Goddess and the God, as I think I also told you; not anything the law would recognize."

"You said it was binding between them."

"Morally. Magically. It's a sworn oath before Powers I'm not really sure you understand or accept."

"Does that matter? Wouldn't it be the actual promise that counted?"

He kisses the hair he has twined in his fingers, does not look at me.

"It would count with *me*," I say, very serious now. "But I don't know how it would, or should, count with you."

He smiles. "Why don't you let me worry about that part?" He sits up, takes both my hands in his, assumes an appropriate and traditional attitude. "Miss, I have the great honor to ask if you would do me the *very* great honor of handfasting me."

I hear his words and do not hear them; they seem to be bypassing my ears and falling directly upon my soul, like blows upon a distant drum. I feel as if I am going to faint, or explode, or just float right up through the white-flowered branches above us and out into space.

He looks so young and happy as he says this to me, handsomer than I think I have ever seen him look, his whole face alight with joy. And looking at him I know that I will hold this picture of him in my heart forever, no matter what may come after. But I have not answered him —I am still too staggered by the question—and he begins to look a little anxious at my silence.

"Patricia?"

I take his questioning face between my hands and look at him; I do not smile. There is a kind of joy that is too great for smiling.

"Oh Jim," I say softly. "Oh yes."

He kisses me gently, then again passionately, and leaps to his feet, grabbing my hand and pulling me up with him.

"Let's go."

I am laughing. "Where?"

"To buy a ring, where else?"

We cross the park, arms around one another's waists—startling the wits out of an Elektra secretary sunning herself on the grass, who recognizes us both immediately, and who calls Pauline in a state of high dither as soon as she gets back to her office (Pauline just laughs)—and stop in at the hotel to pick up a jacket for him for later that night.

In the cab on the way uptown—we are both a little giddy with the romance and the suddenness of it all—we agree that we will go through the ceremony the next time he is in New York; there's really no time this trip and I want to talk to my coven about it anyway. In a tiny Irish import shop on Lexington Avenue in the Seventies, we find what I have in mind, though Jim is still astounded that I have firmly rejected Tiffany's.

"Some big old gold fender?" I jeer. "I *don't* think so! A claddagh is what."

"What?"

"Clad-da," I say patiently. "Irish wedding ring, design dates from the sixteenth century. Two hands clasping a crowned heart; it's very romantic, you'll like it."

We pore over the selection: different castings, all sizes and weights, quite a few nice antiques—satiny silver, mellow dark gold. I choose the ring I want, one of the few small enough to fit my finger, in a glowingly patina'd silver.

Jim seems disappointed. "Only *silver*? It's not very—grand."

"Well, silver is sacred to the Goddess"—this in an undertone, lest the elderly County Cork shop owner should hear; and with difficulty too, Jim is pinching me and groping me and tickling me, trying to get me to lose my cool—"and gold is sacred to the God."

"Right—well, I'm getting you a gold one, too," he says, and does, picking it out himself.

"What about yours?" I ask shyly.

He looks a little surprised. "I don't wear rings usually—not very often, anyway."

"Well, you wouldn't have to *wear* it. Just *have* it. And for the ceremony, too. But yours—"

"—would have to be gold," he finishes triumphantly. "See, I catch on fast—and yeah, I think I *would* like one."

After we pick out his ring, Jim takes the antique ring he gave me in January and puts it on my finger next to the silver claddagh.

"That'll be the engagement ring, right?" I tease.

"As long as you're happy, honey—" he says, a little uncertainly.

I fling my arms around his neck; the shop owner beams maternally on us.

"M'darlin', you have no *idea*."

By mutual decision, I keep the rings until such time as they will be needed; we stop back at the magazine offices, then go out to dinner at Trader Vic's in the Plaza, with Pauline and Janice. After, he drags me all the way up to the New Yorker theatre, to see a horrendously dull Godard flick, *Two or Three Things I Know About Her*.

And he falls asleep! I can't believe this! I pinch myself to stay awake, knowing he will quiz me on the damn movie when he wakes up. With perfect timing, he opens his eyes just as the credits start to roll, turns to me with a look of delighted surprise and asks, "Whose little girl are *you?*"

I hit his arm, half-amused, half-appalled. "Well, yours, I hope!"

"Oh, Patricia, I was teasing—"

To punish him, and also because I have to in the line of duty, I in my turn drag him back downtown, to catch Jefferson Airplane's eleven o'clock set at the Fillmore East—Diane Gardiner has made me promise. But she didn't know who I'd have in tow tonight . . .   We stop at my apartment first, to drop off the rings and freshen up—now it's my turn to change clothes—and Jim stages a brief mutinous protest over a cup of tea.

"It's so nice here, couldn't we just stay here instead of going to the show?"

"We won't stay there long, I *promise*. Diane will kill me if I don't show up, so we'll just go and say hi, stay for a few songs and come back here."

He complains bitterly, but gives in with good grace. It never occurs to me that he doesn't want to go because he doesn't want to be recognized. It sounds ridiculous now, but I never seemed to remember that he was famous, who he was to the public. To me he was Jim, the Jim I loved, and we were just us together, no one else could even see us; or maybe my magic made us invisible.

It is a cool spring night, lovely and clear, and we walk the couple of blocks to the Fillmore. I am still shy of public displays, and he has to ask me to take his arm walking down the street. Outside the Fillmore, he is recognized by a fan—the only time this is ever to happen when I am with him.

"Hey, Jim! Jim Morrison! Where's the Doors, Jim?"

He never looks aside, breaks stride or misses a beat. "I don't know, man, they've all got smallpox."

We go in the backstage door, say hello to the two or three Airplane members that we encounter, and are led by a stagehand up a steep twisty little staircase to the sound booth on the side of the stage. We are joined there a few minutes later by Allen Ginsberg, who introduces himself to us, very politely; Jim returns the civility. Ginsberg gives me this smile that's gallant and incredibly condescending at the same time, you can tell a mile away he thinks I'm some subliterate groupie bimbette Jim picked up outside on Second Avenue, and to whom he must therefore be extra-specially courteous and speak in little simple words.

I smile back every bit as condescendingly, casually mention my title and affiliation, and then slap him in the chops with some very unsimple words indeed about *Howl* and *Airplane Dreams*, which I have just been discussing with Jim. His attitude visibly changes, and after that we all have a fine time.

The concert is a typical knockout Airplane show—I never do admit to Jim that sometimes, just sometimes, I love the Airplane even more than I love the Doors—but there is a kind of steely undercurrent running through group and audience alike, as if things felt by all are being brought to focus here, tonight. It is a few days after Kent State, and emotions are still raw.

Up in the balcony, some stoned kid suddenly lets out an inarticulate bellow of rage and despair. Grace at center stage squints up the spotlight beam and quips, "Yeah, somebody told me Jim Morrison was here tonight..." Against the audience hoots, Jim mutters, "Thanks a lot, Grace," and I see why he was so reluctant to come.

But as I promised, we do not stay long. There is some talk about Allen and Jim and me going out for a beer (" 'Where are we going tonight, Walt Whitman?/The doors close in an hour./Which way does your beard point tonight?' " I quote sweetly, and Allen smiles a weak little smile), but they want to go round the corner to McSorley's, on Seventh Street. This being only 1970, McSorley's Ale House has not yet been dragged kicking and screaming into the twentieth century: Women are still not permitted to cross that piss-stained threshold. Just as well, I say—I mean, what woman would *want* to?—but I still don't much like being told I can't...   Jim giggles about it, and our drinking expedition is regretfully called off.

Outside, in the cool early morning air, he looks hopefully around at the darkened shuttered shops.

"I'm so hungry—is there anyplace we can go to get something to eat? Even a *pizza*—"

"No-o-o," I say, mentally reviewing the local restaurant roster. "We could go to Chinatown, there's lots of places there open all night."

"Too far. Is there anything to eat at your house?"

"Sure," I say with a grin. He gives me one of his I-can't-believe-you-actually-*said*-that looks; I relent. "Oh, all right. There is, but I'll have to cook it."

"Well, would you? Please! Patricia! I'm *starving!*"

CHAPTER 12

THE *REAL* DUCK DINNER:

And so it comes to pass that at three o'clock in the morning Jim and I are sitting sprawled on pillows on my living-room floor, eating, with our hands, happily and messily, hot crisp roast duck just out of the oven. It is delicious, and we gobble it up like pigs, stuffing our faces like two characters out of *Tom Jones*.

"What a great idea, to make me cook this."

"And you said you're not domestic..."

"Yeah, but I never said I couldn't cook. What's so hard about roasting a damn duck? Any halfwit can cook a duck. You throw it in a pan, you put it in the oven, you take it out when it's done. It's not nuclear physics or alchemy or anything."

"Well, it was wonderful, thank you for cooking it. We'll probably both have horrible nightmares, going to sleep after pigging out like that, but it was worth it."

"I'll protect you." I begin to clear away the duck rubble, and he leaps up to help me. After a very domestic interlude washing and drying the dishes, we go back into the living room, and Jim puts some records on, one of them Dylan's *John Wesley Harding*. We talk idly while it plays—he even sings along to "All Along the Watchtower" and "Down Along the Cove," sounding like no one but Jim Morrison singing Bob Dylan.

Then it is my turn to choose the music, and I put on my all-time favorite, Renaissance dance music—pavanes, galliards, Tudor top of the pops.

"Dance with me," says Jim suddenly.

"To *this*? Are you kidding?"

"Well—it *is* dance music, isn't it? Then you can dance to it."

"Well, *I* can," I say. "I don't know about you."

"Let's find out."

I clear the floor of pillows, put on my favorite sequence of tracks and walk into the middle of the room. Standing very straight, barefoot in my red minidress, I curtsy to Jim, right down to the floor, head bent, arms lowered and extended, as gracefully as I can manage. He draws himself up in front of me, bows with surprising elegance, hand on heart, and as I come up from my curtsy he takes my hand.

We do a few basic steps—grave pavane stuff, stately circling round first one way, then the other, palms pressed together vertically at shoulder height. Then, quite without warning, the music catches us into it: the lutes and viols and sackbuts, the candlelight, the dizzying perfume of the sheaves of lilacs, purple ones, white ones, in vases round the room, all combine to take us out of time and place, we dance in tune with the music and with ourselves.

After a few minutes of this—by now we have blown off the Tudor crap and are locked in each other's arms—we collapse laughing onto the sofa.

"That kind of thing always looks so sedate, but it sure takes a lot of energy," he remarks. "We could use some of those themes in our own music, I bet; they're formal, but catchy, they'd sound good as rock."

"*That* I'd like to hear— You're right, though; I used to be a go-go dancer when I was in college, and it wasn't half as much work as this."

He looks at me with a disbelieving grin. "You were a go-go dancer? *You*? Miss Priss of Manhattan?"

"Hey, come on, Morrison, you should know by now I'm not as—"

"Prim?"

"—Well, yeah, maybe—*prim* as I might look. Anyway, I needed to get a part-time job my senior year, so I worked as a go-go dancer in some of the local roadhouses. It was *not* topless, so don't leer like that."

"No, no, this fascinates me! You have no idea. What did you wear?"

"A black leather fringed bikini, if you must know."

"And?"

"Fishnet stockings and thigh-high black leather boots." I start to laugh at his astonishment. "Really! It was all on the up and up; a few of my friends in the dorm were also dancers, and this local guy and his wife managed us—booked us into the clubs and bars, drove us there and back, chaperoned us all night long and kept the drunks away from us. Couldn't have been more respectable. It was the best job I ever had. Too bad it was just before you started making records, I'd have loved to dance to Doors music."

"I'm sorry I missed your act."

"Oh, you'd have liked it. In between sets I'd sit and read Shakespeare or Joyce or whatever for class on Monday, all wrapped up in one of those plaid lumberjack shirts over my costume. I made twenty-five, thirty bucks a night—that was a lot of money back then."

Jim has been howling with laughter for the past minute, finally managing to gasp, "I can't *believe* this!"

"I promise you, it's true," I say stiffly. "I don't see why you find it quite so amusing or improbable, it's *not* very complimentary . . .   But lots of people had to do something to earn spending money at school. I didn't want to ask my folks for anything extra, they were stretched pretty tight already; and I would have made a *terrible* waitress. It was perfect: music *and* exhibitionism. Just like your present job, now I think of it . . ."

"Yeah, I guess so—any other hidden talents?"

"I can bellydance."

"Now *that* I want to see!"

"Another time, I promise." I lean back against the pillows on my end of the couch, just watching him. He is still apparently taken up with the seemingly incongruous mental picture of me as a go-go dancer, since he is chortling quietly to himself.

"Well, you are just full of surprises, aren't you," he remarks at last. "Writer-editor-critic-witch-dancer-exhibitionist. Not to mention genius, and knowing everything—"

"I never said I know everything. What I said was, I'm usually right.

What makes you think I think I know everything? *You're* the one with the soul of a dead Indian medicine man—"

"Hey, *you're* the scion princess of a long line of Celtic shamans, remember? That beats some dead Indian by a couple of miles. Seven miles." He shifts position so that my legs are lying across his lap, and begins to run his hands absently up my thighs and under my skirt. "What's your coven gonna say, by the way, when you tell them you're marrying outside the faith, as it were?"

"Who says you're outside the faith?"

He doesn't answer right away. "If I decided I wanted to, uh, *convert*, let's call it, what would I have to do?"

"Well, you'd have to be instructed, and the senior witches would have to be convinced you weren't just doing it for me, or for fun, but because you really wanted to be a witch yourself. And you'd have to be formally initiated. You know so much about it already, I don't think it'd take you more than a couple of months, if you were serious. *Are* you serious?" I ask, when he does not reply at once.

"Yeah, actually, I might be," he answers with a smile. "I've always been interested in that sort of thing, as you know, and you've taught me so much more about it, just being around you, talking to you. I'll have to think about it some more, that's for sure."

"No, don't think about it. Just—*be* about it."

For the past five minutes, we have been intermittently undressing one another, casually, without urgency, as if the other's consent were not required. I find myself enjoying the sense of ownership and being owned that this brings, the sense of possessing, of familiarity with him and with his body, and I can see that he is feeling likewise.

We go to bed without fuss but with intent; in the middle of love-making he whispers in my ear, "We weren't built to last, Patricia."

(Later, for the movie, Oliver Stone will pick up this line, and will make it Jim saying it to Pam.)

"We are as the beasts that perish," I agree grimly. "I like you enormously, you know."

"No," he says, surprised and delighted. "I *didn't* know . . . I never know where I really stand with you, you're always so damn gracious and polite. I'm never sure whether you're just too well-bred to tell me to fuck off, or whether you really— But, I guess if you didn't want me around, you'd have said so by now."

"Oh yes. I'd have said."

"And you did say you love me." This is more a question than a statement of fact; a plea, even.

"I did say, and I do love you. But I still might not have *liked* you."

He is quiet for a while after we have finished making love, just drowsing in my arms. "You haven't sold out, you know," he says then.

"*What?!* What's that supposed to mean?" I give him a sharp dig in the ribs, but he is very serious about this.

"I mean, about us being together, and you writing for the magazine, and people maybe thinking the wrong thing. You know what I mean."

I flash on that secretary who saw us this afternoon, and I do not smile. "Oh yes. I know exactly what you mean. Somebody been tattling?"

"No. I'm not stupid, though. I know that kind of stuff happens. I just don't want you to get hurt by gossip and all, 'cause no matter what they say, it's not true. I'll tell you what's true. And I know you're not going to *let* it be true—the kind of things they'll be saying."

I shift around until I am lying across his chest. "The reason it's not going to be true is because I'm going to be twice as hard on you as I am on anybody else. I decided that a long time ago. Because I love *you*, not them, and because I hold you to a higher standard than other people, and because that's the only way things are going to come out even in the end. It's not fair, maybe, but that's the way it's going to be. Can you understand that?"

I hear the smile in the dark. "Sure."

"And you don't mind?"

"Not if you don't."

I sigh. "Have you ever in your life given anybody a straight answer?"

"Christ," he says, surprised, "I hope not."

The next day we spend apart, he having things of his own to attend to: Doors business (they have a concert in Detroit this weekend), Elektra business (live album; he wants to call it *Lions in the Streets*, others want to call it *Road Trips*, it ends up being called *Absolutely Live*), book business (an editor-author meeting up at Simon & Schuster). We do not meet again until the following day, when he shows up in the early evening with yet another present for me.

"Oh, I got a present, too," he informs me, as I am almost incoherent with delight at the magnitude of the gift. "I was up at my publishers and embarrassed my editor into giving me this really expensive book on Alfred

Hitchcock. Well, that's what editors are for, really. He doesn't actually *edit* me or anything, fix my syntax or punctuation or any of that stuff. I just saw the book on his shelf, said how much I was into Hitchcock —as a former film student—and looked through it for the whole meeting, just kept saying how nice it was, until he couldn't do anything else *but* give it to me. I think he was a little pissed."

But he's very pleased with himself, and pleased with my pleasure in the unexpected gift. We discuss his poetry book for a while—he seems to have memorized my review, and that makes me a little uncomfortable, until I remind him of what I said the other night, that I would have to be harder on him just to maintain some semblance of critical impartiality. But he's teasing; we sit and drink tea, then do a little cocaine. I don't usually have coke around, but there's maybe half a gram in the little silver pillbox, and we do a couple of lines.

Drugs are never to play a big part in our relationship: the odd joint, a few lines, no more. Nor does drink, strangely enough, despite what tales others will have to tell in later years; perhaps his uncharacteristic abstinence with me is due to my own vastly more temperate habits— I like recreational drugs just fine, but I like staying in control even more, and he doesn't want to seem an undisciplined drunk or druggie by comparison—or maybe it's just because we have infinitely better things to do with our time together than get blasted out of our skulls. Or it might just be that he knows already that I will not give him the permission that Pam does: I am not an addict, I have no guilt to work out, therefore I will never allow him the sort of behavior she allows him—or put the sort of pressure on him that she does.

And perhaps too his sobriety is a function of the fact that we never spend more than a week together at a time, and maybe that's as long as he can hold it together without cracking. In the 60's, we did not understand the nature of alcoholism as well as we do now, of course; it was regarded as a quaint character flaw, almost a positive trait for a would-be poet. Maybe the fact that he stays straight for me is the most flattering compliment he could ever pay me, the greatest gift he can give me. The bravest thing, of course, would have been kicking booze altogether; and it would not only have been for those who loved him, but purely for himself. But that is not the way it was—in the 60's.

So now we have a pleasant buzz on, from the tea and the coke and the bottle of wine I finally open—my idea, not his.

"I can't stay all night tonight," he says with regret. "We're leaving early tomorrow for Detroit, and I've got to get myself organized for the plane."

"You can stay for a while, though?"

"Of course. I didn't want to leave without seeing you again."

He is sitting on the floor at my feet; I am ensconced on the sofa as usual. Now he drapes one arm possessively over my thighs, leans against my knees, half-closes his eyes and starts to sing, very softly.

" 'Love hides in the strangest places,
Love hides in familiar faces—' "

I blush deeply; he notices it, and smiles, but does not stop singing.

" 'Love comes to those who seek it—' "

The verb jars. "Don't you mean 'Love *hides* from those who seek it'?"

He blinks and looks up at me, struck. "Well, that changes the meaning completely—"

"Yeah, I'm hip."

"I wrote it for you," he says then. " 'Love hides in familiar faces'?"

I burst out laughing. "Oh Jim, you did not! I bet Robby probably wrote it."

"He did not. And I didn't write it for Pam, either."

"She once told me all your songs were about her."

"Well, she thinks they are. But they're not. I don't want to talk about her, anyway," he says with sudden energy. "I want to talk about us."

"Not much to say. You're going back to California, I'm staying here."

"That's true, it won't be any more frequent, probably, than it has been all along. But it'll be different, and that's what matters, isn't it?"

"Well, *I* think so."

"Not to mention the fact that, next time I'm here, we'll be getting married."

"Handfasted," I correct him. "Handfasted. I like that word much better, really. Also it's truer."

He pretends to consider. " 'Truer'! Can something be more true or less true, do you think? Isn't it either true or not true? Or can there be degrees of truth, I wonder?"

"Yes," I say flatly. "Yes, Jim, there can."

He glances up with a wicked sparkle in his eye.

"Oh? Then I guess that would be why you saw fit to mention my 'wife' in that review you wrote? Man, I was so pissed at you for that—"

"How pissed?"

He laughs. "Why do you think I asked you to *handfast* me?" He enunciates the operative verb clearly and carefully.

Well, frankly, I am not at all sure why he asked me, though I have reasons I'd certainly like to believe. I am not even sure whom I meant when I wrote the line to which he is referring ("The poems . . . are stuffed with highly personal allusion, images, and events that only Morrison himself, his wife and his press agent could possibly claim to understand"): whether I meant Pamela, who claims the title, or me, who seemed to feel a need to force a decision that had apparently already been taken.

But Jim has no doubts, and seems vastly amused by it all.

"Well, of *course* you meant you, and that's why I asked you, had to make an honest woman of you—"

"I *am* an honest woman!"

"—and couldn't let you make a liar out of me, talk about my 'wife'—"

Now it is my turn to be amused. "Oh, right, so it was purely for the sake of truth in journalism, is that it? You're a prince, Morrison!"

"Well, you said it, now you have to make good on it—" We are by now tussling on top of the bed, he trying to pin me down, I not trying very hard to escape.

"Doesn't take a house to fall on *you*, does it," I say, laughing. "Was Pam pissed when she saw it?"

"Who knows? I told you, we're not seeing each other any more. And I couldn't care less if she is—she probably thought you meant her anyway, if she read it. If she could read," he adds rather cruelly. "But I"—a teasing thrust—"know you *didn't*"—another thrust.

"So? What are you going to do about it?"

"I'm going to nail you to this bed, for one thing."

"You can try."

"Your breasts have gotten bigger."

"You just don't remember from last time. And that's no answer, either. I bet when you came back here to New York, for that Forum gig, and we went to bed, I bet you couldn't even remember who it was that you were balling."

"I remembered. I wasn't even drunk."

"No, I guess you weren't—"

"You're shivering."

"Damn right I am. You scare me."

"ME? *I* scare you? Patricia! I *love* you!"

"That's why I'm scared."

"Well then, if you're scared, why don't you just come under here, like this?"

"—Maybe you weren't drunk after all."

"Oh, Jim—"

"Who's my competition?"

"Nobody I know."

"So, I'm the only one, then."

He reaches down and pulls out my diaphragm, tossing it across the room, immediately renewing his attentions. It does not occur to me at that precise moment to wonder at what a hostile gesture this must surely be, even though it is a safe time of the month, and why he would want to hurt me.

"Jim—"

"Tell me!"

And, after a moment, I do. "Don't you know? Don't you even fucking know? I loved you from the first time I ever laid eyes on you, how many times do I have to tell you that?"

"You have to tell me all the time, forever, 'cause I love you too."

"Took you long enough to *do* something about it."

"I'm here now."

"For a while."

"I'll always be with you."

"We'll see." I never want him to leave my body, loving the feel of his weight on me, never able to get him close enough.

"Why are you crying?" he asks, alarmed.

"Because. Because it's too beautiful. Because I'm still afraid."

"There's nothing to be afraid of."

When the silence has made me a little braver I ask what I have never before had the nerve to ask.

"What about Pam?"

"What about her? I told you, it's finished with her."

"I just want to know who *my* competition is. Or was." I do not believe for one *minute* that it's finished with her; or rather, I believe him because I could not countenance being involved with him otherwise, and I probably believe that it's over right at this very moment, and I even believe that *he* believes it's over. But, apart from how he feels about me, there are other forces at work here, and way down deep I know already that love will not be enough. He needs that permission Pamela alone can give him: permission from a junkie to be an alcoholic, permission he knows damn well he will never in a million years get from me. And, given the nature of addiction, his and hers, I now know too that it is unlikely he will ever find the strength in himself or the cause in me or in anyone else to give it, and her, up. But I want to believe him, so very much, and so for now I allow myself to believe. It is a bad mistake.

"Fair enough." He moves off me, reaches for the silver tankard of water I keep by the bed, pulls me over to snuggle against him while he drinks. "Well, I'll tell you. We lived together for a while, of course, and then we didn't, and then we did again, and then we didn't again. Now we don't, haven't for a while. I told you, it's over. It's been a very on-and-off thing, and now it's off for good. She's not like you, you know."

"Oh, believe me, *that* I know."

"I guess I just felt responsible for her," he says, sounding puzzled by it all. "She's kind of vulnerable, not very independent. She could never do what you do—"

Yeah, about as vulnerable as a piranha . . . "Why didn't you ever tell me this before?"

"I did; or didn't I? Anyway, you never asked. I'd have told you if you had, but this is better." He sets down the tankard and hugs me long and hard, his face buried in my hair, against my neck. "Any more questions? Man, being in bed with you is worse than ten interviews—"

"No more questions. Well, one maybe. *WHY DID YOU PULL OUT MY DIAPHRAGM?* I don't wear it for looks, you know, it serves a pretty useful purpose—"

He smiles a mysterious little smile. "Oh, I just don't want us to have any barriers between us, that's all."

Not good enough; I am more than a little angry, it is incredibly irresponsible of him, but he won't respond to further questioning, and after a while I drop it, unwilling to spoil the mood. But, as he said earlier, he cannot stay the night, and we reluctantly pry ourselves apart a little after midnight and get out of bed. While he dresses—I remain naked, out of some strange need to stay just as I was when he was with me, for as long as he is with me—we talk about Kent State, still major news.

"It's just bullshit political stuff." He flicks a finger at a Times article I have cut out and left on the table. "I'm sorry those kids were killed, there's no excuse for what those soldiers did, but I just don't think things like that have much meaning overall. It's easy to be swayed by dramatic incidents, but in the end what's changed? You have four dead kids and the system is stronger than ever."

It is perhaps the most overtly political statement I will ever hear him make. "You don't believe in the Revolution, then, I take it?"

He hears the sarcastic edge I put on the word, and laughs.

"Revolution! *If* there's really any sort of revolution going on these days, and I for one would like to think there is, it's not with college kids getting killed on campus. Though I would guess that would radicalize you pretty fast, getting shot at, whether it's in Vietnam or over here. No, I don't believe in the Revolution, not by that name anyway. That's one of the reasons I don't care for the Airplane as a band—though I like them as people—that plus the fact that they're the most unsubtle band I ever heard, everybody playing and singing as loud as they can, up front all the time, no delicate interplay like we have, the Doors have. But singing 'Up against the wall!' is easy when you have a limo waiting outside to drive you away after the gig. Limos are fine; so is rebellion. But I'd like to think the real Revolution is bigger than that."

He is dressed now; I accompany him to the door of my apartment. I am still naked, and it is an interesting sensation when we are in one another's arms kissing goodbye; so interesting, in fact, that I just twist my hair up out of his way and we make love again right there, standing up, leaning against the door.

"Listen," he says then, "I should be back here in a month or so. I want to take a little time off alone before my trial starts, maybe go to Europe, and I want to see you first, so we can do the handfasting. I want that to happen really soon; I just won't be able to see you any sooner than that."

"Oh, I know. A month is, what, nothing, thirty days. I didn't expect, you know, that you would."

He smiles. "I know you didn't. That's why I'll be back."

He kisses me again and is gone. I close the door after him, on a room full of the scent of lilacs.

CHAPTER 13

May–June 1970

THE NEXT MONTH PASSES ON A PLANE OF ECSTATIC existence hitherto undreamed-of: Jim calls more than usual, Jim writes more than usual, Jim sends things, Jim says things he's never said before, that no man has said to me before. He even sends a poem he's written to run in the magazine, the first time this particular work of his has ever been published anywhere. And wonder of wonders, I even *like* it: It's called "The Anatomy of Rock" (originally subtitled "The whole thing started with rock&roll/Now it's out of control," but in the course of one of our conversations he asks that the subtitle be eliminated, no reason given; I ask for none, and comply at once). Frankly, I am surprised that I like the poem as much as I do, but it truly is one of his better efforts: taut, telegraphic, full of pace, place, import.

I can't resist telling him so, in a letter, copy of the poem with extensive excessively literary annotations. He calls as soon as he gets it, shyly pleased with some of the things I have said, respectful of the esthetic reasoning that went into the rest of the criticism.

"There, you see, Jim, I *can* be fair about your poetry—"

"I never said you couldn't, or weren't. But I'm glad you like it, anyway; I always like it when you like it."

"Uh-huh . . . We'll probably be running it in the September issue—cover picture of you, not with the other Doors, some more pictures of you inside."

Actually, a photographer has sent us a terrific slide to use on the magazine cover: a portrait of Jim in Maximilian's Palace in Mexico City, taken just a few weeks ago—Jim standing in front of a surrealistic mural by an artist named, wonderfully, Juan O'Gorman. The composition is so lovely, the colors and textures so carefully shot, that it seems Jim is part of the painting, deep burgundy shirt, shoulder-length hair, fabulous cheekbones and all. It is the best picture I have ever seen of him—it is the Jim I am in love with—and for the next twenty years it will be the only picture of him on display in my home.

To accompany the poem, Bruce Harris does a critical exegesis (under the anagram de plume Chris Reabur) called "Morrison Hotel Revisited," one of the more reasoned and reasonable pieces on the Doors to appear of late. (When Jim finally reads it, in Miami during the trial, his only comment to me on it is, "I think you've been talking to Bruce—".)

But by now, spring 1970, most of the rest of the hip press, rolling their eyes and shaking their heads, has gone off the Doors. The Miami and Phoenix antics, Jim's increasingly boorish public drunk act, the obvious fracturing of the once-monolithic group unity and the even more obvious effect on the music—all have taken their toll. Pieces like this one by Bruce (who, with a few others, remains loyal to the end, and not just because he works for Elektra either) are few and far between these days; I'm only grateful I don't have to write it myself.

Rockwise, it is a modestly eventful six weeks or so: Fairport Convention, Al Kooper, James Taylor, Traffic. (You must understand, this was daily fodder back then; it was considered substantial and pleasant, but by no means exceptional . . . it was nice.) But the big event is the Who performing their rock opera (or cantata, as Pete Townshend more modestly, and correctly, calls it), *Tommy*, at the Metropolitan Opera House in Lincoln Center; party downtown at the Fillmore East to follow.

Now *this* is a major scene, not to mention mainstream validation: rock at the Met! Oh wow! I get to wear an evening gown! (Tudor cut, green velvet, a little unseasonal but who cares; though, regretfully, I draw the line at a tiara; however, I do allow myself a garnet necklace worn as a headband by way of compromise.)

But swanning through the doors of the Met and around that fabulous lobby, members of the hip press every bit as resplendent as members of the uptown glitz crowd, is something very special (we have better hair, too, even if tiaraless).

I have always liked the Who, though nowhere near as much as I like the Airplane and the Doors, and I've enjoyed the songs from *Tommy* that I've heard in concert and on record; but this integrated, powerful performance is something else again. The Who, never one of your more sluggish bands, seem tonight to have caught a spark of divine fire; it seems impossible that any musicians can play so hard so well so long. Not to mention that it must surely be one of the single loudest rock moments of all time and space: When I put my hand on the Opera House wall, I can actually feel it shaking under the onslaught of sound. Sure isn't *Tosca*...

At the party afterwards I encounter Eugenie, a friend of mine who works with Bruce at Elektra, and of course the first thing we talk about is Jim. Eugenie is of the opinion that our union is a very good thing indeed for both him and me.

"The greatest thing about Jim Morrison is his curiosity," she says. "Curiosity just might save him; and man, is he curious about *you*."

"Me!"

"You bet. A woman he can talk to, *and* a woman he can go to bed with? This is something new for him, somebody who's his equal in brains as well as in the sack, and he wants to know all about it."

"And I? What do *I* have to do?"

"Easy. Don't fall in love with him."

I don't have to tell her it's already way too late for that.

I don't have to tell the coven, either; we've discussed Jim on several occasions, anyway. But, just for form's sake, at the next regular meeting, in the new-business segment, I officially announce to my assembled witches the news of their High Priestess's impending handfasting, and who her intended mate happens to be. Nobody is surprised in the least degree, least of all Maura and Brân, who have been my confidants all along; and Aengus, my current partner as High Priest, is over the moon with glee, loudly declaring how right he'd been, that Jim will be taking his place beside me as High Priest before the year is out—he even bestows a magical name on Jim to chime with my own; we will use both names in the ceremony, in addition to our real ones.

There is some spirited discussion of Jim's obvious interest in pagan themes and values, and his suitability not only for initiation but for partnership with me; but on the whole it is no big deal, though everyone is of course delighted for us both.

Only Maura expresses doubt; later, very privately. She knows very well how I feel about Jim, knows too how seriously I take my six-month-old duties as High Priestess; and, though she puts it as lovingly as she can, she also knows that what she must tell me is not something I would ever want to hear.

Just something she senses: But I know to trust her sensings . . .

"If you're going to do it"—she uses my magical name, something she seldom does outside the circle except for grave cause, though she softens it with a diminutive—"do it soon. Very soon. Don't wait."

And the terrible thing is, I know in my deepest heart just why she is bidding me make haste; and I know too that she is right.

Toward the middle of June I go up to freaky little Goddard College, way off in the depths of greenest Vermont, to attend a four-day event called the Alternative Media Conference, attended by some 1300 or so of the prime movers on both coasts in progressive radio, underground press, trade and consumer publications, record companies, video and film; not to mention just plain high-energy hangers-on.

It starts out as a deadly serious slate of seminars, workshops, meetings, panels, but quickly degenerates into a sort of stoned MLA convention, a mini-Woodstock for the freak elite. Lots of cool talk flying about alternative media, but nobody seeming to know quite how to actually set them up. There are *Om*-ers from San Francisco who insist on resonating their way through every crucial moment, and the Yippie Cretin Brigade who specialize in gratuitous pig-calling, gossip queens with their clothes off (not an easy memory to live with) running stoned through the fields, doctrinaire ego trips all over the place. I am most dispirited by the whole thing, and end up doing magic alone in the woods, just to calm and center myself again.

I am cheered up somewhat when, upon my return, a letter arrives at the office from political prisoner John Sinclair; he very graciously commends some columns I have done and the points of view expressed therein—his opinion means a lot to me—then concludes with, "Patricia, it isn't ever the *kids'* fault—please remember that. They will support whatever is offered to them if it's offered to them in a way they can

relate to, and it's up to *us* to make the alternative available to them.
Dig that. And right on."

I know what he's saying; but, after Goddard, and thinking back to
Woodstock, I wonder. Can "we" really hold out such vital alternatives
after all? Are we all just a bunch of ego-tripping acidheaded hacks? And
the "kids"—are they not to be held responsible for their own choices,
do they just open wide and swallow anything the current sweeps in? Isn't
enlightenment supposed to enable you to make your *own* decisions, not
just blindly accept and support whatever the media—however hip or
alternative—send down the pike?

I think about it until I get a headache, and resolve to lay it all on
Jim when I see him. Whenever that might be. It's his own fault anyway.

"RED ALERT!! *Morrison's* here!"

The voice on the phone is Eugenie's, from across the street at
Elektra. It is about nine-thirty in the morning, a butter-soft early summer
day the week after Goddard.

"You're kidding."

"No, I'm *not* kidding, and he's on his way over there."

I glance down at my 'engagement' ring and almost self-destruct with
pure delight, but— He might not come after all, don't be *too* thrilled,
he might have forgotten all about you . . .

"It's the middle of the night for him," I protest weakly. "He *can't*
be here—" Deny, deny.

"He took the red-eye. He's here, all right, and he'll be *there* before
very much longer, so consider yourself warned."

I hang up the phone and stare, stunned and unseeing, at a poster
the editor of a Canadian rock magazine has been thoughtful enough to
send me: The First Annual Jim Morrison Film Festival, it announces.
Picture of a bearded and work-shirted Jim in the desert, for the public
premiere of *HWY*, his first serious filmic effort (if you don't count his
UCLA student film, and most people don't); plus assorted Doors promo
films, including the infamous "Unknown Soldier" short. It can't be true,
he would have called first, he isn't here, and even if he is he probably
won't come over . . . I don't know why I am torturing myself like this;
but I brush my hair and fix my makeup just in case.

An hour later, the Tibetan bells on the office door jangle melodi-
ously, and the poster boy himself walks in, greeting Laura by name and
with pleasure; Leon is with him.

I get up and go into the next office. Jim is standing there looking smugly pleased with himself, as if he has done something exceptionally clever, but also a bit unsure of his reception. Pauline comes in to say hi, and I go up to Leon to give him a hug and kiss.

"Doesn't Jim get a kiss too?" he chides.

I am, ridiculously, too shy to kiss Jim in front of everybody. It's only Leon, Janice, Laura and Pauline—three of whom, at least, know very well with whom their editor is sleeping. But still.

Jim rolls his eyes and pulls me into his arms, kissing me soundly, running his hands up along my body. When he finally lets me go, I am blushing and he is laughing.

"I'll get you for that, Morrison," I whisper threateningly, but the smile on my face is a match for his own. After a brief casual chat, Leon vanishes, apparently under orders, and Jim and I go out for an early lunch—the dreaded Ginger Man again—and a walk in the park.

Though we manage to eat a few more bites of lunch than we did last time, again we are consumed in white-hot talk. The handfasting is uppermost in our minds, but we do not really address it until we are once again back in the park, under the same tree where Jim proposed the month before. The white blossoms are gone now, replaced by soft green leaves, and we sit in their cool shadow, Jim stretched out on the grass as before, his head pillowed comfortably on my jean-clad right thigh.

We are discussing the long-distance aspects of our relationship; over the intervening month he seems to have fallen prey to misgivings as to my ability to deal with so untraditional a commitment, however spiritual.

"I don't know, seeing me every two or three months, do you really think you can handle that?"

"To be totally truthful," I begin, perhaps not *totally* truthfully, "I don't really think I could handle seeing you a whole lot more often than that. I like distance, I need distance; for me, it's the spiritual connection that matters most, not somebody's physical presence. I'm a witch, remember?"—he nods vigorously to indicate he has never for a minute forgotten—"I don't have to be *with* you to *be* with you. I'd much rather be on different coasts, and know that we were bound to one another in a true and spiritual way, than have you move in with me here and know you weren't really there most of the time at all—whether it was mentally *or* physically."

He thinks about that for a while. "So just because we wouldn't always be with each other, we wouldn't necessarily be apart from each other . . . I can dig that."

"Yes, I think you can; otherwise I never would have accepted your proposal! Besides, I need a lot of time alone, and I'm sure you do too. I love you, I love the idea of being linked to you, but if we were around each other all the time we'd get bored. I'd hate to bore you, and I wouldn't want you to bore me."

(Plus the fact that I'd never in a million *years* put up with your day-to-day bullshit, Morrison; all this crap I hear from L.A. about your drinking and your slutting around. I am wise enough to know that I'll never be able to change *that*, not unless you want to change it yourself —but at least long-distance means I don't really have to put up with it. Or not that much anyway, and that's no less loving a thought for being a true and honest one. Maybe *more* loving, in that I see it and I still love you just as much, in that I won't let you behave like that around me—and so distance is the only way . . .)

He flexes his neck against my thigh, and I almost faint. "We'd never bore each other," he says in a hurt voice.

"Well, maybe 'bored' is the wrong word," I say, when I can speak again. "Let's just say that now, when we see each other every couple of months, we don't waste time on small stuff or on fighting. The time we have is way too precious for that. That means a lot to me, and I hope to you too; I wouldn't want to lose it, it's too special. Besides, we're always on the phone, or writing letters; it's not like we're ever really out of touch."

"So, you wouldn't even want to be on the same coast with me." He ponders this silently for a while, but does not seem either insulted or displeased. "Well, all I can say is, you're the first woman I was ever with who ever said anything like that."

"That's because I'm not *like* any other woman you were ever with —in case you hadn't noticed."

"Oh, I've noticed, believe me, I've noticed"—now he is smiling faintly—"but don't you want to be mine, want me to be yours?"

I look down at him, but his eyes are half-hooded, as usual. Is this a test or what, *everything* with him is a goddamned test . . . But I sense a fine and to me desperately important line here, between love's natural need to claim the beloved and be claimed in return, and love's higher, nobler imperative to, as the Zen saying is, hold fast with open palm; and I hope I can manage to walk this line correctly.

"No," I say, after a long and rather fraught silence. "At least, not in the way you mean. I want to be with you when I'm with you, and you to be with me when you're with me, and when we're apart we'll still be together. But nobody owns anybody else in this thing. Not you, not me. It was never meant to be any more than what it is—and anyway, we already are, you know, each other's."

His silence is even longer than mine. "I know," he says at last. "I really—know." Then, with a deep breath and a tender smile and a surge of animation, eyes open at last, he looks up and asks, "Well, when's the wedding?"

I sigh; test passed, the cliff we had been so unerringly headed for avoided at the last second.

"Tomorrow night. It's Midsummer Day, according to the old calendar, St. John's Day. Tonight's Midsummer Eve, and that would be cool too—but the officiating clergy, for lack of a better word, have prior commitments."

"A witches' Sabbat—"

"Yes, actually, but not by that name." I wait, but he doesn't ask. "So, is that okay, then—tomorrow?"

"Sure, honey; but"—he turns his head to nuzzle briefly between my thighs, I blush and hope no passers-by happen to notice—"does that mean we can't sleep together the night before?"

"It doesn't mean anything of the sort."

He has business that afternoon with Leon, and on parting tells me to meet him at the hotel at six. I fly back to the office, tell Pauline what the deal is (though not about the handfasting; nobody at the magazine knows about the coven I belong to, though they know in a general way of my interest in such things), then dash home to change into something more respectable (and seductive) than jeans and a Jethro Tull T-shirt.

On the stroke of six I present myself at the front desk of the Navarro Hotel, the elegant small establishment halfway along Central Park South that Jim has been using on his New York stays since at least January. I ask—a little diffidently, a little assertively, *lots* more than a little possessively—for Mr. Morrison. I am informed by the clerk that Mr. Morrison is still out, and would I care to wait. I am turning away to sit down and do so when I hear:

"Join the club."

I look over at a couch against the lobby's far wall. A woman with coarse brown hair is sitting there, and it seems to be she who has just presumed to address me.

"I beg your pardon?" I ask, in a voice like the wind off a glacier.

"He's not here yet. You were asking for Jim Morrison, I heard you."

"Yes, I was, Miss, ah—" (And what *possible* business could it be of yours?)

"Oh, Joanna, my name's Joanna. He sent me a telegram that he was going to be in town, and that I should just meet him here. I've been waiting all afternoon."

"I see." I don't, not really, but on another level I see only too well. But I volunteer nothing, not even my name, and I take a seat as far from the sofa as I can get, never taking my eyes off the hotel street doors. I am furious with Jim, and with myself, and with her, but mostly with him, and I plan to make him pay dearly for this when I get him alone. In the meantime, I have to endure it: Joanna is remarkably voluble with a stranger, going on at great length about what a Doors fan she is, and I smile and nod, nod and smile, pretending it really matters.

I smile a very thin smile indeed when, at about six-twenty, I see Jim come sailing through the street doors with Leon. He sees us both at once and doesn't flinch for an instant.

"Well!" he says to Leon, an aside meant for Joanna and me to hear. "I wouldn't have missed this scene for worlds."

"Like to tell me what's going on here, Morrison?"

We are walking to 57th Street, to a movie theatre showing one of the all-time great double bills: Bergman's *The Passion of Anna* and Mick Jagger's film debut, *Ned Kelly*. Really perverse. Actually, it is a preview screening of the Jagger flick sandwiched in between regular showings of the Bergman; I have passes, and I find it kind of vengefully appropriate that Jim should accompany me to Mick's movie (Jim *hates* Jagger . . .). The party includes us, Joanna, Leon and Leon's friend Skip; Jim and I are walking a little behind the others. He tries to put his arm round my shoulder, draw my arm through his, but I pull away from him.

He seems amused by my silent fuming, and I can tell from his manner that he has spent a good portion of our afternoon apart doing some serious drinking.

"Oh, she's nothing," he drawls. "She's just a fan, she's been in a, well, I guess you could call it a hospital. She had some—difficulties, and started writing to me as a sort of therapy. I felt sorry for her and wrote back, and I guess it was a mistake but I told her I'd be in New York this week and that she should stop by and say hi."

"And you thought it was okay to invite her along with us on the night before our—" I cannot say the word with the others so near, but I don't have to say it.

"I *said* I just felt sorry for her, Patricia. Hey, you want to split, just us, we'll split, right now, we'll go straight to your place—"

"Oh no, no, no," I say with a certain grim satisfaction. "This was all *your* idea, I wouldn't *dream* of interfering. No, we're going to the movies, Morrison, all of us, and God help you if you say we're not."

So we sit through the last twenty minutes of the Bergman and then *Ned Kelly*, in all its unremitting awfulness. Leon and Skip wisely decamp midway through the Jagger opus, but Jim and I and Joanna remain as if nailed to our seats. She is sitting directly behind us, actually, and has a tiresome habit of giggling to herself and commenting aloud, predicting the screen action. Jim totally ignores her, even when she thrusts her face between us to get her point across.

Yet when I say even the lightest word, he turns to me at once, leaning over with exaggerated courtesy until his ear practically touches my lips, his arm draped across the back of my seat and his fingers playing with my hair. It's the first time he's ever played his stupid games with me, these moronic tricks I've only ever heard about, the first time he's ever been less than impeccably courteous or more than pleasantly intoxicated. And in light of tomorrow night's vast undertaking, I cannot help but wonder a little as to what this might not bode.

At last I have had enough—it's maybe nine o'clock by now, Ned/Mick has just met his fate—but when I turn around fully intending to make our *very* firm excuses to Joanna I see with relief and surprise that she has herself disappeared, softly and suddenly vanished away. I nudge Jim, who glances behind him, shrugs, grabs my hand and makes a dash with me up the side aisle and out of the theatre.

In the cab on the way to my place I berate him roundly, but my heart really isn't in it, and all he does is sing the *Ned Kelly* theme song

("Blame it on the Kellys!") and smile seraphically at me until I give up. It doesn't take long.

We go to a neighborhood place for a lateish dinner, then wander round the East Village for a while before settling in for the night. He is considerably more sober now than earlier—another little trick of his, I don't know how he manages to do this.

His mind, not surprisingly, is running on the ceremony, what he perceives as the unknown; it intrigues him, probably scares him a little, but he's also endlessly curious and excited about it, and when we are lying gasping and exhausted after strenuous lovemaking he asks about it yet again. I patiently go through the various details of the rite, answering all his questions—and *never* was there anyone like Jim Morrison for questions—until he seems satisfied.

"Where are those wedding rings?" he demands suddenly. "I want to see them."

I fetch the claddaghs from the silver box on the mantelpiece, where they have been lying in state for the past month. Jim takes them and plays with them for a while, silently, examining them minutely, fitting them on each of his fingers in turn, then on each of mine. His gold ring is too large even for my thumbs.

I watch him, and finally I ask the question I have not dared ask until now; ask it knowing damn well I shouldn't, ask it dreading even as I ask the answer I may get.

"Is this—*real*? For you?"

He does not reply at once, but reclaims both rings from me and puts them together on his little finger; mine doesn't go past the joint. He studies them, still in silence, for a long time, and I begin to grow frightened at that silence, certain that he knows just how frightened I am.

"Oh, it's real," he says at last, and does not smile. "And that's the right answer—"

"Is it the whole answer?"

At that he does smile. "You tell me, honey."

All at once he gets up, goes over to the cupboard where I keep writing materials, comes back with pencil and paper. I watch him as he moves around the bed, first one side, then the foot, then the other side.

"No, stay there," he commands, as I start to shift position. "I want to draw you."

I lean back on the pillows. "Oh right, I've seen *your* drawings! Those snakes-and-ladders things in your notebooks, or those paintings you did for Tandy"—Tandy Martin, his high-school girlfriend in Virginia, now married to David Walley's good friend Jim Brodey—"that sun-face and that alleged self-portrait?"

He grins, shaking his head. "I can't believe you saw those—it's so weird thinking of you and Tandy knowing each other—but this won't be like that."

I am still skeptical, but obedient to his direction I stretch out naked on top of the bed, moving an arm this way and a leg that way until he is satisfied with the pose. He has that look on his face now, that look of an artist at work, any kind of artist: judicial, impartial, a look that the unsuspecting might well take for that of a mechanic or a scientist, rather than that of a creative person in the act of creation.

It turns out to be one of the most sublimely, supremely erotic moments we are ever to share. We do not lay so much as a finger on one another: The sensuality lies in the forced immobility, the focused intensity. It is in fact another form of lovemaking, and the impersonality of it is so tremendously exciting precisely because it *is* so impersonal: Our knowledge of one another's bodies, our experience of what they have done together, is the subtext.

Apart from all that, the sketch he diffidently proffers after about ten minutes is surprisingly lovely, a vivid, graceful pencil rendering, maybe not the greatest work of nude portrait art ever achieved, but for one in the morning, not half bad. It is full of tension and plasticity and life; recognizably my own body, even.

I stare at it, amazed. "No one's ever done anything like that for me before," I say humbly. "It's beautiful—thank you!"

He smiles with shyness, with wickedness. "My pleasure—and that's because the guys you've gone out with have been clods."

"Evidently."

His pencil is busy now on another full-length, then on a head sketch: He turns my head this way and that, tilts my chin up, lowers it, pulls my hair forward over my bare breasts and shoulders, shakes it into fullness around my face. Three minutes for that one; though he can't quite get the hair falling the way he wants it, and it ends up a collaborative effort, with me doing my sketched hair myself. When he finishes up the second full-length nude pose, and puts down the pad, we fall on each other.

But in the night he turns to me out of sleep and nowhere.

"Something that can't change," he whispers, kissing my shoulder, my neck, my breasts. "Can't be touched—with you—not with anyone else—with you."

It is as much of the whole answer as I will ever get, or he can give.

PART THREE

A midsummer day's night's dream
her long hair chains his hands
his length upon her
did the earth move?
no the galaxy shifted
Are they possessors
or just possess'd?

CHAPTER

24 June 1970

WE ARE STANDING IN MY SMALL LIVING ROOM; IT IS about ten o'clock at night on Midsummer Day. Candles all over the room flicker gold against the deep purple walls and silver tin ceiling; on the marble mantelpiece stands a cut-crystal vase filled with peonies. Huge, puffy blooms—some are pink, some white, a few of the white ones are tipped with blood-colored streaks.

Jim and I are hand in hand before a waist-high table of carved oak, pressed into service, as it usually is, as the altar. He and I have had our ritual baths—quick purificatory dips in salted water, a few passes with a lighted candle, anointings with consecrated oil, a prayer—and now we are dressed in long black robes, the ritual garb of my Celtic coven. The robes are floor-length, loose and unbelted; underneath them we are naked. I wear some silver Celtic jewelry, and upon my forehead is the moon crown of the High Priestess—a silver browband with a Pictish crescent moon at the front, mark of my office. Jim wears a vaguely classical-looking wreath of woven willow and laurel, very Dionysian against his long hair.

I am holding Jim's hand because he is nervous; but so am I, a little.

Catching sight of ourselves in the tall pier mirror, I laugh: We look like the woodcutter's children in a fairytale, hand in hand for comfort in the halls of the elf-king.

"I have to help set the table," I tell him, gently disengaging my hand from his clutches. "The High Priestess shouldn't have to do it herself."

"I thought *you* were the High Priestess," he mutters.

"I am, but not tonight. Lady Maura and Lord Brân"—I give them their full coven names and titles—"are officiating because I can't perform my own wedding ceremony, and you're not an initiated witch anyway. It's okay. You'll be fine. Just say that prayer I taught you."

He rolls his eyes, but seems to calm down as he mumbles the brief prayer to himself, over and over, as if there is reassurance in repetition, and watches the final preparations for the rite: setting up a small cast-iron cauldron to burn incense, lighting more candles, putting out the many ritual implements on the altar. The familiar drill soothes and calms me as I go along: Goddess candle, Goddess statue, athamé (the ritual black-handled dagger, tonight used for another purpose than invoking), sword, water, salt, censer, God statue. And then the special things for this particular rite: the quaich to hold the consecrated wine—a wide, flat, double-handled silver bowl that, as Jim remarks, looks like the Holy Grail ("So *you've* had it all this time!"); an ornate eighteenth-century silver chalice; a braided red silk cord; my wand of willow wood, bound with silver and sealed with a bloodstone; the claddaghs we bought last month, one silver, two gold.

Jim and Brân are talking earnestly, obviously guy stuff. I can't hear what they are saying, but Jim is nodding comprehension, and, although grave-faced, he does not look scared or unhappy. He catches my eye then and gives me his full, rare smile, that wonderful scything of delight right across his face. I smile back, but I have sudden tears in my eyes as I look at him.

Maura nods to me, and I go to Jim and take his arm. "Come on, we have to stand over here. The High Priestess will cast the circle and bring us into it. We don't have to do anything yet. Just watch."

Brân, Jim and I stand off to one side as Maura begins to create the sacred space. Jim tells me afterward that it seemed to him as if she stood at the center of a great sweep of movement, the stillness at the storm's heart.

But to me it feels as it has always felt: intent and power creating

something more where only a room has been until now. I center myself
as Maura raises the great black-bladed ceremonial sword and scribes the
circle three times round in the air. Back at the starting point, she invokes
the Quarters, calling the powers of North and East and South and West
to attend and witness and protect, welcoming them to our rite. The
circle forms immediately: a sphere of blue light, not quite visible to the
eye, stretching from floor to ceiling along the line of the candleflames.

"What is between the worlds does not concern the worlds," she
says then, and I feel Jim startle a little beside me. When I ask him about
it later, he tells me that at that instant he felt the room being taken out
of time, the sensation of being outside an otherness of place was made
utterly real to him.

Maura lifts and lowers the sword, cutting a gateway, and holds out
her hand to Brân, bringing him in with a kiss on the cheek. Brân brings
me in likewise, and then I bring in Jim. I take the sword to seal the
circle behind us, then lean it against the altar and turn again to Jim,
taking his hand and turning him to face the altar.

"What did you *do?*" he whispers fiercely. "It was like being dropped
into a vacuum." (Throughout the ceremony, though naturally the ritual
is paramountly serious, all four of us will exchange conversational asides
and even laughter at the occasional flub, and the moment never seems
to suffer.)

"You felt the circle being formed and sealed," says Brân. "You're
obviously sensitive to it. It's been done so often here Patricia doesn't
even really need to cast it formally anymore."

"It's like—the vibes are bouncing off the *walls!*" Jim gestures around
him; he looks pleased and excited, and, in the candlelight, very beautiful
and ridiculously young.

The rite begins in earnest: Maura and Brân invoke the Goddess and
the God to bless and sanctify this joining. They cense us, anoint us with
consecrated oil, sprinkle us with water, smudge our foreheads with burnt
rowan ash. Brân steps forward, holding the black sword point uppermost;
I take the rings from the altar and slip them onto the tip of the sword.

Going back to Jim's side, I speak for only him to hear. "These rings
symbolize the Sacred Marriage, the union of the King and the Goddess.
When we put them on—and later—that's who we'll be for each other,
in this circle and after. You have to be absolutely sure you want to go
ahead with this. We can stop now, if you want, and it'll be okay. There's
no way this would hold up in court or anything, it's not legal and you

could marry someone else publicly any time you wanted to. But it is a valid religious ceremony, and it will create a real bond between us. There's no 'till death do us part' about it. Death *doesn't* part; only lack of love."

I have been looking him straight in the eye through all this; now I lower my gaze briefly, then bring it back up to him. He is smiling slightly, very serious, his whole being intent upon me and my words.

"This is it, Morrison," I say with a smile. "This is the 'speak now or forever hold your peace' bit, so you better be absolutely certain you want to go through with it. If you've changed your mind, I'll understand; it won't change anything between us. I love you, and I'll still love you if you decide now that maybe you'd rather not do this after all."

I am a little breathless from this speech, and a little fearful that maybe he *will* change his mind, even now, though I can see perfectly plainly that he is totally caught up in the rite; something here is speaking powerfully to him. He raises my hand to his lips and kisses it, and such an expression of love and tenderness is on his face that I can scarcely bear to look upon it.

"No," he says, shaking his head, smiling down at me, then glancing quickly over at Maura and Brân. "Oh, no! I'm sure."

Maura smiles at us and begins to recite the Charge, a sort of list of what the Goddess requires of each of the partners in this union; Jim and I listen attentively, our eyes fixed on each other's. Then Brân holds out the quaich, half-filled with red wine, and Maura takes up the little black-handled knife, the athamé, from the altar.

This is the part that Jim has been most nervous about from the first; but it is also the part that has most engaged his imagination: the atavism, the primitivism, the ancientness of the bond of blood we are about to make between us—the cro-cotaig of our Celtic ancestors. A bond not privileged to orthodoxly wedded couples: They have no link between them as Jim and I shall have—this sacrifice to love and honor, courage and union . . .

I take the athamé from Maura—it is my own, a sgian dubh, a traditional Scottish dagger—and, after a glance up at Jim, I make two tiny cuts on the inside of my left wrist, carefully over the bone; we don't want to slice any arteries here. It stings a little, but not much; a few beads of blood well up immediately, hardly what I would describe as rivers of gore, and I hold out my wrist to let them fall into the wine in the quaich: three or four drops, no more.

Then it is Jim's turn. He takes the athamé from my hand, puts it to his own wrist, then shakes his head.

"I don't think I can do this," he says with a rueful smile. Then, sensing my instant hurt recoil: "Oh, no, *no*, I didn't mean I don't *want* to do it—Patricia!—I just mean I can't do it *myself*." He hugs me to him and kisses the top of my head. "Oh honey, I'm sorry, you thought I meant I didn't want to go through with this—no, I just can't, you know, cut myself. Is it okay, is it okay in the rite, if you do it for me?"

I begin to breathe again; for one terrible moment I did indeed think he wanted to stop the ceremony.

"No, *I* can't . . . but the High Priestess can—"

Before Jim can flinch or even blink, Maura takes his hand gently but firmly and makes two barely visible nicks on his wristbone. He stares a little unbelievingly as Brân holds out the quaich to catch the few droplets.

"There, that's it, it's *done!*" I say to him. "You're not going to *faint* or anything, are you?"

"No!" he replies indignantly, and we all laugh.

Maura presses our wrists together, binding them with the braided red cord that Brân has earlier blessed, and which has been lying coiled round the foot of the Goddess statue on the altar. Taking a deep breath, I recite the handfasting vow from memory; then Brân gives Jim the words of his vow, a line at a time.

There is a long living silence, in which Jim and I look only at one another. Brân holds out the sword for me to take Jim's ring from the point. I take the gold claddagh with my unbound right hand and slip it, awkwardly—it is hard to manage with one hand tied—onto Jim's little finger.

"It's a little loose," he says. "I guess my fingers were fatter when we bought the rings."

"Well, then I'll just put it here—"

I slip the ring onto the finger it best fits; then he takes the silver ring and puts it on my hand—the usual wedding-ring finger. As he does so, I look only at him. All of a sudden we are amazingly relaxed, giggling a little, even. Brân, smiling, whips off the red cord that has bound our hands and puts it back on the altar.

Maura, who has been holding the quaich while all this went on, now gives it to me, and I turn to Jim.

"You'll like this part . . . Link hands with me on the Cup; as we drink, think with me on the bond that we have made."

The ritual requires that the couple drink from the quaich at the same time; this proves to be all very well in theory, but trickier in practice. We manage only a sip or two before the wine starts making a bid for freedom. We break up, and try very hard not to spill the stuff all over us.

"I think it's easier this way—" I take the quaich and drink off a swallow, then pass the bowl to Jim, who follows suit; we pass it back and forth between us until Jim takes the last draught. I reclaim the quaich, set it down on the altar and blow out the center candle.

When I turn back to Jim he is looking a little dazed, but there is one more thing we need to do . . .

"Step over the sword with me," I whisper to him, taking his hand. Maura and Brân are holding the huge black blade at knee-level between them, and Jim and I step over it to end the ceremony.

Without warning Jim reels a little, staggers a step or two and then goes down, knees caving in right under him. I struggle to hold him up, but he slumps rather gracefully to the floor, and I throw myself to my knees beside him, cradling him in my arms, terrified and guilt-stricken and half-laughing all at once.

"*JIM!* Jim, are you all right?"

He has not passed out entirely, it turns out; it seems to be just a brief fadeaway, and after fifteen or so tense seconds he opens his eyes and focuses on my face.

"Hi, honey!" he says with a faint grin.

"What *happened?*"

"I felt—I *felt* something bigger than anything I ever felt in my *life*," he says very precisely. "Is that all? Is there more? Please, Patricia, no more! I wouldn't have fainted if we'd done this at City Hall or some-place," he adds reproachfully, sitting up with some help from all three of us.

"Well, no, probably not, but it wouldn't have been as much fun either . . . Are you sure you're okay?" I gather him into my lap, holding him protectively; the ends of my hair feather across his face, and he gives them a teasing tug.

"Sure. Usually when I pass out I do it for much less, uh, *noble* reasons," he says with a grin for my concern. "I'm *fine*, I *promise*, I just want to stay here like this for a while. Just hold me. —So we're really married?" he asks after a few moments.

I laugh, relieved. "Weren't you paying attention?"

Maura, getting out the wine and cookies from their usual place under the altar, hears this and smiles.

"I think all this was a little more than you were prepared for, Jim."

"No, Patricia told me—"

"I know, but it's still hard for someone who's not used to it—the circle, the intensity of the power that's raised, coming for the first time into the presence of the Goddess. It's a very physical thing."

"You're telling *me*!" mutters Jim with feeling, and my spirits soar at the returning normalcy in his voice. He resettles himself more comfortably in my lap, intent, sorting his reactions, analyzing. "It was like— *imploding*, this incredible pressure and haze, something huge pushing down on me from all directions at once. I never felt anything like it, not even on acid."

"You felt the presence of the Lady." I ply him with cookies and a little wine; he is looking more himself now, though he does not stir from where he is, stretched out with his head in my lap.

"To answer your question, Jim," says Brân, passing the wine to Maura, "certainly you two are married; handfasted, rather, in the sight of the Goddess and the God and with us as witness to it. Patricia explained all that to you, before the ceremony."

"Well, yeah," he says. "But *still*."

We laugh, talking quietly for a while over the wine and cookies; after Jim recovers himself, we sign two documents that I have been preparing. They attest that on this date James Douglas Morrison and Patricia Kennealy, having handfasted themselves one to the other in the sight of the gods and in the presence of the High Priestess Maura and the High Priest Brân, declare that they are married in that rite. All four of us sign the papers, one of which is in English and the other in runes, Brân and Maura using their mundane names (nothing will induce me to tell you what they are). Jim and I squeeze out a few more drops of blood to seal our own signatures (themselves in plain old ink), and that concludes the formalities. Or, at least, the public ones...

Jim settles down again, leaning against the wall, and I curl up next to him in the corner on a pile of fur rugs. What neither of us is prepared for is what happens next.

* * *

Difficult to explain, and strange enough even at the time: But as we are lounging around in front of the fireplace, still chatting casually, all at once I feel my attention seized by a force utterly outside myself. I have felt this force before, though under different circumstances, and I know exactly Who it is that now approaches...

Looking across at Jim, I see that he seems to have received a similar wakeup call; he sits up suddenly, his face stamped with surprise—that delightful taken-aback expression he gets when something unexpected and new and pleasing happens—and he looks back at me with questions all over his face.

Maura and Brân do not need a house to fall on them: When they see that Jim and I are looking on one another with the wide dark pupils of desire, they gather up the altar tools, give us oddly respectful salutes, seal the circle behind them and leave the apartment.

Jim and I are alone in the circle—well, *not* alone, actually, and the great thing to me is that he too knows it. I excuse myself briefly to double-lock the door behind Brân and Maura, then return to the living room to re-enter the still-sealed circle. Shedding my black robe, I stand in front of Jim in the candlelight wearing only my silver crown and my wedding ring and three feet of dark red hair.

Jim looks up at me for a long time. "You look like—Someone," he says at last, in a soft wondering half-drowned voice. "Someone I should know."

"You know me." And indeed I feel as if someone—or Someone— has put me on, donning my flesh and form as easily as a mortal woman will don a dress; my body, my being, both raised to a higher exponent. And all those things I had been telling Jim before the ceremony suddenly take on a new and startling significance.

He slips out of his own robe and pulls me down beside him; without another word spoken we fall together naked into the soft heap of pillows and furs. As we make love I hear myself chanting softly to him in Irish, repeating to him the vows we had exchanged during the ceremony— the words we had said as we put the rings on one another's hands, repeated now as we take possession of one another, as we claim one another for the first time as wedded mates:

"Cuirim fad beannacht na greine thu—" ('I give thee the blessing of the sun—')

"Cuirim fad beannacht na gealaí thu—" ('I give thee the blessing of the moon—')

"—na mhara—" ('—of the sea—')

"—na reanna—" ('—of the stars—')

"—na Dé—" ('—of the God—')

"—na mBan-dé—" ('—of the Goddess—')

"Jesus Christ," Jim says after, inappropriately though not at all irreverently, "what was *that* all about?"

I can barely draw breath enough to manage a laugh. "*That*, my beloved, is what making love in a magic circle is all about."

"I like it, I like it—it's kind of a gift."

"Comes with the dinner, Morrison, the Goddess takes care of Her own." We are lying tangled together in the fur rugs, still breathing in gasps in the aftermath of the most apocalyptic lovemaking I have ever known.

"Well, if you ever go in for missionary work, mass conversions, you'll know what to use for a selling point—"

I try to move, and fail, and laugh. "I can't move—I don't think I'm there anymore below the waist."

"You'd better be—" He catches me by the hips and pulls me up beside him, cuddling, kissing my shoulder, playing with my hair; then asks shyly, "Are you happy?"

I close my eyes lest I explode. This is beyond happy: I have it both ways, validated just the way I want to be, bound morally but not legally. "How could I *not* be happy?" I ask in return. "You loved me enough to do this for me; and nobody else has to know about it; and out of it all I've got *you*. It's perfect, it's like eating your cake without having to have it."

We drowse in silence for a while; the candles burn down, the scent of peonies and incense is thick in the room. Jim puts his head on my breasts and is so quiet and so still for so long I think he has fallen asleep. I run a hand through his hair.

"I can hear every word you're not saying," he stage-whispers, and I laugh.

"Oh yeah? What about what *you're* not saying? You've been awfully damn quiet tonight."

He stretches and shifts. "Lot to think about. I don't do this kind of thing every day, y'know."

"Well, you'd better not—"

"Hey, you've been pretty subdued yourself. You sure have enough to say for yourself any other time—man, New Yorkers have something to say about everything, and they all think they're right."

"That's 'cause we are. All eight million of us. All the time. And at least we *do* think, which is more than I can say for—"

He grabs me, laughing. "Oh, man, who is it tonight? Southerners? Or Californians?"

"How about Southern Californians?" We tussle for a few minutes, kissing and laughing and rolling on the floor, then settle down again. "So, you weren't married before after all, Morrison."

He draws himself up with mock dignity. "I assume your not particularly veiled reference—unworthy of you, I might add—is to Pam. I *told* you we weren't married, it wasn't like it was a big secret or anything."

"Yeah, but you lie a lot." I am suddenly unwilling to spoil my wedding night with the specter of Pamela, rattling her chains—well, her beads, maybe—next to our nuptial couch like Marley's ghost. "It doesn't matter. The only thing you can't do now is handfast another witch."

Jim hoots. "Not likely! One's enough for me, especially a High Priestess. Not to mention I wouldn't want to do that knife trick again, either . . .   So, *Mrs. Morrison*, being as you're a June bride and all—are we gonna send out engraved announcements, society page and all that?"

I startle at his unexpected use of the name and title. "Are you *nuts?* A witch wedding? They'd love *that* at Rolling Stone—and too many people know about us already. Anyway," I add smugly, slipping one leg between his and moving it slowly upward, "it's more like you're Mr. Kennealy than I'm Mrs. Morrison. In fact, it's exactly like . . .   In the Craft, the woman always takes precedence, as the Goddess precedes the God; a priestess can act as a priest, but not the other way round. So don't you forget it."

"Oh, you know me," he drawls. "I never forget anything."

"I do know you; and, only when it suits you."

"What did you mean, death doesn't part? Are we stuck with each other *forever?*"

We have made love for the sixth time in two hours; even I, who knew better than Jim what to expect, am a little awed—maybe there is more to the principle of divine indwelling than I have ever imagined.

Jim elbows me impatiently when I do not answer him at once, and I jump.

"No! No, of course we're not. Well, we sort of are. I mean, we could go through an unbinding—a divorce ceremony—should we ever feel the need. But what I meant was only that death will never part us in any real sense, we'll always be together, always be linked on a very real level. The connection will be there as long as there is love; the vow is forever, and so is the bond."

He ponders that awhile. "I find that—comforting," he says at last. I glance sharply at him to see if he is being sarcastic, but his expression is open and honest.

"Why do we have to talk about that now?" I ask, a little more crossly than I mean to. The last thing I want to discuss at this moment is either one of us dying; but especially him dying.

"Oh, I just like to get these things sorted out"—and now he *is* being sarcastic.

"I've told you before, death is *not* the end, beautiful friend. At least witches don't believe it is; death is just a phase, and bonds we make in one life don't end when we start another. We've been lovers before, married before—we've probably been mother and son, father and daughter, brother and sister, friend and enemy; and I haven't always been the woman, and you haven't always been the man. This isn't the first time we've ever met, you know."

"There were sparks when we met," he says, savoring the memory. "That knocked me out—*you* knocked me out."

"You were pretty impressive yourself . . . But you always recognize people you've known before."

Jim brushes a hand across my forehead, tracing the line of the silver crescent moon where the ritual crown still gleams. He begins to tease the crown out from under my tangled hair, gently pulling the headband off at last, combing out the snarled strands with his fingers. I lie very still and just watch him; he looks intent, serious, loving, at peace—and I realize I haven't the faintest idea what he is really thinking.

"I may already know the answer," I say then, "but why did you do that?"

He turns the crown over and over in his hands, then sets it aside.

"I've been making love to a goddess all night, now I want to make love to my wife."

"I don't really like that word," I say honestly.

"Well, what word *do* you like?"

" 'Consort.' 'Consort' is good, I like 'consort.' "

He snorts. " 'Consort'! Why don't we just go right for 'Lizard Queen'?"

As we start to make love again he is laughing, but I get in the last word.

"See, Jim, didn't I *tell* you it would be more fun than City Hall?"

CHAPTER

15

THE NEXT MORNING I WAKE UP BEFORE JIM; BEFORE I
even open my eyes I know he has a raging fever—his side touching mine
might as well be aflame.

"Jim, you're burning up! How do you feel?"

"Fine."

"What a liar you are." I rummage through the nightstand drawer.
"Here. Put this in your mouth."

He grumbles, but opens wide for the thermometer. When I take it
out, I see to my horror that the mercury stands at over 101.

"A hundred and one! You're staying in bed, don't you dare even
think of getting up. I have to run out to get some stuff for you."

I hate to leave him alone, even for the few minutes it will take to
dash down to the corner grocery and the drugstore on Second Avenue.
But I need things for him I don't have in the house just now. I consider
antibiotics—tetracycline or some such, as a longtime self-medicator I've
got plenty of assorted brands in the house—but decide against it, who
knows what he's allergic to, and I will rely on plain old aspirin to bring

his fever down. Coming home, laden with invalid gear, I feel like Nurse Nancy.

Jim is fitfully asleep, his skin still fiery to the touch. I phone my doctor, who lives three blocks away and refuses to come over on a house call. He advises a hospital emergency room via ambulance, which seems a bit alarmist; but when I wake Jim up again to take his temperature, and see it now stands at 103, I reconsider.

But no other doctor I call will even ring me back; I can't find Leon, even. In desperation, I phone my mother for advice—she works with a doctor, the measure of my desperation being that I don't care she will know thereby that Jim spent the night with me—decide to apply home care as she suggests and see what happens by lunchtime.

I wake Jim up periodically to stuff him with aspirin, give him alcohol rubs, which he shudders at, and pour vast quantities of warm soup and cool water and flat sweet ginger ale down his protesting throat. He is a little delirious by now, and when I command him to drink still more fluids, he rebels.

"I can't drink any more—"

"Well, you can't be drinking enough, Jim, 'cause nothing's coming out the other end."

"C'mon, honey, the snake's seven miles long, it takes a while—"

"Not good enough! Get into that bathroom and don't come out until you drain that lizard dry!"

"Won't." He burrows down into the blankets and afghans I have heaped on top of him: wool, on a lovely June day, but he is shivering and his skin is still hot to my hand. "I've got a hollow Columbus anyway, y'know," he adds. "Just don't give me any more of those damn alcohol rubs, I promise I'll drink more water."

"Okay, but if your temperature isn't down in the next hour, it's the hospital for you."

Amazingly, it drops three degrees in half that time, and by noon it is normal again. Fever spike with a vengeance—I have never seen anything like it. When he asks me for something to eat I almost cry with relief, and make tea and toast and soft-boiled eggs, as he has requested. When I rejoin him, he is out of bed and on the point of getting dressed. I put a stop to that right there.

"Oh no, you're not going anywhere, Morrison. Just get back in bed and I'll feed you; you can get dressed later, if you're good. I'll try to phone Leon again."

This time I get through to Leon, who is concerned but not overly so. He says he'll try to come over later that afternoon, that I'm obviously doing all the right things and just take care of Jim in the meantime. I pass this on to my patient.

"You cured me!" he says, clear-eyed and bright-faced. "I think I was just overtired, we had kind of an exciting evening last night."

"To say the least." I give in to his pleadings, and let him out of bed, to curl up on the couch with pillows and blankets; I read to him while he dozes.

"Do you know Rimbaud?" he asks. " 'The Drunken Boat'?"

"Not only do I know it, I know it in *French*, and what's more, I can recite it. Well, some of it, anyway." Which I do, to his approval, and follow it up with another poem in French, a college favorite of mine, a haunting thing called "La chanson du spectre."

" 'Qui donc êtes-vous, ma belle?
Comment vous appelez-vous? . . .
. . . Je suis la mort, dit-elle.
Cueillez la branche de houx.' "

I have been deliberately trying to soothe him back to sleep, but he is drowsily attentive.

"You speak beautiful French—can you translate, too?"

"Well, not for the U.N. or anything, but I did study it for eight years. I *think* I could manage a conversation."

"Great—I heard Jean-Luc Godard might be in town, thought I might like to get together with him, but I can't speak French. You could translate for us."

I am less than thrilled at the prospect of translating between a director of movies so boring they make my hair hurt and his happy fan Le Roi Lézard, but I say Sure, fine, no problem. Jim drifts off into a doze, then into a real and restful sleep; I let him do so undisturbed.

But I watch him, hawk-eyed, while he sleeps, lest he should perhaps stop breathing or something; I want desperately to hold him, protect him, *save* him—but I know even as I wish this that it is the most forlorn of hopes. All I can begin to hope for is what I already have: him, here, now; and last night's ceremonial joining and the rapture that followed; and whatever will come of any of it, for as long as he will be—in the largest sense—around.

Leon shows up with Skip at around six, by which time Jim is awake again, fresh as a rose, lively as a monkey, brow as cool as a mountain stream. I have no idea how he does this, it must be magic. Leon, reassured, goes out to dinner with Skip, while Jim and I stay and cuddle. He apologizes profusely for putting me to so much trouble and worry, saying he doesn't mean to insult me but he's just too exhausted and maybe the best thing would be for him to go back to the hotel and fall out.

"Whatever you want, it's fine, believe me," I keep telling him. "That was a nasty little fever, and I just want to be sure you're resting."

In the end, I accompany him to the hotel anyway, spend the night; we even make love a few times in spite of our weariness. The remainder of that week passes in a dazzle and a dream: The next day, Jim is looking a million times better, refreshed, clear-eyed and alert. With shy pride he hands me a piece of paper: a poem he has written for me while I slept. It is not the first poem he has written me, nor will it be the last; but to me it is by far the loveliest, lyrical and achingly erotic, and I start to cry.

Jim is gleefully delighted with my reaction, and not above a dig.

"Well, *that's* a first! The critic weeps—is this the same girl who usually gives me 'Reread Aristotle's *Poetics!*' right in the chops?"

It's not the only thing he gives me as a wedding present, though surely the most precious: He surprises me with an incredibly lavish gift of jewelry; I reciprocate with a more modest gift of my own.

But that night we decide to take it easy, going for dinner to a Japanese restaurant a couple of blocks from the hotel: a small, inexpensive second-floor establishment across the street from City Center. We sit on tatami, shoes off, legs tucked into the little dugout under the table. About halfway through my teriyaki I feel a distinct nudge against my bare foot, repeated almost immediately. How sweet, I think, Jim's playing footsie with me. Until I glance down and see that it is a large gray *rat*. It looks domesticated.

"Aaaagghh!" is all I say. Jim thinks it's hilarious, and continues to tuck undaunted into his sukiyaki; I have suddenly lost my appetite. He chuckles about it all the way back to the Navarro.

Where there is a message awaiting us from Leon: Joanna was back, but Leon told her that Jim and I have gone upstate together, and she went away apparently reconciled.

"I wish we *had* gone upstate," he says mournfully. "Some nice old inn, somewhere in the mountains—well, next time."

I do not ask when, where, how; but we spend that night at my place again, unwilling to chance Joanna's untimely return.

On what will be our last full day together this trip, we get up early and wander around downtown; over to the White Horse Tavern in the West Village, Dylan Thomas's old haunt; many bookstores; then back to my apartment, where I change into something more suitable for our last night.

Jim approves. "Nice dress," he says when I emerge from the bedroom. "Well, what there is of it—"

I look down. Okay, it *is* short, and it does have a neckline that necessitates no bra—that tits thing again!—but it's perfectly respectable, a red cotton Betsey Johnson A-line, with long sleeves and buttons all the way to the hem, which ends in fact a foot or so above my knees.

It doesn't stay on very long, so who cares anyway—Jim is obviously fully recovered from whatever it was that had afflicted him—and after, we head back uptown to the Navarro. Since he will be leaving in the morning, it makes more sense for us to stay there that night. It is raining lightly by now, so I wrap my big fringed shawl over my hair and we venture to 57th Street for dinner, at a place called Wine and Apples, serendipitously downstairs from our first-ever dinner venue, Piraeus My Love—it was only last year, but it already seems a hundred years ago. After dinner, we walk hand in hand along 57th Street, stopping at a bookstore across from Carnegie Hall ("Why don't the Doors play *there?*" I ask, but he is doubtful), where he chooses for himself a two-volume poetry set, *The Hundred Thousand Songs of Milarepa*, some Petrarch, and a couple of Allen Ginsberg's books, picking out for me some works on Celtic mythology.

After we have ensconced ourselves for the night at the hotel, one strange incident troubles our idyll: Joanna comes to the door, shouting something about "Well, are you going to give me a divorce or will I have to kill you?"

" '*Divorce*'!?" Jim whispers, with a grimace of disbelief.

"Mick Jagger was really the one, you fucking bastard!" she informs us in a jet-engine howl, then with a final bash on the door—bolted, thank heaven—she is gone. Jim and I look at one another in silence.

"*Another* wife?" I tease.

He laughs. "No, you're the only one— Let me call the desk to make sure they don't let her up again." He does so, then visibly dismisses it with a shrug. "Let's go to bed."

"It's only nine o'clock!"

"So? I have to get up early to make the plane, and that means you have to get up too. We can read for a while, if you're not inclined to anything more, uh, *taxing*."

Oh, like at any time *ever*, let alone this week, I've ever indicated otherwise? "Sure you wouldn't rather go for a walk in the park or something?" I taunt back.

"It's raining."

"You won't melt. Don't you like rain?"

"Yeah, I'm human, I like rain. I just don't feel like going out for a walk in it—not when we can be in bed instead."

"Oh, well, if you put it like that—"

The Betsey Johnson dress comes off even faster than it did this afternoon; he doesn't even unbutton it, just rips it off me and throws it on the floor. It's my very favorite dress, but somehow I don't mind very much at all, and I look at him as he moves, naked, to the window to draw back the draperies, letting in the rain-glinting city light upon us both.

I say, very slowly and carefully, "I know I've said this before, but you are the most beautiful thing I have ever seen in my life."

It's a lie, of course: He is the most gorgeous creature that has ever walked this planet since the dawn of time. But I can't tell him that . . . It has never ceased to be delight and wonderment to me, how perfectly he suits my ideal of what I find attractive in a man, what comprises for me a man I can love: the physical, the spiritual, the mental, all in link, and all so totally instinctual from the start.

In soberest truth, I could not have *designed* somebody I would find more perfect—somebody handsomer or more intellectually challenging or more seductive or more desirable. All the elements are here in him, and the fact that the rest of the world seems, incredibly, to think he's gotten fat and sloppy and obnoxious merely reinforces me in the correctness of my opinion. Not that that really needs reinforcing—right again, as usual!—but really now, what fools these mortals be. Who *can* they be looking at when they say this?

Not at this man now in front of me, obviously; and the one thing that truly troubles me, that tiny detail of his drinking, is very far from us both just now. And I know, somewhere way far away, that I will do well to remember it, that forgetting it will be an error in judgment that will cost me dearly. But as I look at Jim, as he is this minute, here, with me, all my thoughts clear to one, and that one is, I have married this man. This man is my husband.

Oh, not in the eyes of the law, certainly, or even in the eyes of his friends, if they knew about it, which they do not; and, yes, extralegally, pseudojuristically, unsanctionedly, quasiofficially, whatever negating qualifiers you please, they're all true and I will ever be the last person on earth to dispute them.

But the fact also is true: In my religion, the only way that matters to me, I have wedded the man I love, and he for his part has loved me enough to wed me as I wanted—for whatever reasons, but I see no reason to doubt the word he has given me: that he did it because he loved me and because he wanted to. Twenty years later, his word is still good enough for me . . . and no matter anything or anyone else, private or public opinion to the contrary notwithstanding, that fact remains fact and always shall.

So he grins now, shyly, as I tell him how beautiful I find him, and slides into bed beside me.

"Well, you're not so bad yourself—"

"Oh, thanks for the crumbs!"

"Oh, Patricia"—he gives me a little shake—"don't you know by now you have to take everything I say with—"

"With a grain of salt?"

"With a salt mine."

"Everything?" I twist round in his arms to look at him. "Does that include the other night? The ceremony? After?"

He looks back at me for a long time before he speaks. "No. Not that. Not—that."

"I'm just asking, you know. You change your mind a lot."

He gives me a quick glance of wry amusement and grudging respect. "You're getting dangerous to have around, honey; you're starting to know me too well."

"Is that a problem?"

"Not yet."

We make love a few times, then watch the late news on the TV, just snuggling and quietly talking. I ask him something I've always wanted to ask, about whether he reads the reams of stuff written about him, and what he thinks of it. Being as guilty as the next critic in this regard, I naturally would like to know.

He smiles, a little wearily. "Yeah, I read it all; well, maybe less now than I used to. I guess to find some kind of insight from outside, some sort of key to what I do and how it gets done, whether it should be different. Just trying to understand."

I say unthinkingly, "Maybe if you ever understand how and why, you won't be able to do it anymore."

It's a mistake, and he leaps on it with something like joy.

"Well, well. I think you'd better explain yourself, miss."

That'll teach me . . . "If you understand something completely— I mean intellectually comprehend it—how it works, its inner mechanics, somehow it's a loss of faith," I say laboriously; I really have *not* thought this out. "You lose your faith in your art, like if you all of a sudden doubt you can ride a bicycle and so you immediately can't, you fall off right away. But if you just *do* it, you can't ever fully understand it, and you wouldn't want to, and you don't need to try. That's faith, that's what makes you an artist. If you do the other thing, you're a critic."

He laughs shortly. "Suppose you can do both?"

"I don't know what that would make you, but God help you if that's true. *Is* it true?" I ask, after a pause.

"No," he says at once, but he sounds doubtful, and he does not smile.

We make love all night long, with a kind of violent urgency, as if we not only can't get enough of one another but can't get close enough to one another. Coupling to mere ecstasy does not suffice: What is wanted here seems to be utter molecular fusion; which seems at first not possible, and then, all at once, it is.

Neither of us is the least bit interested in actually *sleeping* together, not tonight; neither of us wants to miss one minute of the other's presence. Early on, Jim does an encore Princess-and-the-Pea number, again pulling out my diaphragm—and this time his self-indulgence, or brattishness, or hostility, is to have terrible consequences. But in spite of our resolve to wakefulness and apparently inexhaustible desire, we finally fall asleep, exhausted after all: for a whole two hours, until the wakeup call from the front desk shrills us both back to startled consciousness.

Jim answers it, sounding a little dazed, then turns to me. "We have plenty of time to get it together," he assures me. "I had them call early on purpose—stay in bed, I want to take a shower."

My arms do not loosen around him. "I'll come with you."

He picks me up and carries me into the bathroom; I barely have

time to pin up my hair out of harm's way before the steaming hot water
is blasting us both. We scrub each other soapy, rinse off—so much for
the later canard that Jim Morrison never changed his clothes or washed
his person, this was not the only time I was to see him in close proximity
to soap and water—then, *very* carefully, make love under the shower,
not the first time for that either.

At last Jim turns the water off, wraps me in an armful of towels
and carries me back to bed, both of us dripping and shivering in the air-
conditioned chill of the room; I wonder what the maid will make of the
drenched sheets, then decide she's probably seen far worse. We make
love one last time before Leon calls to check that Jim's awake and about.

"You don't have to leave now too, you know," Jim says, hanging
up the phone. "Why don't you stay and sleep a while longer, they won't
throw you out of the room."

But I am already searching for my scattered clothing. "Hey, I *live*
here, remember? I have a home I can go to— Anyway, I want to go
over to the office for a few hours. I didn't do a lick of work all week
with you here, and I still have a column to write."

"Are you gonna put *me* in it?" he demands eagerly. "I want to be
in it—"

"Certainly. Which anecdote would you prefer, 'Lizard King Jim
Morrison and his new bride, drinking blood at their wedding . . .' or 'As
Jim Morrison said to this reporter, while they were fucking each other's
brains out in the shower (on the floor, against the wall, on the bed,
under the bed) . . .'? Either one sounds good, but you decide."

He gives me the snake-eye, the one where he knows you're probably
kidding but he's not quite certain.

"Be a best-selling issue, that's for sure."

"Oh, we're not that desperate to raise newsstand sales . . .   Anyway,
I think you've got enough troubles along that line already."

I regret it immediately: The shadow of Miami has been held off all
week by the blaze of love and passion ignited, and the spiritual high
imparted to us both by the wedding ceremony, and I wish to hell I had
not reminded him of the impending trial—most especially not in these
last few precious moments.

But he lets it pass, goes round the suite collecting our clothes from
where they were flung in haste the previous evening. I notice with some
amusement that several buttons are missing from my dress, and one seam

is even torn all down the side; I hope my shawl will mask the gaps until I can get to the office and mend them. (In the end, I never do sew the buttons back on, never stitch up that seam . . .)

Jim is packed now, both of us fully clad.

"Is that all your luggage?" I point with some disbelief to the rather small bag standing by the bedroom door.

"Yeah—I travel pretty light. They have stores in Europe, if I need something more I'll buy it." But he leaves the books he bought with me ("till the next time I'm here"), some other things as well.

The moment is come at last, and both of us know it. He takes my hand, looks down for a long time at the silver ring, then kisses it (his own ring is on a chain in his pocket, I saw it earlier while he was getting dressed).

"Don't you forget me now," he says softly.

"Oh Jim—don't *you* forget *me*."

"Hey, I'm the Elephant's Child, I never forget—wouldn't want to forget."

"No—but you do lose track of things from time to time."

He grins down at me. "Pa-tr-r-r-is-s-s-eee-ahhh"—again the teasing twist he had given my name the first time he ever spoke it—"don't *you* remember? Signing oaths, taking vows, drinking blood, *fainting*? Not to mention making epic love all week long, which maybe I'd better not mention— And you're worried I'm gonna FORGET?"

"I wish you weren't going," I say, muffled, into his neck.

"Me too, now . . . But I really need some time by myself before the trial starts— I still say you should come down to be a character witness."

I laugh, a bit shakily. "Oh, right, they're really gonna believe *me*! 'On the stand to testify, Mr. Morrison's witch wife, Patricia—' No, somehow I just don't think that would work out."

"Well, maybe not. Anyway, we can't have you radical New York agitators stirring things up."

"As if you hadn't done enough stirring up of your own—"

"I didn't do it," he whispers into my hair. "I told you that."

"Yes, you did tell me that. Well, now I guess it's all up to a jury of your peers."

"I have no peers."

"I know."

We hold each other for a long time, in silence.

Down in the lobby, I receive the muted morning civilities of Leon and Skip, and cling to Jim until the last possible minute.

"I'll call you as soon as I get back," he promises yet again. "Maybe I'll even stop off here first—but I do have to be back in L.A. for at least a couple of days before the trial starts, to talk to the lawyers, maybe buy myself some trial clothes—"

"*You?* In a *suit?*"

"No, I think some of those Mexican wedding shirts, maybe an embroidered jacket or something— So maybe we should just plan on meeting in Miami. But I *will* be back soon. With you. I promise."

"I know."

He kisses me tenderly and deeply, says something to me he has never said to me before, and steps into the cab. See you later . . .

I watch until it vanishes in the early morning traffic, and even then I look after it for a few minutes longer. Then I walk the three blocks west along the park to the office. I already know I am pregnant.

CHAPTER

16

July–August 1970

"WELL, BETWEEN YOU AND JIM, KENNEALY, THE KID'LL have *great* hair."

That is Susie: I have just told her the news, and she is not being flip or cruel or cavalier about my situation, but trying desperately to keep me from thinking of doing something, well, desperate. And she knows the best way to do this is to make me laugh; that, for me, laughter serves, always, to keep things in perspective. It is a valiant effort, but doomed: This, just now, is too big for even laughter to help much.

I laugh anyway. "And enough personality problems to land it in a padded cell by the time it hits puberty," I predict. "Oh, I know you're only trying to help, but, believe me, I'm way past that already."

"Then you know what you're going to do?"

"No. No. But I know what I *have* to do."

"What's that?"

"Tell *him*."

It is the end of July, and I have missed my first period. I *never* miss periods, so— Anyway, I knew even before the bed was cold that I was pregnant by Jim: just some little psychic signal telling me I was no longer alone in this vehicle called a body. It is a spooky feeling, and I do not like it at all.

I try to think of everything: every possible alternate ending, every imaginable variation on this age-old scenario. It always comes back to the same one: Jim will want nothing to do with this. In spite of the fact that of course he had *everything* to do with it: If he hadn't played Little Jack Horner with the damn diaphragm I wouldn't be in this situation right now. (Well, I might; other friends of mine have gotten pregnant behind diaphragms, it's not foolproof. Certainly wasn't in Jim's case . . .)

But assigning blame, though it passes the time agreeably enough, can take you only so far. After a while you know very well that decisions must be made, and you are the only one who can make them. This does not sit well with me, who, historically, prefer to let things decide themselves. But that is a luxury I cannot afford in this particular situation; I will, indeed I *must* decide. The scary part is that you know so well— overwhelmingly, all-consumingly, obsessively well—that you are not deciding only for yourself, but for a potential someone else too. The thought of that Other is never absent for the smallest instant from your mind.

Or what passes these days for your mind. Emotions have already got in there to muddle things up, have been in there all along, actually; only now there are some new ones, very powerful ones, ones I have never before had to deal with, and I feel ill-equipped indeed to do so. I decide I need more information, can't make a decision without data. So I call Diane: For some months now, her upstairs-next-door neighbor in a pleasant though modest West Hollywood bungalow block (*nothing* like the way it will be depicted in the Doors movie . . .) has been none other than Pamela Susan Courson, and the way I figure it, proximity equals truth.

"Tell me about Jim and Pam," I command. "Are they really married?"

I can hear Diane rolling her eyes all the way from L.A.

"Not *legally*—ooohh, that terrible Pam. But you know she goes around *calling* herself Mrs. Morrison, and sometimes she even wears a wedding ring— She came over to my place once, *really* pissed off at Jim, just raved on and *on*. Well, get a di*vorce*, I said. Oh no, no, she said, they weren't really married, at all, ever, they never got a license, they never had any ceremony—no, no, they're not married."

"Good."

"Well, *why?*"

"Because I'm pregnant."

"Ohhh *Patricia*—and it's Jim's, well of course it is, what a stupid thing to say, but is it good or bad? For *you*, I mean, who cares about Jim?"

"It's good that they're not married. I don't know yet about the rest of it."

But I do know. It is Jim's cosmic stupidity, and I am going to pay for it through the cosmic nose. I try to think of how it can be partly my fault too: if I hadn't gone off the pill and started using the other thing, if I'd insisted he wear a rubber (yeah, right), if I'd told him I'd cut it off if he didn't pull out, if I *had* cut it off when he pulled the diaphragm out—

At the end of all this I still don't see how it's my fault, and I feel even worse than before. Because there seems to be more to it than that: It feels, dare I say it, almost fated. Oh, not that I'd *wanted* to get pregnant, I've *never* wanted that. But somehow it almost seems as if this should be happening just as it is, for whatever reasons (because I know he's going to die? Because it's our mutual karma? Because the kid will be the One to Save the World? Do I really believe any of this? Answer: No, and it's dangerous to so indulge): that I should at this moment be carrying Jim's child. I have not heard, not yet, of the numerous paternity suits already reportedly pending against him; nor of one Penelope A.M. Truex of Sea Cliff, Long Island, who after Jim's death will write a letter that *Rock* magazine publishes, in which she claims she bore Jim a son as the result of a one-night stand in Tangier at just about this very time. (Her story, when at last I do hear of it, sounds quite likely to me, but I do not pursue it, save to mention it to Oliver Stone on our first meeting as a possible casting coup—he wonders aloud why the boy has not come forward, but I don't think he follows up on it.)

If I had known about her then, or about all the alleged others— I don't know. I like to think there would have been no agonizing and no question and no delay; that I would not even have told him we were expecting. But liking to think is not the same as knowing.

I can't figure it out. I don't *like* kids, I don't *want* kids; not even his. He is going to cast me off without a kiss or a word when he hears about it. No *way* is he going to provide any kind of support—not financial or emotional or any other kind. And just as certainly I cannot provide on my own for a child—I can just about make it taking care of me.

What it seems to me: some perverted and grandiose flash of déjà vu destiny, my own self made flesh and manifest to worship and cherish and adore without vanity or guilt. And Jim, of course; and Jim. If it were not his child there would be no question—but, also no question, it is no one else's child *but* his, and so the questions are many and hard. The child *as* child—as separate being, as possible person—has nothing whatsoever to do with this. It's all just him and me.

And when I come to realize that, and know it to be true, I also know what I am going to do about it. But it will be a long, hard, painful time getting there.

And I still have to tell Jim.

Time goes by. Prisoner of sex, I get a little fatter, and am sick a *lot*, and start to glow distinguishingly. Jim is back from Europe by now, but I have not heard from him; presumably he is engrossed in pre-trial activities, planning strategies with his lawyers, that sort of thing. Since I need to talk to him, and have no way of reaching him in guaranteed privacy—well, I *could* always call him at the Doors office, I've done that before, but somehow I shrink from it this time—I confide in people I would not ordinarily have chosen to confide in, hoping that sure access will come of it.

Bruce Harris is the first person I tell (well, after Pauline and Susie and Diane). I would have told him anyway; he is a good friend and has been privy to most of Jim's and my relationship. When he hears what the problem is, he damns Jim to hell in several very original ways.

I burst into tears. "It takes two, you know."

"You love him, *don't* you," observes Bruce disgustedly, confirming the only too obvious. "Kennealy, you're a lunatic."

But he does what must be done, speaks to those who need to be spoken to; he finds out where Jim will be staying in Miami, asks if he can tell Jac Holzman, it'll make it easier to get through. I say yeah, sure, whatever it takes, who cares who knows about it anyway (Jac's reported response: "I'm surprised Jim can still get it up").

All of a sudden I am deeply suspicious of everyone's motives, including my own. I have of course still to screw my courage to the sticking place—though that's about the only thing so far that *hasn't* been screwed—and tell Jim. But I cannot rid myself of this strange feeling that I am being managed . . . and I probably am.

"Ask Jim for a lot of money," urges Diane. "He'll respect you for it, it'll show him he can't push you around."

I have never rattled a tin cup with him yet, and I am not about to start now. "All I want him to do is pay for the—procedure," I tell her icily. "I can't afford it myself, otherwise I wouldn't even ask that. The sum total of my hospital bill, and not a groat more."

"Listen, Pam does it all the time," says Diane, with what she seems to think is ace persuasiveness. " 'Give me some money, Jim, I think I'm pregnant.' That's the kind of thing he understands, don't you see?"

Guess not. He may well be used to that sort of behavior—and to the sort of woman who would behave so—but that's not the way I do things.

Getting back to my problem. Being pregnant is unlike anything else on earth, a doubling of being, two bodies occupying the same space at the same time, in beautiful defiance of that prime law of physics. I realize to my vast surprise that, whatever happens in the end (and I know in my bones it will be absolute disaster for everyone involved), part of the ungodly mixed feelings I have just now is a strange and delicate gratitude to Jim for this experience; and no matter what comes after, that will never cease. Regardless of what will ultimately be decided, Jim and I are still for all time the parents of a child, and nothing anyone does—not him, not me, not anyone—can change that.

Two months is unquestionably it, though. The prospect of spending the next eighteen or twenty years raising Jim's daughter or son, alone, impoverished, certainly on welfare for at least the first years, unable to meet either its needs or my own, is utterly insupportable and unacceptable, and I know there is no way I will ever be able to make it be anything else. Not alone. I will not inflict that on a child, and I will not inflict it on myself.

So then it is the other thing, the course of action I cannot even bring myself to name yet in my mind. I would sooner die than tell my parents about this, so seek strength from my friends; and they do not fail me.

"So," says Susie. "Are you planning on maternity?" (Carefully, so as not to offend me if I might be, however unlikely.)

"I *don't* think so!"

"Nor I," she says, more easily now. "If you and Jim were planning on settling down and getting married or something, it might be different and you'd want to have it, but I don't think that's what either of you have in mind."

"Well, of course it isn't. It was terrific as it was, I was perfectly happy and I thought he was too."

"It's legal now in New York State, you know, and the earlier you do it the—less difficult it is. I'm sure the doctor you went to explained it all."

"He did." In fact, my doctor, to whom I had gone a couple of weeks back to officially confirm the pregnancy, had had quite a lot to tell me, ending with, "Listen, you, once you get past twelve weeks, it's a whole other story, and not a very pleasant one. A *lot* less pleasant than the preferred action, and that's bad enough. So go home, talk to your friend if you have to, or need to, and let me know. Soon."

I go away to Block Island for a few days to think about it all; by this point I know pretty much what must be done. I am not entertaining any stupid fanciful thoughts about a shotgun wedding, I didn't even want a legal wedding when I *wasn't* pregnant. The bottom line is that I want several mutually exclusive, not to say contradictory, things: I don't want an abortion. I don't want a baby, either. I want Jim's baby, but only because it's Jim's, but I don't want to raise it, or even to have it —Jim's baby is, after all, not to be thought of as the ultimate Morrison souvenir, sort of a super-autograph. Adoption is a total non-starter: I could not live in a world where a child of mine and the man I love was growing up without us. Above all, I don't want to have to *decide* anything, and more even than that I want things between Jim and me to be just as they were before I got pregnant. None of this is possible, much of it is nuts, and I am having a very hard time.

I sit on the rocks at Mohegan Bluffs and stare at the ocean, wondering how long would it take to drown and would it hurt. Not that I would *do* it (that would be a *decision*), but maybe a tsunami will come and I won't have to decide . . .

When I get back to New York, resigned and resolved and all cried out (or so I think), I learn that Jim is now in Miami for the start of his trial. The other Doors are with him for the first week, but not Pamela. Indeed, she does not attend the trial at all (she herself will tell me, when we next meet in L.A., that this was at Jim's insistence, and not only that but she says he wouldn't even take her calls while he was there). A small mercy, and I am grateful for it.

By now it is about the thirteenth or fourteenth of August. Bruce Harris calls to give me the hotel and room number, and I sit staring at the yellow pad where I have written the information, staring for a very long time. Finally I drop two Percodans, wait long enough for them to kick in, hold my breath and dial.

"Mr. James Morrison, please," I say in my best British accent. "Room 633."

"Just a moment." The hotel operator is not impressed, her What-makes-you-think-he'll-talk-to-*you*-sweetie coming through loud and *very* clear. Bitch thinks I'm just another groupie. She could be right.

Voice on. "Hi!"

"Hello, Jim, it's Patricia." (Here we go.)

"Well, hell, is that all, 'hello'? I haven't seen you for a month or so, y'know. Or have you just forgotten all about me? I warned you about that—"

He seems to be in a great mood, clearly delighted to hear from me. I am seized by doubt: Can it be no one has yet told him? Bruce, Jac, Siddons . . . no one's *said* anything to him?

"How was Europe?" I venture.

"Not much fun alone. You should have come with me."

"I wasn't invited. And I can't believe you were alone, either."

"Oh, it's not as unusual as you may suppose. But what have *you* been up to while my back's turned? You're probably gonna tell me you never want to see me again—"

It just comes out after all. "No, what I *am* going to tell you is that for the past seven weeks I've been the expectant mother of your unborn child."

He never misses a beat. "Well, if it's handsome and brilliant, then it has to be ours, right?"

I still can't tell if this is news to him or not. "Oh, it's ours, all right. Yours— Unless God has seen fit to work a miracle; it's happened before, I hear."

He laughs. "Rock and roll Immaculate Conception? Well, honey, obviously this is way too heavy to talk about over the phone, we have to see each other. Call Bill and have him get you down here as soon as possible. My time is pretty well taken up with the trial, but we're done by late afternoon, and we have days off in between. We'll talk. It's going to be all right."

"Jim—"

"I'll see you later, Patricia."

I stare out the airplane window at the puffy clouds below, at the gun-gray sea below the clouds. Doors manager Bill Siddons has arranged passage; it is Monday August 17, and I am on my way to Miami.

All I want to do is stare out the window next to my first-class seat, stay in my fugue state, gather strength and wits to face the hell I know is waiting for me in Florida. But the man in the seat next to me wants to chat, and he is cheerful and paternal, not hitting on me or anything; just seeing that I am nervous and upset, and being nice enough to take the trouble to distract me. He is a salesman of some sort, and opens his sample case to show me all sorts of arcane bits of computer parts. I haven't the faintest idea of what he is talking about, it's as if I have suddenly lost all memory and mastery of the English language.

But I tell him about Jim, and the Doors, and the trial—even he has heard of Jim, it seems—and the time passes quickly enough. At Miami I am met by Doors publicist Mike Gershman, Jim's lawyer Bob Josefsberg and Josefsberg's wife. We drive to the Carillon, a medium-priced hotel on Collins Avenue at 68th Street, where I get a room on the twelfth floor overlooking the ocean (paying for it myself), check in and, following Mike's advice, cool out for an hour in the tub.

"Jim knows you're here," he had said in the car. "Get settled, wash your face, calm down a bit, and go down to his room as soon as you're ready. He'll be there. He's expecting you."

I had stared at him, a bit unnerved. "Do you know what this is all about, Mike?"

"No, but I can guess. Just remember, you know Jim and you know what he's like under the best of circumstances. You've got an imagination, so project it a little and understand what it's like for him just now. That's all. He's basically in a good frame of mind, if that's what you need to know."

Message received and acknowledged . . . "That's what I need to know, all right."

An hour later I emerge from the elevator and knock on the door of Jim's room, six floors below and about twenty steps down the hall from my own room's location. No response. I rap again, louder and longer this time.

Television noises from within; then a bellowed "WHO'S THERE??" Even through the closed door I recognize that vocal timbre.

"Patricia," I say, a bit more sharply than I had intended. Babe Hill opens the door a crack and peers out.

"Hello, Babe," I snap. "Is he there?"

"Oh, hi, Patricia," he mumbles, sounding a little discomfited. "I think he might have been asleep, let me check."

"I'll wait," I say with a grimness.

Almost immediately Jim slides through the doorway, grabs me by both my arms and kisses me hard on the mouth. "You look like a ghost," he says reprovingly when we finally pull apart.

"I'm not surprised." I am furious with myself for responding to his kiss.

On the way down in the elevator he looks sideways at me. "Did you have a good flight?"

"Oh yes. It might have been an even better flight if the plane had just crashed and burned with no survivors, or maybe vanished into the Bermuda Triangle. I'll manage it better next time."

He visibly flinches at the bitterness in my voice. "You don't really mean that."

"Yes, Jim, actually I do."

We ride the rest of the way in silence. Arriving on the lower lobby floor, I push past him when the doors open; he grabs my arm and steers me gently to the right, heading for a dimly lit, nautically themed bar in the far back corner. On the way, a fan comes up to us and hands Jim a cut mango, politely offering me a piece as well. I thank him in my best manner, but do not touch it; well, I mean, who knows where it's been, or what's in it?

So I pace silently beside Jim in this cool Grace Slick stalk-walk— I am wearing a black tunic and flame-colored silk pants, he comments favorably and often on my appearance—and, in the deserted bar, I seat myself at right angles to Jim, at a table in the farthest, darkest corner.

We look at each other for a long time. He is full-bearded again, his hair down to his shoulders, and he is dressed in a neat preppie-looking striped shirt and black jeans, with an embroidered ethnic-looking jacket. Probably from Pam's shop. His eyes meet mine full on, but they are haunted with things I cannot, or will not, read.

"Honey, I'm pregnant," I say deliberately, still staring him down. We hold the look a moment longer, then both of us begin to laugh softly. It is the laughter of desperation and bitterness and pain and frustration and fear, and it is all but weeping, and there is no merriment in it at all.

He reaches across the table and grabs both my hands. I am shivering now, about half a breath away from tears and knowing that I cannot, dare not, weep just yet, there is too much to do, to say. In silence he rubs his thumb over my rings—*his* rings—but says no word except to order drinks. I join him in Chivas and Coke.

Neither of us knows just how to start talking about what we both know must be discussed; but every time I take a deep breath and begin to address it he skates elegantly away. For the next couple of hours he tells me tales of courtroom drama, reads me stories from the newspapers about the trial, anything and everything calculated to distract me, to charm me into a better frame of mind, to distance himself from something he does not want to deal with.

We have more than a few drinks, then go upstairs again and continue our non-discussion in my room. Again I am balked and baffled by his unwillingness to face up to this: It was his idea to get me down here, I know it's not easy for him, but it's even less easy for me. I can see he's scared, but so am I, and I do not have the luxury of time to coax things along. He's just facing jail time; I'm facing—either way it goes—a life sentence.

He wants to make love with me, and I rebuff him, although I want him desperately. That, after all, is how it started in the first place; he's not going to distract me again, not until we've settled this between us.

I have brought with me a few copies of the September issue of *Jazz & Pop*, the one with his poem "The Anatomy of Rock" and his picture on the cover. He is thrilled with the surprise of it, asks if I could get a couple of dozen copies more, for him to bring to the courtroom, to show the judge and the jury that he is a serious person, a published poet. I say I'll call Pauline tomorrow, we could have them sent by overnight air freight.

I stare at the Jim on the magazine cover: the brooding prince in Maximilian's Palace. Stare, and then without warning snap.

"*There!*" I snarl, flinging the magazine at his feet. "*That's* the man I love! *That's* the man I swore vows to! *That's* the man who's the father of my baby! Who are *you*? Just—who the *fuck* are YOU?!"

I rip the rings off my fingers so violently I tear the skin—both rings, the antique solitaire, the silver claddagh—and fire them straight at his head. He doesn't flinch or move or duck, and the claddagh actually hits him in the face. His expression never even changes. But he goes to his knees to pick up the rings; coming over to me, he takes my hands and gently slips them back upon the proper fingers.

"Listen," he says very softly, tilting my face up to his, "we can't talk about this tonight, we're both too upset. I don't want us to hurt each other, or to decide anything out of anger. I'd stay with you, but I want to make love to you too much, and I don't think I'd be able not to, and I don't think that would be good for either of us just now. So just go to sleep, get some sleep, and we'll talk tomorrow. I have all day free, I don't have to be in court at all. We'll talk. It's going to be all right. I promise."

He turns to leave, then turns back abruptly, strides over to me, pulls me violently into his arms and kisses me passionately, telling me between kisses, over and over, that he loves me, asking again and again if I love him, to the point of desperate, pleading, incoherent babbling. I do not understand.

After the door closes at last behind him, I retreat to the middle of the bed, to sit with my legs crossed Indian-style and my clenched fists pressed to my mouth. I am shaking uncontrollably, as if with burns or fever or the first stages of freezing to death, and tears begin to stream silently down my face. Yet I am not weeping: There is no sound, no sobbing, my face is uncontorted, perfectly in repose. It's just that these tears are pouring down my cheeks, and they do not cease to flow for a very long time.

CHAPTER
17

I WAKE UP EARLY, TO A SHINING HOT FLORIDA MORNING. I have no idea of knowing just when Jim will show up as promised, so am afraid to leave my room for even the smallest chunk of time. Not that I have anywhere much to go—I hate the sun, and wouldn't hang out at the pool or the beach if someone held a gun to my head. I have spent the night in unconsciousness only because I took some pills, but I awaken completely and all at once, in full possession of all my faculties and ready for battle.

But no battle comes. The day drags on—in the forenoon period I make several calls to Jim, he calls back a few times, saying he'll be up before lunch, then it's after lunch, then he's gone all afternoon, my calls go unreturned.

I know exactly what he's done: He has turned tail and run like the coward he is, gone off with his drinking-buddy attendants because he can't face me and talk about this situation of his own making. I am in such a towering fury that, Zennishly, I have transcended fury, so consumed with rage that I am motionless and at peace.

About five o'clock the Zen standoff seems to ease a bit. I am going insane from enforced captivity, so I dare a short walk, a mile out, a mile back. Also I am very hungry, which didn't seem to matter so much when I was so angry; it does not occur to me to call room service, too expensive anyway, so on the way back from my walk I stop at a restaurant on Collins Avenue for something to eat, and at a takeout place to bring some sandwiches back with me for later.

There is no message from Jim. I do some more drugs and cry myself to sleep.

The next morning I am up before the sun and ready to kill. Mike calls and says to meet in the lobby for the drive to the courthouse, today is a trial day. I find to my surprise that I am actually interested in watching this travesty of justice in action; in fact, I spent part of my solitary Tuesday reading Miami papers for their accounts of the previous day's frolic in the fields of the law.

I share the ride with the usual suspects: Mike; Gloria Vanjak, a Rolling Stone stringer covering the trial (coverage given the trial by this and other rock rags—with the exception of Rock, for which Mike is himself filing stories—is minimal to nonexistent; the philosophy seeming to be plaster Morrison all over the cover when he'll sell your rag for you, box him in a page 38 sidebar when real principles are at stake); and Harvey Perr, a free-lance Elektra publicist and playwright (*The War Widow*, among other works) who's also a friend of Jim.

We arrive at the courthouse in downtown Miami (if I have to hear Freda Payne singing "Band of Gold" on the car radio just one more time I will rip someone's arms off): typical governmental-slum architecture, bad public art (is there any good public art? isn't that what this trial is all about?), Middle Americans thick on the ground (and in the head). Somebody tells me renowned jewel thief Murph the Surf is also on trial now, just down the hall from Jim, which seems about right.

I do not see Jim until we get up to the second floor and mill around for a while outside the courtroom. Besides the judges, he and I are the only people there wearing black. He comes right over to me, draws me aside.

"I'm *sorry*—" he begins contritely.

"I ought to kick you in the lizard," I hiss at him, smiling all the while for the benefit of onlookers.

"It was unforgivable of me, I know, I'll make it up to you—"

"Unforgivable, but you want me to forgive you anyway . . . well?"

"I promise we'll talk about it tonight. Just as soon as we get back from this thing." His eyes are shifting, opaque, avoiding me.

I smile a different sort of smile. "If we don't talk tonight, Jim, maybe you won't have to worry about coming to court tomorrow."

His own smile is rather more pained; the doors open, and we walk in together. Some camera crew from a local television station has been filming all this, which does not make me happy.

Inside, we part company. Jim goes to the defense table, on the left-hand side within the railings of the court precincts. I flash my press card at the somewhat bemused bailiff, and am escorted to a seat in the press box, also inside the railings, diagonally across from Jim on my left and the judge on my right, facing the jury across the width of the room. It makes a neat quartering, kind of like a magical circle: Jim in the East, the jury in the South, the judge in the West, me in the North. No other press is there (save for Gloria, who sits in the courtroom proper), and I ensconce myself in lonely splendor, with an unimpeded view of just about everybody.

Jim sits at the table with his lawyers, writing incessantly in his little notebooks. He seldom looks up except at the judge or the witness of the moment; he never looks at the jury and he never looks at me.

The judge, one Murray Goodman, looks at me a lot, though—a new player in his courtroom—and I can see what his tiny mind is thinking: one of them damn *writers*, some hippie troublemaker from that commie-pinko-liberal New York gutter press; or else some groupie slut no better than she should be—he saw me outside with Jim, and even an idiot, even *this* idiot, could not have failed to grasp the fact that the defendant and the journalist were acquainted.

But a more evil-looking bucket of pustulence and bad vibes I have never yet encountered: The little sunken pig eyes rest on me until I feel I need a bath; then they move dully on to consider Jim, and I find myself instinctively leaning forward, wanting to throw myself across Jim like a shield, between him and that black-robed thug on the bench of Dade County justice. I content myself with giving Goodman (later to be busted on bribery charges; and, though acquitted, dead soon thereafter) the evil eye every time he looks my way.

This Wednesday is only the second day of the trial proper, which began on August 10th with jury selection and other arcana. The day's witnesses include a Miami policewoman who is shown by her own testimony to be rather less than the soul of honor (some small matters of

her sworn statements not agreeing, listening to a tape of the concert—
strictly forbidden—and blurting out that fact on the stand), and her
comments are stricken from the court record (the prosecutor is totally
unembarrassed); and a photographer who had taken over a hundred and
fifty pictures of Jim in concert that fateful night at the Dinner Key
Auditorium, and not one exposure showed the least bit of, well, exposure.

Previous witnesses have included a sly-eyed, blonde drugstore cash-
ier, seventeen years old and the sister-in-law of a Miami cop, who professes shame and shock and outrage at her alleged sighting of Jim's
allegedly exposed penis. So overwhelming was her disgust, apparently,
that (though she claims barely to have glanced at It) she did manage to
notice, even so, whether or not Jim was circumcised (which, as I and
many others can attest, he is). Off the stand, she tells a Morrison fan
who has reprimanded her, "Fuck off, you little bitch!", and right in front
of reporters, too: a fine specimen of young Florida womanhood. Her
boyfriend also testifies; admitting that his view was partially blocked, he
nonetheless thinks the "exposure" lasted five to eight seconds, and asserts
he was chiefly worried about the effect that the sight of Jim's unveiled
member would have on his young girlfriend. Hey, I'd be worried, too,
if I were you . . .

After the lunch break, which Mike, Gloria and I take together, we
all go back inside the courtroom to hear more testimony from the photographer, and to gape at a startlingly cynical move by the forces of evil
(read prosecution and judge), which seems to give an unambiguous hint,
if anybody still needed one, as to which way this trial is headed: The
prosecutor actually tries to enter into evidence a negative of dubious
quality, when a perfect clear print is already available—the negative
being open to the interpretation "He did it" where the print unequiv-
ocally shows that he did not. Jim's attorneys and partisans are outraged:
not only at the attempted fiddle, but by the judge's casual amusement
—he actually tells the prosecutor it was a "nice try." We should have
saved our outrage; there will be worse of this sort of thing to come.

We run back to the Carillon after court has broken for the day,
to catch ourselves on the evening news and grab a bite to eat. As we
are leaving the courthouse, Jim comes over to tell me he will be up to
my room at around six-thirty; and, much to my surprise, he is.

"If you want an abortion, I'll pay for it."

I am sitting in the middle of the king-size bed, my knees drawn up and my chin resting on my knees. My defenses, honed by two days of fury and anticipation, are sky-high for this encounter. I look up at Jim, he instantly looks away, and I look down at my fingernails.

"Listen," I begin, hating the tight voice that issues from my own throat, "I'm not exactly thrilled by the idea of a baby, but you happen to be the only man I ever thought was good enough to father a child of mine. And now it's happened—remember that diaphragm you seemed to find so annoying?—and I don't know quite what to do about it. I do think you owe me a bit more than just your checkbook."

He glances quickly in my direction, then away again. "It's up to you, really. A baby isn't going to change my life at all, but it would change yours tremendously, forever."

"You cocksucker," I say unemphatically. "I hear Florida still has a law permitting challenges and duels in matters of honor. I didn't bring any gloves with me, but we could take the gauntlet as flung. I'll even let you choose the weapons. How about it?"

"Liberation seems to have gotten the better of you."

"Liberation has nothing to do with it!" I flare, uncoiling like a striking cobra and leaping to my feet. "What I want is satisfaction."

"Well, leaving deeds of arms out of it, what sort of satisfaction could you get, practically speaking?"

"I could take it to court." Jesus, love takes the pipe even quicker than I thought . . .

Jim looks surprised at the idea.

"Another trial? Well, sure, you could do that, and it'd be just like this one we're having now. It'd take a long time, though. First you'd have to have the baby, that'd be, what, another seven months. Then you'd have to set up a hearing; that'd take more time, maybe even a year, with blood tests for everybody and all the rest of it, just to see if you even had a real case. I'd deny the charges, of course, and you'd have to get witnesses who'd say they'd seen me with you in intimate situations, in your house or hotels or wherever, and maybe there wouldn't be any witnesses because I'd buy everybody off first. And even if you finally got it into court you might not win, and there would be horrendous publicity which I wouldn't give a damn about, but I don't think you'll like having your bedroom a feature story in every paper in the country."

He goes over to the floor-to-ceiling window, looks out at the ocean.

"And even if you won the case in the end," he says then, "what would you have gotten out of it? Some money and some satisfaction and a lot of bad press and bad feelings, and a heavy responsibility for the rest of your life. And you'll make us lose what we have now, and we have something so good and real together. I don't think you really believe it's worth all that."

"You seem to have this all figured out," I snap. "Or is this just what that reptile lawyer of yours told you to tell me? Man, some piece of work *that* guy is— If I had an evil suspicious nature, I might think this situation's come up a few times before, and this is just your standard rap to people you've gotten pregnant—   I suppose it makes no difference to you that it's *our* baby, yours and mine, and not yours and Pam's?"

He looks even more surprised. "I—no, *no* difference! None. I won't support a kid. *Any* kid. I can't afford it, and I don't want the responsibility. What would I do, eighteen, twenty years from now, if the kid shows up at my front door and says 'Hi, Dad!'?"

"That would be between you and your child, if that happened . . . But the only way you can't afford it is emotionally. That's part of your problem, isn't it—your *real* problem."

I have never before referred even this directly to his alcoholism; he does not like it one bit, and pays me back at once.

"Well," he drawls, in an oh-come-on-little-girl voice, "wouldn't it be better to have a kid with somebody who wanted to be its father?"

Though I do not let him see it, that was a spear straight through the heart.

"Obviously," I say coldly. "So I guess you're saying you don't want to be your own child's father."

"I'm saying I can't," and now his voice is gentle. "Not now. Of course I already *am* its father, but just now it's not possible that I could *be* its father."

The gentleness has begun to undo me. "It *is* our baby, you know, Jim."

"I know," he answers, with even greater tenderness. "But not yet."

"And you want me to stop it from being any more of our baby. I just want to be sure I've got this right."

"Yes." He will not look at me now, sits playing with my watch, my jewelry, my hairbrush.

I feel calm return, the murderous kind. "I realize all this must be rather old hat to *you* by now, of course, this kind of thing, but not for me. This is probably the only chance I'll ever get at having a child, and you are the only man I've ever wanted to bear a child to—if I wanted

Jim Morrison and Patricia Kennealy, June 1970. © JAZZ & POP MAGAZINE; JANICE COUGHLAN, PHOTOGRAPHER.

ABOVE: James Douglas Morrison, Class of '61, George Washington High School, Alexandria, Virginia. RIGHT: Patricia Kennealy, Class of '63, North Babylon High School, North Babylon, New York.

ABOVE: Patricia with Pauline Rivelli, publisher of Jazz & Pop magazine, 1969.
© JAZZ & POP MAGAZINE. BELOW: Patricia with Tandy Martin, Jim Morrison's
high-school girlfriend, and self-portrait of Jim, 1969. © DAVID G. WALLEY.

TOP PHOTO SEQUENCE: Jim Morrison onstage at the Felt Forum, New York, January 1970. © JAZZ & POP MAGAZINE; JANICE COUGHLAN, PHOTOGRAPHER. OPPOSITE: Circa 1968. FROM THE PRIVATE COLLECTION OF PATRICIA KENNEALY MORRISON. ABOVE: In the Jazz & Pop offices, June 1970. © JAZZ & POP MAGAZINE; JANICE COUGHLAN, PHOTOGRAPHER.

ABOVE: Patricia Kennealy, Los Angeles, 1975. © DAVID G. WALLEY. BELOW: Pencil sketch of Patricia, on which she and Jim collaborated, June 1970. © PATRICIA KENNEALY MORRISON. OPPOSITE: Document signed by Jim Morrison and Patricia Kennealy to attest to their handfasting, 24 June 1970. Signatures of cosignatory witnesses have been obscured to protect their privacy. © PATRICIA KENNEALY MORRISON.

On this Midsummer Day
24 June 1970
Patricia Kennely
and
James Douglas Morrison
do set themselves handfast one to the other
and
declare themselves wedded by that rite
in the sight of the Goddess
as witnessed by
Her High Priestess and High Priest

Patricia Kennely
Patricia Morrison

Morrison

Jim Morrison's grave, Paris, July 1971. © PATRICIA KENNEALY MORRISON.

it, which, quite honestly, I really don't. And what I need you to help me with is a reason. As far as I'm concerned, it's this child, your child, or no one's."

He turns on me, his face a mask of anger. "What makes you so sure it's old hat to me, as you put it? This is the first time for me too, you know, this has never come up with me before."

"Oh Jim, don't give me that! Don't fucking lie to me, on top of everything else! I know about at *least* four others— Let's at least be honest about this, if not admirable."

"No, no, it's not true, I swear it's never happened before." He runs a hand over his beard. "Don't you think this is hard for me? You're not the only one involved here, you know— As you keep pointing out, Patricia, it's *my* baby too . . . And don't you understand yet why I can't let you go through with it, have the baby? Because I'm fucking scared to death by the whole thing. I'm not ready for it. I don't know if I'll *ever* be ready for it. And if you're so set on honesty between us I'll say that *you're* not ready for it either, and maybe *you* never will be."

I am weeping by now, very quietly, making no attempt to hide my tears from Jim, but not advertising them either.

"We're too much each other's person, and our own persons," he continues. "Call it selfish if it makes you feel better, blame me if *that* makes you feel better. All I know is if you have that baby, it'll ruin our friendship."

"It's done that already!" I shoot back at him.

"No, no, it hasn't, honey, don't say that." He comes over to me, tries to hold me, but I pull violently away.

"Don't you fucking TOUCH me, Morrison!"

He sits on the bed instead, gives me a ghost of the old grin. "It'd be an amazing kid, a genius for a mother and a poet for a father."

"No doubt. Except it wouldn't *have* a father, would it." He flinches a little; I brush my hair from my face. "I don't want a child, Jim, not even yours. But yours is the only one I'd ever want— I don't want the other thing, either, though, and I can't do it alone, not without you."

He seems off on another road entirely. "If you did have the baby," he asks presently, "what do you think you'd name it?"

I stare at him. I think we are both out of our minds with pain and grief and pressure, for I say, "Did you know that Sir James Douglas took the heart of King Robert the Bruce to the Holy Land when Bruce died? And on the way Sir James was attacked by Saracens, and when he saw—when Sir James Douglas saw that there was no hope, he took out the silver case with the heart of the Bruce inside, threw it into the midst of the enemy hordes, charged after it, and died."

Silence in the room. When Jim turns to look at me I see that he is crying. Presumably not over the fate of his long-ago namesake . . .

"Patricia—if you have the kid, it'll be your kid. If you have the abortion, I'll pay for it, I'll come to New York to be with you, I'll be right there to hold your hand. We'll go away someplace after it's over, just the two of us."

"And what do you expect us to do about it afterwards?" I manage to say, through the sobs that are tearing me apart.

"Weep about it together, I guess."

He comes over to me, sits beside me on the edge of the bed and opens his arms to me, folding me against his chest. Sure, now that he knows he's won he can afford to be loving . . . We sit holding each other for a long time, both of us crying, talking in disconnected phrases.

"Maybe we should go downstairs, get something to drink," he suggests after a while, when we are both a little calmer.

"Is that always your answer? Maybe—yeah, sure—but you *will* be with me, you won't make me go through it alone?"

"I said I will. I promise."

I shake my head wearily. "No, you won't. You won't be there. You think I can't tell when I'm being lied to, now, just because I couldn't tell all along?"

Surf's *up!* Instantly we are back at it, all thought of drink forgotten.

"I am NOT lying to you! I have *never* lied to you! Why can't you fucking believe that!" He flings me aside, strides over to the window again. "If this had happened at any other time," he says after a while, more calmly now, "things would have been very different—Patricia, Patty, they're out to put me away, I'm not gonna win this thing, you know that as well as I do. I don't know what's going to happen next— and you want to give a baby a convict for a father? If we decide that's what we really want, *when* we decide we want that, then we can have another one; and then it'll be right for us *and* the kid."

He turns around then, and I see by his expression what I must look like. He starts to move toward me, then pulls back again.

"But we would make such an incredible kid between us—"

I explode off the bed. "Why do you keep coming back to that?" I scream at him. "Isn't this torture enough, do you have to make it as hard on me as possible? Or is this another one of your fucking *tests*? Or do you just want to *hurt* me as much as you can, maybe *that's* what this is all about! Of course it would be an incredible kid, nobody's ever said it wouldn't! How could it not be—but this isn't some kind of breeding experiment, to see if two terrific people can produce an even more terrific offspring. You've said you don't want the baby, and I've said the only reason I want the baby is because it's *your* baby, and—the most honest thing I can say—I truly don't think just wanting it because it's yours is a good enough reason to have it. I'm not going to do that to my kid, life without its father, and I couldn't give it what it needs, not alone. I just need you to help me decide that, that's all. Just help me—*know* that. I can do the rest."

"Well—be brave."

I laugh grimly. "Fuck you, Morrison, I can be a lot braver than you can, just watch me! That still doesn't mean I want to do this without you."

"You won't have to! How many times do I have to tell you! I'll be with you, I'll stay with you, we'll be together, I *promise*. Why won't you believe me?"

"Because I know you now, okay? I thought I did before, but now I see that I was mistaken."

That seems to be the last button left to push: Suddenly Jim is enraged, out of control, in such a fury as I have never seen in anyone.

"Don't you understand *any* of this?! Don't you even see what's happening here? You're supposed to be so fucking *empathic*, so *psychic*, aren't you, you're a *witch*, right? Well, you're supposed to be my *wife* too, or didn't that little knife trick at your place mean anything to you after all?"

And that's the last of *my* buttons... "It means *EVERYTHING* to me!" I blaze back at him. "If I'm supposed to be your *wife*—then what's all this even *about*? Just what the fuck did it mean to *you*?"

He grabs me by the shoulders and arms and hair and we crash together into the wall, our faces only inches apart. He pulls my wrist up between us, turning his own sideways, forcing me to look at the tiny white scars.

"I don't know yet what it means," he says then, in the softest and most desperate voice imaginable. "I'm still finding out what it means to me—still wanting to find out. But I'm finding out with *you*. I did it for *you*. Not for anyone else. Remember? *Our* blood, *our* rings, *our* vows—

you to me, me to you. I've never done that for *anyone* else. And you still think this is *easy* for me?"

Abruptly he releases me and spins away from me. *"PATRICIA!"* It is a howl of the purest pain, he is wild-eyed now, almost screaming. "Patricia, I want you to *help* me!"

Incredibly, tears are streaming down his face, he is weeping as I have never seen a man weep before. All of a sudden I am sitting on the bed and he is sprawled on the floor, arms wrapped around my knees, sobbing into my lap.

"I don't know how to help you," I hear myself saying through my own blinding tears, and it is the hardest thing I have ever had to say. "If love's not enough— I don't think you really want to be helped or saved—I think you believe once you're saved, you won't be an artist anymore. It's bullshit, but I think that's what you really think."

"Where do you learn all this, critic school?" Now he is angry again, and I feel my own fury rising to match his. "Or are you just some kind of psychic cheerleader?"

"Fine!" I scream back at him, and leap to my feet, almost kicking him in the face as I do. "Go back to your stupid junkie girlfriend, maybe *she* can help you, the way she's been helping you all along, you fucking alcoholic, the way you *want* to be helped—right into your grave, that's where you *really* want to be! The hell with you, Morrison, I'm having the baby! —No, no, I'm not, no woman on earth in her right mind would want to give her kid a cocksucker like you for a father!"

"Patty—"

"Then WHAT??" I shriek. "What the *fuck?* JIM??"

I am trembling with fury and frustration and helplessness and pain, I feel that with one more word, one more tear, one more turn of the knife, I will explode; or he will, or the planet will—

Jim comes over to me, stares down at me, tears still on his face; then he reaches out and curves one hand round the side of my face.

"Don't you know?" he asks softly. "Don't you even fucking know?" He says something about Pam then and something about me, things that make me so happy I start to cry again. "Why do I have to *tell* you these things?"

For the briefest instant I lean into his touch, his words, it is all possible again. Then I pull away.

"Because you're lying to me, that's why," I say, exhausted at last, he's won, he's beaten me, it's finished. "You won't be with me, you'll

be back with her, everything will be just the same except you and I won't
be having a baby anymore. Just go now, okay? You're going soon enough
anyway—it's safe for you with her, it's easy for you, it's familiar. *She's*
fucked up, so she gives *you* permission to fuck up; *she* tells you you're a
great poet, *she* doesn't suggest you reread Aristotle; you don't have to
work at any of it—oh Christ, Jim, just *go*."

We stare at one another, faces still stained alike with tears. I catch
sight of myself in a mirror: I look like a banshee, eyes blazing, face white
as death, once-smooth hair a red ragged mop. Unbelievably, I want him
more than I have ever wanted him, more than I've ever wanted anyone,
and I can see that he is wanting me just as much. Without another word
we are in one another's arms, kissing desperately, saying incomprehensible things, clinging to one another as if we were each other's last hope
of escape from a burning land. Perhaps we are.

Somehow we are both naked, and he pulls me down onto the bed.

"I'm gonna burn you down," he snarls into my ear.

"I—*don't*—think—so!" I snarl back.

"I never said you weren't a very sexy lady—"

"You never said I was."

"Oh Patricia, do I have to say *everything*? If I didn't say it, it sure
was implied—"

We are still delirious with hurt and pain and madness, and our
lovemaking is more violent even than usual—not abusively, physically
violent, Jim and I were never into that kind of thing together; but
explosive, desperate, ferocious with urgency and subtext and aftermath.
Perhaps it's violence after all.

The phone has rung a few times during the course of the evening
—even after all this drama, amazingly, it is still barely ten o'clock—but
I have not been picking up; and when it rings again an hour later,
I reach out a bare arm and take it off the hook. Jim stirs beside me.

"Who was that?"

"Mike, probably. Does he know you're here?"

"I'd say he's got a pretty good idea."

"Well, let him wonder."

At about midnight, some Doors minion comes knocking. Jim is
deeply asleep, and I do not respond. The safety chain is on, so I feel
reasonably safe in ignoring the inquirer; but he actually has hotel security
unlock the door. They can't get past the chain without breaking down

the doorframe, and I still won't answer his entreaties. I can't believe he would actually go so far, though he might think Jim and I have killed each other. But he goes away, taking the security guy with him.

After a moment's thought, I put the phone back on the hook; it rings almost immediately.

"Is Jim there with you, Patricia? Are you two okay?"

"Yeah, he's here, he's asleep, we're fine. Give us a wakeup call. And don't worry—I'll get him to the court on time."

CHAPTER

18

"Jim! I'm freezing and I'm falling off the bed! Why do you have seventy-five percent of the bed and a hundred percent of the covers?"

" 'Cause I'm a bed-and-cover hog."

"Well, give *over*—" I kick and push and pound and shove until he retreats, laughing, to his side of the bed, pulling me on top of him.

"How's that?"

"Fine with me."

We seem to be reconciled again after the previous evening's storm; we make love a couple of times—there's not that much leeway for passion, court is pressing, what a bummer—and though we know we both have to get up and get dressed very soon, we cuddle for a while all the same.

I am lying stretched across the bottom of the bed; Jim is lounging vertically, and we intersect at right angles somewhere around the knees. I am following a thought of my own.

"You're so shy you insist on creating a sensation," I observe to the ceiling. I look sideways and up at him just in time to catch the expression on his face: His eyes spark, his face comes alive in a smile of delight and surprise at the perception, and he spreads his hands in a gesture of acknowledgment.

"You got me."

"Do I?" I roll over and move up to lie propped beside him. "Do I really?"

"If you want me."

"Oh, I think I might be persuaded—but not just now." I push him. "We have to get up, Mike and your lawyers will kill me if I don't get you out of here on time for court."

"Yeah, right, what's the judge gonna do, start without me?" He leaps up to escape my ungentle prodding in crucial areas, goes over to the window, stretching and deep-breathing and drumming on his chest like Tarzan. I watch appreciatively, a sight I never grow weary of. He looks *so* good, the hair, the beard—

"I feel *great!*" he shouts happily, smiling as if he had not a worry in the world.

I sigh with mock exasperation and throw a pillow at him. "How many times do I have to tell you—you feel great 'cause you were with *me* all night!"

"You always say that."

"Well, if I always say it, it's because it's always true."

He grins. "You could be right—" He wanders over to the dresser, picks up the books I've brought with me: the poems of Wallace Stevens, a book on the making of *2001: A Space Odyssey*, Robert Graves's *Watch the Northwind Rise*—just pleasure reading, nothing heavy—pages through them and then turns to the Miami papers.

I point to the article on the trial. "If you were going to start a riot, Morrison, why on earth did you pick a place like this to do it in? Major city, redneck attitudes—"

He bursts out laughing. "Miss, do you consider this a major city?"

"No, I consider New York a major city. I don't even consider Los Angeles a major city, actually, but I just thought I'd be polite—"

"Well, don't be. It's wasted on these people."

We shower together, scrubbing each other's back—Mike has called, anxious that Jim not be late to arrive at the halls of justice this day— and while I put on my makeup he amuses himself by scribbling in my notebook. We go down to his room, where he changes clothes for court, and then head to the lobby to assemble the entourage for the run across the bay to Miami.

This time I do not sit in the press box, but directly behind Jim in the front row of the spectator section; if I reach out my hand I can touch his back, and I have to suppress the desire, the need, to do so. Whether for his reassurance (I'm here, Jim) or my own (are you here, Jim?) I do not know.

During the breaks and the lunch hour I go around talking to some of the kids who are still attending the sessions (down from SRO crowds only last week to a modest turnout yesterday and today). Did he do it, I ask. Did you see him expose himself? Did he really mean to suggest going down on Robby, or was it just on Robby's guitar, or did it even happen? But by now they have seen that I am with him, and they are wary, or shy, or reluctant, and will not exchange anything more than the barest pleasantries. Mostly they want to know if I'm Jim's girlfriend, what it's like to be a writer from New York, what kind of magazine do I write for.

Actually, the copies Pauline has air-expressed down have arrived, and we bring them to court with us, pass them out to spectators and press; Jim orders a number held back, in case his lawyers think it might be possible to have them entered into evidence. Hey, Your Honor, here's this poem he wrote, actually published in a magazine, he's not just a sodden exhibitionist . . .   Best of Irish luck to you, I think, not sanguine as to his chances.

I look around at Jim's support group: Mike Gershman, bodyguard/Jim-minder Tony Funches, Harvey Perr, Babe Hill, Gloria Vanjak, myself—not much of a court for the Lizard King on Trial. The other Doors were here for opening week, but went back to California; Pam of course (despite Oliver Stone's later license) was never here at all, though I do not learn until some time after that she actually spent the weeks Jim was on trial on a heroin 'diet' in L.A.—snorting smack, falling out, waking up to do some more. Apparently she ended up collapsing and being diagnosed not as scagged to the gills but *suffering from malnutrition!* Slimming through Smack: a whole new dietary concept—probably only a matter of time before it turns up on the afternoon talk shows.

The day's witnesses are a real Zoo Parade—first to take the stand is one Robert Jennings, whom we all immediately dub 'Big Bob.' "He only testified against me so he could get to tell everybody how tall he is," is Jim's assessment later. Six foot nine: which occasions much ribald comment among the defendant's partisans about the nine inches.

The other startling thing about this clown is that out of all the people who were there that fateful first of March at Dinner Key Auditorium (well, nobody ever warned J. Caesar to beware the *Kalends* of March . . .), it is Big Bob alone who seemed to feel the need to sign the complaint against Jim that led to us all being here this day. If he hadn't—Jim wouldn't be here on trial, and if he weren't on trial our discussion about the baby might have gone very differently, and if all those things had been different perhaps Jim might not have entered upon the spiral of depression and despair that seems to have led to his death —or maybe it all would have gone exactly as it did. Things are as they are, and there is always a reason for them to be so.

So the only person in all Miami sufficiently offended by the alleged public display of Jim Morrison's private parts to actually *file a complaint of possible felony* (thus opening the way for extradition) now takes the stand. I'm sure it's just one of those droll little coincidences that he also happens to work in the Miami prosecutor's office, along with two other members of his family (hey, is nobody after this prosecutor guy for nepotism? *I'll* file a complaint!).

Jennings testifies dismayingly well, if perhaps untruthfully, claiming he saw Jim fondling himself onstage, hands inside his pants, and later exposing himself for all to see; he cites what seems to be the State's Official Exposure Time of "five to eight seconds." I mean, were all these turkeys *counting*, or what? Could they look at Jim's penis and count at the same time? Do they know how long eight seconds (or Jim's penis?) really *is* (easily long enough for pictures to be taken—there weren't any—or for cops to move in—they didn't)? Did they maybe have *stopwatches?* Were they *synchronized?* What the hell is going *on* here? (We know, we know . . .)

After Jennings, his friend James Woods is up (so to speak). Now *this* guy says he sat *right next to* Jennings for the *whole* concert and saw no exposure and no "simulated oral copulation" (Jim/Robby/Robby's guitar). Oh, come on now, Woods, you just mustn't have been looking very hard . . .

We are cheered up no end. Ah, Diogenes, there is one honest man in Dade County after all! Our elation is short-lived: Before the gavel falls to end that day's session, Judge Murray Goodman hands down a triumph of jurisprudential doublethink. Community standards (yeah, right, as if Miami *had* standards) of 'obscenity' (the prevailing local attitude to, oh, X-rated movies, strip joints—not exactly unknown in the County of Dade—four-letter words; as well as more general standards—the nudity in *Hair* and *Woodstock*, other books and plays and films—as seen by both the general populace and Jim's own peer group) are NOT TO BE ALLOWED AS EVIDENCE in this case. Considering that the 'community' is supposed to be the offended party here, would not what the 'community' thinks about such matters be, to say the least, slightly relevant?

Max Fink, Jim's perfectly surnamed and utterly Neanderthal lawyer (off-stage, every woman is a 'broad,' every gay a 'faggot,' every black a—well, you get the very nasty picture; and I am also convinced he is responsible for much of Jim's attitude to me since I arrived; he's dead now too, just like Goodman . . .), certainly thinks so, and makes a strenuous argument to that very point—which the jury, having been sent out of the courtroom, is not permitted even to hear.

Goodman is immovable, and I find my thoughts going idly to pins being stuck in black-robed dolls. When I hear his flat denial of Fink's motion, I know Jim is doomed; and as we all rise at day's end for justice's exit, and Jim turns round to me and I see his face, I know he knows it too.

Back at the Carillon, everyone is bugging out, returning that evening or the next morning to Los Angeles or New York or wherever. Before the tribe decamps, however, we all go down to the bar in the lower lobby where Jim and I had our initial encounter Monday night, for a farewell round. The party has swelled to nine by now, the usual suspects and a few new faces.

There is little chance for privacy, so Jim and I just gaze at one another over our Chivas-and-Cokes. Someone offers a toast to "The Miami Nine!"; we all drink and pledge defiance and triumph, but I don't think anyone is really believing it.

I do not expect to see him again before I leave—I am up in my room packing, my plane goes in two hours or so, Mike Gershman and I are flying back to New York together—but he stops in for a brief and more private farewell.

"Don't ask me," I warn him sincerely. "Just—don't. I know I said what I said, but we both said a lot of things, and I still might change my mind and have the baby after all. I don't think I will, it would be hell for it and me, but—I just don't know."

"I didn't say anything," he replies humbly. "I know you'll decide what's best for all of us, you, me *and* our baby . . . I'll send you enough money, you won't have to worry about anything."

"Whatever you like," I say, suddenly beaten. "I'm tired, I want to go home now, Jim, and just—just do what I have to do. You won. Okay? Are you happy?"

He pulls me to him with sudden urgency, holds me very tightly.

"*Nobody* won here! Don't you *ever* think that, don't ever believe you lost . . . Just let me know when. I'll be with you. I told you. I'll hold your hand, we'll get through this together."

I do not believe, and I know he won't. But I say I do, I even tell him so. I don't know what he really believes.

"I love you, you know," he adds. "I really love you—you *will* be all right."

"And you?" I ask, muffled, into his shoulder.

"Oh, I'll be all right too."

The Doors have concerts to play, hence Jim's departure from Miami the following morning. Not many dates, but one or two (literally one or two) did survive the carnage wrought by Judge Goodman's calendar games (canceling, rescheduling, denying, delaying, postponing—the band could plan nothing but that he would seemingly out of spite force them to change it): Bakersfield, San Diego, the Isle of Wight Festival (a disaster; Jim will say after it that he will never perform in public again).

I fly home that night sunk in despair, and do more drugs than I should have done even if I had not been pregnant—mostly grass and Valium, a Quaalude here and there when things are really rough. And am then consumed with guilt for doing so: Suppose I decide I want to have the baby after all? What damage might possibly have already been wrought? The way I've been doping, and the way Jim's been drinking, who knows? But this is no more than a passing guilt, really, and it is no factor in my eventual decision.

I talk to Jim once or twice over the next few weeks—the promised funds duly arrive, and will cover the cost of the procedure at a private clinic on Park Avenue. Assuming, of course, that this is what I decide to do; but I think that by now both Jim and I know very well that I will have the abortion as I have said I will all along. It is best; not easiest, but best.

When I call to tell him the procedure has been scheduled, he is not there. I leave messages, but the trial is coming to an end, and he does not return the calls; and after that I do not call again.

When I go alone to the clinic, for a preliminary examination the day before, they inform me very gently that I am about a week too advanced for the preferred method to be safely employed. They do not even hint that it might just possibly be my own damn fault, that I in my torment of indecision have left it just that one little bit too late.

But *I* think it: What now, I ask, wondering if I am going to have to go through yet another decision, I used up all my deciding strength on *this* one . . .

They tell me what I will have to do if I still wish to terminate the pregnancy: I will have to stay pregnant until twenty weeks, halfway through, another eight weeks or so, till the first week of November, and have a saline abortion.

This is the first time I have ever heard those words. The staff at the clinic explain the procedure to me, and I get hysterical right there on the spot. They are very sympathetic—apparently this is neither an unusual situation nor an excessively emotional response—and send me home with some sissy pills for my 'nerves,' something lame like Librium.

When I do get home, accompanied by my friend Noreen, who is standing in for the absent Jim as consoler and supporter and hand-holder, I say fuck *that*, take four Quaaludes and call Miami. Six times. He is not in, does not return the calls. Noreen talks me out of murder and/or suicide, stays with me for a couple of hours to make sure I really am persuaded and not just saying so.

After she goes home, I am alone with myself and my—*child*. And it is a truly terrifying moment, even more frightening than when I first learned for sure that I was pregnant, or even first knew it, that June morning at the Navarro. The knowledge of pain and awfulness to come is the least of it; it is the utter helplessness that is beyond all endurance.

As ever in extremity, I turn for solace to a place I have always turned: my faith. Witches do not make judgments as do practitioners of some other religions, as to the rightness or wrongness of abortion: They decide each case on its own, considering only the ramifications for those involved—the woman, the man, the potential child.

In the end, it is the words of Maura, the High Priestess who married me to Jim, that help me most now. "You are the only one who can decide. If a woman knows that she can't offer her child anything like the life she wants for it, it's not the worst fate in the world for that child's soul to wait a little longer, to find a better chance of a better life with parents who are better able to offer it."

I look at her through blinding tears. "I know—and I never wanted a baby in the first place, but once it happened, I just wanted so much for *us* to be able to do that for our child, Jim and me together."

"And he's told you that's not possible. Now you have to do what's best for all three of you. I know you can't support a baby, can't take care of it; Jim doesn't want it born and says your relationship is over if you do have it. That's not a lot of space you have to maneuver; and it doesn't sound to me like any kind of decent or caring situation into which to bring a new soul. Babies don't ask to be born to their parents; but they do ask and require to be given a safe and loving life once they're here. And if they can't have that, then it's best that they don't come at all. You're the one who's going to suffer most here, not Jim; only you can decide whether you're brave enough in the end to suffer alone, or whether you're going to make a child suffer with you, for the next twenty years, for the rest of your lives."

"I don't have the strength to have it and give it away, Maura."

"Then you've already decided."

True; but not as simply as that.

One sullen morning in mid-September, Bruce Harris phones me at work.

"I have good news and bad news. First the bad news. Jim's been acquitted on the felony rap. Now the good news. He's been convicted of everything else."

Good old Bruce: Somebody else might have gotten the good news and the bad news mixed up, but he understands completely how I am feeling about it just now.

Well, it is not quite true, as it turns out: Jim has also been acquitted of the public drunkenness rap, and so is found guilty, ultimately, only of indecent exposure and public profanity, both misdemeanors. But still. With luck (I am feeling *very* vindictive, morning sickness probably has a lot to do with it), he could be doing some hard time.

"Did you talk to him?" I ask reluctantly.

"Oh yeah, if you can call it that. He's gotten very weird lately— he knows about the abortion being postponed, by the way."

"How could he know that? He wouldn't take any of my calls, when I phoned to try to tell him."

"Beats me. Maybe Jac or somebody told him?"

"How would *they* know? A fine thing, when half the music biz is in on all your obstetrical details," I say bitterly.

"Well, he'll probably show up here the night before you go into the hospital, you know how he is. Don't give up."

Hey, *I'm* not the one who's giving up here . . . and I *do* know how he is.

Two days before the verdict comes in on Jim in Miami, Jimi Hendrix dies in London of an overdose of downers; two weeks later, Janis Joplin dies in Los Angeles of an overdose of heroin. Jim, now back in L.A. after the verdict and awaiting sentencing at the end of October (Pam is off in Paris with her boyfriend, an alleged French count with a fondness for heroin—shared interests are *so* important in a relationship), is sent by all reports into severe depression by news of the two deaths, and begins telling people that he's next. I have to say I would not be surprised.

October passes. Having made up my mind to do what Jim wants, what even I have come to see is the only possible thing I can do, I am calmer than I have been for some weeks; and resolved that since this, here, now, is as much as I will ever know of this particular condition, I will—not 'enjoy,' that is incredibly the wrong word, but make as much of it as I can, gather in as much of the experience as possible before it is gone forever.

Jim is sentenced in Miami on October 30: He gets the max—sixty days of hard labor to be served in the Dade County jail, for the profanity charge; and for public exposure, six months of same, plus a five-hundred-dollar fine and two years' probation. There is an immediate appeal, and he is free on fifty thousand dollars' bond.

For me, no appeal: On Friday, November 6, I go into the hospital. The night before, I sit up until dawn, trading off between cocaine and Quaaludes (well, it doesn't matter any more, does it), waiting for Jim to call, to show up at the door, knowing damned well that he'll never show up; and trying in the meantime for an overdose.

Neither eventuality—not Jim, not the OD—takes place. I don't know which I'd have preferred.

CHAPTER
19

November 1970

I WAKE EARLY; THERE IS A LOT TO DO BEFORE I LEAVE for the hospital. Clean sheets against my probable return, food out for the cat, finish packing. The chosen hospital is—purposely—not nearby, and I have hired a car and driver to get me there and pick me up after. I am well ahead of schedule as I bump the suitcase through the early morning clinic crowd, on my way to the proper elevator for private patients.

Proceed upstairs; explain why I am here, for the first of at least ten subsequent times—how is it they never seem to remember? Or do they keep asking because they want me to have to keep saying it? "I'm here for a late abortion."

I spend about half an hour in restless waiting in the TV room; I consider bolting, also for the first of many more than ten subsequent times. Could I make it to the elevators before they realize I'm splitting? They probably wouldn't even notice . . . In the hall outside they are trucking babies back and forth in wheeled trundles with see-through plastic sides. Then two cribs go by with not babies exactly but little blanket-wrapped packages, neatly pinned and tucked like Sunday's roast. I feel the panic starting to seep in like icy water, like evil smoke.

Finally, they call my name, and I go into the examining room for a preliminary scan of my swollen belly; a cursory peer, and I am sent downstairs again to Admitting. I wonder briefly at the snaily pace of a hospital; it seems slow and haphazard, too deliberate for a life-and-death locus, but maybe that is why.

Admitting does not take long. I change into nightgown, robe and slippers all bought especially for the occasion. They will be thrown away on my leaving, I don't want anything around after to remind me of this. The admitting officials want to take my wedding ring from me, but I will not let them; instead I wrap it several times in tape against possible theft. I have to have even so much of Jim with me; it's all I have left —or will have.

I get a thin plastic band with 'P. Morrison' on it snapped around my wrist; the attendant takes my street clothes to be placed in a locker, and I am wheelchaired upstairs by an aide. Two very, very young student nurses are assigned to look after me. They are hesitant with their glances and their questions, and I find I am feeling sorrier for them than I have felt for anyone, myself included, for quite some time.

Back to the examining room to be 'prepped'—which means shaved. Then young Dr. Ralph comes in, thirtyish, gives me the most thorough physical I have ever had in my life, catechizes me elaborately on what drugs I take and my past medical history, and inquires thoughtfully if I think I might need psychological assistance after the abortion. Then more waiting. There is very little water in the hospital; the mains have frozen in the bitter cold and burst. I am edgy—water being the only thing I really drink—and hating Morrison and myself.

At about two that afternoon it all gets going. They wheelchair me to the labor room where I am to get the injection; the room is small, square, bare, horribly efficient. I get up on the table, put on a medical gown, shake a little, and hitch it up under me, feet out straight, hands at my sides. I think I have never been so frightened in my life.

A saline abortion is the most physiologically acceptable method of abortion, though perhaps not equally so psychologically. It is in fact the actual birth process, artificially induced: a premeditated and deliberately engineered miscarriage. The only real difference from a full-term delivery is that the fetus is only seven to nine inches long at twenty weeks, totally incapable of life outside the uterus; and, of course, it is dead on delivery.

Saline abortions cannot be performed under optimum conditions of ease and safety before the eighteenth week of pregnancy or after the twenty-second; the twentieth week is preferred, when there is sufficient fluid present in the womb and the top of the uterus is at the level of the woman's waist.

The process is fairly simple and only infrequently dangerous: After injection of a local anesthetic, a long, hollow needle is inserted through the abdominal muscle wall into the uterus, at a point halfway between navel and pelvic bone. A catheter is then attached to the needle, through which half of the amniotic fluid is drawn out of the uterus and replaced by an equal amount of salt solution—hence the term 'salting-out.' The entire process takes about forty minutes; after the solution is instilled, the fetus dies, labor begins between six and thirty-six hours later (twenty-four, for most patients), and, as in a regular miscarriage, fetus and placenta are then expelled. There are labor pains, and they are real ones; real labor, and in the end, of course, one is delivered of a corpse.

Dr. Anita, young and simpatica, assisting Dr. Ralph, swabs my belly bright pink, neatly quartering sterile white towels to leave a small pink open rectangle from navel to groin. The I.V. tree next to the table has two bottles on it, one the saline solution for the procedure, the other plain glucose.

Dr. Ralph prods my arm. "Terrible veins." Guess *I'll* never make it as a junkie.

They decide to go in at a wrist vein. "Open and close your fist, many times, fast." Somebody inserts a needle into the vein on the back of my hand; it is surprisingly painful, there is blood all over, and then I am wired up to the glucose drip.

Dr. Anita skin-pops Novocain into the rosy rectangle, explaining in her accented English that the actual pain will be brief. I look at her, feeling skeptical; and I am right to feel so. Brief, yes; bad, also yes. It quickly modulates to a bearable cramp; my hand actually hurts far worse, where the sugar solution is still dripping in. Then she installs the abortion needle, a huge syringe, and I half-rise off the table. It stands shiny and ghastly emerging from my pink belly, and they push me gently down again.

There is still no water, and they say they could not give me any at this point even if there were. Dr. Ralph working quickly, drains off four tubes of amniotic fluid through a catheter; as each tube is disattached I feel a strangely hot and dry trickle running down my side. I am starting to panic, utterly; I want to get up and run away. Then the saline solution is hooked up to the needle and begins to drip in. I try to keep my mind off the fact of needles and tubes and what is happening inside my body, or else I will start screaming and never, never stop.

Suddenly there are no bubbles in the saline bottle; the drip has halted. What!, I say. Dr. Anita runs over, says sharply, "Cough!" I comply.

"Harder! Again! Again!"

They are afraid, I can tell; sometimes if the needle slips out of the muscles holding it in place, it can puncture and even kill. I think I would not be sorry. But as I cough, the muscles push down against the needle and the uterus together, and I gasp at the pain: dull, heavy, green.

Then the saline begins to drip again; they relax. Fetal part blocking the needle, Dr. Ralph explains off-handedly. At the look of instant imaginative total horror on my face—my conscious kid with its hand over the needle, trying to save its own life?—he changes the story quickly to womb subsidence. Is that like earth subsidence, uterus strikeslip fault, I want to ask. I close my eyes instead.

At last it is finished; the bottles, salt and sugar, are empty. Dr. Ralph, whose first saline abortion this is, pulls out the needles. There is blood all over the floor; everybody says don't look at the blood. I say it's mine, and I'll damn well look at it if I want to. There is a lot of it.

Still no water, though. By dinnertime, the blonde girl across the room from me, Jane, is cramping. They wheel in the Spanish girl in the next bed; her dyed dark blonde hair is darker now with sweat. She was in labor eighteen hours, Jane says with real empathy; as they shift her from gurney to bed her gown falls open, and her bare back is oddly vulnerable.

I have trouble getting to sleep, and when I do there are evil mocking dreams. It is so hot in the room. I spend a lot of time thinking about the pain to come.

They take Jane into the labor room at about five Saturday morning; all night she was moaning like a hurt animal. I try to imagine pain great enough to make me scream with it, like that woman yesterday morning, while I was waiting to be admitted, and can't. Macgregor, the Chinese woman in the left-hand bed to mine, and I have both been cramping; something is beginning to happen.

The baby's dead, milady said . . .   I allow myself to think of it, briefly, the quickest fleetingest thought-touch, all I can bear before it threatens to overwhelm me. There have been no movements since yesterday evening. For about a week there have been the tiniest little flutters somewhere way inside; talk about butterflies in your stomach. I will *not* think of it as a baby, though, not until I must, and my one wish is to get it over with, and fast.

Jim is much in my thoughts, as I doubt I am in his. I think I hate him, quite a lot, maybe even as much as I love him; but mostly I just wish he were here with me for this, as he promised, though I know he is not at all good at that sort of promise; and the desperate futility of this wish produces the only tears I seem able to cry.

I am having short sharp twinges now, nothing too much different from menstrual cramps. It should begin sometime this evening. There have been the oddest painless contractions; experimental, maybe. I think of that lying story, "She had two pains a minute apart and that was it." Some chance.

Jane comes back to the room at around two, looking worn but triumphant; she can go home tomorrow afternoon. As for me, still no action; sometimes they have to repeat the injection—it has been twenty-four hours now from the instillation—and I would not be surprised if they did, the ordeal must apparently be dragged out to the last possible pinch.

I have never been much good at handling physical pain; emotional agony I know like a sister, and can deal powerfully with it. But physical pain—still, can anything be worse than what I anticipate, what I imagine for myself? I will know, soon enough; there is no stopping it now, and perhaps I even deserve it.

Jane says it was not what she expected; she screamed at last from the relentlessness of it, from grinding steadiness without letup, rather than from intensity. Dr. Ralph, appealed to, says no analgesic is possible; but I think he is a liar for a sadistic macho morality. He calmly disagrees, saying anesthetic or painkillers would halt the labor outright, or at best indefinitely prolong it. I still think he's lying, wants to see us suffer for not wanting our babies; but can even he believe anyone would go through this who had even the very smallest and slimmest of other choices?

The cramps worsen, come and go; I move my legs back and forth against the bedsheets, trying to distract myself. I call Bruce and Pauline, who have been so supportive through all this; without their help I don't think I could have retained even the grip on sanity I still manage to exert.

I want Jim very badly, and with all the unreasonableness of pain's producing. Also I want to beat him up for making me hurt. Last night, in the not-quite dark and stifling heat of the room, I suddenly became able, for the first time since Miami, to visualize him. No, I *can't* see your face in my mind, Jim, at least not until now, now that our baby is dead inside me and the pain is beginning to rise. Superstar baby—*my* baby. The meaninglessness of a good thing in isolation. A good thing in a bad context becomes, unavoidably, the very worst thing of all.

No, I did it, and I am if not glad in my choice then at least at peace with it; within the terrible limitations in which I had to choose, I made the right choice. I just want it to finish itself so I can sleep. Jane is asleep now, like a tired child herself; her boyfriend has come and gone, solicitous, caring, concerned, loving. Again I try to imagine Jim sitting next to my bed and holding my hand, and the intensity of that wish astounds me, simultaneously, with the onset of the worst pain yet. Oh hell. This is going to hurt.

I am thirty-one hours gone now from the instillation. I dare a glance outside; quick, because I do not ever wish to look up at this hospital again and be able to say, 'That's the room I was in, where I killed my baby.' The moon is plainly visible over the river; at its worst possible aspect, naturally, between the half and the full. There is a spreading bruise around the intravenous entry on my hand; it looks like a black moon itself.

Abruptly, about ten that night, the cramps escalate. Jane has told me that the real labor pains come round from the back, tightening and then easing off. I have hot flashes, cold chills and have to go to the bathroom a lot. My entire belly south of the navel is round and hot and hard like a grapefruit. And bright pink, not like a grapefruit—the sterile swab wouldn't come off when I took a shower, the one time there was water for more than ten minutes. I stare at the pink stain and wish it were blue. Woad. Sacrifice color. Celt-Pict-British antiquity dye. I *hurt*, goddamn it. I wish I could *really* witch it, throw the pains onto Morrison instead of having to bear them myself; couvade revenge. Adrenaline rises; I think I am going to need it.

Midnight has gone round and I am still awake, still here, still cross and hurt and angry. By two in the morning the pains are bad enough for the nurse on duty to give me a pill. I thought there *was* no pill to help, but I am in too much pain to argue with her. Wax and wane, like that ghastly moon. Is this it, or is there more? I rock my hips from side to side to try to counter it.

There is now no water at all, save for the operating rooms. I drink from the gallon bottle Macgregor's husband brought in, along with a sack of ice cubes, for us both to share. I want to last out the pain as long as I can in the room, because once they take you into the labor area you can't come back out until you're delivered.

It seems to have begun for real. The pains are regular, bad and rhythmic; I have begun to stain. It is not as I thought it would be. So far I have managed to keep quiet.

At five-thirty in the morning I change into the short backless medical gown and ring for the nurse on duty. A very nice aide comes in, and I explain developments.

"We're off!" she says, and goes to fetch a gurney, glad for me that it's nearly over.

"Just let me finish this one," I say.

"Are you kidding, this might be the one! On you get."

I lever myself onto the gurney; it has a sheeted mattress and is a bit higher than my bed. She puts up the railings and wheels me into the hall and down to Labor Room 1. I get a water-soaked gauze pad, no more, though I speak eloquently of the gallon of Poland water back next to my bed.

The pains intensify. By what I judge to be six but could just as well have been three in the afternoon I have been doing some moaning; the contractions are closer, harder, longer and well-defined. They rise to a peak, level off up there and hang on forever, then subside. In between there are cramps, but they seem a welcome nothingness compared to the contractions. My mind is clean of all but the pain. The water-gauze is essential, I have been panting like a heat-struck hound to avoid some of the pains. Sitting up and moving, pulling myself up, stretching and pushing with the pain along the steel-bar sides of the gurney seem to work best. My belly is rigid and incredibly hard; I can feel with my fingers the contractions rippling across.

It is light out now; time in here is meaningless. Pain is blinding me; I have been retching with the convulsions that the contractions have now become, and ask for something, anything to ease it. A day-shift aide, surly and squat, comes in to tell me I have to have pain to get the delivery over with. Well, okay, but will it be much longer? Well, she couldn't say, I'll just have to put up with it; the implication clearly being that it's my own fucking fault . . . or my fault for fucking.

I calculate; that Spanish girl went eighteen mortal hours. I could easily be here till dinnertime, or even later. No way I'll ever last that long; dying sounds pretty good at this point. Just fade out, jump the tracks, cease upon the midnight with no pain . . .

Then without warning everything goes absolutely black in front of my eyes. I hear myself screaming somewhere far away, genuine top-of-my-lungs murderous screams. It seems as though I have been doing it for some time. Pain is supreme. I touch myself between my legs; I am distended, straining, stretched open like the mouth of a jar. Either it is truly almost over or I have pushed too hard, too soon, too much. I catch sight of myself in the glass of a cabinet: I am wild-eyed, pale, hair disordered, sweating like a spooked horse. There is pale bloody discharge, foam and blood all over the sheets. I fade out again.

Screaming does not bring me to release. The surly aide returns, scolds me; I am disturbing the other patients with my disgraceful shrieks.

"Well, they'll just have to put up with it!" I snap, waspishly repeating her earlier advice to me. She scowls and puts a thermometer in my mouth.

"I'll *bite* it," I warn, teeth clenched on the glass tube.

"I don't *want* you to bite it," she says, now a little gentler. "Push with your pains, but only when there's a pain."

I go right on screaming once the thermometer is removed. Being essentially a very reserved person, I cannot believe this noise is really being made by me.

An Asian doctor I have not seen before comes in, either hours later or seconds later. I don't know which because I have closed my eyes and when I open them she is there. She pokes at me, lifts the sheet.

"You are in such pain because you are about to expel the fetus."

Even in my extremity tears come to my eyes. What a strange word for Jim's child, I think, and then, At last. The next scream about to tear through my throat comes out as a whisper only, because all my strength is suddenly diverted, absolutely involuntarily, like a switch being thrown somewhere, into the next contraction. My knees draw up automatically; the copulation analogy has been amusing me, bitterly and intermittently, all along, but I am not amused just now.

There is one all-encompassing pain, a pressure and a feeling where no similar feeling has ever been before—I cannot even recall if I made any sound at the last—and then a hard, wet object shoots out from between my legs, and the pain stops, and the mattress is deluged with water and blood, all in the space of ten seconds.

I instinctively lift my head to look, to see what I have borne; but the doctor swiftly moves to block my view, covering my eyes with her arm.

"It's over," I whisper, it's OVER, feeling nothing but relief. She says yes, push a bit more, the afterbirth has to come out. There is the sharp iron smell of blood in the room. I drift off; the doctor cuts the cord, I hear it snipped.

"You'll feel a sting," she says, and I jerk slightly in my daze as the I.V. is again hooked up to the back of my hand. There is Demerol in it this time, and I will sleep. It is over, and though I am everlastingly sorry that it had to be done, I am not sorry that I did it. Nor am I glad. Oh Jim, I think. Why weren't you here with me?

The aide shakes me out of my semi-postcoital drift. "Sign these."

I struggle to focus on the papers she is thrusting into my shaking hands. Mortuary tags. Death certificate. Burial permit. I am the mother of the deceased, and Jim is the father.

Nobody told me about this part of it—I do not dare read them, just scribble my name and close my eyes, leaning back on the pillow, too exhausted, too devastated in body and spirit to take it in.

The placenta will not come; the doctor cautiously pulls on the cord and it slithers out. She gives me a quick internal, pronounces me finished and in good shape. An enormous wave of second-thought protest and horror at those signatures begins to form, and before it hits me to submerge me in what I think would have been madness the Demerol most mercifully knocks me out.

I sleep. I wake up briefly when they transfer me bodily back into my bed, but then am off again. When I wake again in the late afternoon,

Jane wants to know all the details. Macgregor delivered right there in the bed, they couldn't be bothered to move her fast enough.

Sleep is simple; it solves all problems of thinking. Bruce and Bobbi come to visit, subdued but decisive in their conviction that I have done the only thing I could have done. Pauline calls, Terry visits. I want nobody else. Nobody. I am so tired.

PART
FOUR

& you beside me
breathing
in an iron dawn

O you are a flying bird
not a nesting one
the falcon
not the dove

CHAPTER

20

November–December 1970

I AM LYING QUIETLY IN BED, WAITING FOR THE NEXT examination—there's always a next one—and thinking hard thoughts.

I am to leave the hospital today, Monday. I am exhausted, totally ripped, but the thought of going home produces a kind of vague interest. Who says you can't always get what you want? The trouble is, it's never what you want when you get it. When you do get it, after anguishing over it for however long it takes, it always turns out it's the one thing you can't *stand*, no *way*, starving for bread and it chokes you, cracking with thirst and water burns your mouth, dying for need of love and it kills you when it finally arrives. If I had to put it all in one sentence, it would run 'Jim, you fucker, you've done it to me again.'

If you want to get simplistic about it, I think dully, it came down to saving my baby or saving myself—and maybe saving Jim along with me. But things are never as simplistic or as easy as that, and maybe it is not even true.

Superkid, right, a goddess, a god, born of Jim and Patricia, the one to save the world . . . Nice fantasy, and not one I could afford to indulge in to that kid's cost; the child would have been the one to pay in the end.

But it would have been his and mine, so did not that make the great difference? With the first clear vision I have had in months, I see; and I see that the answer is no. To have a child to worship yourself and the man you love made flesh incarnate: not good enough. Not for me, not for him, not for the child. I am weary of reasons. For the first time in my life I have made a hard decision—*the* hardest, where no matter what I decided I would be wrong—*I* have decided, not had this decision made for me by someone else or by my own inaction. I have the rest of my life to agonize about it if I feel so minded.

I walk out of the hospital that day wrapped in apartness, feeling entitled to a good wallow—but not too much, that way madness lies. I get into the waiting car, and the driver immediately heads south. I suppose I should let Jim know it's over, not that he would really care; but for my own peace of mind if nothing else, because that's how it should be, he *should* know. Send him a telegram, maybe; something short, literary, appropriately withering. Maybe even something he wrote himself, there must be some line somewhere I could use. And anyway, he couldn't hang up on a telegram.

I begin to shake, the winds of eternity shivering my bones right there in the car. To counter it, I deliberately call to mind how much I love him. Did. And do. And will. Just love: all bare and only, apart from the hassles and the frenzy and the lies and the scenes. My love for him alone and somehow mythic in an elemental state, freed of all qual-ifiers and usages. Not even anything to do with *us*, in reality, or with what love he has for Pam, or with what love he has for me (and it does exist, others' opinions to the contrary notwithstanding—or my own).

But the doubt beats on the outside of my shield, like a wind battering at a Volkswagen on an open freeway. How much of all this is really Jim, how much is what I wish and want and need him to be, and—most horrible thought of all—how much is merely a reflection of myself?

Fuck it, I think with some heat, and let the driver assist me out of the car in front of my building. No, I love him, all right, and that knowing somehow makes the absolute horror of the last four days recede before it, stamping it as valid and true. Love lifts; or perhaps it's merely the substitution of one loss for another, a red herring drawn across the track of my pain, making me thankful for the diversion of one anguish to another. Which will hurt worse, now that I am free to choose—losing the baby or losing him?

"Oh Jim," I say aloud, closing the door of my apartment behind me and leaning back against it—the very place where he and I once made love—letting the memory of him here with me come in with a rush, "I don't think I'm going to be able to *stand* it."

But I already know I will.

I go around for a week or so thereafter looking like Astarte, Fertility Goddess of the Euphrates: At the hospital they gave me a shot to stop milk production, and the result is breasts hard as pears and just about as flexible—unbelievably painful, and twice even their usual size. Incredible. Bras are right out; in the end I just tie myself up in a soft cloth and leave it at that.

Jim of course never calls; though he does speak to Bruce Harris, who is very curt with him ("How is she?" "Physically in pain, mentally despondent. Other than that, Jim, she's just fine"), and one or two of my other friends. I keep my hands off the telephone as long as I can; when I do break down at last and call him in L.A., it is a most unsatisfactory conversation—I end up screaming, he is as remote as one of Neptune's moons, and I have the oddest feeling he's with someone.

I am doing cocaine these days, which I don't much like (the fact that I am doing so much of it, not the coke itself—*that* I like very much indeed); it seems to be the only thing I feel like doing. I also take the odd Quaalude to give my nose a rest, and I have scrip from an obliging doctor for Percodans when the hospital's parting gift of codeine runs out.

I write Jim a letter—I can say things on paper I could never in a million years say in conversation—which runs to eight or ten pages, maybe more, detailing the abortion, the aftermath, my state of health and mind. (The telegram went the day I got home from the hospital; it read in its entirety: " 'Aborted strangers in the mud' "—a line from his poem *An American Prayer*.) Needless to say, I get no answer to either.

I have gotten a few letters of my own at work, bad letters, from hysterical little girls who spell poorly, all shrieking that I can never *possibly* love Jim half as much as they do. And here I thought nobody knew anything about us . . . how do they find out these things? I never say a word to Jim about it, not even when we are speaking again, as we shortly will be; but after Pauline finds me crying in my office one day with a couple of the little horrors in front of me, I tell her and Bruce Harris. They both counsel ignoring and forgetting. Not so easy.

I need to see him, or else I will go not so quietly nuts. Salvation comes from an unlikely quarter indeed: Creedence Clearwater Revival invites about forty members of the New York rock press out to Oakland, their home base, in order to introduce their "new music" to us and in general improve their image with those who are perceived as tastemakers.

Janice Coughlan and Terry Towne (our new advertising director, daughter of a top Billboard magazine honcho) are also invited; I am pleased to accept a trip to San Francisco, even with strings attached, but my purposes are clearly other. The Bay Area is a lot closer to Los Angeles than New York is, and there are planes flying down there all day long, and friends with whom I can stay once I am there. Jim and I are going to be discussing this whole thing in person a whole lot sooner than either of us may have thought.

It has to be, whether he likes it or not (probably not); I know very well it will be my own efforts that will get me safely out of this dangerous frame of mind, but I also know that Jim must help me. I need to *cry* about it, and there is only one person in the whole universe who can hold me while I do it. It won't be over until then; and maybe not even then.

Two weeks before Christmas I get on a plane in New York with it seems just about everybody I know—and most of whom I detest. I would happily go down in flames if it meant I could take the rest of them with me . . . But it is not to be.

This is my first trip to the West Coast; indeed, my first trip anywhere out of the greater Northeast (Ohio to D.C. to Boston), save of course to Miami. California proves—interesting, and Creedence's hospitality is lavish: They put us all up at the Claremont, a fabulous old Victorian-looking barn of a place, like a hybrid English manor house/Spanish villa, up in the Berkeley hills not too far from the great university. It's terrific—creaky corridors, bordello of a lobby strewn with those weird tufted-velvet stumps that pass for benches, palms all over the place.

It feels most foreign, and, in fact, is: I look out the window of my room and see San Francisco across the bay, dimly rising through fog and palm fronds. The strangeness is cut somewhat by drugs, both local and imported from home, and by the many too-familiar faces infesting the hotel halls and dining room and bars and gardens. I am sharing an elegant

room with Terry, which is of course fine, and Janice is just down the
hall; but other New Yorkers, friends as well as foes, pop up every few
minutes, as if this were merely some exotic rock twist on one of those
English house-party-murders. I expect Agatha Christie to come tottering
along any minute, and amuse myself by speculating on who's likeliest to
turn up dead, and at whose hands.

The next afternoon we are all bused over to Cosmo's Factory, a
funky warehouse on the Oakland waterfront—Creedence headquarters
and rehearsal hall, where a spread has been laid on for the guests, rumaki
and tacos and chicken and teriyaki and Swedish meatballs; and where,
that night, the band performs a knockout set for our benefit. Nobody is
quite sure how this is supposed to recast Creedence, whom most of us
like just fine as they are, but there it is.

Some of us split the afternoon feed a little early: Terry and I light
out across the bay to San Francisco, where we have an appointment with
the renowned tattoo artist Lyle Tuttle; and in his immaculate studio off
Market Street, she gets a red and blue flower on her right hand and I
have a black Pisces sign incised into the back of my left wrist.

The party breaks up on Sunday: Most of the contingent returns to
New York, but a sizable cohort heads south to L.A., for business or just
to hang out, in the teeth of a howling windstorm that has even the flight
attendants strapped down for the trip. Looking out of the window, far
to my left I see a comb of snow-covered peaks: the distant Sierra, lifting
their heads above low cloud.

Diane Gardiner has invited me to stay with her in West Hollywood,
and picks me up at the Burbank airport. "What do you want to do first?"
she asks, as we drive through L.A. traffic to her place on West Norton
Avenue—downstairs-next-door to Pam. Jim is lodging at present at the
Chateau Marmont.

"Settle a few grudges."

After I unpack, and restore myself a little with a hit or two of the
cocaine I have imprudently toted all the way from New York, we go out
to dinner on Olvera Street, in downtown L.A. Next day Diane drives
me over to the Doors office, a shabby two-story building at the corner
of Santa Monica and La Cienega, a few blocks away. I climb the outside
staircase with the air of someone with nothing left to lose, and announce
myself to the secretary. Manager Bill Siddons waves from an inner office.

"Which desk is Jim's?" I inquire politely. I scribble out a note
informing him that I am in town and commanding him to call me—

giving Diane's number—if he knows what's good for him. Over at the
desk indicated, I throw back my hair, pull an eight-inch dagger from my
waistband, skewer the note and whomp the blade half an inch deep into
the wooden desk-top.

"Tell him I left a message."

It gets even his attention. He calls that afternoon. "I thought I
recognized the phone number," he says. "But where did you learn to
make European numeral sevens?"

Man, who the hell *cares* . . .   "The nuns taught me, okay? We have
to talk."

"I agree. But where?"

"Well, you know where I'm staying."

"And you know who lives upstairs."

"Is that a problem?"

"Not for me. You could come over to the Chateau."

"No, Diane's is fine. When?"

"We're recording, doing work on the new album. Unless you want
to come to the session?"

"Sessions bore me."

"Yeah, me too. Well, tonight at Diane's then, probably, but if not
then tomorrow night for sure."

"See you later."

When Jim does not put in an appearance by about nine, Diane
decides I need a night out. We have dinner at Hamburger Hamlet, then
go to a Christmas fair at some outdoor flea market, where I have some
poems calligraphed (Dylan Thomas), and Diane buys brass fetishes for
presents and a pair of gold-wire Christmas crowns studded with glass
jewels.

Back at Diane's, still no word from Jim, and we go to sleep early,
me in Diane's room and Diane on the floor cushions in the living room.
Next day it is Duke's at the Tropicana for breakfast, and shopping in
little boutiques along Melrose and Santa Monica and Sunset.

"Want to see Pam's shop?" suggests Diane mischievously. "I know
she's not going to be there today." Be that as it may: She woke me up
early that morning, yelling for Sage, her ill-behaved yellow mongrel,
right under my bedroom windows—I leaped out of bed just in time to
see her pigtailed red head going by not a yard from my face, getting into
a dark blue Mercedes 220 with Sage and driving off.

"Do cats eat rats?" I answer. Diane correctly takes this for an affirmative, and we zoom round to the Clear Thoughts building, across the street from Elektra's offices on North La Cienega and around the corner from the Doors offices.

She stops the car, turns to me to say something and instead stares for a moment or two. "Are you all *right*? You're as white as a ghost."

"It's the time change."

"Bull*shit* it is. What are you on? I thought *you* at least had enough sense not to turn yourself into some fucked-up imitation of Pam and Jim."

"Guess not . . .   Oh, Diane, it's nothing. It's only a little coke. And some grass," I add reluctantly, under the pressure of her uplifted eyebrows. "And a few, um, Placidyls. Some Mandrax. And *maybe* a couple of Ritalins. That's all."

She rolls her eyes but says nothing further, and we get out of the car and go into Themis—named for the goddess who protects the just and punishes the guilty. Pam is not there, only a young and hip-looking clerk under the peacock-feathered ceiling; and we poke around among the racks and display counters. For a clothing store there doesn't seem to be much *here*—some Moroccan robes and Indian jewelry and fringed leather bags, all of it vastly overpriced, little of it my style. We do not linger.

That day Diane receives two additional houseguests, in the form of a gnat-brained pop gossip queen with negative cup size (observed at Goddard, back in June) and her no-neck husband, cut-and-paste hack flyweights who fancy themselves a rock and roll Dorothy Parker and Robert Benchley. In your *dreams* . . .   Anyway, they too have been at the Creedence bash, and we all know one another vaguely from New York—they're not the sort of people I hang out with—though they are, as far as I know, ignorant of Jim and me having any kind of acquaintance. So when they go out to dinner with Diane that night I elect to stay in the apartment to wait for him.

I am sitting alone in the darkened room when the phone rings; I debate answering it, but it could be Jim calling, so I pick it up on the sixth ring. As it turns out, it is some woman calling for Pam! Pam doesn't have a phone so she'd called on Diane's! Could I be *so* groovy and run upstairs to get her?

The Goddess works in strange ways, all right, I reflect, and nip lightly up the stairs, as bidden, to knock on the door of 8216½.

The door swings open on something that looks like a low-market import store hit by a series of tornados: Indian spreads and rugs and hangings, vases full of pampas plumes, feathered masks, beaded curtains in doorways, that kind of thing. I only get a glimpse of this, because the mistress of the house puts it all in the shade.

Pamela Susan Courson, naked to the waist above jeans, a comb stuck in one half-braided red plait, pushes her bangs out of the way, looks at me out of wide spacey eyes, and smiles vaguely. I realize immediately that she is stoned out of whatever mind she has.

"Hi!" she says. "Are you the hairdresser?"

Do I *look* like menial help, you scagged-out little twit . . . *YES!*, I long to say, and let's start with a crew-cut. But . . . "There's a call for you on Diane's phone," I say earnestly.

She pulls on a white cotton shirt and comes downstairs with me to take her call. After she hangs up, she seems inclined to hang out and rap for a while, apparently figuring that anyone staying with Diane must be cool and somebody she'd want to talk to. I look at her and wonder how the hell I am going to get into, or out of, this one. Not to mention what is going to happen, inevitably, when Jim shows up, as undoubtedly he will, this is *way* too good for him to miss, he's probably feeling the vibes clear across town.

Pam's drug of choice tonight appears to be downers of some sort (though Jim's remarks about her heroin use do pop into my mind just then). At any rate, it seems somehow dishonorable for me to be in full possession of all my wits while she is whacked out of her skull, so in order to be on a more equal footing I roll some joints, drop the first thing I find in my purse and smoke about six of the joints; just to even the odds a little. After all this, I am still totally sober.

We talk innocuously enough about L.A. and where to buy neat stuff—she pushes Themis; I do not tell her Diane has already brought me round—and New York, and she loses no time telling me whose girlfriend (the word she uses) she is.

When I tell her I am a writer from New York she seems even more interested. "Ohhh yeah—Jim and I went out to dinner one time in New York with this really cool writer, what was her name—"

I see at once where she is headed, and—like watching a car crash—I am appalled and fascinated both. Karma, man; it just *has* to be—

"—Patricia Connolly, Nealy, no, Kennealy—do you know her?"

In many of my favorite books—Sherlock Holmes, Sir Walter Scott, *The Scarlet Pimpernel*, stuff like that—there is often a moment when cloaks are doffed and masks flung aside and rightful identities declared: "*I am Birdy Edwards!*", "*I am the Scarlet Pimpernel!*", "*I am Roderick Dhu!*", and other similar revelations both timely and thrilling.

So it is with more than a little of this feeling that I look at Pamela now and say—no cloaks or masks or anything enter into it—"Ah, Pam? *I am Patricia Kennealy.*"

Light begins to break behind those dilated pupils. "Ohhh yeah—you look different."

Must be the clothes . . . "And not only that," I continue grimly, "but there are a few things I think maybe you ought to know, and I don't know if it will hurt you but I'm afraid I have to tell you anyway."

What I tell her, industrial strength, is that Jim and I have been having an affair for more than a year, have been friends for almost two. She seems unsurprised, and genuinely intrigued.

"Wow, I never met one of Jim's girlfriends before—"

I am stung, and furious with myself for allowing her the opening. "Well, actually, it's a little more than that. Up until last month, Jim and I were having a baby."

That gets her full attention: She reaches for one of the joints I have rolled, lights it and takes a deep drag before passing it over to me.

"Ohhh—and you decided not to have it after all. Oh Patricia, that's *so* sad, that must have been so hard for you."

She sounds as if she really feels bad for me. I reinforce the point. "Jim and I *together* decided not to have it."

"Oh yeah—I see that—but it would have been nice if you could have loved Jim enough to have the baby."

That gets *my* full attention, though I don't think she means it nastily; more a sort of dreamy comment, visions of babies and booties and no reality whatsoever.

"I like to think," I say with considerable heat, "that I loved Jim *and* myself *and* the baby enough *not* to have it! It was the hardest decision I ever had to make, and I'll never forgive Jim for putting me through it, but just to have a baby—even Jim's baby—because you think it might be cool isn't good enough. Not for me, anyway; and certainly not for my kid. I wasn't about to lay that kind of hell on my child and Jim's."

She looks nothing but sad and sympathetic. "Oh, I know, but you could have gone and lived in the country with the baby. Of course Jim wouldn't ever have gone to see you, or given you any money to help out or anything—"

"*I* don't ask Jim for money," I say, meanly and smugly. *That* gets through to her: She flushes and drops her eyes. "He paid for the abortion, but that's all he's ever paid for. I support myself, take care of myself— I just didn't feel I had the right to ask a child to live like that, especially without its own father. It wasn't good enough for any of us."

"Jim and I aren't married, you know," she says suddenly, out of nowhere. "I tell people we are, but we aren't, and we never will be, either."

I stare at her, amazed by the candor. Perhaps it's her way of matching my own revelation. "When I met you at the Garden, the first time we met, at the Felt Forum shows, you introduced yourself as Jim's wife."

She giggles and takes another hit on the joint. "I know—he hates it, but I do it anyway, even when I call the Doors office."

My head feels like an oil-drum with ears; it is trembling upon my lips to tell her about the handfasting—she has not remarked on my claddagh, if indeed she has even noticed it—but I find to my great surprise that I cannot. It would be too—what? Cruel? Boastful? Incredible? So instead I sit there and listen to her amiable babble, about how Jim never pays the bills and she's always too wrecked to make lists and maybe they'll go to Tahiti so Jim can write poetry, just like Gauguin.

And I, who had gone straight from feeling sorry for myself to feeling sorry for her, look at her lovely stoned face and think, What *ARE* you? Where is your reality, your substance? Do you even have any? Have you ever *heard* of any? What is it in you that he seems to find so necessary? Is there something lacking in each of us, that he needs both of us to find completion in a woman? Both fair-skinned, red-haired—are we two faces of the same woman for him—two phases of the Goddess? What is it that he can't seem to get along without? What is it in each of us that he seems to need, to love, to fear the loss of?

Maybe it's the dope, but our thoughts seem to be running on parallel tracks, for Pam suddenly asks me, "How did you and Jim fall in love?"

Right, the actual word . . .   I am startled out of my wits, and go for another joint before I dare to speak. When I do, I tell her about being the editor of the magazine, and going to meet Jim at the Plaza, and how we were friends for so long before we ever even made love, and how when she and Jim and I and the others had dinner together that night Jim and I were already lovers for almost half a year. It all seems perfectly okay to her. I am a little curious, so I ask, "When did *you* meet Jim?"

"Ohhh, it was a few years ago, 1965? September, I think—"

She drones on, but I sit up as if I have been shot. In September of 1965 I was home from college recuperating from a case of mononucleosis so severe and debilitating that it involved major organs and nearly required hospitalization. About the middle of that month, I was suddenly seized by the strangest, most completely overpowering presentiment of total disaster. Something, somewhere, was dreadfully and finally and terribly wrong with someone who mattered tremendously to me, and whatever it was that had happened to this person would change my life forever. I hadn't the least idea of what it might be, or even who—all I knew for sure was that it wasn't anyone I knew just then, not my family or friends or even the young man to whom I was at that time engaged. Nothing to do with any of them. This was bigger than all of them, this was as big as it got. I was inconsolable for this mysterious grief, I wept and wept; and then I wrote it all down.

So now as Pam tells me about meeting Jim at just about this very time (others—biographers of Jim in years to come—will offer different dates and stories, but this is the one she gives me), I tune out on her and wonder. Could that have been it, then? Was I, three thousand miles away and not yet knowing even the name of Morrison, picking up on the vibe of altered karma when Pam met Jim and changed my life? How—*cosmic* of me. I laugh. Jim, I think, you've done it to me again: You were smart enough to know you were destined to conquer the universe with a red-haired woman born in 1946 whose first name began with P and ended with A and whose last name began with a K sound, and you just went for the first one who came along. Can't trust you to get *anything* right . . .

And as I think this I suddenly realize that I am WAY more stoned than I had thought.

"So *did* you come out to L.A. to see Jim?" Pamela is asking, edging her voice so that I know she has asked this once already and I did not hear her. "To talk to him?"

"Among other things." I am back in the moment, and on guard.

We talk for two hours, maybe more. She tells me about another

woman Jim has been seeing on and off lately, someone she calls "Fräulein von Sauerkraut," but who is in fact the wife of a Hungarian filmmaker also living at the Chateau Marmont. Plus the odd groupie, of
course . . .   When she learns I was with Jim in Miami for a week, her
attitude changes yet again; she eyes me consideringly, and, for the first
time, with genuine respect.

"He didn't want *me* with him in Miami," she says. "I stayed here
all during the trial. He wouldn't even take my phone calls when he was
down there—" Down there with *you*, her tone says. Doing who knows
what . . .

"I was only in Miami to talk with him about the baby," I say.
"That's the main reason, anyway—I had to see him, and he was in
Miami, so I had to see him there. And that's why I'm here now—I have
to see him, and he's here, and when I've seen him I'll go home, back
to doing what I do."

"Well, all I can say is you're awfully fucking forceful on your own
trip," she says, with what seems like admiration.

"What the hell *ELSE* would I be?!" I explode, and she pulls back
a little; how uncool, real *emotion*, what a concept. I school myself to
calmness; it's been so civil and sisterly until now, no need to get nuts
at this point. "It's probably the end of everything between us, but I still
love Jim, very much, and there are some things we have to get settled
between us before it's finally over."

Pamela smiles, as if this is so obvious and I am so incredibly silly
not to see it.

"But it's *not* over! Jim still loves you, and you love him—no, it's
cool, it really is. I tell him all the time, Jim, you've outgrown me, you
need to find someone to challenge your *mind*." She looks at me with not
the slightest hint of hostility and says, "I guess he found *you* . . .   Do
you know, Patricia, I haven't balled Jim for over a *year*? It's not what
we're into with each other. What you have with Jim is so different from
what I have with him, and it's cool, believe me, it's cool!"

Well—I am not so sure. It may be cool with her, and possibly even
connected to her heroin habit, and cool with Jim, and possibly even connected to his booze habit, that they don't fuck; but why tell me about
it? Is this something I really need to know? I have fucked Jim until we
both wept with ecstasy, fucked him until the backs of our heads blew
off and our cortexes short-circuited; is this confession of hers supposed
to make me feel better? Or is it some kind of bizarre *permission* I am

being given here—the head wife in the Morrison hareem giving her permission to the second wife?

"I'd never been out of California in my life till I met Jim," Pam is now confiding, taking another huge toke on the current joint. "He bought the boutique for me, just to give me something to do, but he says it's so me he can't hang out there, can't even go *in* there much— But you know, you're lucky, you're like Jim that way, you have your writing the way he has his poetry, you don't need anything outside like that 'cause it's all inside—"

And speaking of outside . . . Sage suddenly tunes up, out on the steps, and from the flat next door below Pam's the neighbors' shaggy little beast, D'Artagnan, joins in. Someone is coming up the path to Diane's door; I know immediately who it has to be.

So, it seems, does Pam. "No, no, Jim, it's only Diane, don't look! Nobody's there, it's only Diane, don't look inside, it's just Diane—"

Jim is laughing as she dashes out, grabs him and drags him upstairs. I sit alone for a few minutes, breathing deeply, smiling quietly. Shouts come floating faintly down the stairs from above.

Pamela pops back in. "Oh God, what am I going to do, Patricia? He knows it was you in here, he knows we were talking, he's gonna *kill* me!"

I calm her down; I can't imagine why she is so afraid. "He was coming over to talk to me anyway, Pam, you knew that, right? Just send him down here. I'll talk to him. It'll be okay."

"Yes, yes, okay, that's good." She vanishes up the stairs again and Jim comes down almost immediately thereafter—it feels as if I am inside one of those clocks where the figures pop in and out, whirl and move. He closes the door behind him, and I face him with all my defenses like a drawn sword in my hand, ready for his attack.

But he does not attack. We look at one another for a long time, I am falling into his eyes, they hold all the light in the room, in the world. Are we talking, are there words, or is that yet to happen; are we seeing, and what is it he sees when he looks at me? Am I there for him? Is Ahab, Ahab? Is it I, God, or who—

"Girl-talk?" he asks lightly, in a soft neutral teasing voice.

He sounds exactly like himself. The spell is broken. "You could say that," I agree. "I see you finally managed to get here."

He smiles, and my heart turns to stone.

"Couldn't resist your note."

"Yes. I can see that."

He comes over and pulls me up from the cushions and into his arms, just holds me for a long time, my face pressed into his chest and his cheek against my hair.

"Oh Patricia," he says at last. "I think we need to talk."

CHAPTER

But in spite of our need, his words, we do not talk just yet: I pull away from him, sit down again on the cushions, roll some more joints. I roll *lots* more joints, I roll every scrap of pot I can find; when I am finished there must be more than twenty of them, all stacked like little logs on Diane's silver coffee table.

Jim says nothing while I am thus engaged, just watches me in silence from a chair on my right. Then, as I sit back and stare at my handiwork, he suddenly says, "You don't dress like this in New York, do you?"

"What? *What* did you say?" I am momentarily blind with fury: I come three thousand miles, and have such an evening as I have just had, which is not over yet, oh no, not by a long shot, and he's wondering about my goddamned *clothes*?!

"No," is all I say, quite calmly. "Not usually."

But he's right, I *don't* dress like this in New York, they'd throw me into the river with anchors tied to my feet. For this all-important, possibly even final encounter, I have chosen (or my evil twin has chosen) to wear: a fringed buckskin vest, long, sleeveless, with silver conchas for buttons; a black Robin Hood shirt; skin-tight jeans; and knee-high fringed buckskin boots to match the vest. What's more, I have actually tied a wine and gold patterned Ukrainian scarf around my hair as a headband—a favorite fashion trick of Pam's—not an easy thing to have to admit to even after twenty years, but there it is.

I pick up another joint, light it, do not pass it to Jim. "Did you get my letter? Did you *read* it?"

Jim is more uncertain than I have ever seen him, an incredible mix of cold withdrawal and genuine concern, apology and bridling arrogance, love and self-justification. His eyes are opaque blue pebbles, his face remote.

"It was like being hit in the face with hot grease."

"Good. Great. 'Cause there's lots more where that came from."

He spreads his hands helplessly. "What did you want me to do, Patricia? Neither one of us could have done anything except what we did. You did it a hell of a lot better than I did—is that what you want me to say?"

"Yes. Among other things. For starters."

"Well, okay then! You were braver and stronger and smarter than I was. Does that make you happy?"

I cave. "Oh Jim, none of this makes me happy! It wasn't some kind of *contest*, for God's sake, to see who could come out of it with the most class—"

"Then what?"

I take a deep breath. "You said you would be with me when I went into the hospital, and you weren't. I told you once, oh, a long time ago, you've probably forgotten, that I could take anything from you, because I love you, anything except a lie. And you lied about that, and, oh Christ, it was *so* fucking important—" I break off, because I am starting to lose control. I know damn well I will be in tears long before this is over, maybe Jim will be too if I am lucky, but not now, not yet—

"I did not lie to you," he says, eyes straight into mine. "I had every intention of coming to New York to be with you. Do you really think I didn't think about you, about the baby?" He leaps to his feet, starts to pace. "All the time, honey, all the time—sometimes I was furious with you for going through with it even though I really wanted you to, sometimes I was even ready to jump on the first plane to New York and marry you—yeah, right, legally this time, the whole fucking trip, the kid and the dog and the white picket fence—and sometimes I was just so pissed at you for even telling me in the first place. Blame the messenger . . .

But I couldn't, I must have canceled a dozen plane reservations, I just couldn't." He laughs mirthlessly, pauses in his pacing to stand beside me, looks down. "I wasn't strong enough, or responsible enough, whatever you want to think, whatever makes you feel better about it. But don't ever think I lied to you when I said it."

I will not meet his glance. "It just occurred to me—this is the first time we've been together since then, since Miami."

He sits beside me, is silent a few minutes. "Tell me about it," he says at last, in a tone of the most infinite tenderness. "Just talk."

I stop specializing in astounding self-control. I give way completely, his arms around me at last, I am sobbing uncontrollably against his chest, telling him what I have not been able to tell anyone else, it's his right to know, his duty to hear it. At the end, he is weeping with me; I have seen him cry only once before, in Miami, and for some reason this shatters me anew.

He holds me tighter and strokes my hair, kisses the top of my head. "I'm sorry," he says over and over. "It hurt for me too, you know."

"Oh, I *know!*" I turn in his arms, take his face between my hands; suddenly it is my turn to comfort him. "I was there, remember? I knew what you were going through, it was the worst possible timing in the world. But I couldn't do anything about it, and neither could you. We just—did what we did. But I was just so—*devastated* that you never called, not even when it was all over."

"I didn't know what to say," he says simply. "I was afraid you hated me. For not showing up when I said I would, for not calling, for getting you into that situation in the first place. I didn't want to *know* if you hated me, Patricia; I didn't want you to hate me and I didn't want to know it if you did, and I didn't have the courage to risk finding out for sure. It wasn't very noble or gallant or anything, I admit, not very admirable; but it wasn't easy for me either."

"Oh Jim," I say in a calmer voice, "I never thought any of this was easy for you. I didn't *want* it to be easy for you, how could it be easy, for somebody I love so much?" I look away and laugh, and there is no amusement in it. "Do you know, all through this, I kept wanting to help *you*, to not put any more pressure on you—because of what you were going through, because of the trial? And all the time I couldn't understand why you weren't there for me . . .   All I could think of was *my* pain, *my* risk—I could have died, women do, even in hospitals—and it looked to me as if you really didn't care one way or the other if I did." All at once I am hysterical again. "Do you know what I had to do, what they fucking made me *do*? They're such fucking savages about this, they get you when you can't fight back and they don't tell you about this part beforehand— I had to sign a *death certificate*! I had to certify, in *writing*, that this was a baby and now it was dead, that I killed our baby because you asked me to, because I had no other choice— The civil authorities of New York City say I am the mother of your dead child, I had to sign a paper to release the remains for *burial*—"

He is weeping openly now, and I cannot stop lashing us both. I go on and on, just flaying us both alive—the heartache and the loss of blood—and when I stop at last it is only because I am crying too hard to speak. We fall blindly into one another's arms, just rock back and forth sobbing for many minutes, holding each other, weeping for all our losses.

Jim is leaning against the wall; I am leaning against his chest, his arms still around me. We are both utterly spent, but calm now, a kind of bleak reflectiveness.

"We had to go through that together," he says very quietly. "I see that now—"

" 'A mental abortion to balance the physical one,' " I say just as quietly, quoting from my letter. "For you as well as for me, you had to have it too, had to hear it. You're the only one I could have said that to, it was you, it was *your* baby too, and you had to know. Otherwise it makes no sense—maybe it never does." I start to shiver uncontrollably again, with reaction and strain, and he draws me protectively closer. "When I was trying to decide what to do, and you weren't there, my friend Susie said something that made a lot of sense to me. She quoted somebody, I can't remember who, who said that when a woman loves, she becomes always, forever, two people: herself, and her child. No matter whether the child of that love and union is born and dies in childhood, or grows up and dies in leaving her, or never is born at all and so dies before birth—the child lives always in the woman and in her love. Maybe it's true, maybe it's just sentimental garbage—but it helped."

He is silent for a long time. "Are you sorry?" he asks softly.

"Sorry that I had to do it," I say as softly. "Not sorry that I did it. In the end, not sorry. But not glad, not ever happy about it."

We sit huddled together for a long while thereafter, peaceful with that exhausted ravaged quiet which comes after screaming pain; we speak lovingly to one another, consolingly; we even laugh a little. We talk of Miami, of our feelings for each other; Jim even says haltingly at one point that having another baby together might not be out of the question, when things are better, when we are more settled, better able to handle it, when we could both be there, for the child and for each other. I do not respond.

So we sit, and drink a bottle of wine I have brazenly appropriated from Diane's winerack, and then start on another. It is about this time that Diane and the No-necks return from dinner, to find Jim and me cuddled up together on the cushions, talking quietly and intimately.

Diane is unsurprised to find us so, more concerned for my state of mind than anything else. The gossip queen, however, is astounded to see Jim, plainly pissed to realize that he's there to see *me*, and even more pissed to realize that obviously something *major* is going on here and *she didn't know about it* (and, concomitantly, that it is to me that she owes this meeting—if he hadn't been here for me she'd probably never have met him—a fact she will conveniently forget in years to come). I introduce her to Jim as an afterthought; she is gushing and sycophantic (as usual), Jim is distantly polite and not pleased. Diane, unflustered, goes out to the kitchen to get more wine.

I for one would have liked more time to finish our discussion, to come down off the emotional Everests that Jim and I have been scaling, without a rope, for the past couple of hours; and looking at him I can see he thinks so too. But what can you do?

"We *could* get the hell out of here," I whisper in his ear.

"How?" he whispers back, kissing my neck as he does so. "I had too much wine and you can't drive."

"Not 'can't,' just don't." I consider. "I could get us to the Chateau, no problem; it's just, what, right up Havenhurst. I'll drive fast, so they won't catch us and find out I don't have a license."

Jim starts to laugh; I feel the gossip queen's stare snapping like burning pot seeds, singeing holes in my back. Eat your heart out, you septic bitch . . . The cast is added to, rather more dramatically, when the door opens again and Pamela comes in. She is better dressed than earlier—she's even got an embroidered vest on over her shirt—and her red hair is neatly combed and braided into two pigtails. Maybe the hairdresser showed up after all . . .

From where he is sitting with me half in his lap, Jim aims his face at her. "What's the matter, just couldn't stand the party noises another minute, could you?"

Pam seems to think she'd better get her licks in fast, uncertain which way the wind is blowing.

"Jim, why don't you come upstairs, I have this really great dinner in the oven—"

"No, I'm staying here. With Patricia," he adds, just in case she hasn't yet gotten the point. "We have important things to talk about, and we haven't finished talking about them."

I am naturally pleased to hear this, but think it's a little cruel all the same. By now pretty much everyone is into the joints I so industriously rolled earlier, or the wine, more and more bottles of which keep regularly appearing—kind of like the loaves and fishes—or both.

From somewhere someone produces a pack of cards; oh, like if we're playing cards we can't kill each other? Jim, Pam and I start to play War, a simple game for simple stoned people. Very appropriate. He beats us both to hell, every time. It figures. He and I start playing Strip War; I lose my scarf and vest in the first two minutes.

Pamela is still trying to persuade Jim to leave with her, and he is still refusing, getting more mulish by the minute. Finally Diane steps in out of mercy, gives Pam some amyl nitrate and escorts her back upstairs.

I look vaguely after her, not feeling particularly triumphant; more like empathetic. "Is she mad, Jim, do you think?" I ask aloud, ungrammatical for one of the few times in my life.

"As a hatter," he replies without a second's hesitation.

The No-necks retire, perhaps reluctantly, to the spare bedroom—it is very late—and Jim, Diane and I finish off the last of the wine. But at last she too bids us goodnight ("You're both so *faaaabulous*..."), then pauses, and goes out to the kitchen to fetch something. Coming back, she crowns Jim and me, very solemnly, with the gold-wrought Christmas crowns she bought at the fair, kisses us both and goes to bed.

After the coronation... The Lizard King and his Queen-consort are alone.

"We could still go to the Chateau," Jim suggests tentatively.

"In that incredibly ugly car?" He drives this lurid Day-Glo-green Dodge Challenger ("Nobody has a good word to say about it, it *must* be cool"); rented, but still. "I'd rather be dead in a ditch."

"Yeah, well, we probably would be if I drove, and I don't think you're a whole lot straighter than I am right now. We can sleep here on the floor, Diane won't mind. I love you, you know," he adds. Only for about the twentieth time that night.

"I know."

We take off the crowns, and one another's clothes, and stretch out on the couch—really just a wide, thick, velvet-covered cushion plumped right on the floor. The knowledge that the others are just a few feet away—and possibly listening in—is soon forgotten, and we make love for a long time; if rather more silently than usual, just as passionately as ever.

By now it is past three in the morning; everything is very still, in the house and outside, dark and cold and quiet. Jim starts to drift off to sleep, then complains that he is freezing. I pad naked into Diane's darkened bedroom, where I brazenly pull her grandmother's quilt off the foot of the bed and some unused pillows out of the closet. She does not wake up.

Back in the living room, I wrap the quilt around Jim, then slip under its meager warmth myself, tucking it in, scooting the pillows under his head, bracing my back against the coffee table. This is going to be one uncomfortable night . . . I put an arm across Jim's chest, as much for anchorage as for affection, and snuggle close. We talk quietly for a while, coming down, cooling out. It has been an exhausting evening; and it is not over yet.

All at once he turns to me with an unreadable expression.

"What would you do if I died?"

I stare at him, by the light of the one candle we have left burning; I am not at all sure it is not tempting fate sorely, to speak so. But he asks again, insistent on an answer.

"Well—I would mourn you, of course," I say with difficulty. "What the hell else do you think I'd do? I'd behave like a widowed queen, okay? I'd wear black for a year, and I'd cry a lot, probably forever, and I'd buy Catholic Masses for your Presbyterian soul, and I'd do magic rituals to push you through your passages . . . oh, you know, the same old stuff everybody else does."

But he will not leave it. "Would you kill yourself?"

"I'm sure I'd want to," I answer, with a gravity to match his own. "I might even try; or want to try, at least. But I don't think I would, not really."

"So, you wouldn't kill yourself. Would you marry somebody else? If I was dead?"

"Probably not. No. No."

"Why not?"

"I mate for life. My life."

"Well"—he shifts around a little, trying to get more comfortable, settles me closer against him—"suppose you met somebody you wanted to fuck, and I was dead."

"Then I might fuck him, if I felt like it; but that's all it would be. Maybe ten years, twenty years from now. Maybe I'd even meet more than one, two or three even; maybe none at all."

"In ten years? Twenty years? *Life?*"

"You know how fussy I am. Besides, I promised at the handfasting that death wouldn't part us, and I take that vow very seriously indeed. So did you promise, if you recall."

He grins. "Oh, I remember. I just wanted to see if you did."

Now it is my turn to insist. I raise myself up on one elbow and look down into his face. He is so beautiful in the candlelight, and I am more than a little afraid; a slow, cold, chilling certainty steals over me.

"What's going on here, Morrison? You planning on checking out anytime soon? Want to tell me about it?"

"Well—you never know, honey. You just—never know. Look at the other two guys."

He means Jimi and Janis, I know; their deaths a couple of months ago have deeply shaken him, to the point where he has actually told people (not me, not yet anyway) that they're looking at, or drinking with, Number Three. He has fallen asleep now, and I hold him for a while, staring up at Diane's ceiling.

This is the biggest thing that has ever happened to me, or that ever will happen to me. This is the kind of love you usually only read about in books: the Tristan and Isolde stuff, the Lancelot and Guenevere trip, the love that is little short of possession and insanity, and before which everything else goes down as under a rolling boulder. Well, at least it is for me; I don't really know how he feels about it, despite what he tells me. He has told me many times, in many moods and many places, that he loves me; but I do not know what those words name in his mind when he says them. I know what they mean when I say them—but I accept them because he does say them, and because it is he who says them to me, and I believe them—and him—because I love him.

He stirs in his sleep, twists a hand into my hair for comfort or possessiveness; I settle down next to him and fall asleep myself.

* * *

Gray morning light awakens me, that and the sense of other people wakeful and moving about. It feels about nine o'clock or so. I open my eyes wider as a bare ankle goes past my face. Jim's side is still warm against mine, so I know the ankle isn't his. There comes again the sound that probably awakened me, a thundering on the gates of Hell. Not so far off the truth: It is Pamela knocking on the front door. The ankle belongs to Diane, and now she opens the door for Pam to come in.

"I won't deny they're here," says Diane, and stands aside.

Pam comes forward, stands looming over us. I figure there's not much point in pretending I am still asleep, so I sit up, elbowing Jim hard in the ribs; no response. I look at my watch: after ten.

"Wake up, Jim. We have company."

He turns over, grumbling, pulling the quilt with him. I have been trying to preserve some semblance of modesty, keeping my hair over my bare breasts and the quilt over the bare rest of me, and this move doesn't help. What the hell, I think; she didn't seem to mind if I saw *her* tits last night—and that was when she still thought I was the hairdresser.

I try again. "Come on, Jim, honey. Wake up."

"Goddamn it, Kennealy, let me *sleep!*"

"Say hello to our company first."

He lifts his head, squints at Pam standing there, mutters something like, "Oh, *you?*"

Pamela is not to be denied. She is smiling, but only, I think, because there is really nothing much else to do. (She doesn't even think to go upstairs for the Lugers I later hear she collects...)

"Jim, I only have one thing to say to you," she says in her little-girl voice, "and I'm going to say it in front of all these people." By now the No-necks and Diane are discreetly passing through on their way to the relative haven of the kitchen. "Jim, you always do something to spoil my birthday! You do it every year, Jim, this is the fourth one you've ruined for me, and I'm tired of it—"

She goes on in this vein; I try to assure her that it's really not what it looks like, but, come on, what the hell else could it be... Diane comes back in, takes Pam firmly by the arm, as an idiot child, and leads her away to the kitchen.

"Some orange juice, that's what we all need, and some nice vitamin B-12, that'll take care of *everything...*"

Jim is grinning hugely as we hunt for our scattered clothes and hastily dress. "I'm never going to hear the end of this from either of you."

"Oh, spare me, beloved!" I snap. "It's your own fault, you know; we could have gone to the Chateau, we could have gotten there in one piece if we'd been careful, but no, you wanted to stay here, you knew this was going to happen—"

I am very angry indeed, on Pam's behalf as well as my own—I see perfectly well that he is playing us off against each other, just one of his stupid brattish tricks—but I am also trying very hard to keep from laughing. It is truly hostile and horrible, but, let's face it, also very, very funny. I have a feeling people will be dining out on this one for *years* to come . . .

Pamela, apparently fortified with something stronger than B-12, comes back into the living room, and takes a seat across from Jim and me. She looks about as unsure as I am feeling.

Jim gives her a sour glance. "I really think you owe Patricia an apology."

She obediently opens her mouth to speak, but I get in first, appalled at both of them—her obedience no less than his arrogance. No, California people really *are* some other species; I better get back on my own coast before I start mutating. Look what's *already* happened to my clothes . . .

"No, no, please, there's no need for that. It's really all in the family."

We have a bizarrely casual conversation about one another's ethnic roots—Pamela copping to English and Scottish, while Jim is a Scotsman and I an Irishwoman—but damned if I can figure out the subtext. Then all at once Pamela bids us both a cheerful farewell and trails off upstairs. Jim and I look at one another.

"How about you drive me to the airport?" I say at last. "I think it's time I went home."

CHAPTER

January–February 1971

THINGS ARE FAIRLY QUIET THROUGHOUT THE POST-Christmas period—Jim sends me belated Christmas gifts along about New Year's Day, follows up with a couple of calls. We do not discuss the episode at Diane's, or Pamela, or anything else of major emotional freight, and we both seem to be back on our old level of affection. If we are not, neither of us lets the other one see or sense it.

He tells me with pride and pleasure that the Doors are working hard on the new album, *L.A. Woman.* I tell him I probably won't even be around to give it the review it will undoubtedly deserve, as RCA Records have offered me a job writing advertising copy, and I have just about decided that I will take it.

"It might not be such a bad idea, you know," he remarks, after listening to me moan about how tired I've become of the whole rock scene, what scum most of the people are, how being a critic is really not what I want to be doing, how the magazine seems to be going in directions I'm not entirely pleased with, how the music itself has been steadily losing its appeal for me.

"You've been doing this for, what, three years now," he adds.

"Maybe it's time you did something else for a while. I don't know that writing record ads is enough of a change, but you could just do it until you're in a position to do what you really want to. Write your books on the side"—I have been telling him about a grand project I have in mind, a series of Celtic science fiction novels—"and just work at RCA to pay the bills."

"Yeah, maybe—"

He is always so quick, he hears the doubt immediately. "You wouldn't be selling out, you know—don't think of it like that. Just consider it a subsidy for your art—it's not serious and none of it's real."

But how much of it all *was* real, I want to ask him. After we hang up, I decide: I will go out to California, see Jim, and take it from there. I am certain I will be leaving Jazz & Pop, but I want to settle this thing with Jim first. It's probably over; but I want to find that out from him face-to-face, not over three thousand miles of phone wire or even psychic connection.

And yet he has given me no sign that it *is* over. His letters and calls, no more frequent than they have ever been, are also no *less* frequent, every bit as warm and tender and quirky as ever. Not the traditional way a man deals with a woman he has no intention of ever seeing again; but in the new cynicism Jim has taught me since August (and, yes, Jim, a cynic really *is* only a battered romantic), I find myself thinking him capable of even that. Reason soon reasserts itself: Why, after all, would he even bother? If he and I are indeed finished, and he really is off to Paris to join Pam once the record is done, as I have heard he will be, there would surely be no earthly reason for him to continue to string me along. He'd just walk away, and that he has not done; and in the end, he never does.

I get myself out to California the first week of February, leaving a cold and bleak New York (my favorite kind) for a slightly chilly L.A. This time I do not stay with Diane—I plan on being here for at least two weeks, maybe three, and besides, Pam has not yet left for Europe—but with a friend of a friend. Let's call her Tiffany. In between gigs at the moment (and being heroically supported by her ex-husband, whom she charmingly refers to as her "meal-ticket"), Tiffany is a former record company employee; we have been acquainted since about last fall. She knows all about Jim and me, and when she hears that I am coming to L.A. to see him, she graciously offers me crash space at her apartment.

And, what a coincidence, it's only two blocks away from Pam's Norton Avenue digs, on let's call it Madre Street. How very convenient; but for whom? I think nothing of this at the time: big mistake.

Jim knows I am coming, because I tell him so when I talk to him two days before leaving New York. I settle in at Tiffany's—sleeping on the couch, but who cares—then, the day after I arrive, I go over to the Doors office, where the band is at present still recording, in a home-made sort of way, what will prove to be their last album as a four-man band.

This time it really is the walk to the scaffold: I push aside the glass door to the big downstairs rehearsal room on the ground floor, just past the outside staircase. As I step through (I have already announced myself upstairs—though not so dramatically as last time—to Ray), Jim's voice envelops me like his arms around me in happier moments. I peer cautiously around a corner angle to my right, following the sound.

Jim is sitting in the bathroom, singing. The room has been diverted from its more usual function and is now serving as an echo chamber/vocal booth, miked and wired to the consoles upstairs. He is doing the vocals for "The WASP (Texas Radio and the Big Beat)"; he sounds absolutely fabulous—strong and sure and deep-voiced.

I pause in the doorway. He looks up, nods, smiles an indescribable smile and goes right on singing, not a note missed, no surprise on his face whatsoever (well, they probably tipped him off from upstairs, "Hey, Jim, the Witch of the East is back!"). More than that, though: It's as if I've been out shopping for the afternoon, or maybe across the street for a burger, and now I'm back again. No surprise. With him, there never is; it is *all* surprise. Whatever happens, happens. He seems to like it that way.

I wait there until the take is over. "When you're finished—?" I say pointedly and politely.

He nods again, snaps back the headphones and opens a beer for me, then resumes the song. I take the beer from his hand, sip a little, go back out into the main room and look around. There is a pinball machine by the door where I came in, a couch at the other end behind a grand piano; since I play neither pinball nor the piano, I take my beer over to the couch and stretch out. I have nothing to read, so I just give myself up to Jim's singing. It is a powerful number, more poem than song; he chants it rather than singing it. It sounds terrific.

After a while I discover a couple of Jim's spiral-bound steno notebooks under some rubble at the couch's far end, and I eagerly leaf through them. In fact, I have vague plans to *steal* one, or would if my fringed shoulderbag were only big enough to fit it in, until I see with a jolt of surprise that Jim has scribbled my name and phone number (with L.A.'s area code, 213, instead of Manhattan's 212, but still) all over the inside back cover. I am also touched . . . Well, scratch *that* idea; and so we see once again that crime really doesn't pay.

But then, reading through the other notebook, I come across something that jolts me far more, rocks me like a backhand slap to the face. Poems with some very vivid imagery, some very specific references indeed, to what certainly seems to me, in my superparanoid hurting state, to be my abortion: blood and knives and letters, a "fabulous stranger" being "stopped at the door," someone is pregnant and "will he wed her" and "no one knows for sure"—

I feel as if I have been all at once turned to ice, to salt, to stone, to steel. Later Jim will assure me that this particular poem dates from his very early writing days (well, that's what he will tell me, anyway); but at this moment all I can think, and I think understandably, is that he has *used* me: used my pain, my grief, my loss, my tragedy, to furnish grist for his poetic mill. The fact that even if he did, the abortion story is half his anyway eludes me for the moment. Not to mention the further fact that it is every writer's privilege and heritage to cannibalize his or her own life, or the lives of friends or kin or even strangers, to make creative fodder. A common and nasty habit; and one I myself am not immune from. But just now I am devastated and wrathful and vengeful, all but bereft of ideas as to what the hell I will do next. I can't *believe* this guy . . .

Two other Doors wives come in and begin noisily playing pinball at the other end of the room. They ignore my presence completely, not even so much as a single furtive glance acknowledging me there on the couch, like Banquo's ghost; not that they'd know Banquo if they fell over him, probably. Or perhaps I'm just invisible today? Now I know how Yoko Ono must have felt.

After about an hour Jim emerges from the bathroom/echo chamber, looks around for me, smiles when he sees me watching warily from the couch. I look up at him as he lazily approaches; he looks down. Neither of us blinks.

"Finished?" I ask coldly. I decide not to mention discovering those poems, not just yet anyway.

"Yeah, for today," he says. "Come on, let's go for a drive, get something to eat, talk a little."

In silence I sweep out with him to that godawful bile-green Dodge, parked outside in the little corner lot with its nose to La Cienega. Jim holds the door open for me, hands me courteously and solicitously inside, goes around to get in on the driver's side.

"Don't look so nervous," I say with some scorn as he settles himself behind the wheel. "I'm not about to make a scene in the middle of Santa Monica Boulevard. Someplace *else*, maybe—"

"Where are you staying?"

He smiles when I give him the Madre Street address, but slings the car in the exact opposite direction, westwards on Santa Monica.

"We must have *something* to say to each other, Patricia," he says carefully, five minutes into a tense and crowded silence.

"Must we?"

"Maybe too much," he continues thoughtfully, as if I have not spoken. Then, with a visible change of mood, "Well, honey, where to?"

I smile unwillingly. "Straight to hell."

At that he laughs and seems to relax, and so do I. I sneak a glance to my left: He is looking very good indeed, full-bearded again, shoulder-length hair, handsomer than ever. I can never understand these people who think he looks tubby and unkempt—okay, he's got more hair and more poundage than he did in his Young Lion days, but he's also got a masculine grace, a gravity of presence, that comes with it, which I happen to find sexier than any number of tousle-haired, skinny-chested striplings. He is dressed in somewhat collegiate-looking casuals; in my California mode, I am wearing an open-crocheted knee-length vest over a see-through pirate shirt, gold bellbottoms and clogs.

At a traffic light Jim reaches over, not looking at me, and runs his hand under my hair at the back of my neck.

"Listen—let's not get into it just yet. Whatever it is. Let's just— have a good time together."

"Whatever you say." Suddenly the freeze is off, and all the way west we chatter like two high-school kids; it's as if we've been apart for spring break, and now we are so happy to be back together. He talks excitedly about how the new album is going, that it will be the band's best since their second LP, *Strange Days*.

I smile. "After he heard that one for the first time, a friend of mine—well, my college boyfriend, actually—said, and he meant it as a huge compliment, 'With _Strange Days_ the Doors bowed out of the human race.' "

Jim roars with laughter. "_That's_ the idea! So, you went out with one other smart guy besides me."

"Any guy who goes out with me is a _very_ smart guy, Morrison. You should know that by now—and you're the only guy who's been knowing that for the past year and a half."

"I know," he says gravely. "And I don't deserve it."

"_I_ know."

We stop somewhere in L.A.'s western wilds, where Jim disappears into an office building—as he tells me, to get some money from his business manager. I wait for him in the parked car, amusing myself by devising various anagrams of his name—MORMONS LAG: RISE, O JUDAS!; JESUS' IRON MORAL DOGMAS; JAMMIN' OR ROSES; MOM IS IRON, JR.; MR. MOJO RISIN' (and no, I don't know if I'm the one he got it from); MAJOR IN EROS, MS.; ROME'S MAJOR SIN—and reading Pam's traffic tickets, an impressive sheaf of which I have discovered on the floor of the front seat. All of them made out to Pamela Courson (LAME ACORN SOUP) or to Pamela Susan Courson (NAUSEA SCOURS NO LAMP), by the way, _not_ to "Pamela Courson Morrison" (O, NO RUMOR IN L.A.—PAM SCORES) nor yet to "Pamela Susan Courson Morrison" (IMMORAL SCORER UNSOAPS NO ANUS); well, well.

After half an hour or so, Jim returns, and we drive on to Westwood, his old college stomping grounds, where we have lunch in an upstairs Indonesian restaurant. We start out with drinks, and I can see right away that his intake is, since the last time I saw him only a month ago, off the chart.

"I ought to retire after this album, _really_ retire," he says after a long and thoughtful silence. "Who'd miss me, after all?"

"When _you_ quit," I say, rising dutifully (and truthfully) to my cue, "they'll retire your number."

The old grin flashes. "Yeah, right . . .   But I told you a couple of years ago, even, that I didn't want to still be doing rock much longer than, well, about now."

I push some satay around my plate. "Well, being a poet isn't exactly the world's best-paid occupation. Probably not the kind of groupies you're used to, either."

He raises an eyebrow. "Probably not... Oh sure, but I hope I wouldn't *just* be doing poetry. I want to get into films, too—but it wouldn't be just for the money. If it came to that, I guess I could always get the guys together once a year to make an album. No touring, though. But it's the writing I really want to get going on. You told me once, I remember you said once, and I never forgot it, that I had—you called it 'a gift for compression,' 'telepathic shorthand.' "

He brings out the quotes like jewels, proud that I said them, proud that he remembers them, proud that he deserves them.

"And I put it so well, too, didn't I," I agree. "But that's what makes the damn songs so great! And do you really think you could give up your audience, the Doors audience?"

"Well, hopefully I would find another audience of my own, or some of them would come with me. Anyway"—he looks straight into my eyes, that direct blue gaze I never fail to fall for—"I think that audience is past us, really. They don't need us—me—and when I needed them, in Miami, they were nowhere to be seen."

He drops his eyes then, abruptly shuttering them, one of the things he does when he feels he's given too much away, or when he's telling half-truths. I continue to look at him, and am still looking at him when he brings his glance up again.

"Don't you ever stop looking at people?" he says angrily. "Got a stare like a fucking cat—always *lookin'* at me—"

"Afraid I'll see something I shouldn't?"

"Afraid! I'm not afraid—I'd just like to look at you without you looking at me, that's all."

"Then you better just close your eyes, 'cause I'll *never* stop looking at you."

"Well, what if I'm not here?" he challenges.

"Especially then."

We finish up lunch after a couple of hours, trail downstairs and spend a couple of hours more poking around Westwood, mostly in bookstores (in one, synchronistically, he buys me a young fantasy author's first novel, with the observation, "This looks like your kind of thing." He must be second-sighted: Many years later, the author will become a friend and a spiritual guide; in fact, with her husband, she will sponsor me to knighthood in Scotland, in the fall of 1990. And the bookstore itself will sell my own novels one day...).

"Where to now?" he asks gaily, back behind the wheel.

"Hey, it's your town—how about Venice Beach? Your old haunt, right? I've never been there."

Out at Venice, we walk along the deserted beach, and he tells me tales of his early days here, after college, sleeping on the sand or on rooftops, penniless and happy, perpetually tripping, writing his heart out.

Now he looks out over the water, gray today, slow-moving. "Maybe it's time to be moving on, sign somewhere else."

"You mean leave Elektra, go with Atlantic or Columbia?" I am a little confused: Did he not just tell me over lunch he wanted to quit music entirely?

"Among other things, maybe, yeah. The contract's up with this album anyway, and frankly, I just haven't been that jazzed with most of the people up there for a long time. Except for Bruce [Harris] and a couple of others, I don't think all that many of them even knew what we were trying to do."

"You mean like—" I mention a particularly noxious exec.

Jim giggles maliciously. "Yeah, him especially. You know, he's got the skinniest cock I ever saw—you could pick your teeth with it."

"E-e-e-e-w-w-w, no thanks! But how would *you* know?"

"Oh, every now and then over the years we've been side by side at the urinal . . .   He thinks we're friends, but the guy's a remarkable pig —with a prick like a pencil."

"He's even piggier than that—he tried to put the make on me once, a few years ago, until I threatened to tell his wife. What I should have done was get him busted for attempted rape or something—except he probably couldn't have gotten it up with a splint."

"I'll fucking *KILL* him—" He really means it, is suddenly angrier than it seems the anecdote warrants, and I look at him curiously.

"No—I think just *being* him is punishment enough. But let's talk about nice things."

I slip my arm out of his and put it round his waist, leaning into his side and circling him in front with my other arm; he drapes his round my shoulders, tangling his fingers in my hair for good measure. And so, happily encumbered with one another, we cling together, scuffing along through the sand of Venice Beach for about a mile, talking and laughing and kissing and every now and then falling over each other's feet.

The rest of the day is spent wandering around Santa Monica and West Hollywood and even as far afield as downtown L.A. We just drive, in that horrible green car, getting out wherever and whenever Jim feels like stopping, shopping or browsing for a bit, then back into the car to drive some more.

On the shopping front, he buys a few things for himself, more for me—against my honest protests. I get really uncomfortable when Jim buys me stuff, and though I love the things because they are from him, I would be happier ungifted. I don't even like it when he pays for dinner or cabs or whatever, and always offer to pay my share—something that never fails to amuse him, though he never takes me up on it. But I would feel—sleazy if I didn't offer, and am always prepared to pay.

As to the gifts, perhaps it's because I cannot yet reciprocate on the same lavish level (though I have managed a rather nice belated twenty-seventh birthday present, which I give him that afternoon to his genuine delight); or perhaps it's because I feel he's only buying me stuff out of guilt, or as some kind of payment, or because he thinks I expect it of him—or because other women *do* expect it and he feels he must do no less for me.

Chiefly, though, it is out of pure generosity. You have to be very careful what you admire around Jim, because invariably he will buy it or provide it or obtain it. He has the gift-giving instincts of an Arab prince: He tells me he recently bought an antique American Indian eagle-bone whistle he'd taken a fancy to—rather pricey—and when a friend's wife admired it he'd felt obliged to give it to her, admitting to me now that he'd really wanted to keep it himself. But he liked her, he says philosophically, and it didn't matter anyway.

And it doesn't: His own material requirements are astonishingly low. He owns no property, though I hear something about a ranch, and someone tells me years later that he once bought Pam a small bungalow in Topanga Canyon. After the demise of his Shelby Cobra, he rents all his cars. His wardrobe is barely more extensive than the clothes on his back at any particular time.

I know nothing of his overall financial situation, of course: He doesn't support me, so there's no reason I would know. The Doors sell lots of records and concert tickets, but of late even that is not what once it was. About a quarter-million or more of Jim's own money drained into Pam's boutique Themis; there are costly legal bills for his Phoenix and Miami trials (justice doesn't come cheap, even if you don't buy the judge. Especially if you don't . . .). Presumably he can afford to kiss off recording for a while, go to Paris and write; but he won't like living in a garret, and I'm sure he doesn't plan to (or Pam doesn't plan to, anyway). But what about afterwards?

But we have not yet discussed the matter of his imminent departure, however, and I find I cannot bring myself to do so. Not just yet, anyway, and perhaps he feels the same. We are too much in our moment to address the future.

Back in the car, he starts to cackle gleefully to himself: that insane cartoon giggle.

"What's so funny?"

"I always know when you're mad at me," he observes blandly, eyes on the road. "All I have to do is read your latest review."

I grin back at him. "That's *really* why I stopped being a critic, you know," I say confidentially, though it isn't entirely true. "I knew that would happen sooner or later, once you and I got involved. Journalistically speaking, I can't be trusted. My prized critical integrity all shot to hell, and for what?" I laugh at his indignant bridling. "Oh, you were worth it, all right, don't worry. Though musicians *are* mostly irresponsible pigs—"

"Me? Am I a pig?" He sounds eager, hopeful.

I laugh again. "Yeah. A *special* pig. The worst and the best."

Pam being yet in town, we cannot stay at Norton Avenue, and there being no privacy at Madre Street, I cannot bring him back there. So that night, after dinner at the incredible Ontra Cafeteria—this 30's timewarp in the middle of downtown Hollywood, peach lighting and movie-set decor and tiny dowagers in tiny veiled hats sitting ramrod-straight in corner booths all alone—we go to a hotel. Not my most favorite thing to do, but he seems well used to it (well, he would be). Anyway, the only other choice is the car.

As we go upstairs in the elevator, I look sideways at my beloved and am suddenly afraid for him. Jim is somehow gone, the man I know, and in his place is Borges's "blank-faced man with a beard." I do not leave this to my eyes, but reach out psychically for him, as I often do; but this time I cannot find him, though he stands beside me. My senses seem to close on nothing, and that is not as it was all day today, or indeed ever before. Rock and roll Caliban, Pig Man of L.A., St. James the Martyr of La Cienega (Santiago de Los Angeles?)—who *is* this man next to me? An extra in his own movie, a plot device in his own novel, a spear-carrier in his own opera . . . He is fading: It has been barely six weeks since last I saw him, and already he is less than he was, less here, less—*him*.

But we fall upon each other as soon as the hotel-room door closes behind us; whatever else is going on, we still want one another as much as we have ever done, maybe even more, if that's possible—that at least has not changed. We make love fiercely, for hours; after, we cuddle and talk as we have long been accustomed to do. But his mind is running along dark roads this night.

"What do you think death is like?" he asks out of nowhere.

I startle a little in the curve of his arm; this sounds suspiciously like the conversation we had on Diane Gardiner's floor, back before Christmas—is this what lay behind the shoot-the-moon lovemaking? Has it been there all along?

"Well, witches think it's life," I say at once. "A different sort of life, where the soul assimilates the lessons it has learned and prepares itself either for its next chosen incarnation or to move up to the next plane of existence. It's always the soul's choice, what to do. You judge yourself; and the judgment is always perfect and correct. God just watches you do it."

"But if you didn't want to come back?"

"You wouldn't have to—the soul in the presence of the Highest knows what it has to do, and whatever it decides, it won't be wrong."

He is plainly uncomfortable with the answer. "Yeah—but don't you think it would be so much nicer to just, well, *sleep*? I want to sleep forever when I die—I think it would be just the most restful and peaceful and perfect thing."

I laugh, which annoys him. "Oh, honey, you are going to be so *surprised*— With that kind of attitude, and with the kind of karma you've been cooking up for yourself this time around, you're gonna have to work so hard when you die, Jim, that this life will look like a piece of cake by comparison. So you can just forget about the Big Sleep."

He smiles, unwillingly. "So, you think you're right about all this and I'm wrong—yeah, yeah, you're always right, Kennealy, I keep forgetting. Well, I guess I'll just have to stay alive forever, then . . ."

"Well, if I *am* right we'll all come out ahead, and if I'm *not* it will still have cost nothing to have believed it all along, so either way I think it works out fine."

He says nothing for a while, just traces the outline of my body with a fingertip, over and over.

"Well, what about this, then?" he asks presently. "What about you and me, about us? We're together now, but— Are you really happy about the way it is? Seeing me every two or three months? Knowing sometimes I'm with other women? Knowing I'm going to be with Pam in Paris for the summer? Does that make you *happy*?"

Oh, man, here we go . . . "No, Jim, it doesn't make me particularly happy," I say very carefully. "Is that what you want to hear, what you want me to say? All right then! It makes me fucking NUTS, okay? But I know it's never going to be any different with you, that this is the only way I can have you, and so, well, that's it. I'd rather have you like that than not have you at all, no matter how insane it makes me. Anyway, I've said this before, and I really mean it: I don't ever want to live with anyone, not even you. If I said, Jim, come to New York and move in with me, and you said, Sure, Patricia, whatever you want, I'd think we'd both lost our minds. We'd both end up dead—either we'd kill each other, or I'd kill you and then blow my brains out. I love you, I love what we have, I love that we're linked on a level that's so far past anything anyone else has—and I don't want us to lose it."

I run out of steam, and wait for what I think is sure to be a sarcastic reply; but he makes no answer. I kiss his shoulder and tighten my arm across his bare chest. "*It* doesn't always make me happy, but *you* make me *very* happy. Always. Forever. Happier than anyone else has ever made me, or ever will. That counts for something, don't you think?"

"Yeah," he says finally, "but I make you *un*happy too."

"Part of the package."

I start to drowse off, but he wants to make love again, and is flatteringly insistent.

"Oh Jim, just let me *sleeeep*, please, just a little nap, then we'll fuck some more, I'm so tired—"

"Later." He is all over me, whispering in my ear; he's turning me on beyond belief, but I refuse to give in.

"Sorry, honey, you're going to have a headache."

He laughs and pulls me on top of him. "You're such a hard-ass, Kennealy," he tells me lovingly. "The only time I can ever get anything out of you is when you're just too drunk or too stoned or too tired to help it."

"You bet," I agree, waking up again. "It's self-defense. You're so arrogant with the people who love you, you know. You think it's a weakness on their part, some kind of tragic character flaw, or maybe just a strategic error, that they allow themselves to love you. Maybe it is. You take their love and you hold it over their heads like a weapon— not just me, everybody, the Doors, Pam, the fans, your friends, you probably used to do it to your family too. Well, I'll be damned if I give you another weapon to use on me. You've got quite an arsenal already, and you wouldn't think twice about doing me in with it."

"Now, would *I* do that to *you*—" That damned low soft caressing voice, the one that vibrates through your very bones even as you know with every fiber of your being that you are being suckered yet again.

"You wouldn't even think *once* about it, if it suited you."

That actually silences him. "I just—" he begins, then starts again, in quite a different voice from even his usual. "Maybe you're right. I guess I've never been straight with anybody that way. I just never thought I could trust anybody that way—with, you know, love."

No suckering here: There is real pain in words and voice and face, and my eyes fill with tears.

"Oh Jim—oh God, sweetheart, don't—it's okay, it's fine." I pull his head to rest between my breasts and just murmur soothingly to him. Yet still I find a tiny corner of myself wondering cynically at how he's managed to turn it round yet again: Is it all just a game to him after all, yet another of his masterful exercises in manipulation, one of his ever-lasting tests? Or is it something else, something more: Is it, dare I even think, *real?*

I do not know. I will never know. Perhaps he does not know himself.

We go out for breakfast the next morning at Duke's, then take tender leave of one another, at least for a few days. Pam will be leaving for Paris shortly, and until then it would probably be best for both of us to stay apart. Anyway, he still has the record to finish up; the Doors are mixing, and since they are themselves the producers, Jim of course has to be at the sessions.

So I hang out with Tiffany, who seems only too pleased to hear all about Jim. I'm a little down, I think with good reason, missing Jim, wanting to be with him, and I confide in her extensively, thinking nothing of it, believing her interest to be sheer sisterly concern. After all, she's been a sort of friend of mine for a couple of months now; why *shouldn't* I tell her what's going on with Jim and me?

It has, of course, occurred even to naive little moi that she only found the place on Madre Street—with all L.A. to choose from, she just *happened* to move in two blocks from Pam, what wild fortuity—*after* I told her, having been asked for housing input, what street Diane (and thus Pamela) lived on. But I dismiss the thought as evil and unworthy; and anyway, I need a place to stay until Pam leaves. Life is just a series of trade-offs . . .

I have a surprisingly good time: I do a couple of interviews, check in with friends in the business, go out to Malibu where a colleague has a house, shop with Diane and go riding several times, always a favorite pastime—most notably with Alison, another publicist pal, way north, up by Newhall.

Though the very excellent horses carry Western tack, which I as an English hunt-seat-trained rider scorn and despise, we have a nice day's hacking. Strangely, the horses were reluctant to come to us, apparently preferring to clump together in a little herd, way off in the far fields. But eventually they allow themselves to be lured in, and we set off on a very enjoyable afternoon of cantering up cliffs and slithering down gulches. The horses seem to be having a good time, too, though still spooked and restive, easily startled, apparently listening for something, ears swiveling like radar dishes.

On the way back to town, I look around at the landforms; you can really see that all this used to be at the bottom of the ocean. And perhaps will be again very soon: There has been much newspaper and TV coverage lately of wild earthquake predictions, Edgar Cayce stuff, lurid forecasts of California finally falling into the Pacific, tidal waves turning Nevada into desirable beachfront property.

I *love* this, actually: I have been passionately interested since my childhood in volcanoes and earthquakes and their attendant frills (such as tsunamis), and I find the Caycean uproar intensely thrilling. Well— I wouldn't want to wish disaster on any state, not even this one, and especially not while I myself am personally present in it, but—

"I hope there's an earthquake while I'm out here," I say spontaneously; equally spontaneous gasps of horror and protest from the others in the car. "Oh, not one that would *hurt* anybody, just a little one, big enough so I would really know I'd been in one. I think that would be so cool."

We discuss seismic topics for a while, then forget all about it and go out to dinner at Musso & Frank. At about one minute to six the next morning, I zoom awake on the living room sofa-bed, bolt upright out of deep sleep, looking wildly about for whatever has so abruptly awakened me. Nothing. I am just settling my head back down on the pillow when there it is, right underneath me, underneath the sofa-bed, underneath the building, underneath everything, shaking and shaking and shaking: Earthquake! And a big one too.

I have never moved as fast in my life as I move now: straight to the window, to see what it looks like! In the other room, Tiffany leaps out of bed and dashes into the living room, where by now I am hanging out the casement in my nightgown, entranced by the sight of the ground actually undulating up the street. This is *terrific*... There is a sharp smell of ozone or something in the air, and blue flashes all around, not from snapping power lines but which are apparently emanating directly from the ground. I am not making this up. And the sound of it is, well, like nothing on earth.

Tiffany is yelling something practical about standing under the door-frame lintels, that's supposedly the strongest structural element, hence safest. I reluctantly haul myself back in over the sill. The quake is still going strong, I can see cracks zigzag their way up the plaster walls, right-angling before my eyes.

In the midst of all this seismic excitement, the phone rings! It is Alison, who tells me in no uncertain terms that if I *ever* say, write, hint, *think* or otherwise suggest that I'd like there to be an earthquake in L.A., she will come over and personally rip my tongue out. *

Just when we think we might actually want to run screaming into the street, the shaking stops. Before the rest of the Los Angeles Basin can get the same idea, or at least get it together enough to act on it, we dive for the phone. I call my parents in New York, Tiffany hers in Ohio. They have not yet heard about the earthquake—not surprising, it's barely a minute since it stopped—but they immediately start making all sorts of parent noises. We reassure them, give each the other's number, in case we can't get through from here later on. They want us to come home at once; we say right Mom, sure Daddy, and hang up.

There are aftershocks all day long, and some of them nasty big ones too; we know they are coming because a dog in a neighboring backyard starts to howl about thirty seconds before one comes rolling along. This causes me to speculate: I seemed to sense the quake about half that

---

* (But the *really* spooky thing is that, approximately four hours after I finished writing this section you are now reading, an earthquake measuring 6.0 on the Richter scale struck Los Angeles, at 10:43 a.m. EDT on 28 June 1991. Maybe I shouldn't be allowed to talk about —you know—at all . . .)

interval before it hit, but I do not sense most of the aftershocks beforehand, except for the two biggest; but the dog knows, and the horses
seemed to know yesterday that this was coming, that was why they were
so skittish, why they preferred to stay safely out in the fields. Hmmm.

By now, of course, my initial delight and euphoria have vanished:
We see pictures of the devastation out in the Valley—TV footage of
huge freeway interchanges pancaked and broken, hospitals collapsed,
scores of people killed, hundreds hurt. Not fun at all.

By now, too, I am pretty well scared to death, now that I've had a
chance to think about it. Every aftershock sends me into some sort of
guilt-stricken psychic tizzy (it's *my* fault! *I* wished for it! *I* made it happen!
I called it and it heard me and it came!); all I want to do is cower under
a blanket and stuff junk food—Cheez Doodles and Twinkies. A sure sign
of stress reaction: I *hate* Twinkies.

The stress is not eased much when all sorts of wild rumors start to
float around L.A., each wilder than the last. The one with widest
currency, at least in the rock community, is as follows: If there is a
magnitude-5 or greater aftershock within four days of the main quake
(epicenter at Sylmar, we have learned; not all that far from where we
were riding the afternoon before—those horses really did know what was
what), then the *Really* Big One, the Monster, the feared and fabled,
sooner-or-later, 8-or-better-on-the-open-ended-Richter-scale one, will
hit a day after that. You can tell that just tons of painstaking seismic
scholarship went into *this* one (oh man, stoned at the lab *again*. . .), but
nobody is really thinking clearly anymore.

If I am jittery, Tiffany is utterly terrified, and on the eve of the day
the Big One is due (there *was* a 'herald' aftershock/foreshock, giving still
more credence to the prediction; but it was only a piddling 4-pointer),
she actually makes us gather up our portable belongings and *sleep in the
car* until dawn (and I get the front seat; as I'm five-eight, and she's five-
five, it seems hardly fair).

Though all this is of course insane, still it is less insane than Alison
and a couple dozen of our colleagues wanting me to join them in a rock
biz caravan to safety, driving in convoy across the Mojave by night to
Las Vegas, hopefully just ahead of oncoming tsunamis—a haven to which
I am quite sure death by geology would be infinitely preferable.

It goes on like this all week: talk of continental shelf collapse one
minute, the very real threat of the Van Norman Dam's collapse the next.
I eat a *lot* of Twinkies.

CHAPTER

23

"YOU CAN COME OVER NOW," SAYS DIANE ON THE other end of the phone a few days later. "Pam left this morning for France. I *know* that's all Jim's been waiting for; you know, for her to leave so he could be with you."

I say nothing for a moment. I consider Diane one of my good friends, and over the past months she has been a source of great strength and support and sense, especially with the desperate trauma of the abortion, both before and after; but isn't she supposed to be Pam's good friend too?

"Really," I say then. "How's her French count?" The junkie aristo, Le Prince du Smacque—obviously a boyfriend who knows what she likes.

"Ohhh, *Jean*—Pam said before she left that she just *had* to have one more go-round with him, she'd probably get her chops busted good this time, but she was going to go do it anyway."

"What a gal." And, oh, how I know that feeling.

I go over to Norton Avenue later that day; Diane and I have a pleasant afternoon, drinking wine and talking. I notice a picture on her mantel: Jim and Pam, apparently together, or once together. Somebody has very decisively scissored it straight across vertically, right between the two formerly back-to-back figures. Diane tells me the cut job is Pam's handiwork, a neat comment.

There are some scraps of bright red hair beside the picture. "Oh yeah," muses Diane, as if only now remembering, "I trimmed Pam's bangs before she left, they were getting so long she could hardly see."

I consider a split-second, then pocket a pinch of hair; you never know when it might come in handy (no, no, I'm just *kidding*...). In a burst of guilty candor having nothing to do with the stolen hair, I confide to Diane some of the self-recriminations I have been indulging in of late: guilt about Jim and Pam, uncertainty about Jim and me.

Diane smiles. "She's just the Hollywood Homebase girl; he's known her for years, they have this weird thing—that's where she fits in. So what? That has nothing to do with *you*, or where *you* fit in in Jim's life. He's as faithful to you in your place as he is to Pam in hers. He's true to you in his fashion, you're true to him in yours. Just think of Jim as some sort of wonderful male Justine, Patricia, and enjoy every minute of it ...   As our dear wise friend Grace Slick tells us, we come and go as we please, and we all need more than one person to get that special fulfillment. It doesn't mean that we love, or are loved, any less for it."

This seems to make so much sense that I wonder if I have in fact lost my mind to earthquake terror. After a while, Diane goes out for the evening, leaving me to await Jim's return. When I hear the boots on the stairs, going above and next door, I give them a chance to get inside; and then I grab the bottles of wine I have brought with me against just such possible need, and five minutes later follow the boots upstairs.

When the door opens to my soft tap, I look up straight into Jim's face.

"I have this wine I can't get open, do you think you could—"

He opens his arms without a word or a smile, folds me against his chest like a flower he's afraid to crush, and draws me gently inside.

The place sure looks different from the last time I was up here: It is now of course mostly empty, the furniture all gone into storage. Now there is only Jim's purple-upholstered Victorian carver's chair, drawn up to the white iron-and-glass garden table in the living room; a mattress and box spring plunked down on the bedroom floor; some cinderblock-and-board bookcases beside the bed; a small portable TV with a built-in alarm clock; a Delta Airlines blanket thrown over unmade silky sheets. In the other room, a lonely Chinese ginger jar filled with pampas plumes sits on the expanse of carpet; some suitcases, a brown leather Gladstone bag, an Army-Navy surplus store duffel bag *exactly* like my own, back over on Madre Street. Some books, a few knickknacks, a small stack of copies of *An American Prayer*, Jim's latest venture into self-publishing. And that's about it.

We sit and talk, and drink some more, and make love once or twice; then we go out to dinner at some Mexican place way the hell downtown on Sunset. I am not a fan of Mexican food, and though I manage to force-feed myself some ropas viejas, the least awful-sounding thing I can find on the menu (and actually not bad, though I will never eat it again for the rest of my life), I would not call this one of our most memorable meals.

"Man, you really are a crank, aren't you," marvels Jim. "I never saw such a picky eater—not over the age of five, anyway."

"*Princess* Picky to you . . .   I told you I don't really care for this particular ethnic cuisine, however noble and historical."

"Yeah, but I didn't think you'd be as bad as this—how can you be in Los Angeles and not want to try Mexican food?"

" 'Cause I just don't like weird spicy Third World cookery, that's why. I'm just not into food adventures; there it is." In fact, I actually make him stop and get Kentucky Fried Chicken on the way home ("Oh, you'll eat pure chemical deep-fried cholesterol, but you won't touch nice tortillas and beans and stuff!"). But first we stop at a bar on Melrose, and then at another on I think it was La Cienega, and one on Sunset —by the time we get back to Norton Avenue, we are both a little drunk.

Jim staggers inside, falls on the bed, laughing at some private joke. "Could you take my pants off for me?" he asks.

"Uncurl your toes so I can get your boots off first."

This is a familiar riff with us; it never fails to amuse him, to have me undress him, and he never will uncurl his goddamn toes . . .   But I don't mind. It amuses me too.

I am tugging on one of the chestnut-colored Frye boots—he has cut off the spur strap, and I have little purchase for my grip—when out of nowhere he asks, "Is Bruce Harris in love with you?"

I lose my grip altogether and fall across his leg in astonishment.

"WHAT?! Dear God, no! He's married. Very happily. He and his wife are both good friends to me." I look down at him. "Don't you have any friends like that?"

He stares straight up at the ceiling. "No. I don't have any friends like that."

"I know." Having gotten the boots successfully off, now I pull the buckskin pants down over the last bit of uncooperative Morrison and toss them on the floor.

"You really like me, don't you," he says in a tone of wonder, "you really love me."

"No. Not specially."

"Ah, sure y'do, girl, it's written all over you. But what *I* want to know is, if I'm as fucked up as you're always saying I am, always implying, how come you love me so much?"

"I guess I must just be crazy." I take off my own clothes and slide into bed next to him.

He snorts with laughter. "Oh, somehow I doubt *that*! But now that you love me, I'll never be able to get rid of you."

"Do you want to get rid of me, Jim?"

He smiles. "No. No."

"Then you won't."

He startles me with the speed and suddenness of his movement: He buries his head in my middle, clinging to me for dear life, and I realize that he is crying.

"Don't leave me, Patricia."

I stroke the long thick brown hair, twine my fingers in the full beard. "Jim, you're going to Paris in a couple of weeks. To be with Pam."

"Fuck her. You and I, we'll go back to New York. Or you could come to Paris with me instead, you can speak French, I've heard you, you can live with me and speak for me and we'll write things together. Say you will, damn you, Patricia, say you'll come."

Even I had no real idea of just how desperately I want to believe this, how badly I want to say yes, how easily I could let myself think he really means it. And the terrible thing is that he probably *does* mean it, at least right now, when he is saying it, if not before or after.

"Ask me again," I say at last. "When it's really over with Pam."

"It *is* over with her, why don't you ever fucking believe what I tell you—"

"Well, because it never is, you know. And it won't be, not until you *make* it be over. You go to Paris, and you take as long as it takes, and you tell her it's over, and then you come to me in New York. Then we'll all see how over it is."

"I love you."

"I know you do, and I love you. But there's a lot more to it than that. You love Pam too, I know that, and she loves you—there are reasons for that, and there are reasons you love me, and they're not the same reasons, but they're real reasons." I run my hands over my face. "If I knew now what I'm going to know after you leave me, you'd never leave. I'd know what to do and say to hold you. But I can't be Pam for you, and sometimes I think I can't even be *me* for you."

He laughs, unamused. "You really understand the best *and* the worst of them all, don't you . . . I really like that about you, Patricia, really love it." Now he is slurring, mumbling, half-drunk, half-asleep.

"You and me, living together—Jim, I just can't see it. So many things would have to change, for both of us, I don't know if I could, if you could—"

"Then we'll change them." He is awake again, and openly weeping. It is like a replay of Miami; I can't keep up with him, the changes are making me sick and dizzy. I am bleeding for him inside, feel my face freezing with inflexibility and pain.

"Come to New York," I repeat. "I'll be there. You know where I live. I'll be there."

"Patricia—" He is burrowing between my breasts like some small lost hurting creature, and I start to cry.

"Oh God, Jim, just don't! Please—just don't, okay? I don't think I can take much more of this."

His reply astounds me. He looks up, that wide-awake look he so often gets—of understanding, earnestness, urgency to communicate, *seeing*.

"That's bullshit," he says softly, as softly as only he can speak. "You take as much as you have to, and you take it for as long as you have to. You just—*do* it."

I am unreasonably annoyed. "Oh, right, like *you* do it, I suppose?"

The mask is back in place now. "When I feel like it, yeah. When I don't—" He reaches down alongside the bed, comes up with the half-empty wine bottle, takes a long pull.

"*That's* bullshit," I say severely, pointing to the bottle.

"Sure," he says with mockery and arrogance. "But it's *my* bullshit." Another abrupt about-face: "Read my Tarot cards."

I get my traveling Tarot pack out of my shoulderbag, divest them of their protective black silk wrappings, and, sitting nude and cross-legged in the middle of the bed, begin to lay them out on the sheets. Jim watches with interest; this is by no means the first time I have read the cards for him, and he has been impressed before now with their appositeness.

"The King of Cups, that's you—a brown-haired, blue-eyed man."

I set out the cards in the cross-and-rod pattern: Paris is there, and Pam and myself—the Queen of Wands and the Queen of Swords—all in a strange configuration. But there are some rather more alarming indicators, cards like the Tower, the Nine of Swords, the Three of Swords, darker cards still; and I am suddenly very cold.

"Just—be careful over there," I say at last. "There's some heavy changes coming. Be careful. That's all."

He smiles quizzically. "Well—sure, okay, why wouldn't I? But I *will* be back."

One way or another... I smile back at him, that smile you do when you are utterly unconvinced and trying desperately to convince the other person that you *are* convinced.

"I know you will." But I don't know. I don't know at all. And I don't need the cards to tell me.

I stay with him for the outside of a week, picking up a few changes of clothes from Madre Street and dodging Tiffany's questions. We spend much time driving: He takes me to favorite places of his, the nearby desert, a beach up past Malibu. He is still working on the album mix with the other Doors, so sometimes I just stay holed up alone in Pam's apartment, reading, or writing in my notebooks, until he comes home; or even pop back over to Tiffany's for a couple of hours while he is out, fill her in on developments.

Our days and nights are utterly usual: out to dinner, back to the apartment, conversation, TV, bed. But Jim is drinking more than I have ever seen him drink; worse, I find myself drinking more than my usual two or three little sherries or vodka tonics, just to keep on roughly the same plane as he—though, given the sheer volume of his intake, that is hardly either possible or wise.

Yet he seems unaffected: He is the same charming, funny, sweet person I have known in New York, and his drinking, so far at least, has not affected either his amorous inclinations or his performance—he is the same tireless, vital and loving partner he has ever been.

One afternoon we go wandering along Melrose and La Cienega,

checking out the many little shops selling leatherwork, lace, antiques, assorted tat; as usual, he buys me some stuff. He even nicks a few things for me from Pam's boutique, bringing them triumphantly back to the flat like captured plunder from some primitive tribe.

"I can't accept stolen merchandise, Jim," I say with great seemliness.

"It's okay," he says dryly. "I paid for it."

We are at Barney's Beanery, near the Doors office on Santa Monica, when our idyll begins to turn to hell. We have both been drinking. I do not even recall what sets me off, but suddenly I am flinging words at him like hail against a window.

"What about that notebook I found at the office the other day? You even wrote a song about it!"

His face is blank with genuine surprise. "About what? What are you talking about?"

"About my abortion, you cocksucker!" I hiss at him, trying to keep my voice confined to our table. "God damn you to hell, Morrison, you wouldn't help me, wouldn't come and be with me, wouldn't call me when it was all over, and then you *use* it!"

He does not deny it, though later he will have a different story; incredibly, he seems perfectly willing to have a scene.

"I'm an artist," he drawls, in that stupid voice I so detest.

"You! You're a fucking basilisk! Everybody who touches you bleeds!"

"I use things. I use everything."

"And everybody!"

"It came at a bad time for me," he says reflectively, back in his normal voice. "We've been through all this, you know, Patricia . . . I had a lot on my mind. You were there. You know how it was, you saw it. It didn't mean I never thought about you."

"Listen," I say with an effort. "All I know is you promised you would be there and you weren't, and you said you'd call and you didn't. And now I find out you actually wrote a goddamn *song* about it. How do you *think* I'd feel? All I got from you was an abortion sales talk, a check, and 'Be brave.'"

"Well? You were. I knew you could handle it."

" 'HANDLE IT'?!" Over at the bar, a few heads turn in mild curiosity; I lower my voice almost by main force. "*Now* I see why you do these things, to me, to Pam, to everybody. I finally see it, and you just *hate* that, don't you?"

He never even looks up. "Don't you ever stop being a critic? If you really love me as much as you say, you'll put up with it—if you still want to be with me."

"If I really love you as much as I say, I'll do my damnedest to put a *stop* to it—whether I'm with you or not."

He stands up, eyes still hooded. "Listen. I know you're upset. But we've been having such a great time together, can't we keep it like that? I can't do anything about the other thing. Don't you understand that yet? I'll see you later."

I stare up at him. God, it drives me directly up the *wall* when he says that . . .

"What the hell does *that* mean?"

"It means," he says, faintly astonished, "I'll see you later."

He walks out through the back door to the rear parking lot. I sit there motionless for a moment or two, then dash after him, rounding fiercely on him in the dim deserted alley behind Barney's.

"Don't you *EVER* walk out on me like that!" I snap at him.

"Or what?" he challenges.

"Or this." I whip my right hand back to shoulder height and belt him across the face with my open palm, before he can even think to move or prevent me. I have never seriously hit anyone before, and I am surprised by the jar to my frame, the crack of the sound.

We stare at each other, the print of my hand already beginning to show red on his cheek above the beard. Then Jim smiles, lifts a clenched fist, and aims it at my chin. I do not look away, but hold his eyes defiantly, and think to myself, I am fucking *dead* . . .

But he very deliberately just brushes the side of my cheekbone with his knuckles, the lightest, gentlest touch imaginable; his fist immediately opens to caress my cheek and jaw and neck, his fingers running into my hair. He pulls me to him; I am crying.

"Damn," he says ruefully, rubbing his cheek with his other hand. "You've got some arm. Did you have to slap me as hard as that? It really *hurts—*"

"Good," I mutter into his chest. "Where there's pain, there's life; or so I've been told."

The peace doesn't hold: By the time we are back at the apartment, we are at it again, snarling all the way from the rear yard where he parks the car, round by Diane's front door, up the stairs. To the neighbors it doubtless sounds much the same as usual.

But by now I am just about hysterical, could probably benefit from a crack across the face myself. Instead, Jim grabs me by the shoulders and shakes me, then hugs me so close I can scarcely breathe. I am sobbing uncontrollably, and he too is on the verge of tears.

"Listen to me!" he says. "Just listen—it wasn't you! Those poems you saw, they weren't you! They weren't anyone—they're from years ago, I just had them in that notebook to maybe do something with for the new album. I'm sorry they upset you so much."

Not one word of reproach or 'serves-you-right' for my prying indiscretion, poking my nose into his private jottings. On the other hand, I have no idea if he is telling me the truth.

"No more lies, Jim, I can't take you lying to me—"

"They're not lies." He won't let me go, though I have been struggling violently to free myself from him for the past couple of minutes. He strokes my hair, speaks so softly in my ear. "Just believe me. If you'd been out here instead of in New York, I'd have been with you for the whole thing, we'd have gone away together, everything. I just couldn't face it in New York."

"Oh, now it's my fault because I don't live in L.A.—"

"Shhh—just shhh . . ." When I am quieter, he kisses my hair. "I won't ever lie to you. I'll do things you won't like, and you'll hate it, and you'll bust my chops for it like you just did in the parking lot, and rightly, but I promise you I won't lie to you, and if you hear certain things, if certain people tell you things sometimes, ask me first, not them. All you have to do is ask me."

"It's hard for me to ask."

Unbelievably, he throws back his head, laughing. "Oh man, do I know that! That's one of the things I love, the girl with the best manners in the universe— But sometimes you *have* to ask, and I just want you to know, to believe, that if you do, I'll tell you. You can believe that, can't you?"

I am still shaking. "Oh sure, I can believe *that*! *Anyone* could believe *that* . . . It's all the rest I have the trouble with."

"No problem," he says expansively. He pulls me down onto the bed, starts unbuttoning my shirt.

"I *think*—" I begin.

"Well, don't!" he pleads. "It's more than I can take just now."

"—you're too drunk to fuck," I finish triumphantly, and stand up again.

He pulls me back down by the seat of my pants. "And you're too drunk to stand up."

"Oh, Jim, I really *am* drunk," I say with genuine surprise. "Don't take advantage of a poor defenseless girl—"

He snorts. "You're about as defenseless as a cobra. Take off your clothes."

"No, you." I hold up my arms and fall back onto the bed; Jim pulls off my shirt with an obliging smile and begins tugging down my jeans.

"That better?" he asks solicitously, when I am nude save for my jewelry ("You don't have to take *everything* off, leave it on—").

"Oh, much, the clothes were making me drunker—I'm so cold, Jim, get in bed fast, before I freeze."

"If I move any faster I'll pass out. Hang on."

He lowers himself very carefully into bed beside me; I fall against him. Oh man, I have not been this drunk for a very long time, never as drunk as this with him, and I am still teary and upset from the fight.

"I suppose you're wondering why I'm here—" I start to say.

He kisses me. "You're here 'cause I'm here."

I ponder that for a while. "That sounds right."

"Of course it's right! Yeah, do that, that's good—"

"You made me so unhappy, Jim."

"I know, and I'm sorry, and I'll still make you unhappy if you give me half a chance."

"Well, why would you do that, you said you love me—"

"I do, I can't help it, it's congenital—"

"No pun intended—Jim, nothing's happening, I told you you were too drunk—"

"No, it just takes a little longer sometimes. Just keep on doing that."

"It *never* takes this long with us, never, never." This is true: Sometimes we haven't even been able to make it to the bed, or get all our clothes off, before being overtaken by the moment.

"Don't worry about it, I'm gonna fuck you all night—"

But it is no good. He is too drunk, I am too upset, we cannot make it work just now.

"Well, you can't spike paper without a paper spike." It just pops out; he laughs as I have never seen him laugh before. "It wasn't *that* funny," I mutter.

"No, no, it's you—"

"Oh, thanks!"

"No, I mean, I never in a million years thought I'd hear some-thing like that pass those incredibly proper lips. You're such a class act, Kennealy, when *you* say 'fuck' it doesn't even sound dirty."

He just makes it worse . . .   "You mean I'm such a hopeless prude it couldn't *possibly*, is that it?" I hit him, laughing. "You're telling me I'm *uptight*? Maybe *puritanical*?" With every adjective I whack him again.

Jim is still giggling. I have an idea, and go out to the living room, where I have dropped my shoulderbag, to get my coke stash. I don't have a lot with me by rock standards, but for me it is a *huge* amount—two grams—and at my normal rate of consumption would probably last me two months.

"Let's try some of this." We have only done cocaine together once or twice before; I don't know what his coke habits are (though at one point he does confide that if he had an Everest of cocaine in his backyard, he'd do it all—because it was there), and of course he is ferocious in his opposition to heroin—though apparently unable to keep Pam from using it, if indeed he ever even tries.

But we do some coke, talk for a while . . .   It takes about twenty minutes, some more coke, and that belly-dance I promised him last year, but we are soon past our problem, and most satisfactorily so, not only for the rest of that night but my entire stay. We chase each other, naked, all over the apartment—stalking, leaping, pouncing, laughing, making love between each pursuit and capture.

Suddenly he breaks off the hunt, and starts rummaging through my bag, looking for something.

"Do you want another hit?" I ask, but he does not reply, just keeps pawing through purse rubble, now spilled out all over the floor.

He finds what he is looking for: my little wheel of birth-control pills. "So, you're not pregnant again—"

"No, and I don't ever plan to be, either. Give me those, please, now."

I hold out my hand, but he jumps up and goes into the bathroom. By the time I can get out the other side of the bed and after him, he has locked himself inside, and I hammer on the door.

"Jim! Give me those pills!"

Water is running in the sink; Jim's voice comes muffled through the door.

"I want to get you pregnant again, want you to have the baby—my baby, for me."

"Absolutely not—Jim, give me the damn pills!"

"No! I'm gonna make you pregnant again—"

"Not a chance!" Actually, I am not too concerned, not even when at last he lets me into the bathroom to see a wet mushy heap of what used to be Demulen in the middle of the sink: I have two more courses of pills back in my duffel bag, and I've already taken today's; all I have to do is go over to Madre Street and pick up another wheel—and make sure Jim doesn't know where it is.

I am rather more troubled, though, by what's behind this: Is it just more stupid hostility on his part, or is he trying to tell me something, and if so could it be better expressed in more usual ways?

I let him see my annoyance. "What the hell was all *that* about?! After what we both went through in Miami, what *I* had to go through in the hospital, you really think I'm gonna let you put me through *that* again? No way, Morrison—"

He collapses on the bed, mumbling something about little babies, and is asleep at once. I lie down beside him, doze fitfully, then wake up suddenly. The lights are still on, and I go out to turn them off. Coming back to Jim, I just stop and stand and look at him for a moment. He sleeps quietly on his side, his back to me, though we generally sleep touching at several points. I turn out the bedroom light and slip back into bed, snuggling up to him in our old familiar posture, spoon fashion, my breasts against his back and my arm under his and across his chest. He is so warm.

But he is not asleep. "Tell me."

"I love you."

He rolls onto his back. "Yeah—but what does it *mean*?"

I will never tire of telling him how I feel about him, ever, and indeed take advantage of all possible occasions to do so (maybe by dint of repetition it will sink in?). Nevertheless, it has occurred to me to wonder every now and then about his almost-constant need for reassurance. Or at least for *me* to reassure him: Tell me you love me, Patricia; tell me you haven't stopped loving me since the last time I saw you, Patricia; tell me you haven't stopped loving me since the last time I made you say you still love me, Patricia... The need never seems to extend to his art—he never says Tell me you still like my music, Patricia—but to be limited, if that is the right word, to whether or not I still care, and how much I care. Perhaps he asks this of all the women he is with, or at least all but the one-nighters, the groupie slags. Maybe even them.

How can I put this— "Well, for me, personally, it means that you, in your persona, your entire being—body and soul and mind—are the sum of certain values that mean more to me than anything or anyone else in the world, no matter what you try and do to make me change my mind."

I am very impressed with myself for coming up with this; Jim seems impressed, too.

"Pretty snappy, pretty neat—but am I the most important person in your *life*? I *better* be—"

"*I'm* the most important person in my life," I say gently—and probably not entirely truthfully (well, of *course* you are, Jim, who the hell else??). "Because if I wasn't that to me, then I couldn't be me to you. I couldn't love you, couldn't be who you love, if I wasn't."

"Well, *do* I love you, miss?" That flip, irritating drawl again.

"Oh Jim, who knows... You say you do. You went through a ceremony with me that says you do. *You* tell *me*."

"Do you believe me when I say it?"

"Shouldn't I?" He is silent, and I smile. "That's for you to figure out, really. I love you, so I believe it. If I'm wrong, then I'm wrong; but even if I'm wrong, I still won't have made a mistake."

And this last seems to move him more than anything else I have said. When Jim is moved, he usually says nothing and he usually makes some physical response: Now he pulls me to him, almost violently, up along his body, my face pressed into his neck, his arms tightly circling me, rocking very slightly back and forth. We stay like that for a very long time.

CHAPTER
24

Our last day alone together begins when Jim wakes me, kissing my neck, softly at first, then with greater insistence, until I start to laugh, no longer able to feign slumber.

We make love right then, and for some reason, no reason, it is all there for us and more besides, one of those inexplicably transcendent comings-together: the same passion, the same technique, the same desire and ecstasy as ever; but, as happens to us all every now and again, this time somehow combining to be so much *more* than that, so much more than *everything . . .*

I am weeping uncontrollably, coming down off this blinding blazing apocalypse. He too is shaking, but holds me and quiets my sobs.

"Why are you *crying*, it was incredible, it was beautiful, it was the best—"

All I can say is his name, over and over, as if naming him will somehow prevent the loss I have so long feared, the loss that this most spectacular of couplings seems only to foretell. If I name him strong enough and often enough and with love enough, then he cannot cease, something that is so named and so loved cannot stop being.

He says my name to calm me. "Pa-triss-i-a. My Irish love with her Roman name—" Later he will write this again, in his last letter from Paris, and I will weep again to read it as I weep now to hear him say it.

But I cling to him all the more; I cannot say his name enough, and I cannot hold him close enough, and in the end, neither will be enough.

I calm down after a while, and we lie abed well into the morning. At last Jim sits up, swings his feet to the floor, turns to look at me.

"God, you're beautiful!" he says; simply, straightforwardly.

I stare speechless at him. It's not the first time he's said that, but no one else has ever called me that. Not someone I love, nor in such a way, with such lack of guile and such depth of feeling; and I have never thought of myself as possessing any particular beauty except, I hope, the inner sort. Not unattractive; but certainly not pretty as Pam is pretty. But "beautiful" is just fine.

"What do you want to do today?" I ask, when I am once again in command of my own voice. He falls back into bed beside me.

"Do you think I'm doing the right thing, leaving the band, going to Paris?" he asks abruptly.

Oh, right, as if it matters what *I* think—as if he needs *my* permission to go off with Pam, kiss off the Doors . . .

"I think that's something only you can decide. I don't think I can answer, I have too many—conflicts of interest, I guess you could call them. But as far as the Doors go—that was something you worked so hard for, something you wanted so much, or else it wouldn't have happened in a million years. You worked for it, and I don't think you're finished with it yet. It's a little off the rails just now, but it's nothing you can't fix. The least thing you can do is take it seriously."

"No, that's the *last* thing I can do—"

I give up. "Then what's it really about?"

"Beer. Is there another one in the kitchen?"

"Probably." I wait, but nobody can outwait Jim Morrison when he doesn't want to get out of bed.

I sigh and throw back the covers and go out to the kitchen to fetch the beer, noting on the counter a list of Pam's, mentioning among other things a "carved narwhale [sic] tusk"—how ecologically enlightened— and a letter to "Mrs. Morris" (also [sic]) from the landlord about how the rent is overdue *again*.

Coming back to the bedroom, shivering a little—it is February, after all, I guess *this* is how cold it gets in L.A.—I hand Jim the beer, not without a disapproving glance.

"What, I shouldn't be drinking beer before breakfast? M'dear, this *is* breakfast—"

I can't believe it. He really *did* wake up this morning and get himself a beer—and here I thought that was just a song. Silly me.

"The perfect picture of the shaman/philosopher-king," I say scornfully. "You and Socrates, swigging hemlock; could give the words 'drinking buddies' a whole new meaning."

"Witch stuff," he says vaguely. "Think you know everything—"

"Mostly everything."

He reaches over to a little box on the bookshelf near the bed and takes something out of it. Extending his hand, he touches my forehead and presses something to my skin. I glance over at the mirror on the back of the bathroom door. It is one of those little stick-on psychedelic mirror discs that look like a flat prism, rainbowed and reflective.

"What'd you do that for?" I ask.

"I'm blindfolding your third eye."

"Well, it'll take more than that." I fix him with The Look. "I can see through stone."

"What a down— Listen, let's do some more coke."

"Oh *Jim* . . ." I know where this is going to end up, and that's fine, but he's already had one beer so far today and I'm really not quite in the mood. He insists, though, so I get out the mirror and the razor and my silver Tiffany spoon and silver straw, and both our stashes. He has a bit more than I do, but not very much more; I scrupulously scoop first my coke, then his, perfectly equally.

It makes an impressive little heap. I do all the chopping and lining because I like to, and I really get off on the ritual. We each do a couple of thin lines; then he blows more coke gently down my throat, and I perform the same service for him. I love this, the immediate freeze and cross-eyed high, the erotic implications, the whole thing. We do maybe half of the ration I have doled out; then I rub some coke on his cock and we make love on the silky sheets.

"I really hate these sheets," he complains.

"No traction—"

"Yeah, maybe *that's* what those chains were for . . ."

I giggle, but the sheets really are slick as glass, I am slipping out from under him as we move. In the end he just rips the sheet out from beneath me and we fuck on the stripped bed, on the floor, on the rug in the empty room, stalking one another all around the flat again, fucking wherever we fall.

It is an exhausting session, and by now it is nearly noon. We head out for lunch—some funky place way downtown that never closes, or that has never closed for fifty years, some such story—and drive leisurely back. He has another session; so I spend the day with friends and meet him back at the apartment later that evening. We go over to Barney's again, get modestly drunk and stop by Madre Street so I can change—and get my pills.

He really should not be driving at all in his condition, but he manages, and has just finished pissing into the grassy curbside verge when a young woman passing by on foot looks twice and says, "Patricia? *Jim??*"

It is Ginny Ganahl, former Doors secretary, who is *really* surprised to see us both. As it happens, she lives not far from Tiffany, in a charming wood-shingled bungalow complex; she has a couple of friends with her, and Jim immediately decides he wants to hang out with his old pal Ginny and these jolly strangers.

My patience is just about at an end, so I tell him to suit himself, flounce upstairs and tell Tiffany all. She is very cross with me, says if I really love him, really want him, I better get my tail right back down there. I reluctantly agree, but I'm not sure just where Ginny lives in the complex.

Not to worry: Jim can be heard from the sidewalk, bellowing some tuneless ditty about trouble from Tangier, that's his name. I knock, and Ginny, a very nice young woman, welcomes me inside.

We don't stay long: Jim is so drunk by now that we don't dare drive home, so instead stagger the couple of blocks to Pam's place. An embarrassing progress, as Jim joyfully bellows "*NIGGERS!*" (a lamentable relic of his redneck roots—it's happened before, most notably, I am told, at a Rolling Stones concert) at passing cars. I am all but carrying him.

I glance anxiously at Diane's windows as we pass on our way upstairs, but her flat is silent and dark. It seems a little strange that I have been upstairs for a week now and not even seen her, but perhaps she is up in San Francisco with the Airplane, or just working hard.

Again we go through the usual riff: "Uncurl your damn toes, Jim, I can't get your boots off."

"Won't!" He is lying cruciform on the bed, arms flung out, staring up at the ceiling. "Nobody ever cares about *me*," he says mournfully, "what *I* might want."

"That is a damnable lie, James Morrison, and you know it."

" 'S true."

"Oh God—well, what *do* you want?"

Now he is sulking. "Nobody's ever asked me."

"I'm asking now! I asked this morning! *Everybody* asks you! Nobody has a fucking *clue*, 'cause you don't know *what* you want!"

"Would you come with me, take care of me?"

I shake my head. "Jim, you're going to Paris to be with Pam."

"So, you wouldn't come. Don't you *want* to take care of me?"

"Not unless you can take care of yourself. It's a waste of effort otherwise. You're the one who taught me that."

"Trouble with chicks like you," he mutters. "Too damn self-reliant, too independent—"

"I thought that was how you liked your women, not *needing* you—well, except for Pam, that is."

"Don't *you* need me? Patricia, *NEED* me, damn you!" He crawls across the bed's width, wraps his arms around my knees as I stand there.

It just kills me to say it, but I say it: "I'll *never* let myself need you, 'cause when I *did* need you, I needed you more than anything, and you weren't there. I would hate like hell to really need you, really depend on you for anything crucial, like food or water or a blood transfusion. It's hard enough as it is."

"Yeah, and when *I* needed, in Miami, where was everybody then? Where were *you*, even? You made those damn vows to me, remember, and now you don't even care, don't care that I'm gonna *DIE*, Patty, gonna die just like Janis and Hendrix—you'll be sorry then you didn't need me, you'll see—"

"Oh, Jim, that's not fair, you know damn well where I was! You're the one who was responsible for me being there—and what about *your* vows, you took vows too—and that other thing, well, it won't happen, Jim. It can't."

By now he is totally incoherent, just babbling drunk, so I cuddle him wordlessly for a while, then gently roll him under the covers and turn out the light. I go into the living room, wrap one of his shirts over my nakedness, sit down in his purple chair with my notebook, as I have done so often this week, and write it all down, pouring my soul out on paper.

I am still shaking from the truth I have heard in his voice: "I'm gonna *DIE*, Patty!" Because I know that he is right. This Jim I have seen is the Jim I have heard so much of from others, but have never quite believed in till now. Until now I have been spared the sight of Jim the alcoholic; and though I do not know what that term really means, I know a problem and a grief when I see one.

But I don't know what to *do* about it, what *I* could do, or even if anything could be done. In 1971 we did not think recovery was something that cool folk such as ourselves could ever stand in need of; and I doubt Jim himself had at that point either the will or the inclination to change. Moreover, as they say in rehab, he had not yet bottomed out—and of course, all we who loved him thought he needed was strength and resolve. But some people bottom out at way deeper levels than others—sometimes death is the bottom. What I have so far seen is painful and terrible; but apparently not as painful and terrible as it can be. The worst is still to come.

I write page after impassioned page in my little leather-bound book. It must be two in the morning when Jim comes up behind me, bends down to me, takes me in his arms.

"Patricia. Don't do that again. Don't."

"Don't do what, Jim?" I kiss him tenderly.

"Shut me out like that. Don't shut me out. Please."

I draw back a little to look at him. Tears are standing in his eyes, and I take his face between my hands, look gravely upon him.

"I would never shut you out. Never. No matter what you do. But if *you* shut *me* out, then I can't reach back to you. You—you have to let me in."

"That's hard."

"The hardest. But I'm here. I'm not going anywhere. I'll always be here."

I do not know as I speak these words that this is the first, and last, lie I will ever tell him.

What is to be our last day together in this life dawns fair and cool. Again Jim wakes me with intent; he is eager and clear-eyed, the night's moods apparently conquered, and we make love ferociously, unaided by drink or drugs. As we head out for breakfast a bit later, Jim suddenly turns back to the bedroom, as if for something he has forgotten.

He comes back into the living room. "Here—take these with you, I want you to keep them for me."

I stare down at what he has put into my hands. "I gave you this for a wedding present," I say with difficulty. "And that was a Christmas present, and this was a present present—" In all there are maybe a dozen objects, not only things I have given him but some personal items of his own as well.

"I know, and I love them, you gave them to me," he says softly. "But I'd feel better knowing they were safe with you in New York than take them to Paris, or leave them here in some bank vault. You're my wife, remember? Oh, sorry, I forgot, I mean my *consort*... Anyway, I want them to be with you." He closes my hands over the items, kisses my fingers. "I want them back, you know!" he says with a grin. "This is only a temporary loan, just for safekeeping. I'll be back for them—for you—in the fall. I *promise*."

Will you? I want desperately to ask, but don't. "I still don't understand why you're going," is what I say instead.

"It's hard to explain," he says after a long silence. "I kind of feel responsible for her. She's not like you, she can't do anything on her own, can't take care of herself—it's over, but I think I owe her this."

"Well, she's going to have to learn sometime, don't you think? It's called growing up, being responsible for yourself. This isn't doing her any favors—"

"I know, I know, I just want to end it off gently—" He goes on for a while about how Pam was so young when they met and she just never matured, she's so dependent on him, he needs her too but for different reasons, he needs me in very different ways... I listen to all this, getting more and more steamed, thinking, Well, *sure* she never grew up, asshole, why would she have to bother as long as she has you to live off?

And then he gets into us, him and me, how we will be together in New York, in the fall, for the start of "the season," as he puts it, how we will get a loft downtown, have poetry readings of his stuff at the St. Mark's Church poetry project where Tandy Martin's husband reads his own work, I can write my novels and Jim will do poems and films, maybe we will even write things together...

I look at his eager face while he details this literary idyll: Leonard and Virginia in SoHo, a downtown Percy and Mary, Robert and Elizabeth on West Broadway. I don't even know what I believe anymore, what I *want* to believe, even. He is about to leave for Paris to be with another woman, a woman he has known by even the most flexible reckoning more than twice as long as he has known me, and still he can say I love you Patricia and we'll be together in New York. Sure, Jim; whatever you say, Jim. None of it seems to make the least difference in either what he does or how I feel, so—

I put the things carefully away in my shoulderbag—noting that his gold claddagh is not among them, and fearing to ask about it—and pop back into the bedroom for my jacket. As I leave, I catch sight of a book on the shelf next to his stacks of *An American Prayer*: a small book with a faded cover, a book whose pages are richly ribbed parchment, with that musty old-book smell to them, whose s's are printed like f's, a book that was bound in "the Crown Colonie of Philadelphia" before this country was even a country. It is my last gift to Jim, my belated present to him for his twenty-seventh birthday. It is *De Senectute*—Cicero's discourse on old age.

Jim sits on the couch between Tiffany and me, watching me roll some joints. It is mid-afternoon, and we have stopped off at Madre Street for me to pick up something; Tiffany is there, and so naturally Jim comes in and is introduced and we all think a joint or a drink would be in order.

I don't really pay much attention to anything but the joint in hand, until I hear Jim say with drawling amusement, "Ah, Patricia, you might want to know that your friend has my shirt half unbuttoned and her hand inside."

I think that would indeed be something I'd want to know about: I stare at Tiffany with utter astonishment. She is totally unembarrassed, grabs my hand, starts babbling apologies but they're not really apologies at all. I don't really understand how she could do this, but let her off with a warning glance like a shot across her pitiful little bows.

We all go out together, Jim driving, and end up in some bar on Cahuenga, or maybe it's Robertson. We are drinking shots of tequila with beer chasers, and as I watch Jim I see that he is the most joyless drunk in Christendom, drinking purely for the sake of getting smashed and obnoxious, it's not even to kill the pain anymore, it's to control the situation by lack of control. Well, he's not the only one . . .

I keep pace with him easily, until about fourteen, where I start to lose count, if not control. By this time the bartender is sending over every third or fourth round on the house. I am at a stage of inebriation I have never before attained to, being basically a temperate person with an innate dislike for alcohol. (Even with drugs I never go too far, just far enough to share the moment and not so far that I cannot remember or control what I do . . .) But this is an almost Zen state, with white-light flashes of water-clear vision; and oddly silent, alcohol clogging the auditory nerve.

From here we move on to the nearby recording studio, where the Doors have been busy mixing *L. A. Woman*, which will prove to be the final Doors album. The studio looks as if Pam had her uncredited paw in the decor: Everything is imitation Tiffany shades and paisley baffles; or perhaps it just looks that way because I am so incredibly drunk.

The band is hard at work when Jim and I and Tiffany trail soddenly in. No one bats an eye, and we are greeted civilly enough by the five or six people present. I sober up fairly quickly as I watch them work: Ray all cool professionalism, calling for tracks and levels, Robby and John listening in active silence, then offering ideas.

I am sitting on the couch in front of the board, later moving up to a chair at the far end of the console. "Riders on the Storm" is pouring out of the huge overhead speakers; the band is engaged in laying in the rain and thunder effects over the light jazz base. All I can think of is that stupid Lou Christie song about lightning striking a-gaa-yin—this is not what I think of as Doors music; the dash and fire of their finest moments is not here, and it makes me sad.

It's fashionable nowadays to trash the Doors as mere musical brats, pretentious tinkerers; or maybe tinkers, itinerant bandsmen. But there was an enormous dialogue they tried to set up in those first days, and even as far down the line as *The Soft Parade* (which was, to quote Bruce Harris and my own fair editorial hand, "an awful lot better than an awful lot of awful people wanted to have to admit"). There was a dialogue in words and music, a power and grace of form and purpose of which the tiresome, fill-in-the-blanks, spiritually bankrupt sampling mechanics who call themselves musicians in the two decades since can only, vainly, dream. I miss it still.

Jim has been sitting in a chair at the other end of the console, next to the jugs of wine and bottles of bourbon or whatever; I have been listening so intently to the mix that when next I turn to say something to him I see to my surprise that he is not there.

"Where's Jim?"

"Oh, he went out about five minutes ago. Right after your friend did."

I catch the subtext; hey, a house doesn't have to fall on *me* . . . And besides, if I hadn't known who I was dealing with here, the carefully noncommittal tone of voice and blank face would have tipped me off regardless.

I go out to the front desk. Nobody around; the lobby is deserted. The two bathrooms are empty also. On my way back to the room I notice that the sliding glass doors to the inner courtyard are slightly ajar. I step through and turn the corner into the wind.

Jim and Tiffany are lying on the cold ground at the far end of the garden, locked in a passionate embrace. I walk up to them, crunching my boot-heels into the stones of the path like Dodge City.

Well, at least they're not fucking yet. "Get up. Both of you."

Tiffany keeps moaning; Jim not only obeys me at once, but shoves roughly at her, a small smile on his lips.

"Come on, Mother says we have to get up."

I loom over them: Patricia, Colossus of Cahuenga. Oh, this is great, this is *perfect*, this is *exactly* what I deserve for that thing with Pam back before Christmas; I do so love it when things balance out as nicely as this. Even if I really hate every fucking second of it.

I am about as far from surprised as anyone can be, and in a way I am almost glad. It makes it easier for me to leave, gives me anger as a way home. Just kiss him off and blow town—but not just yet.

Tiffany says something to me; her voice cracks, I can't tell with what. Terror, probably; I doubt it's remorse or guilt. Maybe it's glee. I allow her to pull me into a sisterly embrace, sensing rather seeing Jim's amusement at the scene he has so successfully engineered. Oh, fuck you all, I think wearily; my inclinations are more to multiple homicide (justifiable, no jury in California will convict me when they hear *this* story) than to groupgrope.

I shove her away. "I want to talk to Jim. Alone."

She moves away, and I look straight up at him, bringing my glance across his like a sword.

"Let me take her home tonight, Patricia." He who attacks first is on shakiest ground: old fencing maxim. Or maybe an old Irish proverb. "You know I'm way too drunk to screw. Anyway, I'm not going to spend another night with you. We'll be together again tomorrow night, not tonight—"

His voice trails off. I continue to look at him. God, I could kill them both, right here, no problem . . .

"I'm leaving tomorrow," I say to my own astonishment (I'd had no such plans till now), "and I don't think I'll ever see you again. Not if this is the way you are—"

The blue eyes shutter obstinately. "I don't want to spend tonight with you."

I feel my own eyes snap on like blowtorches. "Fine. You're not spending it with her, though. Maybe Pam puts up with this kind of thing, but I don't. Not while I'm still here. I don't give a damn what you fuck, as long as you fuck it *after* I'm on the plane."

Jim goes back inside, disgusted. Tiffany cringes as I turn on her.

"You two-faced little bitch—"

"Oh Patricia, don't you see, he's just doing this to hurt you, using me to get at you the way he uses you to get at Pam—"

"Sure. I see that just fine. I also see you're not doing anything to discourage him."

We go back inside after Jim, me dragging her by the arm in a grip so vise-like that bruises will be visible later on that very evening.

Back in the studio, no one has much to say, eyes all carefully averted. Suddenly Jim is extremely interested in the quality of the mix: In fact, it takes until nearly midnight before it is corrected and mixed down to his liking. We then go out to the car, Jim leading.

"You driving?" I ask coldly.

"Yeah, I'm driving! What, you think I shouldn't or something? Come on, get in, get in." I slide in next to him, and after a little hesitation Tiffany takes the back seat.

"Where are we going?" I demand.

"None of your beeswax."

What follows is the Ride from Hell. It is not entirely clear to memory's eye, nor indeed was it all too clear at the time; and the way Jim is driving, nor is it likely to be . . . We are tearing along the roads up by Griffith Park at warp speed, zooming past the Frank Lloyd Wright house, the one that looks medieval-Egyptian. Jim observes as we flash by that it is the only house he had ever wanted to buy, but they were asking too much money for it. I believe the figure he mentions is $375,000.

We end up at Griffith Park Observatory, staggering around clutching at the tourist scenic-view telescopes while Jim pisses in a gravity-defying arc out over the dense stands of rhododendrons or whatever below the terrace. We do not stay long, driving back down Sunset in total silence; by now I am nearly sober again, out of sheer fury and concentrated force of will. Jim pulls into the parking lot of some topless bottomless brainless sleaze palace and shuts off the ignition.

"Would you two lovely ladies care to accompany me inside for a drink and some entertainment?"

I am hating the idea like rats running over my face—he's only doing this because he knows damn well what a prude I really am about this sort of thing—but I nod curtly and we all go in. Jim is a regular here, it seems; his presence causes no stir, and the waitresses and bartenders and performers and habitués alike all greet him cheerfully and casually.

We sit on a banquette along the back wall, Jim in the middle, me on his left, Tiffany on his right. The last show is in progress: Onstage, some blonde with cat ears and whiskers and a long fuzzy tail, nothing else, is rubbing her crotch against the lip of the trash can she is straddling.

Jim calls for drinks, obviously figuring this will fix me for good and all.

"What d'ya think, Tiffie," he says on a long loud belch, "is Patricia a frustrated lesbian or something? I mean, she's not even watching the show, won't even look at those little girls up there, whatcha think?"

Oh, right, *I'm* a frustrated lesbian because this is not my idea of a good time, a fun night out with the man I love: watching some bareassed tootsie hump a garbage pail while someone I thought was a friend betrays me to my face . . .

I look at Tiffany, who immediately turns a shade or two paler, and then I look at Jim. He has a faint smirk on his face behind the beard, and I know exactly what he is thinking. He is thinking, 'You wouldn't let me go home with her, Patricia, even though you knew I couldn't fuck her, so I'm going to embarrass you and hurt you and make you look like a total asshole in front of all these people.'

Well, Morrison, only if I let you . . .   "If I ever wanted to make love to a woman," I say, clearly and coldly and with the most precise diction I can summon up, hating him, hating him for making me lie like this, "all *I'd* have to do is jerk myself off. It'd be a better fuck than you any day."

Take *that*, Lizard King! I cannot believe I have allowed him to make me angry enough to utter such a sentence; not only is it offensive and embarrassing but there's not a word of truth in it. Still, he asked for it . . .   I have spoken clearly and loudly enough to be heard several tables away, judging by the snickers, and Jim is furious with me. Now I've made *him* look like an asshole, and he does not like that one little bit. Too bad.

"I've had enough of this crap, Jim," I say, still in a voice like a whip, "and you're tired. Let's go."

To my astonishment, he stands up at once, throws some money on the table to cover our drinks, and exits the place without so much as a stagger. Left behind by his sudden burst of speed, Tiffany and I emerge into the parking lot only seconds later to find Jim sitting sideways in the driver's seat, feet on the pavement, pissing blithely onto the stanchion.

Somehow we all get back to Madre Street alive, though *that* may not last . . .   Jim pisses yet again in the street before we get out of the car, and collapses on the couch as soon as we are inside Tiffany's apartment.

Tiffany has been crying in the bathroom, and is now crying in the bedroom. Jim shakes his head for a long time.

"I don't think I want anything to do with this," he remarks. "You two just fight it out amongst yourselves, and I'll be here for the winner."

I start to laugh; it is so horrible I don't know what else to do. "I know what you're doing, Jim, and it won't work, I promise you. Besides, you said yourself you'd never be able to get rid of me—now that I love you."

"Oh, don' be like that, Patty, honey, sweetheart, I hate it when you're like that . . ." His voice trails off, and he's unconscious on the couch. I have never seen him like this before, and even yet cannot quite believe it, but I have heard stories, and I figure he's just out for a while.

I'm right: Half an hour later he wakes up, just pops up like a figure on an *extremely* perverted Swiss clock, and goes out to the Pullman kitchen, where he makes a great deal of noise rummaging through the cutlery drawers.

"What the hell are you doing, Jim?"

"I'm collecting all the knives an' scissors an' sharp things, so you can't castrate me in my sleep—"

I laugh in spite of my bogglement. "Oh Dionysus—don't even think it! Maenads, Bacchae, yeah, right, *witches*—we don't need *knives*, we just use our *teeth*, our *fingernails*! Anyway, I've got my athamé with me; you remember *that*, don't you, Jim? Yes, I'm sure you do—it's good for lots of rituals, it could manage a castration just fine. That is, if you think you actually have any balls left worth my cutting off."

He piles all the knives and things carefully under the couch, lies down again. "I really wish you wouldn't castrate me, Patricia . . ." He is out once more, as if I have hit him over the head. Maybe I ought to.

I back away from him, to sit apart over by the window. I am shaking violently, and I clench my fists until I draw blood from my palms to try and stop the trembling. I am not like this. I have never before behaved like this in my life, and I never behave like this again. This is what Jim Morrison makes otherwise fairly well-balanced individuals do. This is what he does to people who love him, and whom he says he loves. This is probably what Pam has gotten from him for four years, though God knows what he's gotten from her. It is, simply, the way he is. Or one of the ways.

It is not, however, the way *I* want to be. It is not the sort of thing I wish to go on having to do, no matter how much I love someone. And, although I love Jim more than life, I am *not* going to put up with this; and it does make parting easier, at least for the moment. There will be unbearable pain later, I know that already; but for now—

I go into the dressing room and start packing my clothes, just throwing them into my duffel bag—the one that's just like Jim's. After a few minutes, Tiffany comes scuttling in like the cockroach she is. And as a native New Yorker I know what to do with cockroaches . . .

"Oh, Patricia, please don't be mad, I didn't know you loved him so much—I just wanted to fuck a star, the one I really wanted was Kris Kristofferson, but I thought since Jim was actually *here*—"

I turn to stare at her in loathing and astonishment. Can anyone really be so utterly contemptible? And how *could* I have been so stupid as not to notice this before?

"You lying slut," I say. "I ought to rip your tits off, if you had any—"

With admirable enterprise—seize the offensive!—she rushes forward, both her hands straight out, and succeeds in knocking me into the bathtub, which is unfortunately right behind me, though fortunately just now dry.

But I reach for a hold even as I fall backwards, and bounce right back up. I have smashed Tiffany's head into the sink three or four times, and am clawing for her eyes when Jim strolls in. He looks at us both with nothing but amusement in his face, and in that instant I hate him even more than I hate her. I push roughly past him without a word.

He talks to her soothingly while she sobs, and I shout invective from the living room. He comes outside again, stretches out once more on the couch, and is immediately asleep. I can't believe this, and I throw the last of my possessions into the duffel; there's only a shirt or two over at Norton Avenue, and I'll be quite happy to kiss those off along with Jim.

I am sitting in a chair, drained, cooled-out, when Tiffany creeps out of the bathroom. She sees me sitting there and approaches, careful to keep out of reach.

"Oh Patricia—" she starts in, groveling, whining, begging for my forgiveness.

I cut her off peremptorily; I hate handwringers. "If you must talk, let's go outside in the hall, wouldn't want to disturb Fucko."

Out in the hallway, we sit at the top of the carpeted stairs leading to the next floor up. No one else is around, the building is quite silent; it must be two in the morning by now. I begin to breathe again, think about salvaging some dignity from the wreck of the evening . . .

Then Tiffany blows it all to hell. What a dear friend I am, she says. How much Jim obviously means to me, she says. Then:

"Isn't it better if *we* share him, instead of leaving him to Pam?"

I know I have heard it, but I cannot believe I have heard it. It is as if my mind has stopped cold. It is as if someone has imprudently pushed a button I never even knew was there. A big *red* button, with a lot of warnings around it in big black scary letters, that say DANGER! DO NOT PRESS . . .

I hear it from an immense distance: Isn't this the same woman who told me not half an hour ago that she didn't care what star she fucked, as long as he was famous, she'd rather have had Kris Kristofferson anyway? What *IS* it with you people, do you not understand how much I love this man? That he is the only man I love, or will ever love? Him. This man. No one else. Him alone—

What happens next is utterly unexpected. I stand up at the top of the stairs, righteous fury surging through me and filling me with the strength of at *least* ten. My sight goes pure crimson, flooded from behind with blood. And even in that screamingly impossible homicidal moment, when if I could have destroyed the world with a word I would have, that writer's brain is hard at work, because I actually hear myself thinking way far away, 'Wow! You really *do* see red! How incredible! How great! I must remember this! For a book!'

But it really is amazing, it is just as if someone has popped a red filter over my eyes. But on to more important things: I hear myself shouting, "My GOD, I think I am going to KILL you!" And then I go for her throat.

Tiffany, frozen stiff by what must be the ghastly sight of this blood-thirsty harpy lunging at her from above, blows it right there. Unhindered by petty resistance, I grab her by the arm and hair, smash her head into the wrought-iron railing and then actually *throw her down the flight of stairs.*

She falls like a poleaxed steer, lies stunned for a moment—well, hey, I am pretty stunned myself—then crawls over against the wall, trying to hide. Yeah, *right . . .* I am terrified, even so, that she will escape, so I just vault over the bannister, drop down a good six feet to the floor, and kick her in the stomach. (*That's* for making me sleep in the car that night, bitch!)

"Please, Patricia, I don't want to fight you—"

Well, so far you haven't—I drag her to her feet, throw her against the wall and give her a karate kick in the solar plexus.

"Fight, you fucking cunt, or I'll *KILL* you," I illogically invite her. The timid counterpunch she offers merely enrages me further, by its very effrontery. Oh, like *that's* the best you can do, you little wimp? Please!

Tiffany suddenly wakens to the need for some serious self-defense, as it rapidly becomes all too apparent that I really *do* mean to kill her. I have not indulged in warrior pursuits for nothing all these years; besides, the direct approach is so much more satisfying than the remove of, say, a Luger. It is no little-girl schoolyard hair-pulling, either: I punch and kick and hit with a fury and, yeah, a homicidal glee that would not have shamed a berserker. Yet somehow, all the while, I have the strangest feeling that someone (Jim? God? My higher self? Common sense?) is holding me back from my full force; which is probably why Tiffany *doesn't* end up a lifeless heap on the carpet. Jim misses it all; I'm sure he'd have loved it.

Anyway, I close in at last and get her by the throat, and wind up for what I fully intend to be the kill. But somehow Tiffany gets her arm up and wedges it between her face and my fist, gazing pitifully at me from behind hair and blood and hematomas.

"Please, Patricia—" she whimpers pathetically, obedient to the law of the jungle, turning up her tummy (figuratively speaking) in craven submission.

The appeal to my mercy is successful. I *am* disgusted—at *her*, of course, not at myself. How can I fight such a totally déclassée opponent, not even worthy of the name? I feel the adrenaline murderousness drain away, leaving me sad and cranky, and I lower my mighty right arm and step back.

Tiffany is sniveling softly in pain, and in gratitude that I am no longer hitting her. "Shut up," I say. Louder sobs and sniffles. "I said shut UP, you septic cow, or I'll beat you up some more—"

I leave her snuffling in the hall, go inside, cry passionately for a few minutes alone in the bathroom—Jim is still oblivious on the couch—and gather up the last of my things.

"Get the car keys!" I snap at Tiffany, still huddled in the hall. "I'm not staying in this fucking madhouse another *minute*, you're driving me to the airport right now." It's about five in the morning, but I don't care. I'll just sit in the departure lounge for as long as it takes. I am not proud of this evening's work. Well, I *am* proud, actually, but I know very well I shouldn't be . . . Even so, it seems to have been someone else who has done all this, not Patricia at all—or no Patricia I've ever known, anyway. Then again, there has never before been reason for her to manifest herself. (Not until many years later, when I first encounter the 'evil twin' concept, do I know whose work this *really* is. Thanks, Trixie!)

The cause of all the blood and heartache and mayhem is lying on his back on the sofa, hands over his crotch, evidently expecting castration at my hands even in his sleep.

I stand for a few minutes looking down at him, memorizing, remembering. He looks waxen, unreal, his skin tinged with a strange sweaty greenish pallor; like something you'd see at Madame Tussaud's. He looks as if he has been dead for some time. Perhaps he has been. This is not my Jim, and it is not his Patricia who looks down at him—

The sofa pillows and back and arms seem to swallow him like the up-holstered sides of a coffin.

This is it, the last time for us, I should think. Goodbye, my dearest love, I'm almost glad you're not awake to see it. I kiss him lightly on the forehead, longer on the mouth, touch his face and hair and hand one last time.

Then I pick up my cloak and my bags and close the door behind me. I do not look back.

Tiffany, still crazed with terror and pain, is waiting for me downstairs in her car. At the sight of her my fury tries for a comeback, but I push it firmly down. After all, I need *someone* to drive me to LAX, and obviously it's not going to be Jim. If I hadn't needed the ride, maybe I really would have killed her. Life really *is* trade-offs . . .

I sling my bags in, get into the front passenger seat. "Move."

She starts the car and heads down La Cienega to the airport; we do not exchange one word the entire journey.

At the terminal, I get out, pull out the bags. Tiffany gets out too, comes round to my side, holding out a trembling hand to me, needing to make some sort of peace, or perhaps merely wishing to ensure I don't go out to buy cow hearts as soon as I get home and stick pins in them —cow hearts with her name on them. She doesn't know me very well after all; and, apparently, neither does Jim.

I look at her and she backs up a pace. Then I glance briefly at her outstretched hand, SPIT at her (not very successfully, I have never had to spit at anyone before; but there's been a lot of things in the past few hours I've never had to do before, and just see how *they* turned out), and spin on my heel away from her.

(Tiffany does not get off unscathed, though I like to think it's just her own bad karma and conscience and not my everlasting enmity: Not many months later, I hear through a mutual friend that she has had a bad accident—though, the laws of karma being all things for each, there's ultimately a hefty financial settlement to ease the pain; a good thing too, since her 'meal-ticket' ex-husband has finally wised up.)

By the time I get to the boarding gate, tears are streaming coldly down my face. Nobody else is around—it is after all not yet six, barely light out, the first plane doesn't go for another couple of hours—but I doubt I'd have noticed or cared if anyone was. I sit there alone, wrapped in my black cloak, rocking silently back and forth, like someone who has just been pulled alive from the most dreadful, most terrible, most tragic accident there ever was, and who couldn't save the one she loved most and best from the wreckage.

The flight home is virtually a private one; I upgrade to first class and curl up in the front row window seat, all alone. Even the cabin attendants stay away, and no one else is there to see that I am crying coast to coast. Incredibly, I fall asleep at one point: or maybe not so incredibly, I have defiantly dropped everything left in my stash, I don't even *know*, Mandrax, Quaaludes, Ritalin, Tuinals, some piss-ant Valium—uppers, downers, inners, outers, carpet tacks, whatever! If it pops it drops!

But I am so beyond wired that none of this has the slightest effect whatever: I wake up after half an hour's fitful doze, totally straight, and thinking hard. I know very well that this was not *entirely* Tiffany's fault, the little weasel—if it hadn't been her, it would have been someone, or something, else. Rather, it was all the awfulness of the past six months—Jim, Pam, me, the pregnancy, the trial, Paris—coming together and finding a focus. But mostly it is Jim: This is the sort of thing he does, the sort of thing he makes *you* do, at least if he hurts you badly enough and you are volatile enough in the first place. I beat up Tiffany partly because she richly deserved it, but partly too because I couldn't beat up Jim.

And as I was in the studio garden, again I am glad, if that is the right word, that he has given me this way out. If it had been different, I do not think I would have had the strength to leave; as it is, anger fairly carries me.

But it cannot last at that pitch, and all at once I am so blackly depressed that I start wondering if I could make the plane crash into one of those inviting-looking mountains several miles down, a likely Rocky; can I just will it, wish it like the earthquake, or do I have to actually go and kill the pilots and tank the thing myself? After a while I conclude that this would probably not be a good idea, so I just stare out the window.

Why does he DO stuff like this? Even so, it is the first time that he's ever done anything like it to me, though he must have known I would never put up with it; even now, even in my pain and hurt and wrath, I know that I have been so right to just get the hell out. People love in many different ways, and some of them love like dogs—loyal unto death, endlessly accepting and forgiving, hit me some more I still

love you—and some of them love like cats—loyal beyond death, endlessly comprehending and considering, hit me once and I'm GONE
I still love you. I will not take this kind of abuse from anyone, not even
from him. Even *I* know that.

Jim knows it, too; calls me a week or so later for my twenty-fifth birthday
(a few days off, but who's counting).

"Don't hang up," he says at once.

"I wasn't going to."

"I wouldn't blame you if you did." He's silent a moment; I wait him
out. Then: "I'm *SORRY!* Jesus fucking Christ, I'm *sorry!* I never thought
you'd just—you know, *go* like that."

"No, you just forgot who you were dealing with . . . What did you
think I'd do, Jim? What the hell did you think I'd do? Hang around like
Pam so you could torture me some more? That's maybe her trip, but you
should know by now that's not the way I do things." A jangling pause,
in which I fight to keep back tears, he is *not* going to have that satisfaction. But it's hard to get the words out unstrangled. "You say you love
me—do you have any idea, really any tiniest little idea at all, how much
that hurt me?"

Well, yes, he does, he's so sorry . . . "I don't know why I do shit
like that," he laments. "I always have to blow it when it's important—
Listen, she was nothing, she wasn't even any good, she was a little
bitch . . ." Now it is his turn to pause. "Patty, I'll be in New York in the
fall like I said, with you, I promise, this really is the end of it with Pam,
we'll get a place together, you and me, you'll see—"

I listen, and I have this sad and terrible feeling that somehow, I
will *never* see, not in the fall, not in New York, not ever anywhere. But
I hear his assurances, his oddly urgent insistence, his reminders of how
great it's always been for us and how we really are linked, joined forever
with one another because of the handfasting, how much that means to
him, how beautiful I am, how smart, how mystical, how terrific . . . And
because I want so very desperately to believe him, I say Yes, sure, of
course, Jim, I know, I feel the same about you—

When at last he tells me yet again he loves me, and I tell him I
love him, and we hang up with fervent pledges of mutual mystic devotion
still on our lips, I start to shake. It's not enough: I see a picture of him
propped on the mantel, just a publicity still I'd liked and copped from
the magazine's files. I lunge for it, ripping it into the tiniest pieces

imaginable and flinging them to the floor and grinding them into the carpet with my boot-heel.

I stare down at the carnage for a long time, then slowly go to my knees, crumpling into a little heap on the rug amid the scraps of photograph—right about where Jim and I had stood during the hand-fasting, where we had made love after—curling protectively around the ruins of the picture, weeping the bitterest tears I have ever wept.

To me, at that moment, Jim died.

PART FIVE

Will you come w/me now
to the house of Night?
& remember always
that you are queen there
& I do not forget

CHAPTER
25

March–June 1971

STRANGE AS IT SEEMS TO ME, I HAVE MORE IMMEDIATELY pressing, if not perhaps more important, concerns just now than Jim and how it might be with him in Paris, to which he betakes himself around the middle of March—just about the time that our child would have been born. I mourn about that, of course, even as I receive a last letter from Jim in L.A. and a belated birthday present, then resolve to put it all aside and concentrate on my new enterprise.

I have begun work at RCA Records, as senior copywriter in the newly established in-house advertising creative group, almost as soon as I arrived back in New York from L.A. The work proves pleasantly different from my magazine chores, and sufficiently distracting even to get my mind off Jim for a while, and of course it also means I will never have to listen to another Doors record again—a thought not without its own peculiar charm.

Well, almost: *L.A. Woman* is released in April, to a critical reception that is astonishingly favorable, better than any reviews the Doors have pulled for a long time (well, now that *I'm* no longer reviewing, I guess *somebody* had better like Doors stuff). I myself find it extremely difficult to listen to the album—doubtless to do with the circumstances under which I heard most of its cuts pre-release—but there is more to it than that. From first cut ("The Changeling") to last ("Riders on the Storm"), *L.A. Woman* seems to me to be one long goodbye.

But that is all behind me now, and if Jim returns with the autumn, well, then we'll see. Just now, I have a new thing to master, and it's as well for everyone that it comes fairly readily. Writing ads, at least in these heady days of the long-copy record ad, is rather like writing mini-reviews, and to my satisfaction I get to work on some classy stuff. I create David Bowie's first American ad campaigns (for *Hunky Dory* and several subsequent albums), and do some nice things for Lou Reed and the Kinks, among others. (One Lou Reed ad shot in a subway car, with retouched graffiti artwork, actually makes the New York Times advertising news when various city agencies chastise us for appearing to glamorize the graffiti plague; and a spec ad for the Kinks on their joining the label—the RCA icon dog, Nipper, with puppy-ready teats, over the line "RCA Records welcomes the Kinks to its warm corporate bosom"—calls down upon us cold corporate displeasure from the very highest levels.)

But mostly it is fun, a new writing form and a surprisingly demanding one too: not just rock to flog, either, but country and classical music; and radio as well as print, which serves to familiarize me with production techniques. All the same, I try to keep a writerly hand in, doing a long piece for Rock magazine, where Sue Donoghue is now managing editor, on the decline and fall of intelligent rock criticism (well, *sure*, now that *I'm* not a critic anymore . . .), and the odd article here and there as the mood strikes.

Yet in spite of all this activity and adjusting, meeting new people and learning a new trade, I am deeply depressed by how things have been left between Jim and me. So that when, in April, I get my first communiqué from Paris (a postcard with a picture of Nôtre-Dame and some cryptic remarks about French history scribbled on the back, with a salutation of 'Dearest' and a close of 'All my love'), I am overjoyed, perhaps more so than it is good for me to be.

Still, May brings a real letter, June two more letters and a small package—the last things I am ever to receive from Jim's hand. The gifts are as they are; but the letters are alarming.

Not so much the first two, save only between the lines: Outwardly Jim speaks with real feeling of the beauty of Paris, but then admits he has been ill and unable to write as much as he would like, that he cannot seem to settle into a productive creative groove, cannot find his writing voice, and this makes him unhappy and uncertain. He speaks tenderly of how he misses me, of how it is winding down at last to the final break with Pam, of how there is so much history there, both good *and* bad, but that this is really *it*, as far as he's concerned; of how much he looks forward to our being together in New York as he has promised, by October at the latest, so he can catch the fall colors. In one of the letters, he encloses a poem for me—all about us, lovely, loving, it makes me cry —and he ends both missives on determinedly upbeat notes, as if he were trying to cheer and convince himself as well as me. Still, the subtext of depression is there in both letters, and much plainer in the second than in the first.

But it is the third letter Jim sends me, the last one, the June one, which genuinely frightens me. And frustrates, for I cannot even write back to comfort or to counsel; even though on this one he has put his rue Beautreillis address, in the ancient Marais quarter of Paris, writing it on the outside of the blue-gray envelope in different colored ink, as an apparent afterthought, as if to invite reply without actually wishing to appear to *ask* for it. But I cannot take the chance of Pamela intercepting any letter I write him, or at least I feel that I cannot . . .

He calls to mind joyful things—our handfasting in June, a year ago already; a long and funny reflection on our first anniversary; a declaration of how he loves me and misses me—but otherwise there is little joy here. He speaks of standing on the downslope to a void and not knowing where, or even if, he is; of crying himself to sleep on a night of rain and wondering if I heard him; says that for the first time he is uncertain where I am, says that he reaches out for me in his sleep but his side is cold with my absence.

He writes that he thinks he really wants to be dead, not mad, after all, and how *I* always thought it was the other way round. He speaks of mad Ahab, who "recalled in replete old age the Whiteness of the Whale." He speaks of Byron, "mad, bad, and dangerous to know," and reminds me that I said that to him the very first time we met, asks if I remember (as if I could ever forget!); says that he lives by a script, I by a saga; says that he feels cornered, says he's not even going to mail this to me after all.

And toward the end he writes that he is tired—calls me Patty— says that he walked for miles and came home limping; says he doesn't really know why he does these things and yet seems to learn so little.

He reminds me that once he told me in L.A. that I hadn't sold out, and says that now he requires that reassurance of me; says he wants me to look at him and tell him that he has not sold anything that could not be bought save by honest coinage.

There is much more in the same dreadful despairing vein: The pages seem frosted with hopelessness; the more I read and reread, the more I weep for him, and the more I want to jump on the first plane to Paris and drag him bodily back with me to safety in my arms, forever, away from his pain.

But his pain seems to be his fellow-traveler, and other people are hearing very different things from him, seemingly, at this very moment: To some he talks of getting back in the studio in September; to others he speaks of having finally, definitely, broken with Pam (it seems she is as smacked-out and sluttish in Paris as she was in L.A.) and wanting to return home before the Fourth of July (bitter irony); to others still he extends invitations to come stay with him and Pam in their Parisian idyll. It is probably all true and meant, and to weep for.

As for the pain—well, supposedly that was why he went to France in the first place, to escape it, to transcend it, not realizing he bore it with him; though why he ever thought the continued company of Courson and *her* fellow-traveler, heroin, would help him do any of that is a mystery, now as then. We will not learn until a long time after, not for certain, just what it is that Pam and her smack will in truth help him to; and ever since I learned it, it has been my prayer that there was, at least, no pain for him in *that*; perhaps, even, pain's ending.

But in the end, I do write, as I knew I would—an impassioned plea for him to save himself, whatever it takes, for me and the others who love him, but above all else for himself. I do not know if he ever got the letter.

In late June, Bill Graham closes the Fillmores, East and West. There is of course a big farewell blowout on Second Avenue, headlined by the Allman Brothers, and thanks to some friendships I manage to score a ticket—harder than it might sound, actually. The Fillmore press officer laments afterwards that she spent three years building up her contacts and blew them all on one night, so many and so mighty those who had to be denied.

Anyway, I go over, clad a little unseasonally in a patchwork buckskin tunic over white leather pants. As soon as I step through those great bronze doors I see about a million and a half familiar faces; I wander around, chatting, reconnecting—and then I see Jim across the lobby.

I freeze, for though I have had the strangest feeling all week that I would indeed see him here tonight, a feeling that amounted to utter certainty, still I had not thought it would really come to pass. But there he is; or is he? I stare at him, wondering what to do; and then the man—tall, dark-haired, full-bearded, white-shirted—turns my way, and I see with an indescribable shudder, relief and regret both keen as knives, that it is not Jim at all. This goes on all night: I must see a dozen different guys and none of them is Jim. Spookier still, several times I see someone I *know* is Jim, but when I dash over to him, there is never anyone standing there.

I leave the Fillmore for the last time as I have left it before, way early in the morning, sky already beginning to lighten; I have a red rose clutched tightly in my hand (there was one pinned to every seat, and twenty years later I still have mine—and the program, and the poster). But I am weary and sad and still possessed of the unshakable conviction that, somehow, Jim was indeed there. Not physically, maybe—he does not of course leave Paris, at least not yet and not like that—but there all the same.

Then, a few nights later, I have a visitant.

It is the deepest, darkest hour of a summer night; I am not asleep, but I know I am not entirely awake—or perhaps I am super-awake, hyper-awake on some other level. There is not a sound anywhere, not even from the street three stories below, and Jim is standing beside the bed, looking down at me, eyes deep in a pale, pale face.

In one of his space-fantasy books, C.S. Lewis writes that people often mistake dreams for visions, but no one ever mistook a vision for a dream. How right he was. This is no dream: Jim is so real, so vivid, so *here* that I can see every line of him, every shade and light on that beautiful face; I even take careful note of what he is wearing, the length of his hair, the fact that his beard is gone (I last saw him full-bearded, and do not learn until much later that he shaved it off in Paris).

And I wish with all my soul that it *were* just a dream, because I know only too well what this really is, and what it betokens. It is in fact the fetch, that phantasm of the living that appears a little before a death, when the departing soul is loosening its hold in the body and its ties to the world, putting its skates on, getting ready to roll. (Celts are partic-

ularly sensitive to sightings of this sort—you have only to check the
literature on the subject, well-attested and well-documented all of it—
and being descended from a long line of wolf-headed shamans probably
can't hurt, either . . .) In that brief time, a day or two at most, the soul
travels to people and places it has known and loved in life, going by the
"low road" of the old Scottish song "Loch Lomond," in which the lover
tells his beloved that, traveling by the low road of the soul, he will be
in Scotland before she will, traveling as she must by earthly highways;
he is, of course, telling her that he is dead.

And as I look on Jim as he stands before me, I know beyond any
last lying desperate hoping doubt that he has come to say farewell. It is
indeed the fetch, that quiet visitation from which there can be no appeal,
and it has come right on schedule. Probably the one night in his life
that Jim Morrison was on time for a gig . . .

We look at one another for many moments; Jim leans over to kiss
me, to whisper to me—I feel him against me, breathe him in, so real is
he that I can *smell* him, even, his own unique indefinable scent of wine
and long hair and clean scrubbed male body. And then he is gone.
I feel him leaving not merely my side but the planet, spiraling out on a
long arcing road, drawing away like a comet that whips round the sun
and back again to space, outward bound. It is goodbye, and all is forgiven,
and I love you very much; I give him the same, and more besides. It is
exceedingly final. I think it was over for us before we had ever even met.

When I open my eyes to the sunrise lighting the room, I remember
it all immediately, and sit up so fast I almost black out. I begin to raise
my left hand to my unfocused eyes, then halt the motion in mid-air. My
wedding ring, my silver claddagh, that never leaves my hand—fitting,
indeed, so tightly upon my finger that I could not get it off without the
greatest difficulty even if I wished to—is on my other hand. Somehow,
in the night, it has mysteriously migrated, transplanting itself from the
wedding-ring finger of my left hand—which it has left only once since
Jim first put it there last year (when I threw it at him in Miami), and
never since he put it there again (right after I threw it at him). It now
sits snugly, correctly facing inwards, upon the third finger of my right
hand.

I stare at it for a long time. So, Jim *was* here last night, after
all . . .   Not only that, as I discover when I rise at last: A picture of him—
a lovely Paul Ferrara shot, with a leather hat and a big grin—has somehow
escaped from its place tucked away *behind* the private-edition *Lords* and

New Creatures, and lies now on the floor between bookshelves and bed, not far from where Jim had stood in the night, where often he had stood in life.

Way too cosmic even for cosmic old me . . . When I am once again in control of myself, I call a couple of friends and recount to them the events of the night past. It is now the morning of 2 July 1971, and I somehow sense that I will be needing some before-the-fact corroboration very soon now. I tell them to remember what I have said, and they promise to do so.

The next day is Saturday, the third of July; it is the holiday weekend, and I have made plans to travel out to my parents' home.

I get up early—a clear, warm day—and go to one of the windows overlooking the street. My intent is to check on traffic, but as I part the draperies I startle back as if I have been shot.

Clinging to the *inside* of the screen is the biggest white butterfly I have ever seen. I recover myself, and slowly move closer; it does not fly away, not even when I reach out a trembling hand to gently brush its wings. It stays there for many minutes, wavering a little in the warm breeze; but when I take a last look before leaving the house it has gone. I have never seen a butterfly, white or otherwise, on my East Village street before or since; and it does not escape my notice that many ancient peoples, from the Greeks to the Celts and round the world, have believed that it is in form of a butterfly that the dying soul departs the body.

And it just keeps on getting weirder: All the way out on the train, I am beset by the increasingly foreboding feeling that something, somewhere, is terribly wrong with someone I love, wrong forever. Wronger far than it has ever been: At every stop along the way this sense gets stronger and scarier, to the point where I actually begin to panic, where I have to fight with myself at every station, every time the doors open, to remain in my seat, not to leap out as every instinct is telling me and catch the first train heading back to Manhattan. I don't know why or when or where or who, though I have a fairly good idea of what is afoot; and as soon as I reach my destination I confide all this in my sister. She understands this sort of thing; and afterwards she remembers.

The world is not told of Jim Morrison's death in Paris on the morning of July 3 until the following Thursday, July 8, when Bill Siddons, back in L.A. after Jim's hugger-mugger interment, makes a brief statement.

I neither see nor hear this, as I am watching an Errol Flynn movie (*The Master of Ballantrae*), and not the late news.

So it is that I am awakened at three in the morning by the phone ringing beside my bed. It is a friend calling from San Francisco, a publicist named Gina Gangi. I know immediately why Gina has called me at three a.m., but I do not want to have to say it myself. (Oh no please no . . .)

"Just tell me," I say steadily, tears already spilling down my face.

But all she can manage, over and over, is, "Oh, Patricia—"

"TELL ME!"

And then, in the softest, gentlest, saddest voice on earth, she says, "Oh honey—oh Patricia, he's dead."

I cry out in futile denial more from a sense of bitter irony and inevitability than from any real surprise. Right again, as usual! He'd *hate* that . . .   I have been shot with both barrels in the three a.m. dark, but no, I am not surprised. How could I be, I've been getting messages from Jim and the cosmos all fucking week . . .   At last he has managed to push himself to where I cannot reach him; or has he? Can I not? The first documented case of grasp exceeding reach. Difficult.

This does not last long, of course. Shaking and hysterical, I phone Bobbi Harris, Bruce's wife; Bruce is himself in California, but surely she will know.

I do not even bother to identify myself, nor yet to announce my reason for calling. "Bobbi—" (NonononoNO . . .)

"Yes," she says. "Yes, it's true."

I remember very little of what happens after that, because I think I go insane. I remember Bobbi and an RCA friend, Elin Guskind, coming over right then, in the middle of the night, to take charge of me (and even in my raving grief I realize that they had to go out alone on Manhattan streets at three in the morning to get here, and I am grateful). I remember breaking a lot of things, wineglasses and plates and stuff, just heaving them at the walls, one after another, until Elin restrains me. I remember them getting some clothes on me over my white silk Moroccan shift—a rag Jim thieved for me from Themis—and taking me uptown to Bruce and Bobbi's, until Bruce's arrival home from L.A. that night, when presumably he will be able to deal with me more effectively. I remember crossing Central Park at four in the morning on the transverse road, sitting between Bobbi and Elin in the back seat of a cab, just about off my head, and out of my daze and storm of lamentation hearing the cab driver ask them Hey, did you hear about that rock star who died in Paris and is your friend having a bad trip or what?

At Bobbi's, I remember nothing at all until Bruce shows up that night; he looks haggard, and I, by now dressed head to foot in black, a bit calmer, am there to meet him. He must have had more details, such as were known, about Jim's death, but I have no recollection. Indeed, the official story is suspiciously sparse: Jim Morrison died in Paris early on July 3, of an apparent heart attack, and was quietly buried in Père-Lachaise cemetery on Thursday, July 8. They—Pamela, Siddons, friend Alan Ronay and the two others in attendance—had kept it so in hopes of avoiding the media circus (as they describe it; actually, there was none) that had followed on the deaths of Jimi Hendrix and Janis Joplin back last fall. Pam has returned to L.A. with Siddons, and is said to be in a state of acute shock. Yeah, there seems to be a lot of that sort of thing going around just now . . .   And I do not believe for one *nanosecond* that Jim really died of a heart attack.

Kind and caring as they are, though, even dear friends like Bruce and Bobbi cannot help me much with this one; and so, after a couple of hours just sitting and talking and weeping together—Bruce loved Jim, too—I take leave of them and return home. It is time for me to begin to grapple with this alone and in full knowledge. But after hours of silence, as if people are afraid to call (oh right, as if anything could be worse than *this*), the phone begins to shrill nonstop. I do not go into work until the following Tuesday, and then only to tell them that I am flying at once to Paris.

To that end, I seem to have been busy, though in my shock and daze I recall little of the actual doing: organizing a passport and plane ticket and hotel reservation and French currency and travelers' checks, cleaning and buying and even sewing some suitable mourning attire, including widow's veils of several styles and lengths, arranging for someone to look after the cat while I am away. None of my friends understands why I *must* go to France—it's a long way to go just to put roses on someone's grave, Elin says uncertainly—why I *need* to go; not David or Susie or even Diane, who calls full of tears and Irish-wake laughter. I don't care: I'm going, and Goddess help anyone who tries to stop me. (The coven, of course, understands my need perfectly.)

But I know very well what the real bottom line is: They do not trust me not to lay violent hands upon myself in my grief, they do not think I can keep my busy little fingers off the downer bottles. For my part I don't blame them for being doubtful, swinging back and forth as I have been doing—the wild Irish mourning dove one shift, throwing china and gobbling Valium, the moblèd queen the next, all tears, alone and palely loitering. But all I want to do is keep in touch, as close as I can, for as long as I can; and I must go to Paris to do it.

I have very definite ideas about one's proper conduct in such situations: I didn't watch Jackie Kennedy for nothing, after all, and, as I promised Jim, lying naked in his arms on Diane Gardiner's floor, I intend to bear myself with the demeanor of a sixteenth-century widowed queen. When I get *back* from Paris—well, that might be a different story.

Bruce isn't buying it even so. "You *will* be back? You aren't going to do something stupid over there, are you, Kennealy? Jim being stupid was bad enough."

"Certainly not!" I say with great indignation. "Of course I'll be back."

Well—either with my shield or upon it, as the dear Spartans used to say. But I'm not going to tell him that.

CHAPTER

26

Paris, July 1971

IT SEEMS AS IF IT ALL HAPPENED FIVE HUNDRED YEARS
ago, or five minutes ago. What a treacherous thing is memory, that
timeless ghost putting flesh on past bones, making chill of remembered
warmth.

I kneel beside his grave and look around me, eyes wide and dry and
stony as bones themselves, as if even now this will all somehow prove
to be dream or illusion—man, the worst trip *ever*—seeking a way out
from among the maze of the tombs and the knowledge that they bring
me. But we are locked in here, he and I; all exits are closed, all gates
are sealed, all vistas shut.

For some reason, Highgate cemetery in London, where I have never
yet been, comes to mind, and I think of Lizzie Siddal as she lies there,
consort to Rossetti; another redhaired lady who loved a poet and was
brought down. That bastard Dante Gabriel, digging her up *years* after
she'd killed herself on his account, the poor cow, just so he could get
back the poems he'd so dramatically placed in her coffin before it was
sealed and buried. Creep couldn't even leave her anything to read in
her last bed... They said that when his friends had opened the

casket—he felt he could not personally attend, but apparently grave-robbing by proxy was just fine with him—her long hair had grown and grown, filling the coffin, veiling the poor sad bones with soft flame.

Maybe I will yet take Lizzie's way out. There isn't a laudanum bottle handy, but thanks to several obliging Feelgoods I have a purseful of truly lethal proportions—just about every downer known to modern medicine, and maybe even a few that aren't. And I think I really mean it, too, just now; or want to mean it. Not wise; and wasn't it dear Thoreau who said, "It is characteristic of wisdom not to do desperate things"? Still, maybe Henry David never had to deal with anything quite like this . . .

In the end, of course, I do not do it, do not even try. I consider, and I utterly reject. Jim does not let me, for one thing; for another, I always have such a hard time dropping anything without water. No—let it be, let it bleed, let it roll, let it rip. I'm going to sit this one out, right straight through to the end.

I kneel there all day, alone for the most part; I see only two or three people in all the hours I am there. Out of my need as well as his, I do rituals, for the terrible truth, apparent to me as soon as I reach out for him, is that he is still here. His presence is so vivid, so tangible, that it seems impossible that I cannot touch him physically. It is a devastating feeling to know him so near, to sense him so lost; but even more devastating is the realization that I will have to send him on myself.

I put my hands to my mouth beneath the veil. I can't *believe* this —that on top of everything else I am being put through, I now have to take care of this too, stamp his astral passport, as it were, see that he gets through the gate and onto the plane. Those 'friends' who left him here last week, did they really think just putting him into the ground was enough? Are they all so spiritually bankrupt, so utterly mud-souled as not to know that burial rituals exist for real reasons, and that they are for the dead as much as for the living? It is criminal carelessness, on a par with that other criminality, the one that put him here in the first place—but more of that later. Right now I have work to do.

And it is fine and fitting that I should do it, I have no complaints about that: I love him, he is my handfast mate, I am a priestess and I know how it should be done. And since no one else seems to have seen the necessity ("There was no service," one of them said airily to the press, "we just threw some flowers and dirt and said goodbye"; yeah, about what you'd do for your dead parakeet), it becomes my place and mine alone to do this for him.

For I see at last that if it did not *occur* to anyone else to do this for Jim, then no one else *but* me can or even should be doing it. This, then, is why I had to come to Paris: No one else saw the need, the duty that is for those left behind—not Pam, not Alan Ronay (who did, as we shall learn, so many other useful things for Jim that no one else might have thought of doing, to such effective result too), not any of the half-dozen people who saw him dead and buried. It is my job to obtain for him safe and protected passage, a smooth crossing; and though indeed I have never ceased to work but to that end since first he came to me that night, I now begin my work in loving earnest.

And more besides: I am completing—though never ending—the equation of Jim plus me plus time plus space that was set up long ago: when I heard him for the first time, saw him for the first time, when we first met, when we first came together in love. All that energy to be first grabbed and then transformed, with love and in knowledge. It is balance. But it is like grasping the lightning, it hurts SO MUCH. I have no words for how it hurts, my mind has blanked it out long ago so that I can survive it. But I learn in other ways, much later, where the pain has moved. I see its path wherever I look.

Late afternoon of my first day in Paris. A bell clangs far away below, and it occurs to me that the cemetery is about to close its gates for the night. My mind stands still in panic and denial: I cannot leave him. Just *CANNOT*. For a moment, in fact, I fully intend to stay there with him all night. Then sanity prevails, and I rise—fighting the motion every inch of the way, every atom in my body digging in its little heels and shrieking its refusal—to take leave of him until tomorrow.

Five minutes later, I am back beside him, weeping and confused. It is as if I had to return just to see that he is still here, that this is still true. And now that I see once again that it is, I can bring myself to leave for the night.

On my way out, I lose myself again; I am finally aimed toward the gates by a tiny black-clad Frenchwoman who looks to be in her sixties but is probably in her eighties, and who has the air and posture of a duchess. She sees my distress and tells me kindly, stabbing the air with a diamonded finger, "Déscends, ma fille! Toujours déscends!" I thank her and flee down the hill, out the gates without stopping and fling myself into a passing cab.

Back at the hotel, I weep for a while, crash for a while, then wake up for real and start to write everything down. No drugs, no dinner either; I am past the need for such things. I write like a madwoman, deep into the night, as the city noises beyond the courtyard begin to fade and the air cools to a fall chill, the only sound a far-off bell marking the hours. I do not sleep, and my thoughts are all of Jim.

Next morning, the sun barely up, I put on yet another stunning all-black outfit—to judge from my suitcase, you'd think that Mrs. Darth Vader and I had got our luggage mixed up at the spaceport baggage claim—and walk for a little, looking for a flower shop. On a narrow cobblestoned street not far from the hotel, shopowners all round sluicing down the pavement for the day's trade and sweeping it with twig brooms, I buy twenty-seven red roses and thirteen white ones—for the years of his life and the months of our union—framed by masses of tiny lacelike white flowerets and fine green webs of fern.

One of those really neat Citroën cabs takes me to Père-Lachaise, this time to the northern entrance; again I walk barefoot all the way from the gate. This part of the cemetery is newer, more orderly than the medieval necropolis lower down the hill. As I draw nearer to my destination, I note on the map that various worthy companions are all nearby—Oscar, Honoré, Edith, Gertrude—but I am not here to sightsee. (In fact, outside of a walk-and-errand which takes me along the Seine to Nôtre-Dame and the Ile St.-Louis, and a trip to and from Fouquet's for a glass of white wine in Jim's honor—all this *after* the cemetery is closed, so as not to lose one instant of graveside time—I see nothing whatsoever of Paris.)

This day I approach the grave from a different quarter, passing under tall trees at a sort of dark spooky roundabout. I have encountered no one on my hajra from the northern gates; it is still very early in the morning, Père-Lachaise has been open barely fifteen minutes.

And no one is at the grave when I arrive there. I place my roses over Jim like a blanket, tenderly drawing it like a coverlet right up to the cross. Then I take out his battered silver pen from a pocket, re-ink the dates of his birth and death I put on the marker yesterday, put JIM over his surname; and, with a real grin for the irony of the thing—he'd *love* this—sigh and shake my head and print 'poète' in small neat letters below 'artiste' and 'chanteur.' You got me, Jim, okay? You had to fucking DIE to make me call you a poet for all the world to see, but there it is in black ink, and I the first ever to set that word upon your grave. I do not begrudge it; but my opinion remains unchanged. (Sorry, honey . . .)

Again today, as I did yesterday and will do again tomorrow and every day thereafter for the rest of my time here, I cast a circle and perform a rite of sending according to my own faith, the faith in which this man and I were joined past death. I remain all day, sometimes weeping, more often just being *with* him, beside him, in silent loving companionship.

Toward afternoon, yesterday's young blond mourner turns up again; beyond a greeting so concerned and respectful as to seem almost obeisance, he does not intrude. Later a French couple come up and stand behind me as I kneel. Perhaps I am invisible by now; certainly they do not acknowledge my presence in any way, but merely comment to one another on Jim, "un jeune chanteur américain," saying nothing of note or to which I could take exception. Probably they do not even think I understand French; or maybe they do think I understand French and that is why they say nothing of note. In any case, they remain only a couple of minutes, and then I am alone again with Jim.

I sense his presence as powerfully and as near me as yesterday, but without the edge; there is a calmness about it now, a peacefulness, perhaps because the work of going, of detaching, is well in hand. But for myself, though I know that this is all that Jim requires of me, I feel the need for more, or other, it's not done yet. And also I remember a promise I made him . . .

It is closing time again, and I quit the graveside with my usual reluctance—noting as I do so two young men sitting on the curb of the cobblestoned lane, politely waiting for me to leave rather than trouble my vigil. And, again as yesterday, five minutes later I am back. The young men are already gone—theirs were apparently brief respects—but today I have returned because I have forgotten something.

I take it out of my leather satchel—a tall, gold-and-green (for Sagittarius) votive candle—and set it down, just to one side of the pottery vase of roses that stands at the gravehead. As a lifelong nonsmoker, of course I have no matches, so cannot light it as I would like; I'll remember to bring some tomorrow.

Then I leave the cemetery, to go in search of someone who can help me keep that promise. It is for this too that Jim has waited.

At a likely-looking church in an ancient part of Paris, I arrange for a belated funeral service for Jim. True, it is not Presbyterian; but apparently he has had no formal services save the ones that I myself have given him. Pam couldn't be bothered, his family do not even seem to care that he's dead (his parents, who on the face of it have no qualms whatsoever about suing for and claiming half of his estate, do not even bother to visit his grave until the spring of 1991—when, apparently unable to keep themselves away a moment longer, they go to Paris and spruce up the plot with a new and pretentious headstone, perhaps with an eye to the Doors movie's imminent release), and Jim himself seemed to like the idea when we spoke of it, so . . . Anyway, France is a Catholic country, and Catholicism has always been a whole lot more pagan than it ever dared let on. So, between the rites I have myself conducted and the ones I now order, I think a suitable farewell will be at last provided for a dead Celt.

In a quiet study, I explain the situation to a keen-eyed, white-haired priest: that my husband died suddenly here in Paris while I was in America, and was buried without proper ceremony before I could get here. Could he, would he, do something for him?

It would be most irregular, the priest informs me, gently and sternly; as if I were incredibly careless to have been on the other side of the Atlantic when my own husband cast off his mortal coil. But at last— and I am not at all ashamed to bully him with tears and grief and dumb-Americanism—he agrees to an ad hoc sort of ritual: more than a blessing, less than a formal Requiem. I thank him profusely, and arrange for future Masses to be said for Jim's soul; and early the next day, the priest and I meet at the church, to go together to the grave.

Oh man, I am so right to do this, this was so needed . . . As he begins to intone the liturgy, I close my eyes under my veil. In my heart I am hearing not the rasping mutter of the French priest but the ancient sonorities of the Latin I have known since my childhood, and I soundlessly say the words over to myself in English for my solace: 'May the angels lead thee into Paradise, at thy coming may the martyrs receive thee and bring thee into Jerusalem, the holy city, and with Lazarus, once a beggar, mayst thou find eternal rest.'

Tears are streaming down my face as I listen to this three-voiced supplication, and I find neither contradiction nor hypocrisy in any of it. I have deep faith and total trust in the Path I follow, and in my own right and power to protect and care for Jim on his journey; but this too is good and right. Besides, it never hurts to be sure.

At the end, after he has blessed Jim and the grave itself, the priest surprises me: He asks me to kneel, and blesses me as well. I gratefully accept his benediction—no blessing, whatever its form, is ever to be scorned; they all come from the same place in the end—and I remain kneeling long after he has gone.

Almost closing time again: I tear some scraps of paper from my notebook, write out some quotations from the works of Chairman Jim —*An American Prayer* and *The New Creatures*—and twist them in amongst the stems of the roses. Someone else has obviously been here, either yesterday afternoon, in the few minutes between my departure from the grave and the cemetery's closing, or this morning, in the brief time before the priest and I arrived: The votive candle I left yesterday was lighted when we got here. It has burned all day now, and perhaps it burned all last night as well.

This makes me happy; but as I rise and turn away, something catches my eye, and I am brought up short. On the rear wall of the facing tomb, a large mausoleum at the foot of Jim's grave, someone has drawn in black magic marker a significant rune indeed: a P and a J intertwined, in a style known to heraldic blazon (though probably not to its perpetrator) as botonné.

I recognize it immediately as Pam's work, and decide too that I— much as I detest vandalism—must do likewise; both of us thereby unwittingly setting the precedent for all those future defacings. But just a tiny one, I think, might be forgiven—not ostentatious like Pam's, but one that only Jim and I will notice, that no one but us will ever know is there—somewhere way down near ground level, scratched with the tip of my athamé into the stone.

Then I smile. I don't have to be a vandal at all. The P and J I would make are already there. P and J for Pam and Jim, J and P for Jim and Patricia: And this makes me happy too.

The rest of that week is unvarying in its routine: up early (I even manage to eat an occasional meal—quick fuel intakes at random cafés), straight to Père-Lachaise after the mandatory stop at the florist's—with one side visit, one only, to the rue Beautreillis; I cannot bear more than a brief glance at the building where he died, but I do need to see it—beside the grave all day, back to the hotel, writing most of the night. And I am doing all this *without drugs*.

But I cannot do it forever, cannot stay in Paris much longer. I have done what I needed to do, what I was needed to do; and even Jim would not want me to stay here in pain any longer than I must.

And so for the last time, up the hill to where he lies, between Mme. Vve. Marthe de Villers, 1969, and le Comte Antoine François de Nantes, 1789. I have to leave Paris today, and I still don't know if I can.

I come round the corner, up to the grave and without a second's hesitation do what I have wanted to do from the first: I throw myself across Jim's grave the way I used to throw myself across him in bed, the little cross pushed out of the way and my face in the dirt and my arms reaching out to hold him. And he is so near, so near.

But wherever he is, though, I know he is surprised, and certainly pissed off at me for being right as usual. No Big Sleep after all, just more damn things for him to do . . .   After a while I push myself up again, to sit there quietly, and only belatedly to worry if anybody happened to notice that little exhibition. Not that I'd care, but still; might frighten the horses.

I look down at my hands, gritty from the clutching they have just done, fighting the dirt for possession of him. Dust films the brightness of the ring he set there himself; and suddenly I wonder about *his* ring, what has become of it. It was not among the items he entrusted to me for safekeeping before I left L.A., and I doubt he would have had it with him in Paris. Probably Pam will find it, throw it out, sell it, maybe even wear it herself if she thinks it's cool . . . but I can't help that.

I do not particularly wish to go on bleeding, but neither do I wish to forget anything; and if pain is the price of memory then by God I'll gladly pay it. But is this really what it all came to in the end, is this *it*? All the leather pants and Lizard Kingdoms and busts and boozing and gold records and silver noses—all that merely sufficed to buy him earth enough in this city to lie in forever, an oblong of gray dirt smaller than the beds we shared.

He sang himself to death, and nobody even listened. How do you follow an act like that? Nobody won here; not me by surviving, not him by getting what he wanted, not the straight society who thought his death only proved their point. What was it Diane had said, "Jim died of old age"—and of course she is right, but it still comes out me bringing roses to the scene of the crime all the same.

Maybe it is just the ungodly mixed emotions I am feeling just now: Beyond grief, there is love, anger, rage and frustration that he could have been so fucking stupid, even gratitude for the experience of having carried his child. And maybe I hate him, now, at the end, almost as much as I love him. Maybe. Almost—but the hate is of the moment and the love will last forever; or at least as long as I do.

Or is it all just hubris, the vengeance of heaven coming down hard on yet another uppity mortal? God's laws are not mocked; and though one may defy with a fair degree of impunity the laws made by men in God's name, the true laws of the Deity—like the true laws of love or poetry—have always paid out a fitting return to those with the daring, the imagination or the plain stupidity to break them.

Well then, maybe he didn't exactly *break* the damn law, I temporize, unwilling to consign this particular job lot to the flame, or even just to a lower level of incarnation. Maybe it was only that he had seen it coming long before the rest of us did, had been hypnotized by it, somnambulized, the Medusa trip, turned to stone by his own unpreparedness or his own sheer courage, his own absolute fearless willingness to look those snakes right in the face as they came writhing toward him. He had no shiny shield to reflect the soul freeze that seizes anyone caught out alone in *that* without a mirror; and though I would have sacrificed my own soul to have saved him—life, mind, heart, being, whatever it took—when it came down to it at last I had not even been on the same battlefield.

But his art should have been his shield and his mirror as his art was his god. He hadn't believed so much in God, though; more in Goddess, but most of all in Jim and the Big Sleep. Was that then his sin, his error? Must an artist be punished for not believing in the art he professes to serve? Here lies James Morrison, gone a-whoring after false divinity. And so he died. He is not the first person to get zapped by it, won't be the last either.

It all sounds faintly Christian to the committed-pagan part of me, and intensely pagan to the vestigial-Christian side. And why not? Whatever faith I came to on my own, I wasn't taught all those impressionable years of youth by the Stormtroopers of the Vatican to forget it now. I have broken a number of laws (if not so many as Jim), most of the

Commandments, and I worship a Goddess who was around long before Jesus, but convent schooling is hard to shake. Jim used to tease me, often, for what he called my "Cathologic." Can't help it, WASP...

I dig my fingers into the loose earth again, to be somehow nearer to him, with a sudden scrabbling desperation; then just as suddenly become hesitant and still, afraid to touch anything lest I trouble him where he is.

All week I had kept saying No, this is *not* true, he *can't* be dead; then looking down I would see that name on the cross. Yet to me it was still not possible that the man who is my heart's blood and the father of my child and my artist-hero of all time could be lying there under the rocks and roses with the breath gone from his body, and no word left for me.

Wasting the dawn—maybe he was right. And maybe I wasted our dawn as truly as he did, but I never really believed there would come a summer morning when I would lie sobbing upon his grave in a far country. Every time I pulled myself painfully together, that MORRISON on the little cross would cut the world out from under me again.

But I was wrong, though; there *was* a message. When our bodies were close, so often Jim and I caught echoes from each other's mind; and when I was with him this week past, the silence was filled as it had always been.

This morning, though, as I lie weeping on his grave, there is more; a sort of wry reassurance and indulgence, that I hear with my inner listening ear in a voice I know, a "Well, Patricia, do what you feel like—you always do, honey—but I think you're being a bit more upset than it warrants. It's only for a while. See you later."

And now it is time to go. I do once more what I did earlier: push all the flowers out of the way and just crumple, flung like the flag of some sad, sad nation across the stones and shells and roses, my face hidden in the veil, save where I have pulled the silk aside so that my bare cheek can press upon bare earth with nothing else between us, as close to him as I can now physically get. My hair spills down around me and over him and my hands are clenched upon the wooden cross. Wasting the dawn.

When I can weep no more, I rise quite steadily, brushing tears and dirt from my face. I remove from my leather satchel—once his—the things I have carried in it all week, waiting the right moment to leave them here: small things, special things. New to this assemblage: several long impassioned letters to him, written at night in my room at the hotel. I thrust it all down deep into the gray earth where no one can find it, and smooth the earth and flowers over him again. I close my eyes and call down blessings and protection and guidance and guarding. I speak to him, and hear what he has to tell me. I say goodbye and walk away without looking back. I have never returned.

And I come home from Paris, and I begin to do what I had once told him I would do if he were to die. To wear black for a year. To comport myself like a widowed queen. To buy Catholic Masses for his Presbyterian soul. To do magic to push him through his passages. And to cry. A lot. Forever.

CHAPTER

27

B U T   T H A T   I S   B Y   N O   M E A N S   A L L   T H E R E   I S   T O   I T . . .
When I get back from Paris, Diane calls, full of loving concern; and
because she knew Jim and loved Jim and is on The Raft with the rest
of us, I pull myself out of my stupor of despair and try to listen.

"I understand now why you had to go to Paris, I didn't before you
went but now I do. Are you all right?"

"Oh sure. I'm fine."

"Like hell you are—oh Patricia, just think of him as this mystical
clown, Jesus Christ with sunglasses, he wouldn't want you to be
sad—"

Well, no, I know that; but I also have a sneaking suspicion he would
probably have personally liked national mourning. Still, Diane is doing
this for me past her own sorrow, so I do not contradict her.

"And the baby?" I ask presently.

"Ohhh, how well you did, it was so hard, I know, but it was right.
He didn't want a child left behind him with a woman he loved so much,
the responsibility would only have made him worry about something he
couldn't help. He knew he was going to die, that's what made him pull

his pants down in front of all those people—can't you hear him laughing about it?"

"Certainly." Though I can also hear him telling me he *didn't* pull his pants down—but I suspect she is speaking metaphorically, about pulling pants down on the larger scale. Not that it matters now either way.

"Pam was asking about you," says Diane then, and my attention leaps to focus. "She was completely in shock, but she asked me 'How's Patricia Kennealy, I bet she's taking it very hard.' She said that as far as she's concerned Jim is just on the road and he's coming back to L.A. in a couple of weeks; that she's going on, and that you should too, and not to feel too bad about Jim. He really loved you, Patricia, you know he did; that's what made him sleep with you on my living room floor while Pam was right upstairs."

A comforting thought; though I can still think of a reason or two otherwise. But I'd rather believe Diane's; and after a few minutes more of mutual consolation, and my offering return civilities of condolence to Pam—shades of Queen Alexandra and Mrs. Keppel—we ring off.

Sometime in October, a small package arrives in the mail; it is postmarked California. I open it unsuspectingly, then stand there as if I have been turned to stone: Contained within is a sealed envelope, folded over once or twice, and my name—all *three* names—written on it in Jim's untidy, unmistakable scrawl.

I look at it for a long time. Somehow I know what is in there, and I wonder whether I can bear to open it at all.

"Oh, this is *stupid . . .*"

I carefully slit the end of the envelope and pour out the contents into my cupped hand. It is Jim's wedding ring, the gold claddagh I gave him at our handfasting; nothing else is inside except the long gold chain on which it has been strung.

I look again at the package's wrappings, but there is no clue for me there: no return address, no familiar handwriting, only my own name and address printed in neat plain letters.

It can only have been sent by one person, or so at least I think: Pamela Susan Courson. But even if this is so, still I wonder greatly. Does this mean Jim had the ring with him in Paris, and put it in an envelope for me before he died? And what about the chain, does that mean he wore it? In front of Pam? Or was it left somewhere in L.A., addressed to me, just in case; and did Pam find it when she returned from Paris after his death? Or did Jim foresee his death, and wanting me to have the ring, put it safely aside so that I should be sure to get it back, addressing the envelope to Patricia Kennealy *Morrison*, one last loving acknowledgment? And what did Pam make of *that* when she saw it? *If* she even saw it: Maybe it wasn't Pam who sent the ring back at all— maybe it was the lawyer, or some Doors lackey clearing things out, or someone else altogether—no one ever does come forward to claim my thanks. And what of his promises to be with me in New York in the fall, were those too part of this obviously intentional act?

I will never know. But whatever the truth of it, it is most decent of Pam, or whoever, to send me back the ring, something I did not look for, a gift I never expected; and for which I shall always be grateful.

That night, I light black candles at the four Quarters and a red one on the altar; I cast a circle and step naked into it. On the altar is my favorite picture of Jim, some of his letters and poems and gifts, a lock of his hair—all to make a link; resting next to all this, in the earth-filled scallop shell I took from the foot of his grave, is the gold claddagh. On my left hand is the silver ring that has left my finger only twice since Jim put it there last year: that night I flung it at him in Miami, and on the night of the fetch. Not even in the hospital for the abortion would I let it be taken from me.

I sit quietly, meditating a little, weeping a little, smiling often, remembering everything. The words of the handfasting ritual are so clear in the silence of the room that I can hear them almost with outward hearing: "Death does not part, only lack of love . . ."

But, like the handfasting, this night too requires its sacrifice; and so, slowly, ritualistically, very Celticly, in mourning and in loving, I cut my hip-length hair to waist-length, and I burn the cuttings to gray ash in the black iron cauldron.

Then I take off the silver claddagh and slip the gold one onto my finger. It is of course far too big, and I put the silver ring on again to hold it in place, the two crowned hearts of the ancient Irish design facing one another. And so Jim is with me in the fall in New York after all . . .   I have worn them thus ever since.

Things go on after that, of course: I settle down to work again after a solo trip to Ireland in October, my first time there. I am glad of anything to keep my mind off Jim and his unending absence; but work and travel are not enough, and I begin writing a novel. It is as much therapy as creativity, a roman à clef called *The Voice That Launched a Million Trips*, in which all the contents of my diaries and notebooks and journals are transmuted into fiction.

It may be flawed as a work of art, but it surely works as therapy, probably the single best thing I can do just now. The Jim character is called Toy Tyler, the Patricia character is called O'Rahilly (just O'Rahilly), and the Pam character is called Jeffie. But I find that even the roman à clef format is too painful for me to deal with straight out, too near the bone for comfort, so I add a self-protective fictive element in which the Morrison character, in his desperate attempt to get to be top-of-the-charts again, murders the Janis Joplin character and the Jimi Hendrix/Brian Jones character.

At the suggestion of a few friends who read it (Pauline, David, Bruce Harris), I halfheartedly shop it around to two or three publishers. Though interested, they all want major sleazoid changes—more sex, more drugs—and I am just not up for it, so I put it away. No one sees it again until Oliver Stone lays eyes on it in 1990.

In 1973, I quit RCA and go over to CBS Records, to write *their* ad copy for a while; I end up staying there six years, picking up two Clio nominations and a bunch of other ad awards, and eventually becoming a copy director.

The tenth floor of Black Rock, as the eerie Saarinen-designed building on West 52nd Street is known, is something of a crucible for quirky talent: The copywriting job I am originally hired to fill has just been vacated by Allee Willis, moving on to songwriting (hits for Earth Wind & Fire, among others), L.A., and gossipdom; Tom McNamee, copy director, produced the infamous Hampton Grease Band for the label (also his wife, Louise, will become Della Femina McNamee, first woman ever to get her name on a major ad agency she did not happen to found); Joel Steiger, the copy director who hires me, moves on a few years later to Hollywood, a creative partnership with Dean Hargrove and a string of TV hits that include "Matlock" and "Father Dowling"; Stefan Bright, record producer for Jimi Hendrix, The Last Poets and Mahavishnu John McLaughlin; while upstairs in the publicity department we have future horror writer Ed Naha and the post-Cashbox, pre-*Ninja* Eric Van Lustbader.

Of all the record company creative departments, CBS's is considered pre-eminent (at least in those days), a haven for creativity and classy work; and, from the standpoint of the inmates, at least, by far the best and least-afflicted-with-corporate-bullshit. It is insanely creative, and creatively insane; so much so that suits from other, more structured departments, or managers in from the heartland sales offices—straights— are routinely taken on tenth-floor tours, Come see our creative zoo. We try hard not to disappoint them: I often wear Arab robes to work, and keep a set of storm-warning flags to hang outside my office door on cranky days; the guys set up rec-room games like foosball and table hockey; there is a perpetual darts tournament for tenth-floor denizens only; and—this being the 70's, after all—we do rather a lot of recreational drugs. Many happy afternoons are spent in tremendous scurryings and phonings and comings and goings to set up buys; and—this being the 70's—the drug of choice is usually cocaine. We are discreet and temperate, always; and we know very well when to draw the line—or to stop drawing lines. Indeed, as other books will later reveal, ours isn't even the real CBS action; it's kid stuff, milk and cookies compared to what's going on upstairs on those seemingly straight corporate floors. But for now we are happy in our own little creative corner, and we produce some very nice work indeed—on drugs or off.

Beginning only days, literally, after Jim's death, stories have been wandering in like Ulysses from the West Coast: stories that Pamela has taken to hooking to support her smack habit (her pimp even punches out a friend of mine, whom he mistakenly suspects of coming on—in a non-business format—to Pam).

Stories more evil by far: tales that Jim did not die of a heart attack after all (surprise!), but of a heroin overdose, and that Pam was the one who supplied him with the killer hit, from her own stash. I believe this as soon as I hear it: No proof, vague facts, few names—but the rumors are persistent, and it all sounds quite horribly logical.

And then the stories start to come with weird and lurid details: Jim didn't die in the apartment bathtub, as per the Official Story, but elsewhere, maybe in a notorious drug boîte called the Rock 'n' Roll Circus, where he'd been scoring smack for Pamela and took some himself on a whim; it was too pure for a nonuser like Jim and caused him to collapse, whereupon he was carried, either dead or dying, to the flat and dumped in the tub, in the vain hope of reviving him.

Which is terrible enough: but there are stranger stories still. Stories that singer Marianne Faithfull and Pam's French count lover, Jean de

Breteuil, were frantically summoned to the Morrison flat by the non-French-speaking Pam in her guilty panic; but by the time they arrived, Jim was dead. The count will himself die of an OD a year later, and Faithfull has steadfastly denied the entire story from that day to this. There is even a rumor that a photograph exists of Jim's dead body with knives stuck in it, and Pam visible in the background, and that people close to the Doors have seen this photo, or have it, or know about it, or have suppressed it.

I listen to all this, from the very beginning, but I do not really hear. Jim was not a junkie. He scorned scag and those who used it (yes, even Pam), and only very exceptional circumstances—such depression as was evident in his letters to me, perhaps, combined with Pam pushing it on him, or maybe just one what-the-hell mood too many—could have made him try it. If he did, which I still do not know for sure, it would have been a onetime thing, not anything habitual—Morrison the eternal experimenter suddenly finding himself experimenting with eternity.

I believe, absolutely, for myself, that Pam gave him the smack, but I cannot prove it, not in 1971, and it seems to make but little difference: Jim is still dead. And as Pamela on the other coast begins to lose herself in guilt and heroin and hookerdom, I begin to wall myself up alive in silence and denial.

I think grief has made me more than a little crazy; in fact, I think I am probably just as nuts as you can be and still be functioning in the world, and this state lasts for more years than I care to admit.

It is, simply, so painful that I cannot deal with it rationally, or indeed at all: My friends do not speak to me of Jim, and I never mention his name to them; they even warn their other friends, their teenage (and naturally curious) children even, never to ask me about him. (As a colleague will say years later, "We all knew about it—you and Jim. But nobody *knew* about it.") I have one picture of him in my apartment. I never, never, never play the Doors records I so loved: When "Break On Through" or "L.A. Woman" drifts in at my window from a passing radio, or when some suburban drunk sloshes out of the bar down the street at four in the morning and stands beneath my windows bellowing "Light My Fire" (oh, not personally aimed at me, I'm sure; just one of those New York things), it's white-knuckle time until long after the sound has faded away. When I walk around the neighborhood and see a Morrison T-shirt coming at me, it's like being kicked in the stomach (it doesn't exactly make the grief process any easier, having to see your beloved's face—a face, not to mince words about it, that's been between your legs—inartistically silk-screened across the chest of every low-life yahoo in the world). I cannot read articles about Jim, or watch Doors videos, or even keep near me all the things he gave me—the poems and letters and jewels and sketches and books have all been removed to a bank vault. My own family does not speak his name to me for twenty years.

And, by and large, that's how I want it. It may be pridefulness at base, but I do not wish anyone to see my sorrow and anger, to know how much I miss him. As I did not want people to know about Jim and me when he was alive, so too do I wish them not to know about us now that he isn't. Either way, it's no concern of theirs; and for many years I cannot bear to have it spoken of, let alone speak of it myself.

Which vacuum is abhorred, not by nature but by self-appointed custodians of the Morrison legacy, who apparently seem to think that as long as I say nothing about Jim and me, they can say anything at all—and do. People for whom I am but "one of hundreds," or maybe at best an inconvenient part of a rigid mythos—which opinion I can see perfectly well is the consequence of my chosen silence, suiting them and their agendas just fine, suiting me and mine not at all.

Yet, though I do not wish to speak of Jim and me, I do want to be able somehow to claim my rightful place in Jim's life, to have our love and bond and time together acknowledged. Simply put, I want to have existed in the public record of his life, to be—for reasons of historicity and plain justice—a part of his story. Not to diminish and discredit anyone else, but just to be given credit myself for having been there— no more than it was, but also no less. It's a problem, and for a long time I see no way to solve it.

And then I get a letter from Jerry Hopkins. A former Rolling Stone editor and well-respected rock journalist, Jerry tells me he is writing a book about Jim; my name has been mentioned to him by several sources as someone to whom Jim had been close, and would I care to speak with him when he comes to New York on his grand interviewing swing later that year.

I am surprised, to say the least. I've never met Hopkins, but I've read his stuff for Rolling Stone, and he seems to be a good, careful, workman-like writer. No gonzo, no glitz; and perhaps the best interview anyone ever got the Lizard King to come across with, for a 1969 issue of Rolling Stone.

I go round the barn with this one for a while: I will, I won't, I should, I can't, I need to, I mustn't, I have to, I'd really rather not . . . On the one hand, I want desperately to talk to someone about Jim; and maybe Jerry, whom Jim had mentioned on a couple of occasions with liking and respect, would be ideal. Maybe a book would be a good thing. On the other hand, however comradely he and Jim might have been, he's still a stranger; I don't know how he is disposed to me (or even, au fond, to Jim), if he toes the Courson/Morrison party line, and I don't know if I can really bear speaking to anyone about Jim at all.

But if not to him, then to whom? I have no plans at this point to write a book myself (nor will have any for, indeed, nineteen years after); Jerry might well be the one chance I will ever have to tell my truth about Jim and me, and I would be foolish and sorry not to take it.

So I do. Jerry comes to New York in the spring of 1973; we meet at my house (suitable for the occasion, I am in a long skirt of Red Morrison tartan, and Jerry shows up wearing a matching tie). We go over to the West Village, where we run into Harvey Perr (whom I last saw in Miami) at the White Horse Tavern; from there, it's dinner in Chinatown, a bar on Macdougal Street, and my flat again, talking all the way.

I tell Jerry things I have never told anyone before; the one thing I absolutely will not discuss is the abortion, and he understands and does not push. He is easy to talk to, and tells me a few things in return: He confirms Pam's hooking and addiction, her ongoing fights with lawyers over costs incurred for Jim's Phoenix and Miami trials (as his only heir, she doesn't want to pay out, but she will receive no money from the estate until she does—thus necessitating her turning to tricking; I guess a job as a typist or something would have been just too demeaning).

At last everything seems asked and told; it is long after midnight, and Jerry is about to leave. I close my eyes briefly and make up my mind.

"Wait a minute—I have something to show you, something I want to say. But you have to promise me first it'll be off the record—you can't print it in the book. I just want you to know about it."

He is a little puzzled, but promises; I go over to the bookcase and take from the top shelf *The Lords*, in its blue box bound with red string.

"Jim's private edition books—"

"Yeah, but that's not what I have to show you." I open the flap, gently setting to one side the dried red rose that rests upon the parchment pages, and take out another piece of parchment, older, rough-edged where it was torn from an antique book, sealed now in protective plastic.

It all comes out in a rush: "This is it . . .   Jim and I were married. In a Celtic pagan ceremony. This is the document we signed, that was witnessed by the people who performed the ceremony. I'm a witch."

I must say Jerry takes it well: His sandy eyebrows go up a little, but that's about it. He takes the parchment from my shaking hand and studies it in silence for a while: Jim's looping signature prominent at the bottom of the page; my smaller, neater one, signing my name Morrison for the first time; the scrawls of Brân and Maura, their real names; and, of course, the rust-brown splotch in the middle of the page—Jim's blood and mine, mingled together to seal the signing.

Needless to say, Jerry is full of questions all over again; and for my part I find a great relief in telling him all about it. Until now, fewer than a dozen people had known of the handfasting, most of them coven members; it will not be until later that spring that I come out about it in public, sort of, listing Jim as my deceased mate at my ten-year high school reunion.

But once again everything seems asked, and Jerry takes cordial if bemused leave; I collapse in tears as soon as the door closes behind him. It has been hell; but I am so glad I told him. And I'm glad I don't cry until after he's gone.

A week or two later, after Jerry is back in California, I get a letter from him thanking me for my candor and openness and honesty, telling me "Jim was lucky to have met you," which makes me cry again. Then he asks very carefully and courteously if I might not reconsider and let him use the story of the handfast wedding after all: that it is an important and hitherto unsuspected event in the context of Jim's life, that it would prove how Jim really felt about me; but more than that, it is something about Jim that needs to be publicly known, for Jim as much as for me.

I hold out a while longer; but after renewed persuasions I finally tell Jerry he can use the story. I am not unaware of Jerry's wish to print a piece of biographical hot poop that nobody's even so much as suspected; and this is not a bad thing, he *should* be thinking that. So should I, even: And I think I am making the right decision. For not only will I be making public the fact that Jim Morrison and I were occultly wedded, but the fact that I am a practicing witch—and that too will have its repercussions.

Besides, I think as I send off to Jerry my written consent to let the story appear, if Pam didn't know about it before, she surely will know about it now—a thought, perhaps, not without a certain appeal.

Over the next year, Jerry and I keep in touch by letter and phone, and come to be friends; I even get my coven, in one of the last things we are ever to do together as a group, to do a couple of Absent Healing rituals for Jerry's deaf son, Nicholas: whose hearing, Jerry will report later—"Maybe there's really something *to* this witch stuff after all"— unexpectedly improves by significant levels after the workings; though of course it could just be coincidence.

(The coven is a direct casualty of Jim's death: I withdraw from leadership, Maura is just as reluctant to reassume control, and it breaks up soon after. Some years later, I hear that Brân has himself died, and Maura moves to Europe. Although I will join a Welsh coven for a time, that too will not last, and I have stayed away from formal affiliations ever since.)

I do not swear off magic altogether, however: When Jerry laments to me that he cannot get Pam to talk to him, I do a little—concentrating; less than a week later, she calls Jerry, completely out of the blue, and requests a meeting. He is impressed but cautious; hey, *could* be coincidence . . .

By now it is April of 1974, a year since we first spoke; and when Jerry calls me in the middle of the afternoon, at CBS, my secretary passes on the call.

"Pamela's dead," is the first thing he says.

It is of course a heroin overdose, and it is of course no surprise. I'm sure the magic had nothing to do with it, and considering what her life has been like since Jim's death, it has only been a question of when, not if.

So I am not surprised, certainly not saddened; but I do feel empathy for Pam, her pain and her guilt and her weakness, and so on my way home that evening, I stop in at St. Patrick's Cathedral down the block, and I light a candle. And kneeling in the dim quiet of the Lady Chapel, where I often go to pray to the Mother, I speak for Pamela to the Goddess.

My days at CBS continue, but they are ultimately numbered: In 1979 a series of purges begins, hundreds and hundreds of people summarily dismissed, in a music-biz reign of terror without parallel. All corporate bullshit reasons, of course; and, happily, I am among the first to go. After the first flush of annoyance, I am genuinely thrilled. Copy-directing (I'm an officer by now) is by no means how I wish to spend the rest of my creative life, and now, for the first time since college, I can afford to be out of a job for a while.

Out of a job, but by no means out of work: Now I have time, and money, and freedom; now, at last, the chance to write. For real. To write the stuff I had told Jim so long ago I wanted to write. Books. Novels. A fantasy series of Celtic legends set in outer space; called, not surprisingly, The Keltiad.

Jim was the first person to hear about these books, back in 1970, when first the idea came tentatively to my mind. He was unfailingly encouraging, if perhaps a bit bemused by the concept. But he had some perspicaciously good advice to give even so: including the counsel to switch from the books I had planned to write first (King Arthur in outer space) to a later trilogy, about a young queen who is driven from her throne and must lead her people through an interstellar war, fought with starships and with magic. He was absolutely right, of course, and the first of the Aeron books, my first published book ever, is dedicated to him. (Well, it would have been in any case, of course; who else, and anyway they are all for him . . .)

But that is still a few years off. I stay home for a year, planning the Keltiad's universe, researching, reading, rereading, creating a history. Also I write another novel I'd been wanting to do, about witches in modern England, a black coven versus a white one led by a twentieth-century Pendragon and his journalist girlfriend, and a magical war over the sacred Treasures of Britain. This book will be put away on a shelf alongside my rock novel; but Keltia will become reality.

Just now, though, I need to go back to work; so I take a job writing ad copy for one of New York's institutions of higher learning. And it is while I am unhappily employed there that Jerry's book sees print at last.

Over the past six years or so, *No One Here Gets Out Alive* (a title I myself suggested to Jerry; it seemed singularly appropriate, since no one did . . .) has been rejected by every publisher to whom it was submitted. So Jerry too had put it away on a shelf; I never see this original pristine version, and it is not until a co-author gets his paws on it, adding all sorts of sleazy and semiliterate dubiety to the mix, that a publisher can be induced to buy it. Whereupon it sells several million copies, is never out of print and will be for many years to come the only book on Jim and the Doors in existence.

Thankfully, there is little public comment about Jim's surprise extralegal wedding, though what comment there is does lead to all sorts of unexpectedness: being mentioned by name by vindictive reviewers (talk about conflict of interest!); being stalked by fans who believe Jim's return in the body is imminent (!!), and that I, as his consort, must surely know all about this (!!!); finding notes and flowers and cryptic communications (one is even fixed to my door with a dagger—imitation could be a dangerous form of flattery, don't these people know I'm better armed and a *lot* crankier?) left for me in my building. But, though disquieting, the run of such incidents is mercifully brief.

A rather more lasting result of my career change (record company exec to struggling novelist) is my decision to change my name as well. I have used Jim's name in addition to my own, on a purely private basis, ever since 24 June 1970; and would have had it changed back then, except that I still worked in the music business and there would have been too many questions from too many people whose business it was absolutely none of.

But when I leave CBS, it seems to me that the time is right, and in December of 1979 my name legally becomes Kennealy Morrison— the name on the passport, the tax forms, the checking account. It's more to link him with me than me with him, a way of honoring him and fact together; I never mean it to suggest anything more than what it is. (As long as I am about it, I figure, I will change the spelling of my birth name as well, taking it back a little to its original Irish orthography; and, one hopes, its correct pronunciation also.) (Or not . . .)

The name change seems to mark another era as well: the beginning of an ability to cope with my past; a willingness, or at least a lessening of refusal, to deal with all this at last.

Strangely enough, it is not anything positive that causes the policy shift, but something a good deal nastier: In the newly released book, speculation is made on the various rumored causes of Jim's death—which of course is to me quite upsetting enough—and one of the theories put forth postulates "a spurned mistress killing him long-distance from New York by witchcraft." Well, who could that *possibly* mean, do you think?

When I read this, I go ballistic. Though I had been given, prepublication, the pages from the manuscript that pertained to me, to vet and approve (and, in some cases, even to rewrite, much to their overall improvement), this particular page containing this particular assertion was not among them.

I find the authorial(well, *co*-authorial)-cum-editorial sleight of hand with regard to this a cruel and nasty piece of work: It seems to me that my trust and candor and cooperation have been repaid with a public slap in the face. And though I do not for one minute think it is Jerry who was responsible (Jerry who knew I had not been "spurned," who would never have described me as Jim's "mistress," who knew that I would never have done such a thing to anyone, let alone to the man I love), still, his name *is* on the book . . .

But I blow it off, as it deserves. The creature responsible carefully avoided using my name (though I don't think Jim knew too many other New York witches; but I could be wrong), to get round the libel laws; and, short of sticking pins in dolls (thus proving his lying point) there seems little I can do. (Well, maybe I could stick pins in *him* . . .)

I think what annoys me almost as much as the outrageous irresponsibility of this butt-headed comment is the implication that I'm the sort of person who would, or could, behave in so skulking a fashion (I'll leave that to whoever wrote the thing in the first place). Believe me, if I had wanted to nail Jim, or anyone else, there would have been no doubt *whatsoever* about who was responsible. I'd have done it at high noon in the middle of Santa Monica Boulevard in front of as many eyewitnesses as I could round up and the local evening news, and I'd have put my feet up afterward and waited for the cops, and then I'd have gone along quietly. But you can't expect jumped-up office boys to understand concepts of honor . . .

Anyway, I have better things to concern myself with just now: I have *real* books to write, and to write them the more easily, I decide to leave the world of advertising altogether. I still need a job to make ends meet, however, and so I work in print shops, as a proofreader and typographer. Night shift preferred: I start at five or six in the evening, work until one or two in the morning, come home and write until about six, sleep until two in the afternoon, and am still free to visit editors and agents.

The world of type is a weird one: lots of ex-hippies like myself, creative sorts doing it for the same reasons—writers, actors, painters, musicians. It's a good way to make an extremely decent living (more

money than I made at CBS) and yet not have to tap any of my creative
energies. When I was in advertising, the absolute last thing I wanted
to do after slaving over a hot typewriter all day was come home and do
the same thing half the night, even if it *was* my own stuff. Another
unexpected benefit of this new line of work is that I become fluent in
typographic considerations: fonts and faces and layout and design—
knowledge that I will soon put to good use with my own books.

Still, it is a strange and demanding schedule: lots of overtime (cutting drastically into my jealously guarded writing hours), working conditions often grotty to the point of squalor, the people not always the
sort of people one would choose to be around. It works surpassing well:
I write four complex books that way. But there are many nights when,
down and unhappy, I feel more like a queen in exile, obliged to work
incognita in a scullery until she can return to claim her kingdom;
underemployed and misharnessed, like Secretariat pulling a plow. The
worst is the night I have to proofread the jacket copy for the first volume
of Jim's posthumous, Courson-published poetry—complete with the in-
evitable maddening factitious reference to "his wife Pamela." Only the
knowledge of the greater goal—the books, the books—keeps me going.

And because of things like that, it is also getting more and more
difficult to continue in my self-imposed silence about Jim, particularly
as more and more people put themselves forward as self-appointed spokes-
men and mouthpieces for him—people he had little or no use for in life,
people with far less knowledge of him (carnal or otherwise) than I have.
And the suspicion grows that perhaps my continued silence, and the
silence of Jim's other true friends, only makes it easier for such saprophytic
opportunists as these to stake their claims unhindered.

But I am an intensely private person, and my relationship with Jim
is the most private and precious and, yes, sacred of my life; I detest the
thought of being made to display my grief and pain as some kind of
credential. My policy has always been dignity and reserve and the unshakable belief that it's nobody else's goddamn business; and it always
surprises me when I realize that other people knew about Jim and me,
because to me it was only us. I never saw anything but him when I
looked at him, never saw the eyes watching or heard the tongues wagging.

Yet that is what I will be courting, in spades, if once I do speak
out; and why it took twenty years and a cartoon movie to get me to do
so. But it has always hurt very deeply to be eternally ignored and dismissed
and glossed over in Jim's life: I may not have fit the canonical require-

ments of the Gospel of St. James of La Cienega according to the various apostles, I may have been a variant few verses of "The Ballad of Jim and Pam," but by God I *did* happen. We *were* together, had what we had. And so when I am asked for the second time to speak for publication concerning Jim and me, I am perhaps a little more easily persuaded than I might, or should, have been.

This time it is a friend of my friend David Walley who is doing the asking, for a book she is writing on women who get involved with rock stars. Not perhaps the format I'd have chosen, but hey, I'm not writing the thing . . . I do not know her personally, but he speaks well of her; and indeed, when she comes to my apartment to interview me she is smart, sympathetic and friendly.

But when her book at last appears, in 1985, I am devastated yet again. She seems to have had a hidden agenda all along: the bleak and stereotypical scenario that nice college-educated middle-class Catholic (especially) girls just have to pick bad boys to fall for, giving up all claim to any career or indeed personhood of their own in the process.

Which is, of course, utter and unmitigated bilge: I can speak only for myself, but I'd have fallen in love with Jim had he been a stockbroker or a white slaver or a priest; the fact that he was a rock star was perhaps the thing I found least attractive about him. I didn't build my life around him, I wasn't dependent on him (financially or otherwise), and I certainly don't think I abdicated my own suzerainty simply because I happened to love him.

So by now I am wild-eyed and gun-shy about discussing Jim at all; I have spoken about him twice in a decade and a half, and been sandbagged twice. Only Jerry Hopkins seemed to have a clue as to what it was about, probably because he knew Jim personally as one adult to another—almost uniquely amongst Morrison chroniclers—and liked the Jim he knew.

I am still unalterably opposed to doing a book of my own about Jim; also, by now I have a creative agenda of my own to fill: My Keltiad has begun. The first novel, *The Copper Crown*, is published in hard-cover in 1984, and I am, well, in orbit. It will be followed by sequels and prequels: *The Throne of Scone* (1986), *The Silver Branch* (1988), *The Hawk's Gray Feather* (1990), *The Oak above the Kings* (1993); and there will be at least ten more to come.

Though the books are what we are pleased to call fiction, science-fantasy, there are certainly plenty of biographical (Jim) elements and even autobiographical (me, or Jim-and-me) elements worked into them for those to find who will. This was not how I had planned it, just the way things worked out—as Jim himself had warned me long ago: the writer's eternal nasty habit. But it is right he should be in them.

I think Jim would like them were he still around to read them: The framework is Celtic legendry—everything I have ever read in a long career of perusing Irish, Scottish and Welsh folklore and myth. But the context and the action are pure science-fiction, set from ancient past to far future, among distant stars.

I had described the outline of the saga to Jim as early as 1970, and for various reasons—his death, my line of work, fear of rejection—had not been able to get the thing going until the early 80's. I console myself with the thought that dear Beatrix Potter was a late bloomer too . . . The Keltiad is *Star Wars* meets King Arthur: Druids and spaceships. But it's also a loving evocation of what was best and worthiest about historical Celtic society: an enlightened system in which bards were held in honor next the king and queen, in which women could hold property (an idea which didn't make it to "civilized" Europe until this very century), outrank their husbands, control the marital property and wealth, and even serve in combat (all ideas which *still* haven't made it to "civilized" countries).

It may sound a little strange at first—ancient Celtic legends in outer space—but it all fell into place so perfectly it seemed almost as if it were, well, meant. The more I read in the historical and mythological sources, the more it sounded as if I were actually on to something; as if I were writing not science-fantasy but non-fiction: references to flaming swords that could cut through any substance no matter how thick (the god Lugh's weapon, or a *Star Wars* lightsaber?), a ship that knew its owner's mind and could sail over land as well as water (a faery vessel, or a computerized brain at the helm and antigravity devices?). Some of what may seem the most outrageous inventions or liberties aren't anything of the sort: I found them, I didn't have to invent them at all.

In any case, it seems to work, not only for me but for other people: The books are well received by reviewers and fantasy fans (a loyal and tough lot) alike; but I find that what I like best and most about authordom is the response from readers in whom a chord has been sounded—people who write to me, or talk to me at sf conventions, about how things of Keltia have real resonance and meaning in their own lives. That, to me, is worth more than anything.

In the autumn of 1987, as I am wrapping up *The Silver Branch*, my literary agent forwards a letter to me, postmarked L.A. It has been sent by a woman named Lana Griffin, and in it she tells me that the long-rumored-to-be-imminently-in-production Doors movie is finally going to be made—not a happy piece of news—and that the screenwriter of the moment would like to talk with me, for purposes of research.

In the event, he never does, apparently deeming my input unnecessary to his concept (and he may well be right), and he ends up off the project anyway. But the die has plainly been cast.

I never wanted there to be a Doors movie. In fact, when first I heard the troubling rumor of just that very possibility, way back in the mid-70's, I put a curse on it.

Oh, nothing major: just some free-form bad vibes aimed its way (and, to be sure, the project already carried quite enough iffy karma of its own), just enough of an all-purpose ill-wishing to ensure that anyone who ever tried to make a movie about Jim would be the sorriest bastard on the face of this planet or indeed any other. No movie.

And scoff all you like, but the fact remains that for nineteen years, despite the powerhouse efforts of directors like Brian De Palma, Francis Coppola and Martin Scorsese, despite the in-your-dreams longings of Morrison wannabes from John Travolta and Gregory Harrison and Michael Ontkean to Keanu Reeves and Tom Cruise and Richard Gere— in fact, every dim hunk in Hollywood was dying (so to speak) to play the part—and despite even the fears and hopes and wants and dreads of the Doors themselves, there isn't one.

I can't take all the credit, of course: As soon as interest begins to stir in a possible Morrison movie, a sharkfight of suitably mythic proportions gets under way amongst the various (self-)interested parties. Scenting money and dangling rights, they begin to circle in the bloody waters, the usual bottom-feeding suspects, demanding control and dictating terms. The three surviving Doors blow hot and cold, unable (at least as far as moviemaking goes) to get themselves arrested (which had been, of course, *no* problem for their late vocalist). And there is also an ample supporting cast of misguided actors, deluded directors and variously obsessed screenwriters, quite sufficient to help me keep the curse going indefinitely.

And so indeed it goes, for *years*—No prisoners!—and I look upon it all and I see that it is good; and every time word drifts eastwards of new life reanimating the movie enterprise, I just put on my robes and take up my sword and light candles and face Hollywood and send out some more orders to the astral realms. In fact, I ask Jim himself to put a stop to it—at least for as long as will be best for everyone, but primarily best for me; I think it's safe in his hands. And—must be coincidence again—the thing goes down in flames, every time.

But it doesn't die; and I suppose it was only a matter of time before some bright Hollywood brain (an oxymoron?) realized that not only is there this rock critic who actually claims to have *married* Morrison, but she hadn't fried her brains with drugs back in the 60's and she hadn't OD'd on heroin in the 70's, and, although a writer (Hollywood hates and fears writers, let no one tell you differently), is maybe even relatively smart; hey, why not *talk* to her?

Which is, of course, where worlds collide: I still do not want there ever to be a movie about Jim, and I had been so upset by the two books in which I had figured that I never wished to speak to anyone, ever again, about Jim and me.

Yet now comes this Lana Griffin, and the producer with whom she works, Sasha Harari (who has been trying since 1980 or so to get a Doors movie made, perhaps the greatest victim of the Kennealy-Morrison Curse). Even worse than that, they're *nice people*—straightforward, personable, understanding perfectly how I feel—and they tell me it might not be as bad as I think, that I should at least talk to this writer.

I think about it. Well, maybe I should; if I don't like him, or his take on Jim, or on me, or his shoes, I can always slap another whammy on the thing... It's worked for all these years, it can work for as long as it has to.

So I say Yeah, sure, I'll talk to him. Then there are various interventions for which I can claim no credit whatsoever: a writers' strike, production companies changing in midstream, options running out, Hollywood stuff like that. By the time the dust clears there is yet another screenwriter on the project, an affable and intelligent soul named Bob Dolman (screenwriter for *Willow*, a sweet-natured sword-and-sorcery tale featuring an actor named Val Kilmer).

Anyway, Dolman comes to New York in April of 1988, and we meet uptown. We talk for five hours, most of it at the Hard Rock Cafe, and by the end of the parley I have decided to lift the siege: At least as far as I am concerned, the curse is off and the movie just might be on.

Or, well, *some* movie might be on: As it turns out, Dolman too vanishes from the scene, rights shift yet again, and Sasha Harari becomes part of a troika of producers (with another threesome of executive producers). (One of those producers is Jazz & Pop's old friend Bill Graham, still tough and forthright and good-hearted; who himself will perish too soon, in a helicopter accident in 1991, on his way back from, where else, a rock concert.) Dolman's second-draft script, which I read in the spring of 1989, seems more of an homage to Ray Manzarek than anything much to do with Jim. I myself appear in one tiny scene, in Miami, fighting with Jim over the pregnancy.

Then, shortly thereafter, I get my comeuppance. The gods punish me for my hubris, or else they reward me by sending me a liberator (actually, it's probably both): Oliver Stone rides into the frame, and nothing is ever the same again.

Now I am in my leisure moments a reader, not a moviegoer: If it isn't some medieval costume epic, I can't be bothered. And therefore the only Oliver Stone opus with which I am personally familiar is of course *Conan the Barbarian*, which he co-wrote and which is one of my all-time favorite movies (right up there with *Lawrence of Arabia* and *The Seventh Seal*).

Mostly this Stone guy seems to go in for heavy-message political diatribe; not my sort of thing at all (I do go and see *Salvador* and *Platoon* as part of my initial research on him—impressive, though I still think it's been downhill for him all the way ever since *Conan*. . .)

I have read a bit about him, too, and I ask people for more input; what comes back is both intriguing and unsettling. He is a contemporary (a dowager boomer, born the same year as Robby Krieger, Pamela Courson and me); has impeccably flaming liberal credentials (this despite the fact that he actually *enlisted* for Vietnam, insisting on grunt status rather than officer class and coming home with medals for valor in combat— as well as a rampant and well-documented drug habit); enjoys a reputation as a belligerent and scarifyingly excessive filmmaker who is hard on his audiences and hard on himself.

All this sounds fine, so far. The down side, as far as I can make out, seems to be a self-indulgent partiality for sweeping overstatement, a fondness for explicit violence and sexuality, a rather distressing penchant for fact distortion and even outright invention, and, worst of all, a real reluctance to deal with strong women characters.

Could be trouble, I think. Might be interesting, whispers Jim.

CHAPTER

November 1989–February 1990

YOU'D THINK THAT AFTER ALL THIS TIME I'D FINALLY have learned *NEVER TO LISTEN TO JIM MORRISON...*

But no, and so it is that on a weirdly mild evening a few nights past Samhain I find myself walking down to SoHo, where Oliver Stone is holding casting sessions in a building on Lafayette Street.

As usual, I am pathologically early; after maybe a twenty-minute wait, someone comes to fetch me and I am escorted to the office next door.

He comes out from behind the desk and halfway across the room to meet me, smiling, hands outstretched; we shake hands, murmur how nice and all that, but our eyes are already lasering each other for strengths and weaknesses. I think we're both a little surprised: I was expecting Macho I, Barbarian King of Santa Monica, and plainly he was steeled for Wanda the Wacky Witch—the sort of flaked-out, pentacle-bedecked overenthusiast we snider, more tasteful pagans like to call Bimbo Wiccans—or, at the very least, Glinda.

Instead, I am in Armani and pearls and he is this charming, courteous truck driver with a writer's keen-eyed focus. Oddly exotic-looking

—less white-bread than I'd been told—with a marvelous soft voice that reminds me at once of Jim's.

But we're here to cast me, not him; and as that fact begins horribly to dawn on me—that possible actresses are being considered to play me in this movie—I try, vainly, to control face and voice and gestures.

If Stone notices this he gives no sign, but leans back in his chair, smiles engagingly and opens proceedings by comparing James Douglas Morrison to George, Lord Byron. Too easy! I counter this practically in my sleep, once again relying on dear Caro Lamb.

"Jim like Byron? You mean was he club-footed, or just 'Mad, bad, and dangerous to know'?"

His eyes light up and he leans forward, scribbling madly on a piece of paper; I helpfully repeat the quote for him, ve-ry slow-ly. I can't *believe* that he's going around making this soooo obvious—and not altogether accurate—comparison and yet seemingly had never heard this equally obvious quote; then again, he is a Yale dropout... As we talk, he takes prodigious notes, scrupulous to ask me if I mind that he's writing all this down; I indicate that I would mind a lot more if he weren't.

His primary focus is of course Jim: what kind of man he was, what he did and why he did it and what I thought about it; and I will certainly not be the production's only or even major source of such information. I say at one point that I have never yet seen a book or an article that showed Jim as the Jim I knew and loved, and that I sincerely hope and trust that the movie will manage to pull this off: the Jim who was the chivalrous Southern gentleman and the genuinely shy Romantic and the thoughtful, articulate UCLA graduate with so great a love for, and knowledge of, the written word.

This seems to interest Oliver intensely—who, you will do well to keep *firmly* in mind, never knew Jim, or met Jim, or even ever saw the Doors perform live, whose entire picture of Jim is therefore second-hand and vicarious and fantasized and imagined—and we discuss those aspects for a while. Then he gets into the more personal side of the relationship.

Needless to say, this is not quite so much fun; but in the end, we talk for well over an hour, and I do everything but juggle with plates to get my points across. My chief concern, I inform him immediately and often, is that above all Jim should not be portrayed as he has so often been portrayed in the past: Typhon, Destructo-Lord and Bozo Princeling, out of Rabelais by way of Fritz the Cat; with a little dash of Blake thrown in—Rintrah, roaring and shaking his fires in the burdened air, only with leather pants and a hand mike.

Jim was that, of course, and that too must be there. But he was a lot more besides, and I am understandably anxious that that other Jim be accurately reflected by the guy who claims Jim as one of his personal heroes. Also, and I think not at all unreasonably, I would very much like to be able to live comfortably afterwards with Oliver Stone's portraits of both Jim and myself.

Or, as I now put it, "I don't want to have to throw myself in front of a train after this movie comes out, Oliver."

He smiles; I add, after a beat, "I *really* don't want to have to throw *you* in front of a train after this movie comes out, Oliver."

He bursts out laughing, but makes no promises, and, as sooner or later it must have done, the discussion turns to Jim and other women.

"I don't want to hurt or offend you," he says, watching me closely as he prepares to do exactly that, "but you know there were others." He mentions a trollop or two; just groupie trash.

Well, fuuuuck *YOU*, Stone . . . "What about them?" I say evenly. "They had nothing to do with Jim and me. What he and I had was— different." The implication clearly being, 'And far better than anything they—or you—can possibly imagine.'

He is still waiting for something more; mere implying, apparently, is wasted on this guy.

I sigh and say condescendingly, to Oliver or to Jim I am not quite certain, "Oh, let's just say he was easily distracted."

Stone grins, but pushes it no further, probably figuring I'll go for his throat if he does; and he's probably right. On parting, he courteously walks me out to the elevators. We shake hands, and he startles me considerably by reaching out to grab a fistful of my hair. Just as Jim did at *our* first meeting, though this I have not mentioned to Oliver—

Jim, however, said my hair was beautiful. Oliver asks, with a big grin, "Is it *real*?"

I roll my eyes and reclaim my tresses. "*NOOOOO*, Oliver, it's the scalp of the last director who gave me aggro . . . Of *course* it's real!"

I leave the meeting with this goofy crush on Oliver; well, not really a crush, more a sort of high, composed chiefly of astonished gratitude that he was actually civil and charming and, at least tonight, not the arrogant fuck everybody took such glee in telling me he was; and I begin to dare to hope that maybe, just possibly, this movie might actually be a good thing. The high lasts for about as long as it takes me to walk back to the East Village from SoHo. Longer than that wouldn't be fun. You can see he's nuts. Brilliant, creative, charismatic, intense, dead set on his own trip—and crazy as a road lizard. And so, of course, was Jim.

Over the course of the next two months, while pre-production is booming along (I am asked for everything from chunks of my unpublished manuscript roman à clef to sketches of clothes I wore with Jim), I talk to Oliver on the phone, get a letter or two, send him masses of stuff, am periodically wiped out by tsunamis of doubt and second thoughts.

Those second thoughts are largely to do not with the ultimate wisdom of the undertaking but with Oliver himself, with what I have been learning, from many sources including my own research, of his creative integrity.

It is more germane to the situation than it might seem to anyone not so deeply involved: How will that inexhaustible go-style of his, that relentlessly unreflective, often superficial rush to non-judgment, serve to convey to an already biased public the private side of an incredibly complex man? How will the Prince of Polemic ever do right by the Idylls of the Lizard King? And, of course, there *is* that tiny thing he has about women . . .

So naturally I am nervous and concerned. Not so much for the public Jim: He's out there already, onstage—drunk, dramatic, eminently filmable; and he made himself that way on purpose. No, the other Jim is still the one I'm worried about: Will Oliver Stone be capable of comprehending the subtleties of Jim the unsure, Jim the vulnerable, Jim the spiritual seeker, Jim the humorous self-critic, Jim the lover and Jim the beloved? Not to mention Patricia: Will she come off as a real person, with her own ideas and her own worth and her own identity (a worth and identity *not* derived from Jim, or from a borrowed status as Jim's ornament or appendage)? Or will she just get processed through Oliver's bimbette mill like all his other female characters, to end up looking like just another idiot who fell for Morrison's line? Stone often publicly claims respect for and awareness of the strength and intelligence of women, or of a particular woman (in this case, me), but somehow that respect and awareness never seem to get translated through to film.

And what about the witchcraft? Oliver Stone has not been notably singled out among directors as an avatar of advanced spirituality: Are we going to see powerful pagan themes and values, however unfamiliar they might be to the masses (and hence potentially laughable), treated right out of the gate like something from sitcomland, played for giggles and/or cheap sensationalism? If Oliver has little sensitivity, he has less class . . .

I begin to feel massive doubts assaulting my already shaky certainty, far off still, but real enough, and worrisome (and it doesn't help at all to hear that actor Val Kilmer, who will be playing Jim, is already referring to the film as "tits 'n' acid"); and I begin to dream, endlessly and vividly and with such reality as to cause me to awaken many nights in tears, of Jim.

So when Oliver calls in early January—since I am quickly learning that with him upfrontness is rewarded and reserve gets flattened—I convey these doubts of mine to the guy on the other end of the phone.

What he whispers back to me—*great* telephone voice—is not to worry, that he doesn't for a minute think of me as a bimbette (and he laughs, God help him, when he says it), or of Jim as a sodden cipher in leather pants, or of witchcraft as something to be sneered or snickered at; he goes on to speak of his casting choice, now signed to the Patricia role: Kathleen Quinlan.

After I offer my sentiments on that (she's beautiful, you can see onscreen how smart and strong she is, but maybe he's cast me more as I am now, not the Patricia of twenty years ago; he dismisses my fears), out of nowhere General Stone drops the Big One.

"How would you feel about playing the High Priestess who performs the wedding ceremony? I mean, actually being in the movie yourself."

Incoming! How would I *FEEL??* Right now I feel as if I've just stopped a bullet . . .

"I didn't even know you were putting the handfasting in the movie at all," I say, to gain time. "The other script just mentioned it as having happened."

"Well, I think it's important, it shows a side of Jim that should be seen, ties into other elements—do you think you might want to do it?"

What I *really* want is to know exactly why he is asking me. It is a princely gift and no mistake; but, though I know he often uses real-life people in cameo roles (Ron Kovic in *Born on the Fourth of July*, for instance), I get the feeling that the motive behind this particular casting decision is more like, oh, fire insurance.

Maybe he thinks that if I am in the movie I won't have time to spend sticking pins in Oliver Stone dolls. Or maybe he feels that this will give some kind of Morrisonian imprimatur to the project. Or maybe he's just being kind and generous and respectful of me for Jim's sake. (Yeah, right . . .)

But the fact is that au fond I do not trust him. He has done nothing so far to merit the wariness—well, except for not allowing me to see the script—but I just have this feeling . . . I am thrilled and terrified and grateful beyond words for the offer; but *my* motive is more like, oh, hall monitoring. I think maybe if I am actually *in* this movie, I will be able to exert more influence than would be the case if I were not; maybe if I am actually personally involved, maybe Oliver will not be tempted to indulge in as many fabrications as he might otherwise have done.

I am dead wrong in thinking this, of course, but I am in good company: Two of the surviving Doors, plus several other members of the Doors circle and other associates as well, seem to be thinking along these very same lines, figuring it's better to have a foot in Oliver's camp than not. We'll all be badly mistaken; but, hey, at least, unlike some who just held their noses and sniped from afar, we'll have *tried*.

The thought also fleetingly crosses my mind that Jim, damn him, is probably enjoying this no end. I bet it's his idea in the first place, just wafted into Oliver's head one night, one soft-voiced lunatic charmer astrally whispering to another. Which probably explains what I can hardly believe I now hear myself saying.

"Oh Oliver," I say. "I'd love to."

I regret it immediately, of course. Regardless of what others may think, now or later, I am not doing this for my own personal glory: I don't enjoy public appearances, not even the ones I do for my own books, at conventions and such; I detest the sound of my own voice; and the thought of being up there on a screen for the rest of recorded time (or at least for as long as film stock survives) is absolutely appalling. The alternative—*not* doing it—is worse. Anyway, I have a couple of months to get used to it. It will not be enough.

A few days after that conversation, Oliver's outriders start arriving in New York. First to show up is producer Sasha Harari; after him comes production designer Barbara Ling; and then, in the first week of February, Kathleen Quinlan comes to town.

And now I find I must come to terms at last with the fact that, short of death or disaster, this movie is really going to happen. So far, I have managed to effectively deny it, though by now I am contracted as a consultant, a character and an actress. But when a well-respected, *real* actress shows up at your house, and tells you to your face that she is going to be playing you in a movie that will deal in excruciating detail with some of the most painful and personal events of your life, you kind of have to believe her.

So I open the door to Kathleen Quinlan on a cold windy night, and think to myself, What *HAVE* I done? (Jim, you fucker, you've done it to me *again*... which only goes to show you that you can't be too careful whom you made love with twenty years ago.)

She is shorter than I by several inches, slightly and finely built; yet for all her smallness she has an air that suggests she's about as fragile as cold-rolled steel. Not hard or harsh, but strong and tensile; it does not surprise me when she later mentions she had been a competing gymnast. The hair (not like mine or Pam's at *all*, which was of course part of the whole point) is mid-brown and shoulder-length; the eyes are hazel and the brows are arched and fine. She looks strong and smart and sure, she looks as if she wouldn't take crap from anybody. There is nothing in the least bit Hollywood about her, and that is probably why I like her on sight.

We are both a little shy and nervous to start with, but get past that in about thirty seconds; she asks questions about *everything*, not just Jim and me and other obvious stuff, but about my books and paintings and clothes and furniture, things Jim gave me and things I gave him, our shared Irish ancestry (Oliver's heartfelt cry of woe and/or wonder: "I can't *believe* how many people on this fucking movie are IRISH!").

It's a little scary and a little exciting, and nowhere near so difficult and troubling—except for certain particularly sensitive areas—as I had expected it to be. I mean, the woman *is* an actress, after all; even if she privately thought me a tiresome loony she'd never have let it show. It doesn't hurt either that she is so intelligent, and so open to mystical matters too—we have long conversations about the Goddess and paganism and Celtic religion and spirituality, and she is not unfamiliar with the terrain—and so incredibly easy to talk to. I tell her things I haven't even told Oliver (well, *especially* not Oliver), and I even give her a silver witch symbol to wear in the movie (she does, all through it).

But every now and then, she gets this look in her eye, sort of a measuring, considering look, a look I've seen on Jim's face and on Oliver's, a look I probably get myself when I'm writing. And then she'll say something about the way I speak, or my accent, or my mannerisms or posture or eye contact; when I point out that it doesn't really matter what kind of accent she uses, or how I sit, or whatever, nobody knows or cares, it'll make no difference, she just smiles. Because it makes a difference to *her, she* would know it wasn't right— It is an interesting glimpse of a fellow artist at work in a different medium, and it is utterly unnerving to realize that the medium, this time, is oneself.

We talk a little about the character Patricia; I am at a bit of a disadvantage here, as she's seen the script, of course, and I have not (and I never do, not until a full month *after* the movie is released).

"She—" begins Kathleen, then laughs. "You? Me? Who?"

"She," I say very firmly, in my novelist mode, distancing for safety. "Her."

"Well, she's a little darker than you; not evil, but she's definitely got more of a dark side. But that's Oliver, really."

This does not make me happy, confirming as it seems to all my worst fears; but I do not say so. "Yeah—he did tell me the character would have to have certain composited elements—things I never did, but maybe other women in Jim's life did do. With only two hours or so to fit everything into, you can't have forty different characters each doing one thing, you have to combine."

"And that doesn't bother you?"

"Certainly it bothers me! Especially since I know damn well I'm going to end up getting criticized and blamed, probably, for things I never even did. As a historian it bothers me; and as a person it *really* bothers me, I don't like anybody, especially Oliver Stone, playing around with the facts of my life, or Jim's life either. But I'm a novelist, I understand about composite characters . . . So I just told him that it's okay for her—the Patricia character—to do things I didn't do in real life, but I just don't want her doing anything I *wouldn't* have done in real life. And if there's a character in this movie who's a rock journalist from New York and who marries Jim in a witchcraft ceremony and who gets pregnant by him, that character *has* to be called 'Patricia Kennealy.' I don't really care what else she does, what Oliver makes her do: but any character who's shown handfasting Jim can only be me, and I want her called by my name."

Kathleen raises an eyebrow. "There's a pretty intense nude love scene, you know."

I blush a little. "So? Jim and I made love, I think I can handle that—but Oliver does seem to show a lot more skin in his movies than I'm used to seeing onscreen."

"Yeah," agrees Kathleen, laughing, "and it's a lot more skin than I'm used to *showing* onscreen—we are both gonna be in such trouble for this . . ."

The next two nights are even more fun: We talk for hours, and by the third night are comfortable enough with one another to sit on the floor swigging champagne from the bottle, comparing notes on men. I am boundlessly and subtly reassured: If there *has* to be a movie, and even I must now concede that there really must be, sooner or later, then maybe this particular movie will succeed in being the movie I have hoped for—the true, perceptive, thoughtful, honest picture of Jim no one yet has painted. And I am thrilled and honored and flattered out of my mind that I myself am to be portrayed—no matter what havoc Oliver will wreak upon me in the end—by Kathleen.

Still, over the remaining month before production actually begins, every now and then reality steps brutally in and will not be denied, administering one of those savage little body checks, knocking me over, reminding me in no uncertain terms just why all this is really happening—because the man I love *DIED*—and I am left shivering and in tears. It is good for me to remember this. I hope that everybody else, and especially Oliver, is remembering it too.

At the end of February I go out to Los Angeles for a rehearsal, with Oliver and the other three actors involved, of the handfasting ceremony scene, in which I will play the High Priestess—will play Maura.

It's all very Hollywood: Fly out Monday, rehearse Tuesday, fly home Wednesday. I am, quite naturally, nervous about the whole undertaking; on the drive from the hotel to the production offices on Tuesday afternoon, terror gets the better of me at last. And when I am scared and in California, quite naturally, I talk earthquake.

And when I talk earthquake in California (and even not in California; it happened once in *Bolton, England*), earthquakes very often happen. I don't know whether I just sense they are coming and that's why I get scared and talk about them (well, that's what I like to think happens), or if they happen because I talk about them and get scared (let's hope not). But the attested fact remains that I talk and they happen; and today, after I have talked earthquake nonstop from Santa Monica to West L.A., one happens again.

We are sitting—Davidson Thomson, the actor who is to play the High Priest in the scene, myself, and a couple of actors from other scenes—waiting for Oliver, who is busy with still more actors and running very late. When all at once, ever so gently, the building twitches from side to side, like a cat—a very *big* cat—lashing its tail. I try to ignore the amazed and accusing stares of Davidson and the driver ("She *said* there'd be an earthquake, she couldn't shut up about it!"), and go over to the window to see if the street has begun to ripple yet, when the ground twitches again, a lot more assertively this time.

There is a blur in the hall: Oliver, dashing past, the platoon leader all set to evacuate his troops, sees me, stops dead and points a dramatic finger.

"*You! You* did this! You brought it with you!"

"Didn't!"

He's grinning, but I think he really means it. "You just got tired of sitting around waiting and thought you'd shake things up a little, remind me you were here—"

I have recovered my cool. *"Moi?"* I ask, in my best Miss Piggy manner. "Never!"

But he's still not entirely convinced, and for the rest of the day does not let me forget it, pulling my hair every time he passes me and muttering half-jesting imprecations in my ear. Only *half*-jesting: But it's good for him to be a teensy bit unsure.

On my way back from a trip to the fridge for Evian, it's my turn for uncertainty: I catch sight of Jim in front of me, walking down the hall to Oliver's office. His back is to me, and though I know perfectly well that it is of course only Val Kilmer, apparently already deep in character for the part, I say slowly and quietly to myself, "Ohhhh my GODDDD—"

From a rear elevation he is perhaps two inches too tall, his hair maybe three inches too short and several shades too light; but all the rest is right on the money: the walk, the posture, the clothes, above all else the *air*. And there in the dim hall where no one can see me, I begin to shake.

At last Oliver is ready for us; as I enter the room I am greeted warmly by Kathleen, who mutters darkly that I'd damn well better remember what she told me in New York—not to 'activate' the magic circle and inadvertently marry her to Val. I promise faithfully; then take a deep breath and turn round, as Oliver says, "Patricia?" and introduces Val Kilmer.

Oh, Oliver's been waiting for *this* . . .   In fact, I get the feeling they all seem to be expecting me to, oh, I don't know, faint, or cry, or gasp, or something. Well, fuck that . . .

I smile and look up at Val and say, How nice to meet you. Seen close to, he bears both an extraordinary resemblance to Jim and absolutely no resemblance whatsoever. How can I put this: The physical likeness, though at first glance fairly astonishing, is really superficial—it's as if Jim's face has been put through a trash compactor and then inexpertly applied over Val's; Kilmer is coarse-featured, a bit simian, even, and Jim, after all, was unbelievably beautiful. There is a faint air of mental/psychological likeness, conscious product of the actor's craft. But there is of course no *psychic* likeness, no sense or feel of the real Jim—nor can there ever be—and therefore to me, at least, there is *no* likeness.

If I am less than overwhelmed, Kilmer is less than friendly; no, more, he is distant, to the point of open hostility. I wonder briefly why this should be, then have other things to worry about, as Oliver looks at me and says, challenge glinting in his eye, "Well, you're the only one here who knows what really happened, why don't *you* take the rehearsal?"

It is not a suggestion but a command. And so that is how I make my directorial debut, feeling like an idiot because I certainly should have seen this coming. But I push past my sudden selfconsciousness and start blocking the scene, describing the ritual and working out the action to go with the lines—*my* lines, since I'm the only one who says anything. We go through the ceremony step by step, then we all sit down around the table to talk.

Or at least Oliver and I talk; and, to a vastly lesser extent, Val. Davidson wisely retreats to the couch against the wall, out of the line of fire; Kathleen, on my right, is mostly quiet, occasionally hooting at Oliver and challenging some of his dumber utterances. Though I am aware of Kilmer's looming hostile presence on my left, I also know very well that the man facing me across the table is the only one who matters.

I can see that Oliver is prepared to listen to me, even heed me, up to a very specific pre-determined point. I can see that he has this personal Jim Morrison of his own firmly lodged in his head, in which he has invested heavily, which probably he and Kilmer (neither of whom, you *will* recall, ever knew Jim or met him or saw him in concert, whose experience is totally hand-me-down and pseudo and paraphrastic) have cooked up between them out of their own needs and wants; a Jim that, nevertheless, Oliver very much wants me to validate. I can see that he is not going to get his way. And, I can also see, neither am I . . .

His questions become gradually more personal and pointed, though to his *eternal* credit he does not ask me what Jim was like in bed. But he does push, though at one point he actually says, with what sounds like admiration (or maybe it's just amazed scorn for humility and reserve, two qualities he seems to have little experience with, or use for), "You've been very modest about all this."

Meaning, I suppose, that he's surprised I've never proclaimed myself to be the One True Right Source of the One Real Only Truth about Jim Morrison, as certain others have done or are now doing. But that's always been my policy, with Jim as with witchcraft: Those who talk most know least, those who know most talk least. Still, Oliver seems impressed, telling Val with apparent sincerity, "She's been a very valuable asset to me, a tremendous help to the production—anything you want to know, just ask her." Well, hey, that *is* what I was hired for—but Kilmer doesn't seem to want to know very much, for he asks me nothing at all, then or ever.

Not so Oliver: At last he asks me one question too many, too near the bone—about the abortion—and I snap at him. *Really* snap. We are all surprised, me more than anyone, and Oliver leans forward with a kind of weird happy enthusiasm, as if at *last* he's proved there's somebody home after all. Finally he nails me with The Look—this really great hooded fruit-bat stare—and says in that damn soft voice, "Jim pretty well destroyed you, didn't he?"

Oh, you're not getting away with *that*, Stone . . .   I give him the cold tiny smile Zorro gives the Commandante—you know, the one where he's just sliced through the candles with one swipe of his sword, only they don't fall over until he flicks them with the blade-tip—and say, " 'Destroyed'? *I'M* here. *HE'S* not."

Kathleen lets out a tremendous shout of laughter, and Oliver completely breaks up and laughs for half a minute, nodding as if to concede, Yeah, okay, Kennealy, nice score . . .   I don't look at Val. After that, somehow, we all seem to know where we stand, and I mine some poor eloquence from somewhere and hold the floor against all comers for many minutes, expostulating largely on Jung and the Shadow, Jim and God.

Then I turn to reply to one of Val's infrequent comments and it is not Val sitting next to me anymore but Jim. The hair may not be entirely there yet, but all the rest is: posture, voice, tilt of head, expression, inflection, the slow smile, the lowered eyes, even the little forward body movement with which Jim always prefaced an important question.

I take it like an arrow in the chest: My first, utterly instinctive reaction is to jump out of my skin and yell, "Great Mother! Don't *DO* that!" But a quicker, even more instinctive reaction prevails and prevents it: It seems crucially important, somehow, that nobody, and particularly Oliver and Val, should see how badly this has shaken me. I don't really know why this matters, but it does, and I go with my instinct.

Kilmer does this a few times more over the remainder of the rehearsal, fading in and out between Jim and Val like a bad signal on the car radio, and I can't tell if he's doing it on purpose to get me to react (in which case fuck him) or if he is, in fact, possessed. It is unwholesome, and unexpectedly creepy; more like a zombie than any approximation of Jim's reality. Perhaps we will have to conduct an exorcism after shooting wraps. Maybe two exorcisms—one on Kilmer, one on Stone . . .

I still haven't figured out why Val doesn't seem willing to acknowledge me, why he doesn't want to talk to me about Jim. As the only woman who ever got Jim Morrison in front of an altar for a wedding ceremony, even a pagan one, presumably I would have things to tell his would-be impersonator that no one else could impart. After all, Oliver's told me Val's talked at great length with just about every Morrison associate, sycophant, hanger-on, groupie slut and loopy fan in Christendom, or at least in the Greater L.A. area; surely one more impression won't hurt. (Or will it? Because it's mine?)

He does make an attempt at political face-saving, comes puffing up as I am leaving, to assure me that oh hey, yeah, he'd really *like* to get together and talk, but nobody ever told him I was coming to L.A. (oh right, did he think I'd just send my *stand-in* to the rehearsal?), but he's got this music session with the other movie Doors, maybe I could stay over an extra day, no that wouldn't be any good either . . . By now I am watching his performance with real enjoyment, and I doubt if I'm a good enough actress that none of this big uh-*HUH* I am feeling shows on my face.

Strangely enough, it all seems to confirm what I sensed from him as soon as I met him: He doesn't want to hear what I have to say about Jim. He's got his own private little Morrison all sewed up, and he doesn't want some redheaded Irish warrior sorceress ex-critic from New York ripping out his stitches. (At least Oliver *listened* . . . not that it changed anything, but he did at least hear me out.)

Obviously, I am just the tiniest bit peeved. But I head home the next morning resigned to my fate (if not quite so to Jim's), and for the first time I can see why other Doors connections refused to cooperate with the film—some of the Doors themselves, as Oliver bitterly complains to me during one of our phone chats.

But I know now, as I have pretty well known all along, that joining Oliver's tribe—even so far as I do join it, as a sort of visiting queen-priestess from a faraway Eastern clan, consort to the dead shaman-king —was for me the right thing to do.

Anyway, it's out of my hands, has been for some time; no longer my problem or my karma. And that thought brings a certain peace and freedom. For myself, I am feeling rather proud, actually, and hoping that my Jim (not theirs) is proud too, of how his Patricia (not theirs) has managed. I'll have to ask him when I get home: 'Cause, Jim, honey, I don't think you and I will be seeing one another in this movie after all.

CHAPTER

29

April 1990–March 1991

IN THE LAST WEEK OF APRIL I RETURN TO LOS ANGELES for the filming of the handfasting scene. They will be shooting on location in downtown L.A. for two days, on the set that purports to be my apartment—Oliver has, for reasons of his own, moved the location to SoHo and made it a loft; he has also moved up the time frame, from the veridical 1969 to 1967. I don't know why he has done this.

At six-thirty in the morning I am standing in the middle of the sidewalk, wondering where to go, when Kathleen comes running up. After an affectionate greeting she tells me she is pregnant—talk about life imitating art imitating life!—and I offer her and Bruce warm congratulations.

"What did Oliver say when you told him?"

" 'Oh fuck, oh damn, oh hell, oh shit' . . . "

This is Kathleen's first day of work (I'm only here today to approve the set, at Oliver's order), and she has a major scene with Val scheduled, involving extensive nudity and intensive emotion. The scene alleges to depict Jim's and my first lovemaking, and I really do not want to hear about it, though I *am* deeply thrilled to learn that Kathleen's lines include the bound-to-be-immortal "Come on, rock god, fuck me, fuck me good!" (When friends rather cautiously inquire if such a line in my character's mouth upsets me, I just laugh: Though I think the appellation used in real life may well have been "Lizard King" and not "rock god," I have to admit that I did on occasion say something not entirely unlike it to Jim myself. Tongue firmly in cheek, I hasten to add—which, irony not being his strong suit, is probably not the reading Oliver's giving it here . . .)

As we head over to Kathleen's trailer we are hailed by a cheerful young man. "Hi, I'm Stunt Butt!" he informs me, by way of introduction. I look my question; and he explains that he's Val's stand-in and sometime body double. Though Kathleen (and just about every other woman in this movie; even Meg Ryan, who plays Pamela, shows her tits—bigger than Pam's, in case you were wondering, and I *know* you were) must strip off completely for the camera, Kilmer refuses to unveil his own nether regions. Hence, Stunt Butt to the rescue.

Well, whyever not, I wonder: Cellulite? Shyness? Embarrassing tattoos? Anatomical anomalies that simply don't bear thinking on? Maybe *that's* why Val was reluctant to talk to me: He feared my possible devastating revelations about Jim's rear end . . . I guess we'll never know.

Upstairs, on the actual set, it is magical. I didn't know starving young rock critics could afford pads like this. It is easily ten times the size of my actual tiny flat, thirty-foot skylighted ceiling and one wall that is nothing but window. I covet it insanely. It has been furnished in eerie detail with my own Victorian Gothic taste; even the contents of my bookshelves have been faithfully duplicated. My family coat of arms appears on the curtains, and when I look on 'my' desk I see letters and bills addressed to 'me' at this fictitious Wooster Street address. I am tremendously impressed, and I tell Barbara Ling, whose work this is, that I am moving in directly the cameras are out.

For the occasion—Patricia's first day on the set—I am wearing, having given the matter considerable thought, a black leather jacket, black leather pants (yeah, yeah, I know), thigh-high boots, a cabochon ruby pendant the size of a duck egg, and a purple T-shirt reading "I SLEPT WITH JIM MORRISON."

The reaction to the shirt is fascinating and instructive: All the women on the set scream with laughter, all the men seem rather shocked. I try to figure out why: Possibly they are sexist prudes? Perhaps they find it difficult to think of me in a sexual context with the film's protagonist?

Maybe I'm just not taking this SERIOUSLY enough? But I figure, if *I* can't kid about it, who can?

At Kathleen's gleeful urging, I go up to Oliver and pull open the jacket like Clark Kent changing into Superman.

"Yo Stone! Read my chest!"

He does, and laughs, but I don't think his heart is in it. We tour the set, and block the next day's scene in situ; then Oliver walks me arm-in-arm to the elevator. They're ready to start shooting, and it's time for me to go: Because of the nature of the scene, it's a closed set.

"I'm sorry you can't stay to watch the scene," he offers apologetically.

I look at him. Is he NUTS? Two actors—well, three, counting Stunt Butt—playing Jim and me making love naked in bed, and this clown's sorry I can't *WATCH*??

"Just as well," I say, and leave the set and go back to the hotel, before Oliver or anyone else can see that I am shivering uncontrollably, and trying very hard not to cry.

NO VET SOILER. I LOVE STERNO. LOVE NOT SIRE. SON TO REVILE. LOTS O' NERVE, I. ENVIER'S TOOL. NO ELVES RIOT. NO ROTE ELVIS. VIOLENT EROS. VOLES TORE IN. SENOR VIOLET. REVOLT IS ONE. TIES ON LOVER. LIVE O'ER SNOT. LIES NOT OVER (is *that* one prophetic!). NO LOSER VET, I . . .

I am waiting in my trailer to be called to the set for the shooting of the handfasting scene; it is about eleven in the morning, and I have been here since six, waiting for them to finish up the scene of the day before. Plenty of time and lots of reason to get nuts, so to combat boredom and terror, I have sought humble distraction—as once I did while waiting for Jim—in devising anagrams. And Oliver's name is proving astonishingly apt to the sport.

By the time I have done *a hundred and fifty-nine* anagrams of OLIVER STONE (not a complete list), I am rolling on the floor, and batting them out at a rate of one every six seconds. It is anagram nirvana, they just don't quit; and if nothing else the exercise serves to take my mind off what is waiting for me upstairs.

At last someone comes with the fateful words: "They're calling for you on the set, Patricia." I go upstairs; Oliver (SOVIET LONER) comes over at once, looking pleased and jaunty, and we engage in a discussion about the number of candles to be used in the wedding ceremony.

Not wishing to appear piggy, I suggest four; Oliver (RESTIVE LOON) is silent a moment, then says, "How about *forty?*"

I assure him forty would be terrific and appropriate.

"It won't get me into trouble with the Witch Society or anything? I wouldn't want to offend anybody—"

Oliver *Stone* (EVIL NOSE ROT) doesn't want to *offend* anybody? It has often been suggested that for him, giving offense is something between a hobby, a religion and a physical addiction . . .   I tell him not to worry his pretty little head about it—well, not about *that*, anyway.

I am of course now in full costume and makeup—crown and robe and everything—and shortly am taken aside and instructed in the mysteries of the prop dagger—the stunt athamé, as it were, an exact duplicate of my own, with a squeezable handle controlling a reservoir of fake blood. I try it out, squeezing the haft and putting the point to my arm; a thin stream of 'blood' trickles alarmingly out. Wow.

I practice for a bit, thinking about the premise. Though neither Jim nor I thought twice about this element of the wedding ritual (well, maybe he did, a little, at least about the cutting part of it; though he never disputed the necessity), perhaps allowing this particular element of ritual to appear onscreen is a mistake.

I have consulted with a number of witches about it, of course, and the consensus was Do it. But I have no doubts whatsoever that Bible-belt Middle America will see this as unbridled Satanism; and perhaps seriously disturbed suburban teenage metalloids will in their ignorance see sanction for their own unsavory fantasies. (So will the Bible-belters, come to think of it . . .) Practices of Celtic warrior days will mean nothing to this lot: It's all just blood and sex, with drugs no doubt in there somewhere (they weren't, but you *know* they'll find them!), the Lizard King and his witchy bride, Godless pagans the pair of them (well, scarcely godless). They will never see the symbolism, or the actuality, that the blood represents: love's willingness to sacrifice for the beloved (not unlike a priest's tonsuring at ordination); to them it is just dark and evil and nasty and depraved—an attitude which only reflects their own mind-set and paucity of spirit.

Perhaps, too, though, in this Age of AIDS, it's a little irresponsible to appear to be condoning ritual bloodshed, even between two consenting and uninfected adults, and twenty years in retrospect. In the end, I decide it's not my problem. It's what happened, and I won't lie about it, or diminish it or deprecate it or apologize for it. I am not ashamed of it for the least instant, I'd do it again with Jim in a second, and if people choose to denigrate it for their own purposes, or to misinterpret it out of fear and ignorance and intolerance, or if Oliver himself has chosen to misuse it just to make some sleazy point of his own (as I am beginning to fear, when I hear that Val and Kathleen have swigged 'blood' all through the scene just filmed), well, that's not my problem either.

Now we are really moving: Kathleen, in her black velvet witch wedding dress, comes over to stand with me; Davidson joins us; and then, last of all, as stars do, Val shows up on the set.

If I did not already have so much to think about, if I could allow myself the luxury of reaction, if I did not wish to give them all the satisfaction of seeing me come unhinged, I would flip out and never come back. He is of course now in costume as Jim—long brown hair (never once the right color, at least judging by memory and the lock of hair Jim gave me), that beautiful dark red velvet Cossack shirt and leather pants outfit, the one Jim wore at the Fillmore East concert that I was in the third row for—and this is the first time I have seen him so. Though Kilmer's slack-jawed impersonation is still vastly wide of the mark, even so it is quite good enough for me to wonder, not for the first time, if I am going to get through today alive after all.

Oliver comes over, whispers in my ear, "I'm relying on your intelligence."

"And I on yours, sweetheart!" I snap right back, and he laughs. But he has come to tell us that we're ready to roll.

After hours of what has seemed like empty waiting, everything happens at once: Marks are put down, tape measures are drawn from the cameras and lights to the actors' faces, makeup and hair touched up one last time; the boom mike moves in overhead (I am already wired for sound), the sword is put in my hand, and everyone but Val, Kathleen, Davidson and myself vanishes behind the dusty wall of lights and filters.

Now even I have seen movies about moviemaking, and I have this idea you stand there until the director says Action, so I do. I hear "Rolling" and "At speed" and something that sounds like a slug for the audio track, and they really do come up and smack that clapper thing in your face. And finally Oliver quietly says, "Action."

I have been standing with both hands on the sword-hilt and head bent; now I raise the huge claymore at arm's length, lift my head and slowly revolve three times to cast the ritual circle. I bring the sword point down and hold out my hand to Davidson, who enters, kisses me on the cheek, then brings in Kathleen in like fashion, and she in turn brings in Val.

And as Val takes her hand and crosses into the circle, he gives her a look of such love, and a smile of such sweetness, that I am blasted back twenty years in one instant. Suddenly, without warning, it *is* Jim and me; and in that instant I think, No, I cannot *POSSIBLY* go on with this, this will kill me, right here, right now. It is simply too real; and I feel for a moment as if I myself, not Jim this time, am about to faint in the circle. The total dislocation, seeing with my own eyes, now, twenty years after the fact, what and how Jim and I must then have looked like to Maura as she stood with Brân in the circle to marry us: It is like being wrenched inside out and forced to watch it happening—a true out-of-body experience, only in full consciousness and volition. And I wonder briefly, belatedly, if Oliver really knew what he was asking of me when he asked me to do this; if *I* knew, even, when I accepted.

Then all at once I am past it. Jim *is* there, and not just imperfectly in Val but truly, for me to know and take strength from; and I am there thrice over—in my own self, and in Patricia/Kathleen, and in my own younger self. And all of it is both real and unreal at the same time: I become wonderfully focused, mindful only of what I must do here, my lines and action, the action of the other actors. There is so much to remember here and now that I cannot indulge in remembering there and then; and this is both a blessing and a trouble to my soul. I want desperately to live again in the moment, more than memory; but I know even as I wish it that I cannot, and in any case the moment has never ended.

We shoot the whole scene as rehearsed, the complete ritual. In the finished film, however, it will be edited down beyond recognition, pruned to an incomprehensible few seconds and stuck in the middle of a confusing montage sequence. I don't think viewers will have the faintest idea of what is going on here—true to form, and sloppy storyteller that he is, Oliver never bothers to set it up; the Jim character never proposes to the Patricia character, we never hear a word about witch weddings, let alone why Jim Morrison should want to have one of his very own—only the very astutest filmgoers, or the most knowledgeable Doors freaks, or any pagan, will have a clue as to what this strange scene is all about.

But as I stand there, still reeling, I am struck by a couple of revelations that rock me with all the force of Celtic prophecy. In my preoccupation with how much like torture this was all going to possibly be, I have not realized until this instant that there are actresses on both coasts and everywhere between, famous actresses, who would *kill* for this part, even this little tiny part with, what, three or four lines; and what a great and wonderful gift Oliver has made me.

To me, though, the real and greater gift is the freedom he has given me to face up to my own past, to confront it and take possession of it at last; to accept and acknowledge it easily and publicly, as well as within myself, and to blow off anybody who doesn't like it. And for two decades, I had for all my fond beliefs to the contrary been able to do nothing of the sort.

Twenty years didn't seem to make much difference in how I felt about Jim, though it did give me a bit more insight into why he had behaved as he did. But as long as I did not face what I still so deeply felt, I could heal only so far, and never to the point of being completely at ease with the truth. It had become so huge and difficult and charged a burden that it took something as big as this film, someone as forceful as Oliver Stone ("This is a job for Superman!"), to get me past it.

And it comes to me also as I stand here that *this* is why, at least for me and maybe for all of us, it could not have happened before—why it took eight years for Sasha Harari and nineteen for me—why Oliver wasn't free to do the film in 1985 (*Platoon*) and why he was unexpectedly free (*Evita*) to do it now—why John Travolta and Tom Cruise and Richard Gere would have been so abysmally wrong and why Val Kilmer, substantially flawed as he is, is still so right: Because now is the time for it, and because this really is as good as it is ever going to get. It will not be good; but it could not be better.

It makes me extremely happy to think this, even if it isn't true; and that is why, no matter what hell will evidence itself in the final cut, no matter what has been done to or for or with my character, no matter what weird skewed evil awful twist Oliver has put on me or on Jim or on anyone else (and I know there will be many), I will always be deeply grateful to him at least for this.

The rest of the day seems to fly: It seems only a few minutes later that Oliver is saying that's it, let's move on to the closeup and hand shots. Val has already left the set, so Stunt Butt fills in for his absent mitts.

I find myself hurt and surprised that Kilmer has decamped without even saying goodbye, much less anything more extensively gracious like, oh, I don't know, 'Not a terrible job,' maybe, or even 'Nice to have met you, hope you live through this.'

I know he's got a lot on his shoulders just now, and more on his mind—in the end, it will be his performance that will make or break this picture—and that this is hard for him. But, just possibly, it might be even harder for me, don't you think, especially today; and I can't help feeling that a word or two of comfort or cordiality or even just minimal politeness on the part of Val Kilmer to Jim Morrison's ex votis widow—whom, let's not forget, Jim would absolutely not be best pleased to see so treated—would have been so much to offer. Val Kilmer quite plainly still has major lessons to learn from the man he purports to impersonate; whose leather pants, frankly, he isn't good enough to *sniff*, let alone try to fill out. I know very well I'm not the star here, not the main event; but courtesy costs nothing, and once again I have been made to feel irrelevant and of very little account, irrelevant to my own life and love and history, unimportant even to the filming of my own wedding—and I wonder a little bitterly just how well I have done after all.

We finish Kathleen's closeup, and the hand work, and then it's a wrap! Only a twelve-hour day today! Oliver thanks everybody and heads for the elevator. I call him aside and say that I have something that belonged to Jim, which I would like him to have now as a gift from both Jim and me.

He grins. "What is it, one of Jim's semen samples?"

I recoil sharply, absolutely staggered that even he could be so breath-takingly crude and insensitive. After all, I'm giving him this out of genuine liking and gratitude for what he has done for me personally, never mind what the movie will be like (in fact, probably in *spite* of what the movie will be like). It is something that means a lot to me, a fitting closure; is nothing sacred or solemn or special to this asshole? I had thought, perhaps naively, that surely something that belonged to Jim, that Jim's consort passed on to Oliver, would hold meaning; instead, he offers this unbelievable bêtise—

I do the only thing I can do, short of either killing him where he stands or slapping his face in front of the whole crew: I laugh.

"NOOOOO, Oliver, it's even nicer than that—"

In fact, it is a silver Celtic cross that I had given Jim, engraved on the back with an intertwined P and J; and which has been resting on the altar all through the day's shoot. It was one of the things he gave me for safekeeping before he went to Paris, and I had been keeping it against his return, when he came to join me in New York as he had promised.

But it is time to pass it on; and, amazingly, inexplicably, from the moment I met Oliver Stone, despite all sequels and lapses and uncertainties, despite all the upsetting things I have heard about the script I was never permitted to read and the things my character does in it and the things Jim's character does to her, despite the fact that I may very well hate this movie when it comes out and feel utterly betrayed and sold out and lied to and abused, despite all this and more besides I have never for one instant thought to give Jim's cross to anyone else. And even now, despite what he has just said to me (and people have perished for lesser offense), I am still not sorry I do so.

I take affectionate farewell of him (I like him, you can't help it, his vibes are likable), and of Sasha Harari and Lana Griffin, who have been so patient and caring and protective of me throughout all this, thank everyone else and go downstairs with Kathleen, who has shanghaied me to take me to her house for a couple of hours to cool out.

We head for her truck; but before we get there, about five or six production members come up with copies of my Keltiad books for me to sign.

Now I have been, I think, so brave all day long; I was *so* well-behaved and I hadn't cried and I hadn't even *thought* about earthquakes and I tried so hard to come through for Oliver and for Jim and the cast and the crew and myself. But *this* brings tears to my eyes at last, and I am so proud and happy and honored and touched that they are asking me.

Kathleen leans against the car and teases. "God, Kennealy, you're worse than a movie star!"

"It's the first time I've ever kept a movie star waiting on *me* signing autographs," I assure her, and everybody laughs. Then we drive up the coast road to the remote canyon in which she lives.

We sit and talk: about Jim, about the film, about Oliver, about the weeks of shooting she still has ahead of her. I am so happy she was the one to play me in this movie (well, since the twenty-six-year-old Diana Rigg is obviously no longer available). She will make me look so good— We do not resemble one another physically, but onscreen you can see that this Patricia person had a brain and an attitude, and that's why that Jim guy was attracted to her; and that's all I really care about.

We'd like to talk all night, but we are both very tired, and she's pregnant besides; so at about ten she drives me back to Santa Monica and my hotel, and we take leave; hugs and kisses and promises to keep in touch (which we do). It has been an extraordinary experience, I think for us both.

I go to the airport early the next morning. Oliver has invited me to drop by the day's shoot—the New Haven concert, where Jim got busted—but although I am tempted, I decide to pass. After yesterday, not only would it seem anticlimactic in the extreme, but I just don't think I have sufficient inner resources left to get me through the sight of Val Kilmer pretending to be Jim onstage singing, and the audience pretending to respond, and me, not pretending at all, remembering.

In fact, I don't have sufficient inner resources left to get me onto the morning plane. I consider calling somebody to drive me to the set after all, but in the end I spend a really therapeutic four hours, until the afternoon plane goes at three, decompressing all alone in the departure lounge—and allowing myself to remember, without pain, the last time I waited all alone in this same place, weeping and all but annihilated, to get on a plane for New York after parting from Jim for the last time in life.

But strangely this is a healing, now, and I am so aware of Jim's presence, as I have been almost constantly these past months: Jim with me now, as if he and I together are comforting that younger Patricia, are telling that sad young girl's ghost that she came through after all, and not badly; and perhaps even she heard our voices back then, and knew she would. And I am happy; this is the best thing I could have done. All of it.

The plane is empty and quiet, and when I arrive at JFK at midnight the production office has a car waiting to take me home. Back in my familiar old Victorian lair, a wounded Captain Nemo back aboard the Nautilus—and Jim is here too—I cry for a while, then crash for a week. No dreams.

On Thursday, February 14, 1991—twenty years *to the day* since Pamela Courson left L.A. for Paris and I went upstairs to Jim's arms with a bottle of wine and a forlorn hope (just one more twist of irony's knife, this *unbelievable* timing)—I enter an uptown screening room, give my name to the publicist on duty, take an isolated chair in the farthest darkest corner I can find (not far and dark enough by half), and prepare myself for hell.

It has been an eventful ten months—shooting wrapped last July, I was knighted in Scotland in September, Kathleen had her baby in October, Oliver called a few times, I've gotten back to work on my woefully overdue fifth novel. Apart from letters and calls from Lana and Kathleen giving me periodic updates, I hear very little about the movie, not until the pre-release publicity begins to gear up right before Christmas.

By now friends have told me things, specific things, *bad* things, about how my character has been tampered with; and, as the film draws closer to opening day, I start once again to take it out in dreams. And worse: Soon I cannot eat, cannot sleep, cannot stop throwing up, and above all I cannot stop crying.

Sasha and Lana and even Oliver call (he is no help whatsoever, but I appreciate the gesture); but it is Kathleen who is the one to save me, calling four times in the two days before the screening. And, little by little, I begin to calm down from the verge of genuine flip-out; and as I calm down, I begin to remember certain things.

I remember that it is, as Kathleen has told me, *only a movie;* when it comes out on video people will be watching it while clipping their toenails in bed—or worse. I remember that it was my decision to talk to Oliver Stone, to accept the offer of the part and the job as advisor, that it was I who insisted the character be called by my name, that I have never regretted any of these actions and do not regret them now. I remember too that Oliver, mad and delightful as he is, is also often an insensitive clod and an erratic filmmaker, and that above all else he is a man who did not know Jim.

And last of all I remember some things about me: I remember I am a priestess. I remember I am a knight. I remember I am Jim's consort. I remember that Jim loved me and I loved him. I remember that all this can only get to me if I myself allow it.

And when I remember all these things, I know that I will never forget them again, and now, sitting, waiting for the lights to dim in the screening room, I remember them better still.

I am in black from head to foot, of course, and I am wearing talismans for strength and comfort—things Jim gave me, things that belonged to him. In my pocket I am clutching a little leather amulet bag with a tiny figure of the Goddess on its thong, that Kathleen has sent me for luck and affection; I have filled it with earth from Jim's grave.

Nobody bothers me or speaks to me; when the lights go down at last my pulse is over a hundred and sixty, and I am trembling violently in what I think is the purest terror of my entire life. Worse even than the fear I felt before the abortion, because there at least I knew what I was facing, and here I have not the smallest clue. But it is here at last, after two decades, and I must see it and know it and get past it once for all. That's what all this has been about; Jim—and I too—would not have it any other way.

This must surely be the only alleged biopic ever made where the two real-life lead characters were far more beautiful than the two actors who portray them on the screen. Though Val Kilmer and Meg Ryan are pretty enough, next to Jim and Pam they look like dull unattractive urchins, with bad hair (wigs, but still).

As the film progresses, I begin to lose the edge of my terror; but in its place comes something else, something strange. I had been expecting to feel shock, fury, tears, pain: Except for the tears—I do not weep, not one single tear, my eyes do not even mist over—all those feelings come along in due course. But what I feel most as I watch this movie is unbelief. Not *dis*belief (though that is there too). *Un*belief. What I am watching is something that never happened. No matter that there is a character named Jim, a character named Pam, characters named Ray and Robby and John and Siddons and Holzman and Nico and Warhol and Rothchild, even a character named Patricia—I do not know these people. I never met them, never saw them do what they are doing, never heard them say what they are saying.

Yet they bear names I know, their actions bear a strange distant resemblance to things I know occurred . . .   It is an alternative universe, Stoneworld—Olliewood!—where all things alter beyond reason yet not beyond recognition, so that you can see it and say, Yes, that's sort of it, I remember something kind of like that, but it really isn't anything like it. You identify it; but you do not confirm it. And you *never* lived it.

I had thought, going in, that the scenes between the Jim character and the Pamela character would be the most difficult for me to handle; that I would not be able to deal with seeing the characters together, loving, sharing. Although just about every bit as hard as I thought it would be, that proves to be the least of my troubles.

As for seeing myself onscreen—well, that too is about as hard as I had expected it to be. In fact, I can't even look at this High Priestess (who doesn't seem to look very much like me; which I guess is the idea, she's not Patricia, she's Maura), not past a fast half-second glance; I just close my eyes and listen to lines I vaguely remember having said coming out of the speakers all around me, in a voice that to my ears bears no resemblance whatever to my own.

Thankfully, it's over pretty quickly; Oliver has edited the scene down to about thirty seconds or less (never thought I'd be thanking him for *that*): totally unintelligible, revealing nothing about Jim or me or us, adding nothing whatsoever to the fabric of the film. Typical.

It's easier to watch the character me: I have survived the sight of her making graphic love with the Jim character (Kathleen looks gorgeous), chasing naked all over the loft (which also looks gorgeous, though I could have done without *Carmina Burana*), even an aerial shot of the two of them coupled and thrusting away on the bed (so *that's* what it looks like! How extraordinary!). And all this is fine. Even the "fuck me, rock god" line is fine (and funny).

But when she suggests they cut each other's wrists and drink some blood to cure his temporary inability, and assures him that not only does this work, it's what real witches do (oh yeah, she's also just told him she's a witch), that's where I start to get nuts again.

When the Patricia character and the Pamela character confront one another at a party in L.A., and the Pam character is made to snipe, "You actually put your dick in this woman, Jim?" (never mind the insult, never mind the fact that few people in the 60's ever used the word 'dick'—it was almost invariably 'cock,' Jim's own word of choice), that's where I start to shake again.

And when the Jim character and the Patricia character are together in a Miami hotel room, and she is telling him she is pregnant with their child, and I hear the actors say the lines that Oliver Stone has put into their mouths to say, that is where I realize I can still want to kill.

I sit there white-faced and rigid and shaking all over, as on the screen Val Kilmer and Kathleen Quinlan hurl hateful words at one another. Now, though most of this scene is pure twisted Oliver, many of these words are in fact words that Jim and I did fling at each other; searingly painful for me to hear, even now after all these years, booming out of the speakers, but true words; and I can bear truth.

What I cannot bear is what I now hear: Kathleen storming at Val, "Those vows were forever!", and Val drawling back, "I was stoned, it seemed like a fun thing to do at the time."

And people laugh.

When I can see again, breathe again, think again, my mind clears to two coherent thoughts, two only: I will rip out the throats of whoever it was that laughed; and I will rip out the throat of Oliver fucking Stone.

BECAUSE IT IS A MONSTROUS EVIL BASE DIABOLICAL SAVAGE TREACHEROUS COCKSUCKING LIE. What they are laughing at is no truth of Jim's and mine, but Oliver's lie.

Somehow, the movie continues; and, at last, it ends. The lights come up; I remain unmoving in my chair until nearly everyone else has left the screening room. I am quite certain that nothing shows on my face of how it is with me just now, that my countenance is impassive and free of emotion. But later that week a reporter will call for a story, saying that a friend of hers saw me at this screening, and according to him I "appeared visibly upset." Well, scratch another myth...

All I can think, the only thought I can hold onto, as I make my way to the lobby is that it's a damn good thing for all of us that Oliver wasn't here tonight, because if he had been he soon would *not* have been—just a black oily smoking patch on the carpet where he had been standing.

Outside in the lobby there is a queue for the one elevator, and as I wait my turn I overhear someone say, "Boy, I didn't know all that stuff about Patricia Kennealy!"

And I fade back about ten yards. I do not know him, do not wish to confront him, not even as a stand-in for Oliver, but I do know I do not want to hear what he thinks about what he believes he has just seen. And I think, Right, dude, and you *still* don't know any stuff about Patricia Kennealy...

Then a woman getting into the elevator with me rolls her eyes and flings out her arms dramatically and addresses the car at large.

"God," she announces laughing, merrily throwing back her head, "I thought he'd *never* die!"

I get home. I talk to Lana, to Kathleen; I even talk to Oliver. Then I go catatonic for the next four days. Really catatonic. I do not eat or sleep or speak. I do not take calls. I do not go out. I do not move. I lie huddled on top of my bed under my grandma's Jim-vintage afghan and just—am. I do not weep or rage, even; it's way past any of that by now. All I do is stare.

For what all this really feels like is that Jim has died all over again. Jim has died yet again, and this time it is Oliver who has killed him. Once more I was powerless to save him, once again I have lost him. What I have been doing for the past four days is grieving . . . But it cannot go on—I've learned that much, at least, in twenty years—and so on Monday I pull myself together and start returning calls.

When the movie actually opens two weeks later (oh Oliver, you always do something to spoil my birthday!), it's worse—twenty-year-old jealousies and envies come crawling out from under, well, stones; cunt-loads of spite issuing from the usual suspects—but I consider the sources and blow it off. I do some interviews for TV and print in which I try to be as honest as possible (which means saying conscientiously that I like Oliver but hate his movie); most of them only want to hear the latter part.

The insanity (and, indeed, inanity) goes on for a few weeks longer; then, as the film dies (maybe that curse never got completely lifted, after all . . .), so does all the fuss.

Which is just fine with me, and not a moment too soon. Kathleen puts it in perspective when she calls at the end of March with a fabulous story: When she returned home after a full weekend of movie publicity chores, lying stretched in the driveway of her house was "the biggest LIZARD you ever saw, Patricia, it was the King Lizard, and it was *dead*, and there was *blood* running from its mouth! It came to *my* house to die!"

I'm sorry for the lizard, but I scream with laughter at the cosmic joke: How absolutely *perfect*, a dead King Lizard for the woman who played the Bride of the Lizard King. But it shakes me up a little, too.

"Did you bury it? Oh man, you should have sent it to *Oliver*—"

"No, what happened was even better, listen: A bird of prey came down and carried it off! An eagle, or a red-tailed hawk, they live in the canyon . . . Is that incredible or what? It's a message from Jim!"

You bet it is. But what is he saying? And to whom?

CHAPTER

30

April 1991

AN ANSWER OF SORTS IS NOT OVERLONG IN COMING:
Round about the seventeenth anniversary of Pamela Susan Courson's
death in Los Angeles of a heroin overdose, I get a fax from a British
writer who has recently interviewed me. It is an article that appeared in
a London newspaper, taken from a longer article that ran in Paris-Match:
Alan (or Alain: the spelling seems to alter from source to source) Ronay,
Jim's friend from college days, who hung out with him in Paris just before
his death and who was one of the five persons present at his funeral,
turns out to have arranged a good deal more than just Jim's interment.
He has finally broken his twenty-year silence on the true manner of Jim's
death; and glad as I am that truth (or as close an approximation thereof
as we've so far seen, or may ever get) has been served at last, it is still
not an easy or a pleasant thing for me to hear.

I suppose one of the things that have never ceased to amaze me about
Jim's death is the fact that so many people could have bought what passed
as the Official Story for so long, just opened wide and swallowed it and
never thought twice about why they seemed to gag.

Some, of course, thought a lot more than twice: There have been dozens of theories floated over the years, each more crack-brained than the last, as to how and why and even *if* Jim died. No one with half a functioning brain stem ever fell for the heart attack/pulmonary infection/blood clot taradiddle that ex-surfer Bill Siddons and the Doors organization were pushing (it was generally known in rock circles that by 1971 Jim was not abusing any substance but alcohol, and was in excellent health despite it—no strange mysterious ailment he had been neglecting, that suddenly turned critical and killed him). But no one else had a more substantive explanation, or indeed any real proof. And nobody ever really seriously took Pam's word for *anything*, not even that Jim was in fact actually dead . . .

Stories that Jim had died of not a heart attack but a heroin overdose were circulating before he was even buried: A Parisian d.j. was telling people about it at a hip club, the evening following Jim's death, and the rumors got over to New York and L.A. pretty quickly. The difficulty with the heroin scenario was that anyone who knew Jim at all well had big problems accepting smack as the cause of his death.

And not just because he was really scared of needles, either (a fear perhaps allied to his reluctance to make the ceremonial cuts upon himself for the handfasting): *If* Jim had ever wanted to do smack, in Paris or anywhere else, he could always have snorted it. And it was always obtainable; he had only to ask Pam.

But Jim's horror of heroin was deep-seated and strong, well known to those who were close to him. He never evidenced to me anything other than loathing and distaste for the idea of the drug, and contempt for those who used (oh yes, including Pam). Although he tolerated her habit (being himself an addict to alcohol, he must have scarcely felt in any position to bust someone else), in all the time they were around each other he never joined her in her indulgence. But addiction was still the basis of the long tight death-hold they had on one another, the foundation of their poisoned bond.

I myself will never believe Jim was a junkie: that he habitually used heroin and none of us knew it, or that we would have kept quiet about it if we had known. And despite what has been said elsewhere about Jim's friends' heated denials that he used (our fierce assertions that he wasn't into it must surely only show "where the shoe pinched"), I and others will go to our own graves unshakably convinced that Jim would never, in ordinary circumstances, have had anything to do with smack.

Since he died of it, the circumstances must therefore have been far from ordinary; and, if only to judge from his letters to me from Paris, they were. They conjured a scene I could well believe, a subtext to make me weep: Jim depressed, down about his writing, lost in a foreign country, unable even to speak the language, feeling adrift in his life and work, feeling marooned, *being* marooned with a woman whom perhaps for the first time ever he was seeing as she truly was . . . who knows?

There have even been some veiled suggestions made, intimations by people who knew Jim well in a professional capacity and who were hearing from him at that time, that Pam, sensing her hold on Jim had finally evaporated (that "break" he so often spoke of having been at last achieved), might not merely have offered him the smack but aggressively pushed it on him, out of her frantic need to exert still further pressure and control, to keep her lifestyle and habit intact and funded—if not out of even darker motives still (she was his heir, after all). As to that, I cannot say: There was certainly no such thing suggested in his letters to me, at least; and Pam is not here to speak for herself.

But to me, all those years, the truth of it mattered little: Jim was dead. What did I really care how he had died? He was still dead; even if I knew beyond any faintest doubt how and why and at whose hand, it still would not bring him back to the world or to me.

So now I read the piece the British reporter has sent me; and then I read the full French text of the article from Paris-Match, which Alan Ronay wrote himself. I read them, but I am not seeing them.

Instead, I am seeing a bathtub in a flat in the Marais district of Paris, where the man I love is bleeding and dying, while someone who has loudly claimed the title of 'wife' shows the true nature of her 'wifely' devotion by leaving him there, going to bed, nodding out on smack, and letting him die.

And I find myself in the blazing grip of the most profound anger I have ever known. I did not know I could still get as angry as this, I thought I had evolved a bit past it, this is unlike any wrath there ever was before. I was not possessed of such a fit of fury even with the bitch Tiffany, twenty years ago. Not with anyone ever. Not even with Oliver; but then, Oliver only ambushed Jim. He did not kill him.

And I think, How wise you were, Pamela Susan, to have smacked out yourself in 1974, because if you were alive right now I would be on my way to California to kill you. If I had learned what I now know while you were still breathing, you would not have been doing so more than New York–L.A. flying time past my learning it. Be glad you are dead. Be very glad.

It is more terrible than I think I can bear, more dreadful than anything I have ever pictured: Jim and Pam snorting heroin for two days; Jim depressed, playing all the Doors' records one after another, then going in to take a bath; Jim sick and semiconscious in a tub of warm water, hemorrhaging violently from his nose and vomiting pure blood into a pot Pam holds for him; Pam not bothering to call a doctor or even take him to an emergency room, but going back to bed, nodding out as junkies do, waking up in the early morning to find Jim dead, in warm water tinged pink with his own blood.

It is the sheer inhuman—no, make that *sub*human, *un*human— indifference of all this that sets my rage to flashpoint: The man she professes to love—on whom she has been urging heroin for whatever reasons—is dying in his blood a few feet away from her and so much does she love him that she just lets him die. The self-concern, the animal self-preservation instinct of the true junkie: If Pam had not been afraid she herself might be busted—for drugs, if not for worse cause—she might actually have done something to save his life. He might still be with us.

But, of course, that would not have occurred to her. And that is why, if she had not been safely dead, I would have killed her. No wonder Jim came to me the night before he died: He just couldn't stand being around Pam any longer than he had to. And then he didn't have to, and I doubt he is today.

Still, Alan's confession is a revelation, and fits neatly in with some of the points at which logic had strained over the years. In fact, what Alan Ronay has confessed to, in public and in print, is a masterful coverup, improvised on the spot, that has held for two decades against all comers. Out of what he says was his concern for Jim's reputation, his wish to avoid the druggy taint that clung to Janis and Jimi, his desire that hordes of distraught fans should not follow Jim to copycat deaths (yeah, *right*), and above all his resolution (out of whatever motive) to allow Pamela Courson to evade the weight of the law's majesty crashing down on her for her actions, Alan Ronay lied systematically to the French police and firemen and medical examiners, to the U.S. embassy officials in Paris, to Jim's friends and family and fans, and to the world forevermore, thus enabling Courson to profit by what she had done and failed to do, to carry on her fantasies and her addiction to the day of her own death, and allowing her family to perpetuate and profit by all of it thereafter.

Whatever one may think of Ronay and his actions (and I bet this *still* isn't the entire truth about Jim's death), one must admire the cool dispatch with which he orchestrated the coverup, thinking on his feet on a grand scale. It must have been a hellish scene: Jim dead in a bloody bathtub, firemen emergency squad on the way, police too, filmmaker Agnès Varda and Ronay arriving in the middle of all this, Pam in a damp white djellaba, crazed with guilt and smack and terror, agreeing to anything anyone suggested so long as it wasn't the truth and kept her famously freckled ass out of a French prison.

She was right to be afraid: Besides possession and distribution of heroin, presumably she could have been charged even with murder, criminal manslaughter, negligent homicide, whatever—serious charges indeed. Perhaps the best she could have hoped for, given her own junkie history, would have been complicity in a drug suicide or accidental overdose, if her lawyers had been as fast on their feet as Ronay.

He cleared the rue Beautreillis flat of all traces of heroin (though Pam seems to have needed still another score to get her through the funeral: When Bill Siddons arrived in Paris a few days later, he noticed a box full of white powder on a living room table—when he tried a taste, it nauseated him, and he commented later that it was obviously something he had never tried before). He interpreted for Pam to the inquiring officers (which means that two chief witnesses to the circumstances of Jim's death were not separately interrogated). He concealed Jim's identity as an internationally famous rock star (which revelation would certainly have prompted a far more intense investigation, that could not have failed to implicate Pam). He helped Pam cobble up a fable of recent bouts with a mysterious pulmonary infection that supposedly sent blood clots roving all around Jim's thorax until one lodged in his heart (this tale was meant to hoodwink the medical examiner, and obviate the necessity for an autopsy (standard procedure—even in France—for someone as young as Jim). He even reversed the order of Jim's names (Douglas James instead of James Douglas), so that the trail might be further muddied (the source of the guard's confusion when I came seeking Jim's grave at Père-Lachaise, only a few days later; he had even been listed so in the cemetery records). All of which got Jim safely buried without any autopsy (a post-mortem would have revealed the heroin in his body, and that would have nailed Pamela immediately, irrevocably and absolutely deservedly right to the wall). Let's hope she was properly grateful to Alan for his assistance . . .

But all the fancy footwork in the world could not distance Pamela from her guilt, and she knew very well what Alan had saved her from. After her ignominious return to L.A., she is said to have told people in the Doors circle that she killed Jim, it was her fault, it was her dope, they had been doing smack all that night and the night before, and he'd had a lot more of it than she'd had, and he wasn't used to it because he'd never done it before but she gave it to him anyway, she shouldn't have let him take it, she should have checked on him when he kept vomiting blood, should have called a doctor, but she nodded out from the smack she'd taken herself and when she woke up he was dead.

(Ronay adds a startling little footnote: Pamela was permitted to keep Jim's body, packed in ice and wrapped in plastic, in the apartment for the several days between his death and burial; Ronay's uneasy perception being that she'd really have liked to keep Jim that way forever, that his presence "gave her comfort." Well, I guess that *is* one way of ensuring someone doesn't leave you—or maybe it's just the only way Pam knew she could have kept him . . .)

So: the coverup, the untruth, the falsehood, the taradiddle, the subreption, the whopper, the lie. Even Oliver Stone, that soi-disant crusader for ugly truth, goes along with the furtherance of the fairytale: Pam's parents are said to have given him no choice, requiring him to do so as ransom for permission to use Jim's poetry—poetry to whose copyright they had fallen heir after their daughter's death intestate. They even try to prevent Pam being shown, in the movie, as any sort of drug fan at all; and in the event there is but one scene that does so. But the biggest ransom demand the Coursons reportedly make is that Oliver Stone cannot depict their daughter as having had anything whatsoever to do with Jim Morrison's death.

When I hear that, during production, from several very highly placed sources indeed (it will later be confirmed in print), I know beyond the last of my doubts, and they had never been very many, that Pam had had *everything* to do with Jim's death. So Oliver caves, and the Coursons win: The movie will immortalize Pamela Susan as a sweet, ditzy, much-put-upon, pixie-voiced flower child, who through the evil influences of decadent Eurotrash (Count Jean) and the unending excesses of Jim Morrison is forced for reasons of purest self-defense into the martyrdom of sluttery and smack. Nary a mention in the film, natch, of the profession she pursued after Jim's death, just an ambiguous postscript to the effect that Pam "joined" Jim three years later—oh, like she just caught a later plane, I guess.

So that when I read Alan Ronay's remarkable public unburdening (And why now, I wonder? After twenty years' stony silence? Did the statute of limitations finally run out? Did the need for penitence and shriving overwhelm him at last? Or was Paris-Match just too persuasive?), I am uncomfortably aware of a really nasty feeling of smug satisfaction. (Hey, I'm only human . . .) Right there alongside the fury and the grief and loss renewed, the tears and frustration and anger at the utter useless stupidity of it all, I am puritanically pleased that the truth is out at last. The goddess Themis (there's only one Goddess . . .), protector of the just, punisher of the guilty, has spoken; don't name your boutique after Her unless you're prepared to take the consequences. Justice may be late, but justice always comes: Public images will require radical rethinking; revisionistic biographers and ill-informed movie types and fans who have sung Pam's praises at Jim's grave will know at last just what sort of creature it is they have been lauding: an unfaithful junkie before Jim's death and a plain whore after. And they will know too that she died a killer as well.

But when my wrath cools at last, and I get past my own judgmental, angry self-righteousness, I see that in the end it still makes little difference, I was right about that from the start. Unrecovered, Jim would have been dead sooner or later; Pam may have given him the smack, urged it or even forced it on him, but Jim was the one who put it up his nose. And whether that freely chosen act was to him "suicide [or] slow capitulation," as he himself once put it, only Jim knows for sure.

Pam existed after Jim's death in a prison far worse than any French slammer: the prison of her own guilt. Even I could not have wished on her a harsher punishment. Her hellish life after Jim was a fitting sentence, her own end a verdict she passed on herself; and both verdict and sentence are perfect justice. Themis is not to be denied: Sometimes instant karma is the best and most merciful after all; and my prayer for Pamela (oh yes, and often) is that she will manage things better next time around.

So now this book is written, the tale that for twenty years I had hoped I would never have to write, had sworn mighty oaths I would never commit to print, had prayed that others would tell well enough and true enough and fair enough that I would never have to break my silence and tell it myself.

It didn't work out that way, obviously, and the portrait of James Douglas Morrison that emerged in the two decades since his death was one of a posturing, drunken, sadistic, drug-benumbed clown who couldn't keep his pants zipped in public—or in private, either.

He was that, of course. But that wasn't all he was.

You never really know another person. The only thing you ever can claim to *know*, at the last, unqualified, is that side of his life which has touched a side of your life. All the rest is hearsay evidence. And that one little bit you think you are so sure of—well, even that could be hallucination. Given that this was, after all, the 60's, maybe it was.

For certainly the Jim I knew, the Jim I have tried here to evoke, is not the same Jim others have chronicled in print and on film. No two people who knew Jim Morrison seem to have known the same man, even; how then can those who never met him be expected to get it right? You have only to compare the accounts: He was an alcoholic/No, he hardly ever drank when he was with me. He was cold/No, he was loving. He was a cruel monster/No, he was considerate and generous and sensitive. He was impotent/No, he was a strong lover. He was a pig/No, he was a prince. All you know is what touches you. One saw what one saw, knew whom one knew; and so of course did everyone else.

And, seeing so, knowing so, all one can do in the end is speak one's own truth; no more nor less valid than anyone else's truth. For twenty years I have kept my counsel on the truth that was our own, mine and Jim's, and perhaps that was my mistake. Perhaps that silence only served us both ill, betrayed us both into the hands of the honestly ignorant or the willfully misjudging or the deliberately malicious; only made it easier for the vacuum to be filled, in the absence of real substance, with all manner of cruel and hostile and invidious speculation. Half-truths, or less, set forth as gospel by those who did not, or could not, or would not, know or accept what another's Jim had been.

The clichéd wisdom is that truth hurts. Well, truth *never* hurts. It's only the crap that people go around passing *off* as truth that gets in there and gnaws. And so there comes a time, inevitably, when it is at last less painful simply to speak one's truth and let folk make of it what they will. They will in any case; but at least I shall know that I have set out our truth as we knew it and lived it, as only we can know it, as a small fragment of the Morrison mosaic necessary—whether some like it or not—to the true finished picture. Anything more than that is not mine to command: But the more true perspectives there are on Jim Morrison, from the more differing viewpoints, the more dimensions of his reality can be the more truly known. I cannot make people believe; but I have done what I could to bear witness.

For myself, then, I only know, and thus have spoken of, the Jim I knew and loved, who loved me (oh yes), and who does not seem to be the man whom others have written of, or put on film, or turned into some sort of cash cow: the Jim who was the shy, funny Romantic; the courtly Southern gallant; the creative genius who wrote some of the most stunning songs of a great musical era, songs that will outlast forever the bubble context of their time; the man with whom an intelligent woman could reasonably have fallen deeply in love; the man who could have fallen in love with an intelligent woman; the man who could make a commitment to her that will last past time and beyond law; the man who became increasingly trapped by the iconic persona he had so ironically invented, and who was destroyed by it in the end.

As for the truth of it, Jim knows; and he knows I know, and to me he is the only one who matters, who has ever mattered or ever will matter. What others think or say is not our concern: We did not have as much time together as should have been, or might have been, or as others had; but I will set what Jim and I shared against anyone's challenge.

Time is not the sole nor yet the final judge of anything real, anything that lasts. It's not over yet between Jim and me, nor will it ever be; we haven't yet finished with one another. We will never be apart, and I would sooner have been handfast with him for one year than married to any other man for fifty.

PART SIX

Say that you saw
& did not fear
Say that I loved
& did not run
Say how I
Died

Why are you doing this interview with yourself?

Because nobody else ever asks me the right questions, okay?

Well, you've had a whole book to explain yourself in.

Not exactly. Throughout the book, as I'm sure you've noticed, I have very deliberately refrained from hindsight, except in one or two instances where it couldn't be avoided (and even then it was more like foreshadowing future knowledge). It's been strange, really: Writing the book as I wrote in my journals and notebooks back then—present tense, first person; but knowing all the time that it's really twenty years later, that I know all this stuff I didn't know then, about Jim and about myself. All this new knowledge, insights, perceptions—I thought it was important that people should know.

But I couldn't put it in anywhere else: If I'd included it in the relevant passages, everybody would have been totally confused in time, never knowing whether I was talking about how I felt and what I knew in 1969 or '70, or whether I meant how I was feeling and what I was knowing now, or whatever. It would have choked the flow of the book—falsified the contextual memory, impeded the narrative—and this is, after all, a story. A love story, mostly; the vehicle for emotion, not reflection.

But the reflection is important too: Indeed, the love story cannot be understood without it. I've had twenty years to think about all this, and in my own poor opinion, some of the things I've thought matter—to me, if to no one else. I wanted them known, that's all, on the record: to say what I wanted to say, what needed to be said, the way I wanted to say it.

Besides, at least with me interviewing myself, I can be sure there'll be *one* interview where I won't be misquoted—and I can ask myself harder questions than any interviewer alive.

So why did you write this book?

Because of Jim and me. Because I got tired of the thing owning me, and *I* wanted to own *it* at the end of the day. To take it away from what others have made of it, to make it Jim's and mine again. To forgive him. To forgive myself. Because the pain of not having written finally outweighed the pain of writing. So that, having read this, remembering Jim, people might think of something more real and true and fine than what they usually think of when they remember him. Because it is the last thing I have to do for him, the final thing I can do for us.

How do you feel about people saying you're just cashing in on Jim like everybody else?

Well, first off, I'm not *like* everybody else. As for cashing in, that's more problematic. For twenty years my pride (and resolve) was never to make a penny out of my association with Jim; and, for twenty years, I haven't. I wasn't with Jim for the money when he was alive, and I'm not in it for the money now. I'd have kept to that resolve still, if I were in a position to do so, but that is not the case. Anyway, considering all the people who have for the past two decades been growing rich off Jim's name and life and glory, most of whom have far less valid connection with him than I have, I don't think anyone's really got a right to be throwing this in my face. And, if they do, fuckem. I think of it as astral alimony; and Jim would be the first one to tell me not to fret about it.

I've always thought that the people who loved Jim best and most, the ones who cared for him as a person and not for what he could do to enhance their bank accounts or their self-esteem or their gross receipts—the ones Jim loved best in return—are the ones who boasted least about his place in their lives, the ones who weren't utterly consumed by him, the ones who had a life of their own before him and a life of their own after.

The people who have put Jim and their love for him and his for them into the context of their lives, not made *him* the context: *Those* are Jim's real friends. Not the ones who see him as a cottage industry, a meal ticket, a windfall they can grub up—venal saprophytes with dubious credentials, carrion-feeders from here to eternity, people Jim had neither use nor time for in life and less in death: the self-appointed or the court-justified, people with whom he had no kinship he would himself ever have acknowledged, who had to go to bed with the lawyers and doubtful pronouncements before they could belly up to the trough. Jim had better friends than that, truer kin; and he knew it.

You don't talk much about the other Doors here.

Well, because Jim didn't; and naturally I take my cue from him. Besides, there's no reason why I should; the book is about Jim and me. I met them a few times, on social occasions or by chance; I interviewed John and Robby once—that's about it.

Save for speaking twice with John, in the summer of 1990 (he called me, to ask if he could use a photograph I had taken of Jim's grave for his own book—I said yes, sure; as a result, I am not once mentioned in the book and my name on the photo credit is misspelled; I guess I'll just never learn . . .), I haven't talked to any of them for twenty-odd years. As for Doors associates, I have spoken once with one of them (who reportedly later said in a radio interview that Jim never got married in a witchcraft ceremony; I mean, was he *there?* Did he *see* us? How would *he* know??); never with Jim's parents or Pam's parents or anyone of that ilk. Jerry Hopkins and I are friends, but otherwise I stay far, far from the borders of Doorsland, and that's how I plan to keep it.

*What is your opinion of the well-publicized acrimony between the Doors et al.
on the one hand and Pam's/Jim's parents on the other? Or that between the
Coursons and the Morrisons, for that matter—they did go to court over control
of Jim's estate?*

A plague on all their houses . . .   You're asking my opinion of the sort
of people who'd arm-wrestle for money over the dead bodies of their
children? People whose own son claimed they were dead rather than
have anything to do with them? People who never once visited his grave
until the movie publicity apparently made them think that cleaning up
the site might be politic, or that a quick belated visit was maybe the
least they could do for the money? No comment.

*Thoughts on Pamela Susan Courson? What about these new depictions of her
as having been tough and forceful, that she really pussywhipped Jim and called
all the shots in the relationship?*

The Redheaded Remora? The only shots she ever called were the ones
in her arms . . .   As for the New Thinking on Pam, well, consider
the sources. You generally find that sort of revisionist swill oozing out of
the word processors of people who needed to suck up to her parents for
permission to use poetry quotations and suchlike, in books, or, say, a
movie . . .
      For my part, I can speak only of the woman I met, the woman Jim
occasionally spoke of, the woman some of her friends told me of; I have
tried not to weight the stats.

So?

The Pam I knew was a user—in all senses of the word.
      By no means charmless, extremely pretty, she had the incredible
strength of the weak and the grasping and the parasitical; of those who
feed on anyone rather than take the responsibility for feeding (and not
just in the alimentary sense) themselves.
      As far as I know, though I'd gladly be told otherwise, Pam never
had a real job in her entire life (lazy; sense of entitlement). She couldn't
even manage to run the boutique Jim bought for her (no attention span;
irresponsible), and gunned a truck through the shop window to hasten
its demise (breaks her own toys). After Jim's death, one of her closest
friends told me she had reportedly all but driven her own parents to

bankruptcy (though they came out well in the black after *her* death), ended up selling her jewelry and her camper, and went from there to selling her body. I mean, had the woman never heard of WORK? Was the exotic concept of GETTING A JOB to actually EARN A LIVING totally foreign to her? Or did she just think she was entitled to be taken care of and didn't mind too much who did it—Jim, her folks, a pimp?

There have been some suggestions made that it was her "incredible love" for Jim, her strength of commitment to him, that really destroyed her. Do you think that's what it was, and that they really loved each other?

Oh, sure. Though "incredible" might be just the word for it . . .   No, I think there was probably genuine feeling beween them, at least sometimes. They'd been through a lot together, and that always creates a bond; and sometimes that bond's hard to cast off, even though it would be best if it were.

But I also think they loved one another's weaknesses, not strengths; they fed off each other's addictions and self-indulgences. Frankly, that's not my idea of love. People seem idiotically impressed by the fact that Pam never really left Jim: Well, of *course* she never left him, she wasn't *that* kind of stupid! Where else would she find somebody to support her so well for so little substance?

That's probably also partly why he found it so hard to make the break with her he told me so often he had made, or wanted to make: They needed that hellish permission they gave each other, needed it too much to risk losing, though each of them would probably have been far happier with other partners. But other lovers would have made too many real demands; would have demanded, indeed, that they be real, and it was a lot easier not to be.

I think Jim tried several times, perhaps most seriously (and unsuccessfully) in our own relationship, to break this cycle of dependence, to get into something a little more normal, a little more equal and substantial and real; but it was way too little much too late.

What struck you most about her?

Well, she seemed to have no inner life or higher self whatsoever: no spirituality, no interior resources, no intellectual curiosity or life of the mind. I never could figure out what she and Jim talked about.

Basically, she was a totally dependent junkie who had nothing in her life but Jim; and she was, understandably if not admirably, maniacally jealous and paranoiacally terrified of losing him. Well, why *wouldn't* she be scared of losing him? Somebody as bright as Jim wasn't going to hang around someone like her forever—and he was her meal ticket, her social identity, and apparently all the sense of self-worth the poor girl ever had.

In the end, Pam was a sad, sorry sort of person, not anyone I would have cared to have for a friend. I don't know what her childhood was like—I understand she came from the same sort of authoritarian mulch as Jim—but there are many reasons besides inner insufficiency for addiction. Abuse, trauma, neglect, heredity, environment—who can say where it starts, to end in someone like Pam?

As for the various apologists who zealously assert how much she loved Jim, well, let's just see, shall we: She was flagrantly unfaithful to him while he was alive and became a prostitute after his death. She had a heroin habit that she concealed from him out of guilt and shame, yet seems to have had no problem about supplying him with the scag that killed him. She let him die bleeding, unattended and alone, while she slept off her own smack attack down the hall. I don't think it gets too much more loving than that, do you?

Biographers of Jim have made much of the fact that Pamela "edited" his poetry, that she encouraged him endlessly to concentrate on his poems rather than on his songs; indeed, to quit the Doors and just be a poet.

Well, at least we know whom to blame . . .   I've always contended that the best of Jim's poetry *is* his songs. Besides, my idea of editing someone's poetry is just a teensy bit more complicated than "[going] through it and [taking] out all the fucks and shits." (And do you *really* think Pam would have let him quit the band? A full-time poet could hardly have kept her in smack and Saint-Laurent . . .)

You've been much more charitable about Pamela in other interviews you've done. How come now you're such a bitch about her?

I didn't know then that she had been the proximate cause of Jim's death, did I . . .   Besides, I didn't trust the interviewers to get it right. It's a complex opinion I have of her, after all, and rather than have them distort everything I said and then blame me for sour grapes on top of it,

I chose to emphasize (perhaps overemphasize) the positive: She was pretty, she was charming, and so on.

Also, and by no means least, I wanted to make Jim look like less of an asshole for associating with her. But I truly do believe that, as Jac Holzman told me after Jim's death, Jim needed us both. He needed the "Oh Jim, you're a poet!" he got from her, and he needed the "Take *that*, Lizard King!" he got from me.

Actually, I think Jim just had his first and second wives at the same time: Pam was first-wife stuff—sweet, pretty, girl-who-knew-him-when and who was content to live in his shadow—and I was more your second-wife material, with a career and identity apart from his. Legally, of course, he never married either of us, or anyone else—I was the only one who got any sort of wedding ceremony—but neither Pam nor I was any more Jim's legally wedded wife than Ray was. You could call it extralegal bigamy—with activities on the side.

But Jim and I hardly ever talked about Pam. She had nothing to do with us. Oliver Stone washed her face for the movie because he had to kiss up to her parents; Meg Ryan opined in an interview that "Pamela thought she was evolving into someone who was really whole," that "*they* [Italics mine—PK] made her who she was." Yeah, right—which just proves that the dog must have eaten Meg's actor's homework that particular school night: I doubt Pam had ever had half so reflective a thought in her entire life.

It was Pamela herself who made herself who she was, and what she ended as, and how she ended. And as a friend of mine once said in another context, "You make your own limitations."

Summation?

She was a slut, a junkie, a whore and possibly a murderess. She was less than honest with her friends and family, and she fed heroin to the man she claimed to love, leaving him dying while she nodded out. She didn't have a brain in her head or a moral in her body, and in my court she killed Jim and should have been tried for it. And I guess she has been. Pity she didn't OD a few years sooner—Jim might have actually stood a chance.

She should be damn glad she's dead, because if she weren't I'd kill her with my bare hands. I hope she died in agony, and I'm only sorry I couldn't have watched. Any more questions?

Uh, no, I think you've made your feelings pretty clear. Let's move on. In the various Morrison biographies, you've been treated rather—variously. Some chroniclers slight you or ignore you, others are kinder. Any opinions?

A great many, most of them unprintable. Actually, I think the difficulty Jim's biographers seem to have with my role in Jim's life is that it's been so uncanonical—up to now, anyway. It's not part of the Official Story, doesn't fit the narrow parameters of the accepted mythos; and my keeping so silent for so long hasn't exactly enhanced my visibility in his legend.

But their own stereotypical—and male—thinking is also to blame: They are confronted with an admittedly untraditional relationship, and they don't know what to do with it, so after they describe it (usually straightforwardly enough), they then feel compelled to hang condescending little labels on it like "weird" or "bizarre" or "grotesque"or "eccentric" or whatever. It's almost as if they're afraid of it. Well, they're men. Guys. Not women. I don't really expect them to understand.

But I put it to you that if these same writers had been describing their own similar relationship, they would *never* have used such words, or seen it so. It would be perfectly understandable; it seems weird or bizarre only because it's a woman dealing with a love relationship as if she were a man—a *person*.

I did not take the traditional rock wife's role in my romance with Jim, and it seems that his biographers, lost in sex-chauvinism or wish-fulfillment, cannot get it into their tiny minds that I didn't *want* to be with Jim all the time, didn't *need* or even *wish* him to support me, didn't *care* that my marriage was unsanctioned by the laws of the State of New York (to me, the gods are a slightly higher authority). I had other things in mind, and a life and career and creativity of my own; and *I* chose to share them with Jim (not the other way round), the way *I* wanted to.

It's the way only a fairly secure woman, or any man, might think of a relationship; and the fact that here is a woman insisting on such an arrangement, twenty years ago, at a very young age, really seems to throw them, and they don't know how to speak of it; they feel impelled to diminish it, downplay it, ridicule it or dismiss it or even claim it never happened.

Well, I say the hell with them all. It happened, all right. It was what it was, whatever that might have been, and it was what Jim and

I both wanted. It was real. And I won't go away, and I won't apologize for it, and I won't keep silent about it, and I certainly won't pretend it never was. Those days are over.

But about the Jim books themselves?

Oh, those . . .   Well, with about two and a half exceptions at the time of this writing, I don't really think much of them. Not only are they for the most part indifferently if not poorly written, they're full of factual errors: things like Pam being buried in Jim's plot in Paris (unless she's been moved, as of 1992 she was still where she's been since 1974—in an urn in a mausoleum in a cemetery near Disneyland), or Jim's family background being Irish Catholic (that's *mine*! Try Scottish Presbyterian—that's what he told me, anyway), stuff that even the most basic plodding researcher should have managed to get right. And if they can't be accurate about stuff like that (I even corrected, for one recent book that actually took two people to produce, the spelling of the name of the Paris street in which Jim's flat was located; they'd picked up the error from the Rolling Stone obituary piece and never bothered to check further), how can I really hope for accuracy about Jim and me?

Let's not forget that most of these books are written by people who NEVER KNEW JIM PERSONALLY. Let's not forget that most of them are WRITTEN BY MEN (with testicular agendas probably best left unspoken of). And, more than anything, let's not *ever* forget that most of these books are written by people who needed to grovel before the various controllers of Jim's creative legacies—who have very different agendas, in which I figure not at all.

Which, of course, is fine. But now it's my turn, and I certainly have agendas of my own, which have to one extent or another been served herein. I have tried not to be too Procrustean about it, hope that I have not tortured too many facts into submission. Honesty in recounting, honesty in hindsight: I hope too that I have let events and actions and indeed people speak for themselves. I won't be the judge of that.

You seem to remember everything you ever wore.

Not everything. But no woman *ever* forgets what she was wearing at majorly significant moments with a man she loved.

And everything you ever said.

Again, not everything. Obviously, I couldn't recount five-hour conversations word-for-word even if I could recall them; you can't do books in real time any more than you can do movies so. All conversations represented here, then, are condensed, in that sense; necessarily. But every word reported here is genuine, and I stand by my quotes. I was trained as a journalist, I know how to remember things, especially when taking notes is impossible (as with the movie, for instance; Oliver would have gone ballistic if he'd seen me taking notes on the set, so I took notes where he couldn't see me doing it—in my head).

In most cases, I went straight for my notebooks the minute Jim left the bed, or the room, or the house, or the planet. I'm a writer; that's what I do, write things down. I have included in this book, therefore, only what I could remember (some things are burned into your brain . . .) or what I had written down somewhere. It's not so remarkable, if you think about it—consider the memory feats of oral cultures, for instance—and if it had been *you* with Jim, I don't think you'd have forgotten a whole lot either.

Up until the movie came out, you were pretty much a mystery figure in Jim's life—by your own deliberate choice, I might add—which only made it easier for people who were ignorant of the real story to dismiss you as "just one of hundreds." In retrospect, has anything angered you about your having chosen to keep such a low profile? Do you regret choosing that way?

I don't *ever* regret choosing a way of dignity and reserve, but yeah, a couple of things piss me off.

First, the widespread belief, put about by individuals with bread of their own to butter, that Jim and Pam were married. Without going into all that again, tout court, they weren't. In truth, both of them, on separate occasions and totally unprompted, told me in no uncertain terms that they were not married, and never had been married, and never would be married. Now maybe I might not have believed Jim (at least not at first), but I sure as hell had to believe Pam . . . Not only that, but she described herself to the French authorities as Jim's "cousin" (as, presumably, only a blood relative could be allowed to bury him, and the status of "cousin" was less checkable than that of "wife") and "friend," never as his wife (though according to one source, apparently her lawyers actually changed the Père-Lachaise records—*three years after her death*—

to read "wife" and not "cousin"—well, one fiction for another; presumably to give her family more of a lock on her claim to Jim's estate). She is listed as his "friend" on the official U.S. Embassy death certificate (guess that one was a little harder to creatively tamper with), and Jim's *own will*—naming Pam his heir—states that he is an unmarried person. So much for that; I wouldn't have given so much time to it, except that the contrary is so widely believed even now.

The other thing is the accusation that I murdered Jim by witchcraft. This was published first—my name carefully not specified—in the earliest of the Morrison biographies, and apparently some of Jim's more, ah, credulous fans fell for it.

Let's get a few things straight, kids: I wasn't the one with Jim in Paris. I wasn't the one who gave him the heroin. And I certainly wasn't the one who took it. I loved Jim. Jim loved me. He handfasted me. I didn't kill him. I would have died for him, and I nearly did, and I would still, and I may yet; and if certain elements can't accept or handle that, too bad.

In my grief and long seclusion, I never really thought that anyone could possibly be stupid enough to take this suggestion of a semiliterate ex-gofer at all seriously: that I had murdered the love of my life and the father of my child by sorcerous means. And never in my worst nightmares did I think I would have to be defending myself years later against the still-circulating toxic fantasies of a piece of feculent vermin with all the intellectual capacity of pillow drool.

Unlike certain other people (I can hear Jim snickering now, "You really mean 'lesser mortals,' don't you, honey?", and he's absolutely right, I do), I have never lied about this and I take full responsibility for what I do and say and mean. I didn't have to say anything about any of it: I could have kept quiet about the handfasting—indeed, about Jim's and my entire relationship—and spared myself notoriety, ill will, lascivious curiosity (that means all you delightful souls wondering about our sex life), and a great deal of pain. I didn't have to publicly declare myself a witch, either, and risk ridicule, suspicion and people wanting to burn me at the stake. By choosing silence, or continuing in semi-silence, I could have preserved my peace and privacy, could have kept my Jim for myself.

But that peace and privacy would have been bought at the price of lying, by that self-same silence, about the thing I value most; and that was too high a price to pay. I'm not sorry, ever, for finally making known the whole truth about Jim and me, here or elsewhere. People may still not like it, may even choose not to believe it, but that's their business. Mine was telling it, and now I have.

You were very hard on Jim as a poet, even in print. Pamela would be telling him to quit the Doors, that he was a poet and not a rock star, and you would be hitting him on the snout with a rolled-up thesaurus and telling him to go sit in a corner and reread Wordsworth and Aristotle.

Yes, and he knew I was right, too. Pam told him what she thought he wanted to hear, perhaps thinking he would love her for telling him; I told him what he knew he needed to hear, whether he wanted to hear it or not. Jim had as healthy a creative ego as any artist, but no creative person, ego or not, wants to be told something is good when it isn't—you're grateful for the loyalty, but sooner or later you have to be contemptuous of their judgment . . . and of them.

Jim paid me the supreme compliment of acknowledging my fairness: He knew I would be honest, if hard on him; he knew I wasn't cowed by him and was every bit as literate as he was. He knew there would be integrity in what I told him; no personality crucifixions. If I gave him a belt in the poetical chops, it would be on strictly literary terms, for strictly literary failings. He knew, too, that I would tell him where it was good; where it was right on track, where it went off the rails, and what he could do to re-rail it.

That he would think so, would trust me so, was more than a compliment: It was an honor, and I didn't dare be anything less than scrupulously truthful with him, in reviews or in private. (And any man who could read the reviews I gave his poetry and still want to go through with a wedding ceremony—and a ceremony involving a knife—was obviously not only a man in love but a very brave man indeed.)

I would have failed him, though, had I not told him where the flaws lay, had I been as slavishly (or self-servingly) 'supportive' as Pam. I can speak to this from my own work, how I want people to look at it. I _want_ them to tell me where it's weak or scant or wrong; and I _require_ it of friends. How else can I fix it? Besides, any honest craftsman—poet or carpenter—knows very well where the shaky spots are; you just like to have another of your guild confirm it.

To my mind, Jim's poetry was always too self-indulgent in too many places, too sloppy and self-referential (in the worst way: All art is by nature self-referential, it has to be; but Jim's poems did nothing to bridge the gap between reader and poet, and that's a flaw in any kind of building) for its, or his, own good. He was such a master of word tension and freight—how much he could pack into one word or phrase or symbol!—in his songwriting that I always felt disappointed the poems didn't measure up.

Not that they would always have failed to do so: I think he would soon have found his creative footing outside his songs, and I doubt very much if poetry would have been the end of it, or even the main of it. He was fascinated with my plans for novels, for instance—asked me endless questions about how you put together something of that length and scope, how the characters come, how the plot is worked out, how you handle the exposition, how you maintain your artistic discipline for so long and keep your control over so many things—and confided that he would love someday to be able to write fiction himself, but didn't know if he had the discipline. He said novels seemed to him like *being* a movie, you had to be writer and actors and director and cameraman and costumer and producer and everything else—poems, he said, at least had the advantage of being shorter.

Yet in spite of my own feelings about Jim's poetic works, I have very little patience with self-proclaimed literati who sneer and jeer, at Jim for daring to write and at us for presuming to admire. To them there is little to say—they wouldn't hear it anyway—except that they are more than welcome to the sort of thing they apparently prefer, of which I hold the same opinion, in spades, as they have of Jim's efforts or indeed of my own.

What do you think of Jim's posthumously published books, Wilderness *and* The American Night?

Although I find it rather amusing that Jim and I should both have new books in print, I haven't read the works you speak of; and wouldn't read them even if someone held a gun to my head.

I don't approve of posthumous publishing. The idea of someone who did not create the work (and who is perhaps not even a creative person at all) daring to presume, even with the best will in the world, that he or she can determine what was in the creator's mind is to me absolutely chilling. Such an invasion: And the image of people rooting through Jim's notebooks like hogs after truffles, in search of marketable nuggets, is not particularly edifying either, however noble they claim their motives to be. Jim never meant anyone but himself to see those unfinished or half-finished works; I'm perfectly willing to give his "editors" the benefit of the doubt on motive—but I still think it's a tacky and reprehensible practice, and I don't think Jim would disagree.

There have been frequent charges made, in the movie and a few books, of Jim's alleged violence and brutality, actual physical abuse, against women he purported to care for.

Not with me. Never the least tiniest hint of physical abuse, though I did hit him, of course, that one time . . . In fact, until the film and those book accounts started appearing, I never even *heard* about any alleged brutality, to Pam or to other women.

Were you ever afraid of Jim?

Never. *NEVER*. But, sometimes, although I loved him more than I've loved anyone before or since, I didn't always like him. I may not have been afraid *of* him, but I was often afraid *for* him.

It's difficult to think on now. I never saw Jim violent ever—physically violent, that is; we certainly had enough killer *emotional* scenes—and I saw him out-of-control drunk only once. If he had come back from Paris and moved in with me in New York, as he'd been promising, I wonder now how long that exemplary behavior I saw would have lasted. Assuming that those stories are even partly true, how long before he started throwing *me* around the bedroom, threatening *me* with knives, locking *me* in burning closets?

Probably not long, *if* indeed that's really what went on, because I doubt if he could have controlled his drinking the way he did when the relationship was long-distance and our times together weeks and months between. How long would I have put up with it if he *had* gotten violent? Not one fucking second.

And I think part of the attraction I had for Jim stemmed from the fact that he knew I wouldn't put up with it, that I did strike back, that I would stand up to him. He knew that if he wanted to be with me he would have to behave, that I wouldn't take any of his bullshit; knew too that he couldn't manage to stay off the bottle, not seriously, for more than a short period, and that's maybe why a week or so at a time was about as long as we were ever together.

I think it was the greatest compliment he could have paid me, that he drank so little when he was with me, that drugs too (save for the very occasional joint or line, which I myself enjoyed) were out of it altogether. But it was a compliment he could not sustain; and a compliment he never managed to pay himself.

Though I never saw Jim violent, I surely saw him vicious: emotional abuse, not physical. He could and did say the most cutting, flaying things; and, sometimes, so did I. For what it's worth, Jim was a real person. Sometimes he was one way, and sometimes he was another. Sometimes he had reasons, and sometimes he didn't. Just like anybody else.

If he beat up other women, sodomized them, as has been said, maybe it was because he thought that was what they expected or deserved from him (I'm not *condoning* this; just speculating). If he didn't do any of that with me, maybe it was because he thought it wasn't what I expected or deserved. If he didn't drink to the point of impotent oblivion with me, maybe it was because he simply enjoyed the physical aspect of our relationship too much to allow it to be diminished or impaired.

Why do you think Jim was like this?

Nobody ever said to Jim "That's ENOUGH!" until long after it was way more than enough—Enough!, Or, Too much, as dear Blake put it. That's why the bullshit and the sadism (emotional or physical) went as far as they did: he was always testing people's limits, and very often he got away with going much too far. Jim never laid a hand on me in physical violence, but he certainly made up for it in other forms of torture. I saw my full share of Jim's dark side: He could be meaner than anybody in the world, and people who claim he wasn't like that are just kidding themselves. Jim *was* like that; but Jim wasn't *only* like that, or even *mostly* like that. I wouldn't have put up with him for five minutes if he had been.

I personally believe that some of the roots of Jim's cruelty go far and deep into his past: Though we discussed his family on a number of occasions, Jim never really spelled out in so many words what the thing had been to cause him to hate his parents so virulently, though he dropped a few hints. It must have been terrible, for his was the coldest, most undying hatred I have ever seen—Celts know how to hate—and I would never have pressed him to tell me. But children love utterly and unconditionally until their trust is betrayed; it takes a *lot* to turn a child's love to hate, it doesn't just happen because of quarrels over homework or haircuts. And, as in adults, the hatred is always in direct proportion to the love betrayed—he must have loved them very much, to be so angry and hating and hurting for so long after he'd cut them loose. Only Jim knows if they deserved either the love or the hate.

Still, childhood trauma—assuming the speculation has at least some basis in fact—and resultant escape into alcoholism, though a common story in recovery confessionals, were not considered by me as grounds for permitting Jim to act out as he pleased. And maybe that sounds harsh, but I wasn't about to let him compensate for a hellish past by allowing a hellish present and condoning a hellish future. I didn't think forgiving more abuse was the way to have helped him, and I busted him on it every chance I got.

And, you know, it often seemed as if Jim was *glad* I called him on it, as if (Mommy!) he *wanted* somebody who loved him to say, "No, that's too much, you've gone too far there, I love you but you can't do that to me, and if you do I won't stay around for you to do it to me again." It was the one thing he wanted; but it was also the one thing he couldn't endure when he got it.

So the physical violence that's been alleged—

As I say, I never saw it, just the psychological terror tactics, which only pissed me off. I suppose it's possible, but I just don't think so. He never gave me a vibe of it, anyway, and I think I'd have picked up on *that*. Although other people close to him—members of his own band, even— have said they thought him psychotic, capable of violence or even murder, I never thought that, and I was never afraid of him. Maybe because I just figured I could beat him to the punch or the draw or the sword any day of the week; but I don't believe Jim would ever have physically harmed me.

So, I never feared Jim or the violence that may or may not have been in him; but I certainly did fear the violence he brought out in *me*. He made me madder than anyone else I was ever with; angrier, too. I've never lifted a hand in violence from that day to this; but Jim made you feel and do and think things you never felt or did or thought before, and not all of them were good or wise.

Why did you decide to come out about being a witch, as you did for the first time to Jerry Hopkins when he interviewed you for No One Here Gets Out Alive?

Because it's the truth. Because I was tired of paganism and the Craft being labeled black magic or Satanism or evil fu. Because I wanted to show people that it was possible to be a witch, and be known to be a witch, and yet also be seen and known to be an intelligent, reasonable, religious, moral, good, unfanatic person just like anyone else.

The downside is that once you declare yourself out of the broom closet, as it were—whether you call yourself witch or Celtic pagan or follower of the Old Religion or whatever—you inevitably run head-on into stereotypical and bigoted thinking. After the movie came out, newspaper hacks labeled me a blood-drinking predatoress or devil-sex practitioner or black-magic worker; TV critics (and even some movie ads!) described me as a depraved Satanist. (Thanks a bunch, Oliver!)

People are ignorant and uninformed about Goddess-worship, paganism, the Craft; and because they know nothing they fear (and secretly hope) the worst. Well, sorry to disappoint all you God-fearing souls, but pagans are merely people who happen to worship older gods than yours, and fear is not part of our package.

It's just a different way of looking at God, Who is neither male nor female, or beyond both male and female, or both male and female together. Even the early Christians, before Paul and the other patriarchalists got their mitts on the wheel, saw a feminine face to the Divine Power: the Sophia, the Shekinah, the Ruach, the One who brooded upon the face of the waters—God the Mother. (And just what do you think Mary's all about? Actually, you'll find Miraculous Mother and Divinely Born Child motifs in every world religion from ancient Egypt to Micronesia.)

I worship God/Goddess in Celtic forms because that is my ethnic and cultural heritage; it has spiritual resonance for me, and meaning, and logic. I'm not only a witch: I also belong to a couple of esoteric Christian orders, orders that make up in tolerance what some hierarchs might think they lack in orthodoxy. We respect and worship and acknowledge all traditions, all under the love of God the Father and God the Mother, God the Daughter and God the Son; and if, pagan or Christian, you have a problem with that, all I can say, in caritas, is, Go pray about it.

I personally see more sense in worshipping the Great Mother of us all than in adoring someone who was born in a cave on December 25 while shepherds watched, who grew up to redeem mankind. Oh, sorry, did you think I meant Jesus? No, I was talking about Mithras, actually (check it out!) . . .   The point is that Christianity was not above stealing from earlier religions—faiths it then immediately branded as heathen devilish idolatry—to make itself more acceptable to recruits in its shaky early days.

The Craft, at least, has its roots in life, the life of the land, the seasons, the natural forces, the life of the creatures who live upon the land, the great cycle of living and dying and living again—and, these days, the life of the planet itself, the system, the galaxy. It's the true Green religion; it teaches a respect and reverence for the natural world—soul and body working in harmony with nature—where other religions seem to have nothing but contempt for it. And just see where that's got us.

So you don't believe in a Devil, an evil force?

I never said that. Certainly there are devils, personifications of the ugly spirit of divisiveness and negativity and hatred; witches see a lot of that sort of thing, and very often it's directed straight at them. It's ironic, that so often the people who accuse pagans of being devil worshipers are doing more of the Devil's work than any truly faithful witch has ever done.

We don't do the Dark's work, and we do not love those who do it. So don't call me a devil worshiper because I pray to the Goddess, or because my wedding involved a couple of drops of blood, freely shed; and in return I will not hold you personally responsible for a few things done in Jesus's name, like the Crusades, the Inquisition, Jimmy Swaggart or the Vatican bank scandal.

Maybe if more attention were paid to the Light that is in other ways besides one's own, rather than to imagined darkness put there by fear and ignorance, God in all God's wondrous forms and shapes and faces would be far better served. God has no limits; it's blasphemy to put limits on a Supreme Being. God has as many faces as there are souls to look upon them; it's only the bigoted, frightened and jealous and terrified that someone else might have a bigger or better piece of God than they do, who seek to limit God so.

If each of us sees a different face of God, knows God by a different syllable of the Divine Name, surely that does not lessen God but expand mankind. The more faces and names and traditions of God we have, the more God we have. Where is it written that God must be looked upon from a single window, known by a single name, held to a single path or gender or function?

In the end, we're all talking about, and praying to, and being loved by, the same Power. It's merely a matter of personal choice what we call Her.

Do you think Jim truly believed in the shamanistic principles he seems to have practiced?

Absolutely. He was very serious about it indeed, extremely well-informed about all its nature and requirements. Jim wanted God desperately: He had a God-sized emptiness in his life that he was trying to fill until the day he died. That was one reason he suggested our handfasting: It was a ritual out of the same territory, the same mystical country as shamanism. It carried with it the same kind of spiritual validation, put upon its participants the same kind of psychic mark. Perhaps too, the thought of being wed to a priestess was not without its appeal: a way to approach spirituality through love and a person—it's what we all try for, really.

At the same time, though, he could kid about it; and this, I think, is where most people miss the boat entirely. He was serious about it; but he didn't always have to *take* it seriously. It's a big and critical distinction.

Had Jim lived, do you think he might have taken initiation as a witch himself?

Yes, definitely. In fact, we had spoken of it often—we were discussing it in L.A., even, before he left for Paris, as something to be done when he came back in the fall. He'd certainly read and studied enough on his own to qualify easily, even instantly. He'd have made a fine High Priest to my High Priestess—the coven was looking forward to working magically with him—and in my occult opinion he was a genuine and gifted shaman. Maybe next time.

The abortion?

When you're twenty years older and materially better off and successful in your chosen field, it's fatally easy to look back and say, Well, you should have done this or You might have done that. I'm not going to do that to myself. That terrified twenty-four-year-old girl, who was so in love and so conflicted and so torn, made the best choice she could have made under those circumstances. She was so right and so brave to do it, and I'm not going to bust her two decades later for that choice which was no choice at all.

She saw that she was going to get no help whatsoever from Jim, that she would have to raise their child alone, on welfare because she had no money of her own and would have had to quit her job to care for the baby; that she would never be able to provide for their child anything beyond the bare necessities and maybe not even those; that she wouldn't even be able to give the child its own father. That was not acceptable; and I'm very proud of her for having the guts to realize that it wasn't, against all her own sentimental inclinations, and to accept that it wasn't ever going to be the way she wanted it. She had a great deal more courage than Jim did, and I think it's very much to her credit that she continued to love him as much as she did afterwards, and tried as hard as she did to understand.

Are you sorry?

Of course. But I'd be a great deal sorrier if I'd had the child; and the child would have had to be sorry right along with me. That did not seem fair or right or good to me.

I will regret forever that the circumstances were not otherwise, were not as I so badly wanted them to be—but they weren't, and I will never regret the action I took *in* those terrible circumstances. If Jim had offered the slightest bit of concern or commitment to his admitted responsibility, had held out the least scrap of hope (and *not* an offer of legal marriage, either; that would not have been any kind of right solution, and I would have absolutely refused), I would have had the baby. But when the father of your child tells you to your face that he wants nothing to do with that child, or indeed with you if you have it, I think it would be the acme of insanity and selfishness and destructiveness to go ahead and give birth.

You're very honest in detailing your pain and indecision. Do you think right-to-lifers will try to turn this to their advantage, to discourage other women from having abortions?

That's their business. My business was telling my experience openly and honestly and truthfully; all of it. *Nobody* is FOR abortion; I'm certainly not. But I *am* for choice, and the freedom to make it, and I wanted people (and I guess that includes right-to-lifers) to know the kind of pain a woman must face in making such a decision, and in carrying it out; that it's not ever a decision she makes lightly or casually; that thought and care and concern for everyone involved go into what she decides. And if, ultimately, she decides that the best and only thing she can do for her child is not to have it, that decision must be respected; and she alone must be the one to make it.

I just want people to know that it's never easy, and no matter how right you know you are to do it, you never get over it. For myself, I can take it. But I didn't think I had the right to ask my son or daughter to live a life of pain and abandonment and resentment; being unable to be mother and father both to it, unable to fill its needs, much less its wants. What could I have done, alone, for Jim Morrison's child and mine?

Besides, when the movie came out, I read an interview where someone said that after Jim died, his parents were inundated with photographs of women holding up babies to the camera, captioned 'This is your grandchild.' I'm very glad not to be one of those women, and gladder still that my child, who really *was* their grandchild, never had to beg for their crumbs.

You don't think if you'd just gone ahead and had the baby, gone to live with it in the country, as Pamela seemed to think would be so cool, that might have changed things?

Well, for me and the child, sure, and not for the better. For Jim, not at all. Not in the slightest. You're suggesting that Jim might have suddenly realized the error of his selfish ways, and rushed to join us in domestic bliss? I *don't* think so! That wasn't the way Jim Morrison operated; and what would we have been living on in the meantime, roots and berries?

No, he would still have died, and his child and I would have been struggling along for the past twenty years. I would never have been able to write books; the child, now twenty-one, would probably be one of the lost, angry children I see on the Village streets—given Jim's heredity, probably already in rehab, hating Jim, hating me, hating everything. I would have been bitter and angry myself, and, inevitably, would have been taking it out on the child all that time.

And what would I have told her—or him—when at last she asked me about her father (and how would she be handling it now, in the glare of the public eye, knowing who he had been—and what he had done to us?)? That he didn't want her, but *I* decided she should be born anyway? No. No way. I wouldn't inflict that kind of hell on my worst enemy, let alone on my child and Jim's.

If Jim had died before you had the abortion, would you still have had it?

Man, you are one bitch interviewer... That's the toughest. I like to think I would still have made the choice that was best for us all; but I rather suspect that sentiment and the utter derangement of grief might have overset logic.

And that would have been an even greater tragedy: trying to rear a child in the midst of such loss. It's easy for ignorant busybodies to cluck that the baby would have been a consolation, but let me tell you all, that's facile bullshit.

You don't know until you've been there yourself, what it feels like when the love of your life dies. You *can't* know, not until it happens; you can lose parents, siblings, friends—but you really have no idea. Yoko Ono Lennon was once quoted as saying that in her depth of grief over John's death she turned away from her own child completely, ignoring the boy, not even wanting to be near him, because her own sorrow was so overwhelming that she just had nothing left for him and his, he was only a reminder of what she'd lost.

And when I read that, I knew I had been so right to have done as I did. Sentimental bleeding-hearts and right-to-lifers may differ as they please—and I'm quite sure they will—but they don't know. They do not ever know.

What if Jim had broken with Pam as he claimed, come back from Paris, moved in with you in New York?

Good question. I think we'd have been idyllically happy until he started pulling his old tricks, his alcoholic brat act, his head terrorism. And then I'd have thrown him out on his ear. If he'd gotten sober, stayed sober—well, I don't know. I can't imagine it ever happening.

We could never have lived together like two regular people, though, not and both survived to tell of it. I think it's almost impossible for two actively, productively creative people to live together on anything like 'normal' or even equal terms: Always one person will end up being not only the household manager (if not drudge), responsible for the mundane creature comforts of both of them (or at least for organizing it, if finances permit hired help), but being caretaker and guardian of the marriage or relationship as well. And our society still being what it is, that person is still almost always the woman.

And I wouldn't have done that; not for Jim, not for anyone. I decided very early on that it would be so: As a writer, I require tremendous amounts of time alone, and very few men are able to deal with that. And no man I've ever met would be as supportive of a woman as he'd unthinkingly demand her to be of him, of his needs and wants and requirements.

He wouldn't think twice about it: He'd expect her to take care of all that home stuff, and him, and the kids if there were any; and then he'd say with a straight face, and he'd REALLY MEAN IT, and think he was being so liberated for saying it, "Oh sure honey, you can be a productive creative person too, I have no problem with you being a director, or a rock star, or a novelist." (Subtext: What's for dinner?)

Well, SURE he's got no problem with it, 'cause it's damn well never going to happen; certainly not if it means his lifestyle and convenience will be altered in the slightest because of it. No wonder there have been so few great women artists: No man was ever willing to be the artist's wife.

Relationships since Jim?

Get real! Since Jim, every man I've ever met has fretted that *he* wasn't Jim Morrison, that he couldn't, ah, measure up to the Lizard King; and that therefore he must be lacking and deficient in my sight; that I would always be mentally (or verbally, even) comparing him to Jim and finding him wanting.

Well, I've never expected any other man to be Jim; obviously, no one ever could be, and it was fine with me that they weren't. It just wasn't fine with them, apparently; they couldn't deal with it, and so that was always that.

The short answer is No. And I can't say it bothers me: Jim Morrison is a tough act to follow, and after him I became a lot harder to impress.

The question everybody asks you: What was he really *like?*

All of it.

The question everybody is dying to ask you but not even Oliver Stone had the balls (or the bad manners) to ask you: What was he like in bed?

Eat your hearts out.

Let's talk about the movie. Do you think Jim would have liked it?

Initially, superficially, yes. He was perverse enough to appreciate Oliver's perversity: He'd have loved the film's excesses, he'd have been delighted with the way the music was handled, he'd have enthusiastically approved of the cinematography and the costumes and the sets and the locations and Kathleen, he'd have responded to Oliver's intensity and filmic 'thereness'—because all these are the things I myself like and approve about the movie—but I think that at the end of the day Jim would have been furious and hurt and disappointed with Oliver's vision of him; or, rather, lack thereof. I think he and Oliver would probably have very much liked one another personally; I think maybe even, had he lived, Jim would be doing the kind of films that Oliver is doing—but he surely would not be doing them the same way, and I think Jim would have been extremely pissed off indeed with what Oliver Stone has put on screen in Jim Morrison's name.

Oliver plays fast and loose with the facts in the interest of what he regards as a higher truth; he's done it before, he'll do it again. He's been nailed on it every time, but he does not learn, or change, or even hear. People take biographical films very literally indeed ("Hey, it's in the movie, it *must* be true!"); and Oliver Stone can claim creative license and impressionistic interpretation and artistic homage until the cinematic cows come home, he's STILL wrong.

If people go to see a movie called *The Doors*, I don't think they can be faulted for assuming they'll be seeing a movie that really *is* about the Doors—not some overwrought director's testosterone frenzy, a Valentine-in-absentia to an era he's envious he missed out on. Oliver Stone was in Vietnam (his own idea) for most of the time-frame covered in this movie; but that does not give him the right to indulge his wish-fulfillment by making Jim's life into the kind of unexamined debauch it never really was, or that Oliver himself wishes he'd lived.

It's not The Jim Morrison Story we're dealing with here; it's The Oliver Stone Story, as it is in all his films. Why should this one have been any different?

Anything you'd like to clear up about the depiction of your character?

You bet! I told Oliver I didn't mind him adding things I didn't do in real life; I *NEVER* said I didn't mind him misrepresenting things Jim and I actually did . . .   And though I'm grateful for the public validation Oliver gave me (*and* the best sex scene in the movie!), I'm weary of being busted for some things the Patricia character did that are either Oliver's inventions or things other women in Jim's life did, and I'd like to, oh, divide the spoils a bit.

Additionally, my involvement with the movie has led to the erroneous assumption that I gave it my blessing; well, I didn't, I don't, and, since the release of *JFK* has further crystallized and publicized Oliver's attitude to the facts of history, I'd just like people to know how it really was. So let's take it scene by scene, shall we?

Jim and I met in a private interview, not a cattle-call press op. We did not go to bed together until eight months later, and when we did, our union involved neither impotence nor cocaine nor blood. First, there was no impotence to be cured; secondly, witches don't drink blood to cure it—*ever*—because there is absolutely no Craft tradition that contains such a practice. It's strictly from the Oliver Stone School of Occultism.

(I was told by Pamela Courson that Jim did engage in a blood-and-coke revel, with a woman named Eva—Fräulein von Sauerkraut—at the Chateau Marmont in late 1970. It was simply a coke freakout, nothing ritualistic or elegant or romantic or mystical about it, and certainly nothing to do with the Craft. And though the Fräulein cut her hand, apparently Jim would not cut his, nor allow her to do it for him.)

Moving along, I was not the girl in the shower-room backstage with Jim at New Haven, I never phoned his parents to call his bluff about their alleged demise, and no Door, or Doors minion, ever warned me to stay away from Jim.

The encounter between Pamela and myself was not as the film portrays it (another lie for a cheap laugh at my expense), nor, for the most part, the encounter between Jim and me in Miami. As both incidents have been described at length earlier, I need not go into them again here. All these are just facts cooked by Oliver: It's annoying that I have so often been personally blamed for their untruthfulness, but hey, folks, I didn't write the script . . .   (More's the pity.)

But Oliver's most blatant fabrication is the cruel and false and vicious line about Jim not taking the handfasting seriously. Jim NEVER said such a thing to me, not in Miami, not anywhere else. In fact, quite the opposite: He spoke of the wedding in loving and reverent terms, right up to the end, in the last letter I received from him; he was glad and grateful and proud of the bond, and never said, suggested, implied or hinted to me that he had not been entirely serious in intent about the ceremony.

And so what I want to know is, Just who the hell does Oliver Stone think he is, to misrepresent Jim Morrison in public on something Stone knows absolutely nothing about? The line is an utter untruth that Oliver must surely have known would devastate me, that even as invention is of no use or worth to the film. No wonder he wouldn't let me read the script beforehand... It seems to be purely an act of vicious and gratuitous psychic violence; an act, indeed, of rape.

Did Oliver just think the real-life terrible things Jim and I threw at one another in Miami were somehow not dramatic and cruel and hurtful enough, that he felt impelled to invent fictions whose apparent purpose seems only to be to hurt and humiliate me publicly, in front of everyone (such as their numbers are) who sees this film?

I don't know, and I don't care to know. But I do know that for Oliver Stone to put forth an untruth like that, in a scene like that (and it's by no means the only lying line in that scene), where the truth would have served far better, knowing as he must have known how audiences would react to it, how *I* would react to it, making Jim look like a jerk, making me look like a jerk, only makes Oliver Stone look like the biggest jerk of all.

It was betrayal. And betrayal is the one sin Celts neither forget nor forgive (remember, Oliver, what goes around comes around...).

What about the way Jim is depicted romantically in the movie?

Jim Morrison was the most genuinely romantic man I was ever with, but you don't see any of that onscreen. And I really resent forever Oliver's (perhaps autobiographical?) implication that Jim couldn't get it up without doing something nasty and weird first: drinking blood, throwing lamps, hanging out windows, beating women up, locking them in burning closets—that sort of thing. Some turn-on!

I can only say—yet again—Not with *me* he didn't! Jim and I had a very active, healthy and conventionally enjoyable sexual relationship;

and believe me, I wouldn't *DREAM* of going into such excruciatingly personal and private detail if I didn't think the point well merited my suffering the extreme discomfort of so doing.

To put in terms even Oliver Stone should be able to understand, Jim and I fucked each other's brains out every chance we got. We had *no* problems getting going or keeping going—the most spectacular conjoinings in the most utterly usual configuration. And if people find this too, ah, hard to believe, too bad. I guess it was just a question of whom he happened to be making love with; maybe I just inspired him.

And as long as I'm on uncomfortable topics: There have been some revolting allegations made recently, which I'd like to kill off here and now (and, hopefully, thereby to spike the guns of future biographers less devoted than I to Jim's best interests): allegations that toward the end of his life Jim was supposedly being secretly treated for various dramatic venereal disorders, among them penile cancer said to have rendered him not only impotent and incapable but to have necessitated removal of all or part of his sexual organs.

All I can say to this imbecile piece of grotesquerie is, I *THINK* I'd have noticed! I was extensively in the area in question during the time Jim was presumably undergoing treatment for this mythical condition, and I can assure you under oath that everything in the vicinity was present and accounted for and in perfect working order. I would not ordinarily be dignifying this sort of sewage with a response at all—but it's been said, and, given the public's past gullibility (particularly with regard to certain things I myself am alleged to have done in Jim's life), I choose to err these days on the side of overexplication.

You've said you didn't think Val Kilmer was particularly interested in any input you had to offer him on Jim. Why do you think Kilmer felt this way, and why do you think Oliver and Val blew (as it were) the chance to depict Jim as he really was?

I don't know why Val (or Meg Ryan, for that matter) didn't feel it necessary to talk with me. Despite their numerous boasts in the media of having scouted out and talked extensively to *everyone* who even *remotely* knew Jim and Pam, for some strange unaccountable reason Kilmer and Ryan didn't seem to include me in that category. Which was, of course, their prerogative; but let's not then go around claiming we've got the whole story, shall we, kids?

Perhaps my reality conflicted with Val's preconceived notions of Jim, or of the sort of woman Jim would have been attracted to, the sort of woman who would in her turn have been attracted to him. Maybe he had already adjudged Jim a loser by the time he met me, and therefore only lost loser women could have figured in his life, lost souls whom Jim proceeded to destroy; and Kilmer couldn't get behind the idea of a strong woman whom Jim could *not* destroy, and who refused to destroy herself on his account, being in love with Jim, and he with her.

I don't think Oliver and Val really understood Jim's and my relationship; or Jim's and Pam's either, come to it. Their tiny minds could grasp the groupie crap, the blowjobs in elevators, the butt-fucks in motel rooms—that seems to be the level of thing they can comprehend, and all they really wanted to hear about. Too bad. They missed a lot. They missed making a thoughtful and intelligent and perceptive movie, for one thing, and settled for the only Jim their combined creative talents could apparently handle.

In the end, perhaps it was just that Oliver Stone and Val Kilmer lacked the guts to see the real Jim Morrison even when he was standing right in front of them. Perhaps they did not want to see him. Perhaps they were afraid to see him. Or perhaps it was, simplest and saddest of all, that they could not find that Jim Morrison in themselves.

Summation?

The movie shouldn't have been called *The Doors*. It wasn't about the 60's. And it certainly had very little to do with Jim Morrison.

How do you think Jim saw himself?

As a seeker. A teacher. A point man. More than anything else, Jim wanted people to see that what he was doing, they too could do; not the drugs and the booze, but the moving out, the breaking through, the seeing, the learning.

He never thought of himself as a leader, and he never claimed to have answers; only questions. He believed he was just someone who happened to be doing things a little differently, a little in advance of everyone else, or aside from them. It was that thing of wanting to lead from the ranks, to direct from off the set.

I don't think Jim really loved fame; to him, that was never the point. Although at the beginning he found it a useful tool to help him gain access to people and fora he might not otherwise have been able to reach, in the end he knew fame was a liability, a form of possession, an albatross slung around that psychic mariner's neck of his. There was certainly a wish to be known, but not for vanity, not for the usual ego-monster motives. Jim wanted to be known for what he knew; and just as strong, if not stronger still, was the wish to be only a presence, a syllable on the wind, and to let his words do all his speaking.

So you approve of all this Morrison-mania, all these kids who weren't even born when Jim died taking him to their hearts?

Not in the least. For one thing, that kind of 'devotion' has kept me from his grave for twenty years, and probably always will (and in case you were wondering, if I'd had anything to say about it, I'd have given him a Viking funeral off Malibu, or Scotland; or, at the very least, he'd have been cremated and his ashes scattered over Venice Beach).

No, I don't approve of it because I do not want to see Jim admired for the wrong reasons, by the wrong people. And the wrong reasons are of course all the stupid acting-out excesses, the drugs and the booze and the sluttery and the destructiveness; and the wrong people are of course all those very same impressionable young folk who take all that out of context.

Sure, Jim took drugs; sure, he was an alcoholic. All the same, he was a sane and a serious person, an educated and a literate person. There was wit and thought and intelligence and reason behind his work, if not perhaps always behind his personal life; and no matter what else he did, he always paid his audience the honor and the compliment of addressing them, through his songs and, yeah, his poems, as his equals in mind and purpose.

So pay *him* the same honor and compliment, okay? If you really love and respect Jim Morrison and what he stood for, don't think you're showing it by imitating his worst, or by infesting his grave like psychic maggots, trashing it for everyone else. Don't idolize him for his attitude; in fact, don't idolize him at all, he'd hate that worse than anything. And don't ignore, EVER, the disciplined mind and craft and soul that created the art you all claim to love. (Which translates as: Get some weight into your lives, boys and girls; read some books, write some words, think some thoughts—after all, Jim did; why not emulate *that* side of him?—get something behind your eyes that Jim can be proud to see there. He wouldn't want stupid and shallow fans, and *I* don't want illiterate butt-heads, having watched that movie and not bothered to look any further, thinking they really know what Jim Morrison was all about.)

What do you think killed Jim?

The short answer? Miami and Pamela, not necessarily in that order.

What do you think killed Pamela?

Weakness. Addiction. Indulgence. Not just having the wrong maps, but apparently not having any maps at all. Perhaps if she had something real to do with her life, both before and after Jim died—like supporting herself, for instance—it would have given her a framework to live within and strength to build it; not just earning her own keep, but earning a sense of her own self.

But maybe that was too much like real life; she seemed to prefer to live in fantasy. I think the fact that I had to go to work every day and produce creative things is one of the main reasons I'm still around to be writing this book and all my other books; why I'm here, and Pam isn't. It's humble, it's mundane; but it gives you something to focus on, outside your pain and despair. Knowing that you have to take care of yourself because no one else is going to do it for you, knowing that you *can* take care of yourself, that you wouldn't have it any other way—it's a great blessing, and it saved my life and reason. If Pamela had only felt she could do something else with her beauty and charm and talents besides hook . . . well, I don't know. You can grieve as long and as deeply as you must, and you can grieve *how* you must—I will personally never be done mourning Jim, he's in my heart, my soul, my life, my thoughts, my prayers and my work—but what you can't ever do is not be real in the world.

But Jim?

In the end, Jim Morrison killed himself. Let there be no mistake about that. If Pamela Courson had not been there handing him heroin—there's a fine loving 'wifely' gesture for you (Borgia wife, maybe)—at a moment when he was despairing and vulnerable and maybe wanting an end to the pain, he might have lasted longer.

A little longer: The Jim of the 90's would have had to be a totally committed recovering alcoholic, a transformed, reformed individual, which I like to think he would have been. Otherwise, he would still be dead; and, let's not forget, though Pam may have been pushing the scag—for whatever reasons of her own—Jim was still the one who accepted it.

It was, ultimately, proximity. I doubt very much if Jim would have gone out looking for it. He wasn't a junkie. And he'd never have been offered smack at my house.

The deadly weapon that Jim used on himself wasn't heroin, though, but the fatal dichotomy—self-created, self-inflicted, self-perpetuated—between Jim Morrison the stage madman and James Douglas Morrison the inner vulnerable loving soul. He made this dichotomy of his own free will, and took it unto him; he thought he could control it, he thought he was kidding, he thought that people could see he was kidding. But the dichotomy wasn't kidding, and pretty soon neither was Jim, and in the end no one was kidding at all.

What do you remember best about him?

I think the contradictions of him are what is most vivid in retrospect: the breathtaking cruelty, not just to me, that incredible blank coldness that could descend right down over him like a shutter over a window. You knew it was mostly out of fear, but that didn't make it any easier, any less hurtful; and he wasn't above taking your love and understanding and holding it on you like a gun.

But then there was that other side: the love and warmth and generosity, the most astounding passion and tenderness—and always so much more of this side than the other. I remember us being silly together, giggly and hilarious; and I remember us cutting each other to bloody bits with words. I remember weeping as I have never wept for anyone else, and I remember him weeping with me.

It's been suggested elsewhere that Jim was not a warm person, and perhaps that is superficially true. But what I remember best of warmth, the thing I remember most, the thing I think of first when I think of Jim, is joy. Just joyousness: the way he looked the afternoon he asked me to handfast him, under a flowering tree in a springtime park; the way he would smile when something caught or amused or pleased him, the way his eyes would spark and his face light up and his whole being seem to kindle at something you'd said or done; a smile that warmed the room and warmed you too, so that you would smile and think better of yourself for having made *him* smile—like the sun coming out of a cloudbank, just as warm, just as cheering, sometimes just as transitory. It was all extremes with Jim, but I loved that. I still do.

He was mannerly, charming, joyful, generous, hopeful, loving; he could not have kept so many of us so loyal to him all these years if he had been anything else, or anything less. And though he was other things as well, *these* things made the Jim Morrison that mattered, the Jim Morrison who has lasted.

I remember him best with the right side of my face and my arms around him; and in writing this book I have fallen in love with him all over again, as I knew would happen, though I never once ceased.

Why do you think Jim was attracted to you?

My incredible sexual prowess. No, no, just kidding—well, no, I'm not kidding. . . Oh, because I was as smart as he was, of course! Because we could have the most gloriously satisfying mental encounters and then fall into bed and have the most gloriously satisfying sexual encounters. The fact that the same woman was capable of supplying him with both seemed not to have been without a certain appeal—or perhaps novelty.

What do you think Jim saw in your relationship?

I think he saw possibility, alternative, another way to live his life— maybe even hope, a way out, a road to freedom. I think he saw love, felt love, knew love. We had an excellent physical relationship based on mutual and equal desire and an excellent intellectual relationship based on mutual and equal brains.

What we did *not* have was a relationship based on mutual and equal dependency; he had Pamela for that. The addicted Jim needed Pam, also addicted; the recovered Jim would have wanted me, or at least someone *like* me—I don't pretend to know if we would have stayed together, though naturally I'd like to think so. But given all that had passed between us, maybe even love would not have been enough.

But Pamela was an addict and a promiscuous person, and she fed that side of him; I was neither, and fed a very different side. The best I can say about Jim and me is that it was not possessive; it was about more than that, or maybe it was a kind of possessiveness on a very different, hopefully higher level—a level that is not commonly perceived as possessiveness at all. You can forge bonds at a distance with someone that are stronger and surer and more lasting than those of law or even of habit; it all depends on what you both bring to it to begin with.

I like to think that Jim and I brought love and trust and loyalty and honesty to our union, in a way that we alone understand, and that we continue to bring those things to it even now (death doesn't part, remember?). I know he has kept a protective arm around me ever since; I have often felt his presence, his hand in my life.

I like to think that I honored him, and us, by going on to live a creative and productive and happy life. I became the artist he knew I could be; I didn't dive into scag, or turn tricks, or live in some half-world, or end up in rehab or dead of an OD; and for that I have Jim to thank as much as myself. It depends, too, on what you do with what you're given.

Do you believe Jim really loved you?

Insofar as anyone can believe anyone else when that word comes into it: Yes, I do. I believe he loved me as well as he loved anyone, or could love anyone. I believe he loved Pamela as well as he loved anyone, or could love anyone. I believe the one did not necessarily preclude the other (or even necessarily precluded the groupies); each was different, both were real.

I have Jim's word as to how he felt about me, and that's all I need to have or to know. In things he said, things he wrote, things he did. I believe Jim loved me because Jim said he loved me, and because I loved him I believed him. What others may say or think about it is, beyond a certain natural annoyance, of no concern to me.

They weren't there. I was. I heard what he said and how he said it, saw how he looked as he said it, felt it body and soul when he said it. I am the one to whom he was saying it, and therefore the only one who can judge of his truthfulness in saying it.

In the end, it's between Jim and me and no one else, and it's enough.

Speaking of ends, what would you like for an epitaph?

Quite a lot, actually. Let's see: "She was a great lady, a nice writer and a fabulous babe. She had brains, guts, class and soul. She loved Jim Morrison and he loved her. She died writing."

Pretty pretentious.

Well, I didn't say I *deserved* it. Only that I'd *like* it.

How about something a bit more modest?

"She kept the faith."

What do you think Jim might have liked?

"See you later."

EPILOGUE

3 July 1991, New York

TWENTY YEARS LATER. NOT AS IT WAS THEN, NOT NOW, with tides of international necrotrash washing up against the walls of Père-Lachaise, drinking, drugging, crashing cars through the gate and setting it ablaze. Jim would have *hated* that, and them...

And because of offal such as this, for two decades I have not been able to return to where he lies: because I cannot bear to see his grave, that small, that fine and private place I well remember, so full of love and quietness, as the trampled mire they have made of it, cannot bring myself to sully my memory with their barbarity.

And so because I cannot ever go back there again in life, am banished from his resting place by the maggot hordes, I send my spirit today in my body's stead, my own fetch, to visit him, a black-clad and black-veiled ghost walking those cobbled paths, down the little street to the side gate, up the lane to the right, past other lanes and up the little rise, in between tombs and trees, coming round to where he is. I have walked that path often in memory, and now I walk it again—in mind, if not in life.

I am there; and also I am here, where once we were together: here in my seclusion—casting a circle, conducting the rites as I have done every year all these years, being with him more truly than anyone can ever know, and he with me; going to Mass at dawn in a nearby church, a Mass that I have arranged for him as I promised him I would; returning to a seclusion that is not apart but sharing—it is Jim who comforts me today; this is *my* idea of the way to mark this anniversary day.

Astral mourner: I look upon this grave with inner vision—the only valid kind—and I see not the defaced tombs and monuments, the quagmire gravesite, but a peaceful plot of mounded gray-white dirt, ringed by the scallop shells that are sacred to another James whom pilgrims visit, away south in Spanish lands, a little wooden cross lying flat upon the earth. I remember those shells, that mound, that cross: I remember too that, first of all the many who have followed me here down the years and called him so, I wrote upon his grave before anyone else that one word of all the words, that very little word he wanted so to hear, more than any other: that word 'poète.'

I place roses in my dream-vision, as I did in life: red for love, white for loyalty. I leave another letter for him; I talk to him, telling him what has passed since last I came here—though I have never once stopped speaking to him since he died. Celts speak ever to their loved dead, they are only in the next room after all. I kneel by his side all day long; this is *my* dream, no one dares trouble us.

He is not here, of course; not as he was that other time when I knelt here, not even here as the ghouls at the gate think he is. Yet he is here all the same; and so I bend to kiss the earth above his heart. In my vision it is once again clean dry gravedirt, undefiled by joints and butts and bottles. I weep a little, a lot; I pray in several fashions as I have prayed for him for twenty years, and will for however many more.

I pray as a witch and his wife, as a priestess in her power speaking to the Goddess for her mate. I pray as a knight of an ancient order that, like Jim, died in Paris and lived on in the greater world. I pray as a servant of St. Michael, as a warrior praying for a fallen warrior to a warrior archangel. And last I pray as Jim might have asked me to pray, or prayed himself: an echo from his childhood, the shaman's prayer of a Southwest tribe. All will be heard where they are spoken; and anyway, he knows now, himself . . .

But as I once gave it to a character of mine to say in one of my novels, I would not still be thinking of Jim if he were not still thinking of me, and never with such love.

In the film, Oliver Stone has given the Jim character a line to the effect that women are noble because "they carry on your name with dignity after you die."

I would like to think that I, at least, have done so.

O lion-faced
Roman-bodied
beautiful clown ghost

my most
beloved

—pkm

New York, Miami, Los Angeles, Paris   1969–